PRAISE FOR

Tris Speaker: The Rough-and-Tumble Life of a Baseball Legend

"Timothy Gay has accomplished something special with this book, recovering a great player and a hallowed time from the deep well of nostalgia and bringing them back to life, not as we wished them to be, but as they really were."

—David Maraniss, author of *Clemente: The Passion and Grace of Baseball's Last Hero*

"Carefully researched and documented, engagingly written, and very illuminating. Gay has filled a serious gap in baseball history, and his effort compares favorably with Charles Alexander's acclaimed biographies of John McGraw and Ty Cobb."

—*Booklist*

"Gay, who spent four years researching Speaker's life, has crafted a rugged, no-holds-barred look at a player who encompassed all the complex magic of early twentieth century baseball. Speaker's story exemplifies why baseball holds such an important place in the American imagination. It is our story—a story of sin and expiation, of loyalty and love, of courage and dignity. This should be required reading for any serious baseball fan."

—*Sport Literature Association*

"An eye-opening look at baseball's now seemingly prehistoric 'dead ball' era, which also was rife with gambling scandals, grudges, [and] amoral team owners."

—*Dallas Morning News*

"Tris Speaker was the prototype for Willie Mays as the best center fielder and most complete ballplayer of the dead ball era. Timothy Gay has crafted an enjoyable and important book about one of the most dominant yet underrated players in baseball history."

—Richard A. Johnson, coauthor, *Red Sox Century and The Dodgers: 120 Years of Dodger Baseball*

"Tim Gay has written a terrific book about a fascinating ball player—a .344+ lifetime hitter who still holds the major league record for unassisted double plays by a centerfielder. Every sports fan ought to read it."

—David Owen, author of *My Usual Game*

TIMOTHY M. GAY

Tris Speaker

The Rough-and-Tumble Life of a Baseball Legend

THE LYONS PRESS
Guilford, Connecticut
An imprint of The Globe Pequot Press

Copyright © 2007 Morris Book Publishing, LLC
A previous hardcover edition of this book was published in
2005 by the University of Nebraska Press.

The Lyons Press is an imprint of The Globe Pequot Press.

10 9 8 7 6 5 4 3 2 1

Printed in the United States of America

ISBN: 978-1-59921-111-4

Library of Congress Cataloging-in-Publication Data is available
on file.

To Elizabeth and
our precious "triple A's" —
Allyson, Andrew, and Abigail —
big league by any reckoning

Contents

List of Illustrations

Acknowledgments

First-time authors find themselves, much like Blanche DuBois in "A Streetcar Named Desire," dependent upon the kindness of strangers. The many kindnesses began with David Kelly, a baseball history specialist at the Library of Congress, who willingly took a rookie writer into the bowels of the library to find publications that ceased to be published decades ago. David was unfailingly patient, as were his colleagues who helped a mechanically challenged amateur historian operate the microfiche machines. John Vernon, Connie Porter, and Carolyn Gilliam at the National Archives helped me go through immense databases on various censuses and Civil War records, unearthing information about Tris Speaker's ancestry and dispelling much misinformation along the way.

Very little of the background on Speaker's family life in Texas would have been possible to find without the dutiful pro bono help of Mrs. Cleo Davis, Hill County's leading historian and genealogist. Mrs. Davis, in her eighth decade of life, combed census records, examined real estate documents, explored a cemetery, told me about the central Texas legacy of Bonnie and Clyde, and led me on a wonderful tour of Hubbard and Hillsboro. Cleo, I'm forever in your debt. Several other distinguished residents of Hill County, including retired business leader Bill Jarvis, funeral home executive and volunteer sportswriter Don Sims, Justice of the Peace Gene Fulton, restaurateur Billy Mack Waller, and antiques dealer Nancy York Ryan and her lovely mom, Mrs. Tony York, were generous with their time. The ballplayer's niece, Miss Tris Speaker Scott, spent a few minutes with me on the telephone early in my research.

In New England, I was grateful when distinguished historians Glenn Stout and Richard Johnson not only answered my calls but proved to be incredibly insightful and patient. Their past research and current observations helped shape the book. Dick, who's the curator of the Sports Museum of New England, sacrificed the better part of three days on my behalf, generously giving me the run of the place and allowing me full access to the wonderful diaries of Bill "Rough" Carrigan. Glenn's colorful quotes also adorn the book.

At the Boston Public Library, Aaron Schmidt generously shared the archival files on Speaker and Ned McGreevey. At the Massachusetts

Acknowledgments

Historical Commission, Phil Berman provided guidance. At the Massachusetts Institute of Technology, archival librarian Nora Murphy helped me uncover information about Speaker's World War I aviation training.

At Fenway Park, Richard Bresciani, the Red Sox's vice president of publications and archives, and Debbie Matson, the director of publications, pulled out musty clips from file drawers and storerooms that hadn't been unlocked in some years. Ace intern Henry Maheegan, a recent graduate of Trinity University, put dozens of documents in digital format. Being in the innards of Fenway was cool enough. Being treated with such great courtesy and respect was above and beyond my hosts' call of duty.

Bob Wood, Smoky Joe's son and still thriving well into his eighties, was also generous with his time and files. Sox historian Ed Walton provided great anecdotes and guidance.

In Cleveland, I was honored that Fred Schuld, the former head of the Society for American Baseball Research and a Tris Speaker buff, took such an avid interest in my project. Fred, almost eighty years young, spent a day showing me the ropes in the microform room of the Cleveland Public Library. He also shared with me scores of artifacts he had accumulated over the years – from photographs and cartoons to poems and clippings. Fred, I wish you had gotten to meet the Gray Eagle that day when you thought you were delivering a package to Gray Eagle Liquors. At the Cleveland Public Library, microform room librarians Debra Nunez and Ryan Jaenke were extremely patient in helping me find back copies of the *Plain Dealer*, the *News*, and the *Press*.

Mike Sowell, author of *The Pitch That Killed*, afforded me much time on the telephone. His methodical research on the tragic death of Ray Chapman, also conducted in the microform room of the CPL, helped guide my book. Journalism students at Oklahoma State University now benefit from Mike's wisdom.

Jim Elfers, the author of the beautifully researched *Tour to End All Tours*, provided much encouragement, not to mention pro bono photographs. Jim, I wish we could exhume Germany Schaefer to hear his impersonation of Spoke. But I'm glad we missed the dog-badger dustup in Abilene.

Henry "Hank" Thomas, the grandson and biographer of the great

Walter Johnson, gave me the tip that the original Wood interview with Ritter was still on file at the University of Notre Dame. Hank, your great-grandfather helped save the Republic at Gettysburg and your grandfather gave it much glory in the century that followed. You come from good genes.

Paul Zingg, the author of *Harry Hooper: An American Baseball Life*, was a terrific resource. Professor Zingg's research on the many temptations of Hot Springs, Arkansas, was instrumental in shaping chapter 5. Harry Hooper was a gracious gentleman and so is his biographer, who's now the president of Chico State University in California.

Speaking of magnanimous gentlemen, the *Boston Globe*'s Bob Ryan, author of *When Boston Won the World Series*, provided superb insights into Speaker's legacy. Bob, if T. H. Murnane's observations were ex cathedra in his day, your writing is today.

At the National Baseball Hall of Fame in Cooperstown, New York, Claudette Burke and Freddy Berowski at the A. Bartlett Giamatti Research Center were extremely helpful, as were the Hall's dead-ball era specialist, Cobb biographer and buff Dan Holmes, and broadcast archivist Jeremy Jones. The Hall's executive director, Dale Petroskey, and vice president of development, Greg Harris, were also generous with their time. W. C. Burdick, the photo manager, helped procure some terrific shots of Spoke.

At the Lawrence Ritter collection at the University of Notre Dame's Hesburgh Library, curator George Rugg was very helpful. As was my publisher and editor, Rob Taylor, at the University of Nebraska Press and Bison Books, who has the patience of Job. So, too, does copyeditor Lona Dearmont, assistant project editor Ann Baker, and former marketing director Sandra Johnson.

Neighbor John McNamee, an undergrad at the University of Virginia, did yeoman's work in compiling the index. Former child rodeo star Tad Mizwa of Leona, Texas, provided great insights into Will Rogers.

I would be remiss if I didn't acknowledge my fellow "dead-heads" – the members of the Dead-ball Era Committee of the Society for American Baseball Research. Former chairman Tom Simon, a proud Vermonter like the great Larry Gardner, was supportive from the get-go. Trey Strecker, who teaches at Ball State University, provided excellent perspective on Speaker, as did Mike Grahek, Steve Johnson, Dean Sullivan, Don Jensen, Gene Carney, William Burgess III, Greg Beston, and several others. Jacob Pomrenke found the Hugh Fullerton quotes on the '12 Series. Guys, I'm looking forward to that day when I buy you all a beer and we toast the DEC's patron saint, "Dode" Paskert. Had Dode's shot to right center in the Baker Bowl been a foot longer, Paskert, not Spoke, would have gotten the standing ovation from Woodrow Wilson in the '15 Series. The ProQuest on-line research tool available to SABR members was an extraordinary asset. SABR's ProQuest has to be the best research bargain in America.

Most of all I'd like to thank Elizabeth, Ally, Andrew, and Abby for their love and support. Andrew is surely the only Little Leaguer outside of Hill County, Texas, who celebrates tough catches in the side yard by exclaiming, "Look, Dad, I'm Tris Speaker!" For that reason alone, it was worth doing the book.

When Speaker Swings Out for a Fly

When Speaker swings out for a fly
That leaves a blot against the sky
The Graces known of old, fade out.
Where Form and Art are forced to yield
And Rhythm leaves in utter rout
Before Perfection on the field.

Poised for the sprint on agile sweep
For Texas tap or wallop deep
The poetry of Motion fades and passes onward with a sigh.
And all the Graces look like jades
When Speaker swings out for a fly.

— Grantland Rice

Introduction

Defense to me is the key to playing baseball. I know people say, well, you've got to score runs, but you've got to stop them before you can score runs. And I used to love to run down every fly ball. I used to love to throw a guy out. Of course, I played good offense, too. But I just felt baseball was a beautiful game . . . I mean, all you do is go out there and you're out there by yourself, in center field, and it's just a beautiful game. — Willie Mays

Willie Mays's famous catch in the 1954 World Series is not only an iconic moment in baseball history – it's a defining event in American cultural history. America's national pastime had been integrated for less than a decade when Mays, a descendant of Alabama slaves, raced into the most remote precincts of the Polo Grounds to rob Vic Wertz of extra bases. It's been a half century, yet the Say Hey Kid's catch lives on in lore, celebrated in movies (remember the climactic scene in Billy Crystal's *City Slickers*?), documentaries, songs, barroom banter, and chats around the water cooler.

Mays's play is ingrained in our collective memory because we've repeatedly seen the grainy black-and-white film. It's been heralded in so many commercials and promotional videos over the years that even casual fans can summon the image of Willie galloping into deep right center, arching his neck to corral the ball as it descends directly overhead, then losing his cap as he whirls to throw back to the infield.

No such film exists of an equally spectacular World Series catch made thirty-nine years earlier. Nor is there a still photograph, audio record, or even a lithograph. Considered by many onlookers the greatest clutch play they'd ever witnessed, the moment has sadly disappeared into the ether of baseball history.

It happened in Philadelphia on October 9, 1915, in the bottom of the ninth inning in the second game of the World Series between the Philadelphia Phillies and the Boston Red Sox. One out from a victory that would have knotted the Series at one game apiece, the Red Sox were clinging to a 2–1 lead when the Phillies advanced a last-gasp runner. Up to the plate stepped veteran hitter George "Dode" Paskert, who promptly slugged a ball into the distant reaches of the Baker Bowl's center field. Sportswriter John Foster captured the moment for the *New York Times*: "Everyone but [the Red Sox center fielder] knew the ball was gone for a Philly victory. Off with the crack of the bat from his normal shallow position, [he] reached the center-field fence, leaped and, half his body over the wall, came down with the ball clutched in his tiny mitt."

Phillie partisans groaned as the Sox center fielder held the ball aloft, showing the umpires that he had made the catch. The hostile crowd nevertheless gave him an appreciative ovation as his teammates mobbed him on their way off the field. Among those who stood to applaud was President Woodrow Wilson, who had thrown out the first ball and watched the entire game from a box seat next to the Phillies' bench in the company of his future bride, Mrs. Edith Galt.

The player who drew the presidential approbation was Tris Speaker, a tough-talking Texan from cowboy country who was easily the finest center fielder of his generation and one of the best ever. Yet, like his catch that long-ago afternoon, Speaker has been forgotten; somehow, he's fallen out of baseball's pantheon. Today, his defensive brilliance and pioneering contributions to the game go largely unacknowledged. The few discolored photographs that survive from his playing days show him in uniforms so scruffy that they would have made Adonis look unkempt.

Ask informed observers to name the greatest center fielders in history and they will invariably cite Mays, Joe DiMaggio, Mickey Mantle, maybe Ken Griffey Jr., and a couple of others. Even Duke Snider, whose skills weren't in Speaker's league, will get more nods than Tris. Yet nearly eight decades after Tris's retirement, he still holds American League records among outfielders for most career chances, most put-outs, most assists, most double plays, and – here's a statistic not often associated with center fielders – most *unassisted* double plays. Speaker played so shallow and with such élan that perhaps as many as six times in his career he caught line drives and out-hustled the runner to get a force-out at second base. The only other dead-ball immortal whose defensive acumen was in Speaker's class was Honus Wagner, the gritty shortstop of the Pittsburgh Pirates whose gargantuan hands gobbled up every grounder in sight.

"Speaker was Willie Mays before there was a Willie Mays," maintains baseball historian Richard Johnson, the curator of the Sports Museum of New England. Like Mays, Speaker was a fearsome hitter. Speaker's lifetime batting average was twenty points higher than DiMaggio's and more than forty points higher than Mays's and Mantle's. Tris was much more than just a Punch-and-Judy hitter. If the lively ball had been introduced earlier in his career, many of Speaker's more than a thousand career doubles and triples would have been home runs.

Mays and Speaker, in fact, serve as touchstones in baseball history. Willie personified the best of the postwar era, when Major League Baseball finally ended its shameful policy of segregation. Speaker embodied the best and worst of an earlier era, when baseball was lily-white – and defiantly so. A cantankerous Southerner who never stopped fighting the "War of Northern Aggression," Speaker would have preferred to play only with young men like him, white Anglo-Saxon Protestants from below the Mason-Dixon line.

Woodrow Wilson and Tris Speaker had much in common when their paths crossed in the autumn of 1915. They were both of Southern heritage, both convinced that the old Confederacy had been wronged during Reconstruction, both hostile to the notion of racial equality. That same year, President Wilson had previewed D. W. Griffith's silent film, *Birth of a Nation*, pronouncing it a masterpiece. Griffith's film is essentially a raison d'être for the Ku Klux Klan. The movie's most dramatic scene comes when, to the clamor of Richard Wagner's *Ride of the Valkyries*, a Klan posse literally rides to the rescue of a Southern belle and her family desperately trying to save their home from a group of marauding black soldiers, whom Griffith naturally depicted as bug-eyed and shiny-toothed.

Griffith's scene touched such a powerful nerve that it provoked riots in theaters across the country. If Speaker saw the movie, no doubt he was among those applauding fiercest as that scene rolled across the screen. Speaker grew up in a region of central Texas where the Klan operated at a fever pitch. Local KKK leaders were heroes. Lynching was not uncommon.

Despite his convictions on race, there's some evidence that Speaker was able to overcome at least part of his bigotry later in life. As a spring training coach and special advisor to the Cleveland Indians in the late

1940s, Speaker took great pride in teaching the nuances of outfield play to Larry Doby, the first African American player in the American League. Doby credited Speaker with making him a better ballplayer; the two developed something akin to a bond. Speaker, brought up when the South's Jim Crow laws were at their most virulent, lived long enough to see black Americans, including Doby, fight against fascism in World War II.

The ignominy that continues to surround two of Speaker's dead-ball contemporaries – fellow Southerners and outfielders Ty Cobb and "Shoeless Joe" Jackson – has ironically eclipsed Speaker's star. Cobb and Jackson were brilliant players, but neither possessed Speaker's all-around game. Cobb could cover ground in the outfield but had only a middling arm. Jackson could throw but was an erratic fielder.

Today, Cobb and Jackson are as well known for their failings off the field as for their exploits on it. Cobb, a Georgian, was a scary sociopath. The mere sight of black people so filled him with rage that, on several occasions, he brutally pistol-whipped African American men whose only offense was to share a sidewalk with him. Jackson, a South Carolinian, may well have been functionally illiterate during his playing days. Shoeless Joe was so unworldly that he appears not to have understood the danger inherent in the 1919 Black Sox "fix." Jackson knowingly pocketed crooked cash to "throw" the World Series against the Cincinnati Reds, then proceeded to bat better than .300 and, with the exception of a couple of suspicious plays, field his position more or less on the level – inducing ugly threats from the thugs.

Speaker in his younger years certainly shared Cobb's antipathy toward people of color; Tris told a prominent writer in the early 1910s that he was a member of the Klan. But Speaker was able to keep his supremacist views in better check than the Georgian. Moreover, like many of his dead-ball cronies, Speaker was an inveterate gambler who was befriended by hustlers and bookies. He no doubt "arranged" the outcome of more than a few games, profiting from ill-gotten gain. But thanks in part to some hardball tactics by his attorneys, he was never publicly fingered in anything as infamous as the Black Sox scandal. So, in effect, Speaker has been punished by history because he wasn't as viciously bigoted as Cobb or as ineptly corrupt as Jackson.

Devotees of Ted Williams, Carl Yastrzemski, Lou Boudreau, and Bob

Feller may wince as they read this, but Speaker was the best all-around player in the history of not one but two franchises. He was the leading light on two Red Sox championship teams; then, following a trade that devastated fans in Boston, he led the Indians to their 1920 World Series triumph over the Brooklyn Robins as a player-manager. His wizardry in center field captivated audiences on four continents during baseball's grand world tour in 1913–14. Tris was a heady ballplayer and manager; many of his innovations were emulated in their day and are still in use today. With its reverent tone and classical allusions, Grantland Rice's "When Speaker Swings Out for a Fly," quoted above, illustrates that the leading commentators of the day appreciated Speaker's genius.

Indeed, for much of big league baseball's first half century, Speaker was considered its archetypal center fielder. In 1936, when the Yankees first brought up Joe DiMaggio, Joe deliberately invited comparisons to Speaker by playing an exceptionally shallow center field. Yankees pitcher Lefty Gomez loved to tell the story of facing Tigers slugger Rudy York one afternoon in DiMaggio's rookie season. Gomez happened to glance out to center field during York's at bat and was alarmed to see DiMaggio playing uncomfortably close to the infield. After the game, Lefty supposedly overheard talk in the clubhouse that DiMaggio was determined to "make 'em forget Speaker." Retorted Lefty: "Well, Joe, let's not make 'em forget Gomez. Play deeper."

Leo Durocher, Willie Mays's first Major League manager, marveled at his center fielder's baseball IQ and natural gifts. "Leo the Lip," who played on the Yankee dynasty of the 1920s and had seen a lot of great ballplayers in his day, was in awe of Willie's ability to be in precisely the right place at precisely the right time.

Tris Speaker's contemporaries, too, spoke in similarly reverential terms about his capacity to control a game while standing hundreds of feet from the batter's box. One reporter was moved to write, after he saw Speaker spear one line drive after another, that he possessed "the greatest sense of baseball flight ever conferred on man." Grantland Rice once likened Speaker's movements to the "smoothness of a summer wind."

Tris Speaker played in an era when sportswriters liked to tag stars with hyperbolic nicknames. Lou Gehrig became "the Iron Horse," Walter Johnson "the Big Train," Babe Ruth "the Sultan of Swat." The moniker hung on Speaker, though, was a little different. It paid homage to something other than his prematurely aging hair. He was called "the Gray Eagle," in part because it described the aviary brilliance with which he presided over center field. He swooped and soared, surmounting the game from an aerie few ballplayers have ever attained. What a shame there's no film of that day in 1915 when the president of the United States stood in tribute to him.

CHAPTER 1

October 1912

The mood of many of the fans filing into Fenway Park that October afternoon mirrored the foul weather. Even by Boston's often-dank fall standards, it was a dreary day. Heavy clouds hung over the Back Bay all morning and afternoon, further dampening already soggy spirits. The previous day's game at Fenway had been played in fog and drizzle so impenetrable that even Bostonians in the best seats had trouble seeing what was happening on the field. Considering the way their Red Sox had played, that was probably a blessing.

Boston's "Olde Towne Team" hadn't merely lost the last two games; it had disgraced itself in a way that enraged the city. The past forty-eight hours had been a fiasco. Days that had started with so much promise for Red Sox fans had ended in bitterness and recrimination.

The Red Sox, the American League champions, and the New York Giants, the National League champions, were concluding the 1912 World Series – or, as it was known back then, the "World's Series." It had been a hotly contested postseason that riveted fans throughout the country. Extra trains had to be added to shuttle all the hangers-on between Boston and New York. Torchlight parades drew huge crowds in both cities. Special platforms were erected in Times Square and along Boston's "newspaper row" on Washington Street so that tens of thousands of passersby, in those pre-radio days, could follow the action on mammoth boards with diamonds carved into the middle. Pitch-by-pitch and base-running updates were flashed to board operators via telegraph, then displayed on the diamond, triggering deafening roars and groans. The Times Square board was hailed as a technological marvel; it was run by electricity.

Boston mayor John Francis "Honey Fitz" Fitzgerald, whose yet-to-be-born grandson would become the thirty-fifth president of the United States, and New York mayor William Gaynor engaged in good-natured public jousting. Thousands of people – quite likely the two mayors among them – engaged in not-so-good-natured private betting. Saloon-keepers, bookmakers, and sportswriters all agreed it was the most heavily wagered event they'd ever seen. Gamblers hung out in Fenway's bleachers, hollering out the odds. Scalpers were hawking tickets for as much as fifty or even sixty bucks a throw – double the take from the '11 Series. Many commentators were calling the '12 Series – the ninth ever played – the finest yet.

The Red Sox had gone into the previous day's game holding a 3–2 lead in games won in the best-of-seven series. (The second game, lengthened by a nasty scuffle that cleared both benches, had been called a tie and suspended after eleven innings because of darkness.) A Boston win looked assured in the seventh game, however, because the Sox were sending their ace, twenty-two-year-old "Smoky Joe" Wood, to the mound. Wood had dominated opponents that season, winning thirty-four games while hurling a Gibsonian ten shutouts. Smoky Joe had acquitted himself well in the Series, winning games one and four while striking out a total of nineteen Giants. In game one, Wood was particularly stout, snuffing out a Giants rally in the ninth to preserve a 4–3 win. "I threw so hard I thought my arm would fly right off my body," Joe supposedly declared in the clubhouse afterward.

President William Howard Taft, cruising off the Newport coast aboard the yacht USS *Mayflower* – a floating Xanadu replete with wine cellar and solid marble master bath – insisted that a naval wireless keep him apprised of game seven's progress. Taft was a huge man and a huge baseball buff. Two years earlier he had become the first president to take part in Opening Day ceremonies. In retrospect, perhaps Taft should have been trolling for votes instead of trolling Rhode Island Sound. In less than three weeks he would lose all but two states to the combined forces of Democrat Woodrow Wilson, the winner, and Bull Mooser Theodore Roosevelt, the spoiler.

Despite the interest evinced by their portly commander-in-chief, Wood and his Red Sox teammates had not been enthused about the prospect of clinching the Series the day before. In fact, quite the opposite: two incidents earlier in the Series had incensed them.

First, baseball's governing National Commission, which served as a rubber stamp for the club owners and league presidents, decided not to share the proceeds of the tied second game with the players. The commission reckoned that since there had been no conclusion to the contest, the ballplayers had not earned their stake in the gate.

The other issue that left nerves raw was Boston president James Mc-Aleer's insistence that spitballer Buck O'Brien – not the peerless Wood – start the sixth game of the Series. With the Sox holding a three-to-one advantage in games won, Wood was primed and ready to go in game six at the Polo Grounds in New York. But McAleer doubtless wanted the Series to move back to Boston for one more day of big box office. Despite the protestations of Red Sox player-manager Jake Stahl, second-year-man O'Brien started the sixth game and was battered around for five runs in the first inning. The Sox went on to lose 5–2.

As explored in Glenn Stout and Richard Johnson's *Red Sox Century*, the postgame innuendo floating around Boston was that O'Brien didn't know he was scheduled to pitch until he arrived at the Polo Grounds just before the game started. Supposedly nursing a hangover from too much revelry in Manhattan the night before, Buck was in no condition to take the slab. Joe Wood's brother Paul, under the misconception that his unhittable sibling would start, had bet a hundred bucks – a tidy sum in those days – on the Sox in game six. On the train ride back to Boston following the game, Paul Wood was so bent on revenge that he reportedly baited O'Brien into a fight, inflicting a black eye.

It wasn't the first time that Boston's American League franchise had been suspected of postseason shenanigans to hype the gate. In 1903, the year of the first modern World Series, the great pitcher Cy Young and his Pilgrims (as the team was then called) allegedly "threw" game one against the Pittsburgh Pirates to protest the meager financial incentives – and manipulate more favorable odds for the Boston club for the remainder of the postseason. Young got scuffed up in the top of the first inning, his fielders made several embarrassing gaffes behind him, and the Pirates managed to pull off not one but two double steals – all before a peeved overflow crowd in Boston's South End. Boston's players and the club's owner, the story went, had taken full advantage of those more lucrative stakes once the odds evened out following Pittsburgh's victory. Boston fans knew that story all too well – and they thought history was repeating itself.

Another rumor swirling around Boston pubs was that owner McAleer, knowing O'Brien would falter, had wagered a bundle on the Giants in game six. Patrons of a Roxbury saloon called "Third Base" (so named because "it was the last place you stop before going home") were sure that the Red Sox president was larding both pockets.

The sixth game of the '12 Series was knocked off the front page of most newspapers around the country because it took place the same afternoon as the attempted assassination of presidential candidate Theodore Roosevelt. A deluded bartender named John Schrank shot Teddy in the chest as the former president was working his way toward a stage in Milwaukee. Schrank's pistol shot was deflected by Teddy's metal eyeglass case and by a fifty-page speech that was fortuitously folded in his vest pocket. Undeterred, Roosevelt held up his speech text with the bullet hole in it, vowing to the crowd, "I will make this speech or die." He finished his remarks before submitting to medical attention.

The tension on the field and in the stands at Fenway got even uglier as the seventh game approached. There was no rest day between the sixth and seventh contests; the players got off the train and – bleary-eyed – were back at Fenway after a short night's rest.

Brand new that year, the ballpark was packed to the rafters as it had been throughout the Series, so crowded that standing-room-only sections had been cordoned off on the field itself. Thousands of people were craning their necks behind roped-off areas in the outfield, barely three hundred feet from home plate. Many of them were bellowing the chants for which Red Sox fans had become infamous. One of them, sung to the tune of a popular ballad called "Tammany," went:

Carrigan, Carrigan
Speaker, Lewis, Wood, and Stahl.
Bradley, Engle, Pape, and Hall
Wagner, Gardner, Hooper, too.
Hit them! Hit them! Hit them! Hit them!
Do, boys, do!

But with the first pitch of the seventh game just minutes away, Boston's biggest cheerleaders were conspicuously absent. They were the self-anointed "Royal Rooters," a group of several hundred *über*fans led by Mayor Fitz and Ned "Nuf Ced" McGreevey, the proprietor of the Third Base saloon. McGreevey earned his nickname by thundering "Enough said!" when his customers' arguments over sports or politics grew too loud or long. Either nervous that the Royal Rooters wouldn't show or acting out of spite – or perhaps both – McAleer's green eyeshade deputy, club treasurer Robert McRoy, sold the Rooters' usual seats to fans queued up outside the ballpark. Since the club had sold Series tickets in strips of three games, in management's view duckets to the seventh game could only be secured on a first-come, first-served basis – a pesky little detail that was never communicated to the Rooters, nor anyone else, for that matter.

A few moments later, waving pennants and accompanied by a brass band, Fitz, McGreevey, and company marched through the then-opening in the center-field bleachers, only to discover that their seats had been bartered out from under them. McAleer and McRoy had relegated the Royal Rooters, whose allegiance went back, literally, to day one in the franchise's history, to standing-room-only in left field. Outraged, Mayor Fitz demanded a huddle with team officials, which took place in front of the pitcher's mound. No soap, His Honor was told: the Rooters were stuck in standing room. After their leader's appeal was denied, many of the Rooters went berserk, knocking over a temporary restraining fence and refusing to leave the playing field. Adding insult to injury, fans seated along the third base line began pelting the Rooters with peanuts, Cracker Jack, scorecards, and anything else they could get their hands on. The situation became so frenzied that mounted police were called in to restore order, galloping headlong into the throng from the open area in center field, billy clubs in hand.

Amid this chaos, Smoky Joe Wood was trying to warm up. In forbidding conditions, the start of the game was delayed for more than a half hour as the police and coaches and players from both teams herded the Rooters behind the restraint in left field. Wood's unsettled warmup and the mayhem all around him could not have helped his frame of mind. Like his brother Paul, Joe, too, reportedly had a confrontation with the hapless Buck O'Brien. The two supposedly had to be separated outside the clubhouse a couple of hours before the ball game started; a bat allegedly had to be wrung out of Wood's hands. O'Brien not only had the misfortune of losing game six, he was guilty of another sin in Wood's eyes. Buck was an immigrant kid and a practicing Roman Catholic, a background and a religion abhorred by Wood and a certain faction of teammates.

When the game finally started, Smoky Joe Wood was awful. For the only time all season, he got knocked out of the box early. Before being replaced in the top of the second, he threw barely a dozen pitches, giving up seven hits and six runs. Tim Murnane of the *Boston Globe*, whose observations commanded universal respect (Murnane's pronouncements were considered "pretty much ex cathedra," in the words of modern *Globe* sportswriter Bob Ryan), volunteered that Wood appeared to be "cutting the ball over the heart of the plate." With runners at first and second and nobody out, Wood curiously chose to pitch from a full windup instead of the stretch, allowing the Giants to dash off an easy double steal.

Wood's teammates dragged the Sox further into the mire; behind him, one of the finest fielding teams in history made a peck of mental and physical errors. The hijinks didn't stop after Wood left the game. As reported in the next day's *New York Times*, in the top of the second, relief pitcher Charley Hall tried to pick a Giants runner off second base. Hall's throw eluded both the Sox shortstop and its all-world center fielder. It eventually had to be tracked down by Boston's right fielder as the Giants runners sauntered around the bases.

When the game mercifully ended in the cold and mist, it was 11–4, Giants. The Series was now even at three games each. "When he walked to the pitching mound . . . Wood wore a halo," the *Times* asserted. "But before three hours had gone, fickle fandom was looking about for someone else to put on the pedestal."

To "fickle fandom" – the Red Sox faithful – the whole episode stunk to high heaven. It wasn't just the Royal Rooters who suspected the fix was in; Murnane and other reporters hinted that game seven wasn't on the level. The *Chicago Daily Tribune*'s respected baseball seer, Hugh Fullerton, deplored the suspicious turn the Series had taken. "Stamp out gambling and the end of talk of crookedness is at hand," he snapped in a column that week. Many people feared the worst: that the Red Sox had deliberately thrown the game to recover their losses from the "tied" contest. With Wood pitching, the conspiracy theory went, the Giants had been heavy underdogs. If the Sox players had laid money on the Giants, they would have made a killing.

The Royal Rooters felt so betrayed they gathered en masse on Jersey

Street after the game, singing sarcastic songs of praise to the Giants. Cries of "The hell with the Red Sox!" and "Who gives a damn whether they win or lose!" rang through the Fens. The Rooters' cause was taken up by an editorial in the next day's *Globe*, which likened the club's use of mounted police to Cossacks putting down a Russian peasant revolt.

A coin was tossed to determine the location of the eighth and final game. The Giants' surrogate called "heads"; it came up "tails." The clincher would be at Fenway the next day, October 16, 1912.

Red Sox fans were in a tizzy. With many of them convinced that the team's owner had compromised game six and that their beloved players had thrown game seven, they stayed away from game eight in droves. The Rooters angrily boycotted, with Mayor Fitz leading the catcalls.

Sadly, then, only a half-capacity crowd was on hand to witness the final match-up of the 1912 World Series – one of the best baseball games ever played.

Game eight was everything the previous two contests weren't: beautifully pitched, taut, gut-wrenching baseball. Joe Wood had thrown only a handful of pitches the day before and could easily have been sent to the mound again. But given Wood's mercurial behavior over the past forty-eight hours, manager Jake Stahl couldn't trust him. He turned to rookie Hugh Bedient. Bedient had pitched well as both a starter and reliever during the Series, starting and winning the fifth game, 2–1.

Almost everywhere those seventeen thousand fans looked that day, they glimpsed baseball immortality. Six of the people in uniform were later enshrined in the Baseball Hall of Fame.

Planted in the Giants' dugout was their combative manager, John McGraw. The son of an Irish immigrant railroad worker, "Muggsy" McGraw was revered by his players and Giants fans – and reviled by practically everyone else. He taught his charges to play the rugged brand of baseball pioneered by his old Baltimore Orioles teams of the 1890s. Muggsy, Hughie Jennings, and "Wee Willie" ("hit 'em where they ain't!") Keeler played baseball with sharp knuckles and sharper cleats. McGraw infused the same spirit in his Giants clubs, winning nine pennants and three World Series championships in his three decades as manager. He courted the Big Apple's Runyon-esque characters, counting Broadway stars, bookies, and professional gamblers among his many cronies. Muggsy even owned a casino in Havana, Cuba, which in short order became the wintertime playground of New York's better-endowed hustlers. The considerable girth of McGraw cohort (and some would say past and future co-conspirator) Wilbert Robinson was parked near McGraw in the Giants' dugout. Grantland Rice once wrote of McGraw that "his very walk across the field in a hostile town is a challenge to the multitude." Muggsy reveled in his bullyboy image but despised his bullyboy nickname.

Standing on the mound, in contrast to his profane manager, was the Giants' Christy Mathewson, the former Bucknell University class president whose scholarly demeanor belied a competitive fire. The right-hander was in the middle of one of the most celebrated pitching careers in baseball history. His famous "fadeaway," a screwball that dove away from left-handed hitters, baffled right-handed hitters, too. The "Christian Gentleman," an image he carefully cultivated, captured twenty-three of his 383 career wins that season, compiling an earned run average of 2.12. Mathewson was the closest thing that America had to a genuine folk idol in the early part of the twentieth century – a combination of brains and brawn worthy of the Frank Merriwell books. Writer Jonathan Yardley, in his essay about Matty in *The Ultimate Baseball Book*, called him "the golden god of baseball's true golden age." When Matty died tragically young in 1925, *Commonweal* eulogized him by writing, "No other pitcher ever loomed so majestically in young minds." Chief Meyers, his battery mate for eight years with the Giants, said that Matty's control was so good, "you could sit in a rocking chair and catch him."

In the 1905 World Series against Connie Mack's Philadelphia club, Matty stunned the sporting world by pitching three shutouts in the Giants' drubbing of the Athletics. But in the 1912 Series he was mortal, pitching indifferently in the controversial second game and losing a 2–1 heartbreaker in game five. Mathewson was one of those enviable people who master everything they attempt in life. At a time when the game of checkers was all the rage in clubs and bars throughout the country, Mathewson was the reigning checkers champion in several states, even winning a so-called national competition. He also played a mean game of billiards, bridge, and poker, no doubt sweetening one of the few decent off-the-field incomes from the dead-ball era.

Sitting in the Giants' bullpen was another Hall of Fame hurler. Debonair left-hander Richard William "Rube" Marquard set a record that season that still stands today: he won a remarkable nineteen games in a row. His twenty-six victories that year made Rube the ace of McGraw's staff. Rube enjoyed life in the limelight. In one of America's first celebrity romances, he scandalously pursued vaudeville star Blossom Seely, who was inconveniently married to someone else at the time. After a torrid courtship, Blossom obtained a divorce and married Rube. She was three months pregnant with Rube's child when they exchanged vows. For several years during Rube's off-season, the lovebirds toured the vaudeville circuit together. Their showstopper was a tune called "The Marquard Glide." Alas, Rube and Blossom ended up filing for one of America's first celebrity divorces.

At first base for the Giants was Fred Merkle, one of the hard-luck characters in baseball history. "Bonehead" Merkle had been tarred with his unfortunate handle four years earlier when, in a crucial late-season game against the Cubs, he neglected to touch second base on what would have been a game-winning hit. Merkle's "boner" ultimately contributed to the Giants' loss of the pennant. In center field was another soon-to-be-bedeviled Giant named Fred, the sure-handed Fred Snodgrass, one of the best outfielders in the National League.

Other notable Giants included John Tortes "Chief" Meyers, the Cahuillan Indian from California's missions who was a steady if slow-footed presence behind the plate; Buck Herzog, the no-nonsense third baseman; and second baseman Larry Doyle, whose .330 batting average that season earned him most valuable player honors in the National League. A few years earlier, "Laughing Larry" had endeared himself to McGraw's acolytes in the press box by uttering one of the most feted – and copied – quotes in sports history: "It's great to be young and a Giant."

The Red Sox were renowned for the best outfield ever assembled to that time – and one of the finest ever. Manning the left side was George "Duffy" Lewis, the fleet-footed Californian who excelled at racing up the odd slope of Fenway's left field, which in those pre–Green Monster days curved upward before meeting the wall. Boston cartoonists liked to portray Duffy as a goat perched on a mountain. In deference to Lewis's ability to snare balls off that hillside, Sox fans nicknamed the slope "Duffy's Cliff."

Handling Fenway's cavernous right field was Harry Hooper, who, like Lewis, was both a Roman Catholic and an alumnus of Saint Mary's College in California. Few ballplayers in baseball history have forced a change in the rules, but Harry Hooper did. Hooper had such gifted hands that he would deliberately juggle a potential sacrifice fly with a runner at third base, forcing the opponent to stay on the bag as Hooper inched closer to the infield, patty-caking the ball every step of the way. After witnessing Hooper's juggling act, rule makers determined that a runner could leave the bag after the fielder had made initial contact with the ball, and not wait until the fielder actually controlled it.

In center field for the Red Sox stood a barrel-chested Texan who could be as ornery as the Hill County mules he used to ride as a child. His name was Tristram Speaker and he played baseball with a hell-for-leather abandon that left fans and sportswriters awestruck. In 1912 he was the best ballplayer extant, winning the Chalmers Award (and with it a luxurious nickel-plated Chalmers "30" convertible) as the most valuable player in the American League. He led the circuit in doubles, home runs, extra-base hits, on-base percentage, outfield assists, and put-outs that year. His .383 batting average placed him third in the league behind Detroit's Ty Cobb and Cleveland's Shoeless Joe Jackson.

He was such a hot commodity in New England in the early 1910s that Hassan cigarettes marketed special trading cards depicting Speaker in various poses on the field. Speaker also lent his name to a top-of-the-line straw boater that fetched a full two dollars at finer haberdasheries, plus he shilled for Boston Garters for men. A local jeweler was so taken with Speaker's 1912 accomplishments that he presented the center fielder with a five-hundred-dollar sterling-silver bat.

Tris Speaker's defensive prowess was already legendary in just his fourth full season in the big leagues. Sportswriter Gordon Cobbledick of the *Cleveland Plain Dealer* once mused, "Speaker has been credited with revolutionizing outfield play, but that is less than true. The word 'revolution' suggests followers, and few outfielders were capable of following Speaker's pattern. He played the shallowest center field ever seen before or since his time." Speaker was virtually a fifth infielder. Some six times in his career – including late in the seventh game of the 1912 World Series – he recorded unassisted double plays by collaring line drives and beating the retreating runner to second base. He once raced into the infield and served as the second-base pivot man on a double play ball.

Speaker had a sharp and incisive mind, having spent two years studying at Fort Worth Polytechnic after graduating from high school. Later, during World War I, his facility for engineering earned him admission to an elite U.S. Navy aviation program at the Massachusetts Institute of Technology.

His booming Texas twang dominated a clubhouse in much the same way his feet and arm dominated center field. Early baseball chronicler A. H. Spink compared Speaker's baritone to "rumbling thunder" and likened "his softest words [to the] growl of a mastiff." He didn't suffer fools gladly; at that point in Tris Speaker's world, there were a lot of fools. His piercing dark eyes missed nothing on or off the field. Most of his contemporaries – even the acidic Cobb – managed a smile whenever a photographer was around. But almost all the pictures from Speaker's early days show a dour – even snarling – expression, with his jaw set and lips tightly pursed. His nose was flat enough to suggest that it had been on the business end of more than a punch or two. As a child he was so stubbornly determined to become a great ballplayer that when he was thrown by a horse and fractured his right arm and collarbone in several places, he taught himself to bat and throw left-handed.

One play from the 1912 Series captures the fury with which Speaker attacked a baseball game. In the tenth inning of the ill-starred second game, the Red Sox were trailing by one run when Speaker came to the plate against Christy Mathewson. Speaker smashed a drive over Fred Snodgrass's head into Fenway's center field. Watching him fly around the bases, Red Sox fans held little doubt in their minds that Speaker would attempt to score. As Speaker glanced over his shoulder rounding third, Giants third baseman Buck Herzog turned the kind of trick his manager had pulled dozens of times in his playing days for the old Orioles. Herzog threw his hip into Speaker, causing Tris to stagger. Just then, however, substitute shortstop Tillie Shafer dropped the relay throw from Snodgrass, and Speaker resumed his mad dash for home plate. The ball and Speaker's cleats arrived at the dish at the same intant, but catcher Art Wilson couldn't handle the throw. The ball skit-tered away.

In the recollection of baseball historian Fred Lieb, Speaker bounced up, retagged the plate to be certain his run counted, then – in a rage – headed back up the third baseline to confront Herzog. Both benches emptied as Herzog and Speaker squared off. By the time umpire Silk O'Loughlin and his partners got everyone settled down, darkness had begun to set in. After one more inning, O'Loughlin declared the game a tie.

The Herzog episode wasn't the first time – and it was far from the last – that Tris Speaker felt compelled to put up his dukes. The nephew of Confederate cavalrymen, Speaker didn't hesitate to renew hostilities over what he viewed as the "War of Northern Aggression" whenever a Yankee (on or off the field) or a Catholic or a black person offended his sensibilities. Like many in his generation, the Texas cowboy carried racial and religious prejudices, as well as a healthy chip on his shoulder, through much of his life.

Manager Stahl's gamble to start Bedient in the eighth game rather than Wood paid off. Bedient, a farm kid from Chautauqua County, New York, matched the great Mathewson pitch for pitch. Only in the third inning could the Giants muster any kind of a rally. Red Murray's double over Speaker's head scored Josh Devore from third. The Giants led 1–0.

Harry Hooper saved Bedient from further damage when he made a dizzying catch of Larry Doyle's long drive to right center in the sixth inning. Hooper twisted and turned as he raced backwards, finally diving over the temporary restraint and into the crowd, emerging with the ball in his bare hand. McGraw and his mates howled in protest, but the umpires ruled it a catch.

The Red Sox, meanwhile, could get practically nothing started against Mathewson. In the seventh inning, however, Matty began to tire. Player-manager Stahl's flared single to left and Heinie Wagner's base-on-balls put runners at first and second with two outs. From his perch on second base, Stahl motioned for reserve outfielder Olaf Henriksen to pinch-hit for pitcher Bedient. Henriksen delivered in the clutch, slapping an 0-2 curve ball off the third base bag to tie the game.

Taking Bedient out of the game left Stahl with the toughest decision of his managerial career. He weighed his options, then signaled for Joe Wood to begin warming up. Wood, perhaps not miraculously, rediscovered his touch. Smoky Joe mowed the Giants down in the eighth and again in the ninth.

In the top of the tenth, though, the Giants coaxed a run off Wood when, with one out, Red Murray doubled and Speaker's diving effort to catch Fred Merkle's sinking line drive came up short. Speaker bobbled the ball just long enough to allow Murray to round third and score. Wood gathered himself, struck out Buck Herzog on three pitches, then knocked down Chief Meyers's hot smash up the middle with his bare hand for the third out. His pitching hand, Wood would later tell his son Bob, immediately began to swell.

Things looked bleak for the Red Sox. Mathewson and McGraw, the two old Giants warhorses, were just three outs away from their second World Series crown.

With the ailing Wood scheduled to lead off, Stahl sent Clyde Engle, who'd hit an anemic .234 that season, in to pinch-hit. Matty fooled Engle with a classic "drop," luring Clyde to lift a medium-length fly ball to left center. It was the proverbial "can of corn": Fred Lieb, the bard of baseball's dead-ball era, always maintained "any high school center fielder could have caught it with ease." As Giants center fielder Fred Snodgrass told Lawrence Ritter years later in *The Glory of Their Times*, "I yelled that I'd take it and waved [left fielder Red] Murray off and, well, I dropped the darn thing. It was so high that Engle was sitting on second base before I could get it back to the infield." Snodgrass's infamous muff would haunt him the rest of his life. "Snow" went on to become a prosperous banker and a popular city councilman and mayor of Oxnard, California. Yet when he died sixty-two years later, his obituary in the *New York Times* was headlined: "Fred Snodgrass, 86, Dead, Ballplayer Muffed 1912 Fly."

Up next was Harry Hooper, whom the Giants were playing to bunt. Sure enough, Harry fouled off one bunt attempt. Manager Stahl then bucked the odds and had Hooper swing away. Harry scorched a line drive the opposite way into left center. On the dead run, Snodgrass made a lunging over-the-shoulder catch every bit as fabulous as his muff was dreadful. The crowd gasped for a second time in the last minute or so. Although most accounts suggest that Engle tagged up and advanced to third on the play, the next day's *Boston Post* scolded Engle for not staying on second while the ball was in the air, describing him as "slipping" between second and third. Engle had no choice but to scramble back to second after Snodgrass speared the ball.

Red Sox second baseman Steve Yerkes then worked Matty for a walk. So there were runners at first and second with one out, with the Sox trailing 2–1, when Tris Speaker dug in at the plate.

Speaker was a left-handed hitter whose back foot scraped the edge of the batter's box. Like all great batsmen, his routine at the plate was ritualized. Before he dug in, he tugged his cap down over his forehead, then took his bat and drew a line across the right side of the plate. Next he used his stick to knock the dirt out of the cleats of his right shoe, then his left, before digging his left foot into the back of the box. His stance was severely closed; his front foot was some four or five inches nearer to home plate than his back foot. He kept his hands so low and close to his body that, to one observer, it looked like he was resting them on his left hip. As the pitcher wound up, his bat bobbed menacingly up and down, a habit that writer Tom Meany would later compare to "the lazy twitching of a cat's tail." Tris took a sharp, pronounced stride with his front leg, his right foot coming up off the ground. When he swung, it was with an abrupt, violent, inside-out whoosh that produced vicious line drives.

Early in the count, Mathewson got the best of Speaker. He jammed Speaker with a fastball, inducing a little foul pop-up about two-thirds of the way down the first base line. Exactly what transpired while Speaker's pop-up was in the air has been debated for nearly a century; it's part of baseball's mythology.

First baseman Fred Merkle clearly had the easiest play on the ball. In McGraw's defensive scheme, though, it was the pitcher's job to assign responsibilities on fly balls in the infield. Perhaps Matty was exhausted and not thinking too clearly; inexplicably, he began yelling for catcher Chief Meyers to make the catch. Although Speaker always denied it, eyewitnesses, including Fred Lieb, claim that Tris, too, was barking at Meyers to make the play. The three Ms – Mathewson, Meyers, and Merkle – had the pop-up almost surrounded as, buffeted by the wind, it began descending in foul ground just short of the first base coach's box. But Matty, and maybe Speaker, too, continued to call Chief's number –

and Chief couldn't get his mitt out in time. Merkle lunged but it was too late: Speaker's weak little pop-up thudded to the ground untouched. It was the kind of play that McGraw's Giants should have made blindfolded. But they didn't.

Speaker had been granted a reprieve. As he worked his way back into the batter's box, folks within hearing distance claim that the Texan baited Mathewson by rasping, "Well, you just called for the wrong man, Matty. It's gonna cost you the ballgame."

It did. Speaker smoked a line drive single into right center field. Engle, sliding home from second, scored the tying run, beating right fielder Josh Devore's peg by some two yards, the *Boston Post* estimated. The hustling Yerkes made it to third on the play and Speaker scampered to second. With just one out, Giants manager McGraw played the percentages and walked Duffy Lewis to load the bases.

Mathewson now faced Larry Gardner, who lofted a long fly ball to right fielder Devore. Josh fired the ball homeward, hoping to catch Yerkes tagging up from third. It was all in vain; Yerkes scored easily.

Tris Speaker and the Boston Red Sox had won a World Series that they had little business winning. To win that final game, they had to overcome greed, deceit, erratic play, front-office chicanery, and clubhouse backstabbing – not to mention one of the greatest pitchers who ever lived. Matty, famously impassive, left the mound choking back tears. The odds – something that Red Sox players and fans knew far too well back then – were stacked against them. But somehow the Sox had prevailed.

A minute or two after the game ended, losing manager McGraw, no doubt as devastated as Matty, magnanimously worked his way across the crowded field to shake the hand of winning manager Stahl. According to an account that later appeared in the *Sporting News*, a Sox partisan tripped Muggsy from behind. McGraw did what any self-respecting dead-ball legend would have done under similar circumstances: he jumped up and threw a haymaker at the miscreant. It missed. And so ended the 1912 World Series.

Mayor Fitzgerald, Nuf Ced McGreevey, and the other Royal Rooters swallowed their pride and embraced the new champions. Honey Fitz even managed to wangle an "apology" out of McAleer that was relayed to the rest of the Rooters. The next day, the mayor organized a victory parade that snaked throughout the city and concluded with a raucous rally at Faneuil Hall. The *New York Times* described His Honor as being smartly clad in a greatcoat and stovepipe hat. "I am going to write to Muggsy McGraw – I believe that's what he's called," Honey Fitz declared to the cheering masses, "and tell him that any man like Matty who can give this team such a run must be the best in the world!"

The *Boston Globe* reported that the mayor then handed the Sox the keys to the city and promised them commemorative silver cups. With huzzahs ringing all around him, he anointed them "the greatest team ever," punctuating his remarks by imploring the team's management to lower the price of tickets.

Naturally, before the next season began, the Red Sox raised most ticket prices.

Nearly four decades later, Larry Gardner was reminiscing about the '12 Series with writer Henry Berry. Berry asked Gardner how much his clutch sacrifice fly had meant to him. "It meant four thousand twenty-four dollars and sixty-eight cents to me," Gardner responded, still able to pinpoint the winner's share to the penny. Gardner's birthplace in Enosburg Falls, Vermont, has been converted into a beauty parlor, although a modest sign out front reminds folks of its once-famous occupant.

When both men were in their seventies, Harry Hooper and Fred Snodgrass happened to see each other at a function in Los Angeles. Hooper congratulated Snodgrass on the amazing catch he had made on Harry's line drive in the last inning of the last game of the 1912 Series. "Well, thank you," Snodgrass replied. "Nobody ever mentions that catch to me. All they talk about is the muff."

Movies are produced about Shoeless Joe Jackson and Ty Cobb. Novels are written about Christy Mathewson and Honus Wagner. Cy Young and Walter Johnson still make virtually everyone's short list of best pitchers ever. But Tris Speaker has fallen through the cracks. He's the forgotten superstar from baseball's dead-ball epoch.

All of which is puzzling, since "Spoke" or "Texas Spoke," as his teammates called him, was such a pivotal figure in the evolution of the game. He played on teams that won more World Series than Johnson's and

Mathewson's combined. His .345 lifetime batting average still places him sixth all-time. As a member of the Red Sox, he averaged thirty-seven steals a year. In four separate seasons, he batted .380 or higher. He was a better hitter than Wagner and a far superior fielder than either Cobb or Jackson. He was the only American League batsman in a thirteen-year span to wrest a batting championship away from the redoubtable Cobb. Speaker's record for career doubles – 792 by some accounts, 793 by others – looks like a typographical error; it may never be approached, let alone broken. He got his euphonic nickname early in his career from teammates who would taunt the opposition by yelling, "Speaker spoke! Speaker spoke!" whenever he smashed a hit.

In the July 1987 *Baseball Digest*, Morton Roth debated the merits of the greatest outfielders in history and concluded that Speaker, the "nonpareil among center fielders," topped the list. "What's that?" Roth's article asked, jabbing the reader. "Your memory doesn't go that far back? Dare we dismiss all that transpired before our time? Do we deny the sinking of the *Titanic*? The Battle of Gettysburg?" Speaker's contemporary Donie Bush, who played shortstop for the Tigers and the Senators for sixteen years, once claimed that Speaker could "throw strikes across home plate from any part of center field." His great pal Joe Wood said in a 1963 interview, "I never saw anybody was [Speaker's] equal . . . all around hitting, running, throwing, he was tops."

Along with Willie Mays and Roberto Clemente, Speaker was that rare outfielder whose brilliance tilted the field in his team's favor. In *Of Time and the River*, novelist Thomas Wolfe called Tris "a greyhound of a man." No less an authority than Babe Ruth thought Speaker the finest defensive outfielder he ever saw. When asked toward the end of his life to name his all-time team, the Babe tabbed Speaker as his center fielder. "Spoke was something extra special. Only those who played with or against him really appreciated what a great player he was. In my Red Sox pitching days, I would hear the crack of the bat and say, 'There goes the game.' But Tris would turn his back to the plate, race for it out to the fences, and at the last moment make a diving catch. Not once, but a thousand times," the Babe recalled. Speaker so often threw batters out at first base after short-hopping line drives that his teammates came to view the play as "routine." Will Rogers, Speaker's great rodeo pal and perhaps the most discerning observer of American popular culture in the early decades of the twentieth century, argued that Speaker was the "one man that has never been approached in his playing of center field."

As a player-manager for the Cleveland Indians, Speaker was ahead of his time, platooning players to take advantage of righty-lefty match-ups. He also devised a startling defense against a sacrifice bunt that revolved around him coming in to cover second from center field, freeing the shortstop to cover third and the second baseman to cover first, thereby allowing the third baseman, pitcher, and first baseman to charge the plate and smother the bunt. Tris got the most out of middling Cleveland clubs and did a superb job guiding them to the 1920 World Series championship in his first full year at the helm. Indeed, of the early demigods who became managers – Cobb and Johnson among them – Speaker enjoyed the most success. Tris, furthermore, was the linchpin of the all-star squad that toured the world under the aegis of the "Chicago White Sox" and the "New York Giants" in 1913–14. His clutch hitting and spectacular fielding elicited applause from Tokyo to Trafalgar Square.

One other trait separated Speaker from many of his contemporaries. He was savvy enough to know how much he was worth and brassy enough to fight for it. Few of Speaker's dead-ball compatriots grasped the economics of the game the way he did. He knew what he meant to a club's bottom line and wasn't shy about pressing his case. Using an entreaty from the Federal League as leverage in 1914, Speaker craftily negotiated his way to the highest salary in the big leagues: the astronomical sum of eighteen thousand dollars a year. Over time, he became something of a Will Rogers renaissance man – not just an expert marksman, fisherman, and horseman but also a licensed pilot who treated biplanes as if they were rodeo ponies. Orville Wright had barely hit middle age when Spoke began taking rickety crates up during a brief hitch in the waning days of the Great War. Sportswriter Joe Williams of the *New York World-Telegram* once called the ballplayer-aviator "the manliest of men."

After his retirement, it apparently irked the manly man that so much attention was fawned upon Yankee center fielder Joe DiMaggio. Commentator Bob Consodine once asked Speaker if DiMaggio was the "best" of the then-current crop of outfielders. Speaker growled "no," allowing as to how there must be "fifteen outfielders" in the big leagues better than DiMaggio. Consodine, taken aback, asked Speaker to name them. After a moment or two, Speaker had to grudgingly admit he couldn't. The press's idolatry of "Joltin' Joe" must have gotten under Speaker's skin. In later years, Spoke liked to quietly point out that he had stolen more bases in one year than DiMaggio did in an entire career.

Speaker was also present at the creation of the phenomenon that became Babe Ruth. Tris was a grizzled veteran of six full years in the big leagues when the Red Sox brought the spindly-legged left-handed pitcher up from Providence late in the 1914 season. They were teammates the following year, then rivals for more than a decade. At best, their relationship was prickly. Ruth was the sworn enemy of Joe Wood – and no enemy of Smoky Joe's could be a friend of Speaker's. It didn't help Ruth's dealings with Wood and Speaker that the Babe, raised Lutheran, happened to convert to Catholicism during his days at Saint Mary's school for wayward boys in Baltimore. Despite his dissolute ways, the Babe considered himself fairly devout.

The Red Sox clubhouse, like the city of Boston itself back then, was divided along sectarian lines. Ruth tended to hang out with the Catholics on the team, a group led by Duffy Lewis and catcher Bill Carrigan, among others. Speaker, an outspoken thirty-second-degree Freemason, and Wood, a member of a nativist group that defiantly called itself the Orangemen, led a rival faction of Protestants.

Following Ruth's sale to New York, Speaker famously predicted that the Yankees would rue the day they converted the Babe from a pitcher to a full-time outfielder. "Working once a week, Ruth might have lasted a long time and become a great star," Speaker boldly opined in 1919. Speaker's remarkable lack of prescience regarding Ruth's potential as a hitter now sits near the top of an Internet list of "silliest predictions" of all time.

Tris was christened without a middle name. When he joined the Red Sox, though, the front office insisted for some reason that he adopt a middle initial. So Tris insinuated "E." into his name. He cackled when telling people "it don't stand for nuthin'!" But over the years, writers turned Tris's faux "E." into "Edward." The cackler who loved to munch on blades of grass in between pitches also enjoyed playing practical jokes that bordered on the malicious. Spoke would get so angry with umpires, his Indians' teammate Bill Wambsganss once recalled, that he'd literally turn blue in the face while arguing a call.

While on deck at the Polo Grounds one wickedly hot afternoon in

August 1920, Speaker witnessed the most gruesome moment in baseball history, when teammate Ray Chapman was struck on the temple by a pitch thrown by Yankee submarine hurler Carl Mays. Speaker rushed to his friend's side and stayed with him at the hospital, praying for a miracle that didn't happen. Despite emergency surgery, Chapman died the next day. Chappie's death decimated Speaker. But even in grief, Speaker couldn't contain his religious prejudice, brawling with Catholic teammates over the proper church for Chapman's memorial service. Speaker was such a physical and emotional wreck that he couldn't attend Chappie's requiem mass or funeral.

Observers of the sporting scene thought Speaker "cute," which in the parlance of the day meant he spent a lot of time at the racetrack, in billiard halls, and playing games of chance in back rooms and private gentlemen's clubs. Maybe too much time. The cozy relationship that Speaker and other big leaguers enjoyed with notorious gambler Joseph "Sport" Sullivan raised eyebrows throughout baseball's saloon culture. That curious seventh game of the 1912 World Series was probably not an aberration. Some fourteen years later, Speaker, Joe Wood, and Ty Cobb were accused by a former teammate of fixing a Cleveland-Detroit game played years before. Although all three legends protested their innocence (sort of, eventually, once lawyers got involved and started issuing ultimatums), Commissioner Kenesaw Mountain Landis and American League president Ban Johnson thought enough of the charges to force Speaker and Cobb to resign from their respective clubs and effectively banned them from future management posts. Speaker, one of the most respected managers of his era, was never given the opportunity to skipper in the big leagues again.

"The culture of gambling was endemic back then. It permeated every pore of the game," historian Richard Johnson contended in a 2003 interview. The milieu that big league baseball operated in back then was not much different than prize fighting or horse racing. Far too often – particularly in the postseason – the fix was in. The research of Johnson, Stout, Allan Wood, Harold Seymour, David Voit, and others into the deadball era suggests more than a few "arranged" games, especially in World Series play. Unlike Cobb, who wisely invested his baseball earnings in companies such as Coca-Cola, Speaker left the game without much of a nest egg. American League president Johnson was so suspicious of

Speaker's gambling habits that he hired private detectives to tail Spoke at a couple of different points in his career. Sure enough, the gumshoes confirmed that Tris squandered a ton of money at the track.

In his forties, Speaker was reduced to managing in the minor leagues – and playing a more-than-occasional game to hype the gate. At age forty-one he hit a remarkable .419 in a part-time role for the Newark Bears. In the teeth of the Depression, he made an ill-advised investment in the Kansas City Blues of the American Association. Later in the 1930s, he lent his prestige and wallet to a fly-by-night indoor softball league that quickly folded. His prospects improved when he went into enterprises that would have horrified his Southern Methodist mother: the liquor industry and professional boxing. The marketing of "Gray Eagle Brands" liquor wasn't subtle. Its logo featured a drawing of Tris taking a mighty cut at the plate.

Over time, his ties to Cleveland's business leaders enabled Speaker to pursue a creditable career – and to help establish a wonderful charity for disabled children – but his first few years of "retirement" in the tumult of the early 1930s must have caused some unease. Sadly, after his outlook brightened, he suffered a near-fatal fall at home, then almost died five years later from pneumonia. His twilight years were also far from placid: he was in a serious car wreck while driving to Texas one winter and, two years later, sustained a heart attack that laid him up for months. He never regained full health and died of another coronary four years later.

Commentator Bill Moyers, a native of East Texas, has spent a lifetime studying the tarnished luster of the Lone Star State. In a 1992 commentary for CNN, Moyers had occasion to observe: "Speaker was a Texan. If his flaws were large, so were his virtues." Speaker shared many of the conflicted emotions of such Lone Star legends as Ben Hogan and Moyers's old boss, Lyndon Johnson. These larger-than-life icons – all geniuses in their chosen worlds – were consumed by ambition, hell bent on pleasing absent fathers. They could be petty, vindictive, brilliant, big-hearted, and visionary – all rolled into one incendiary package.

The young Speaker could be, in historian Glenn Stout's estimation, a "bully and an intimidator." Tris was among the roughest in a sport full of rough customers. Ballplayers from that era had little choice but to be rough. Virtually everything around them had a jagged edge. They played for unscrupulous owners. There was next to no job security and very little money to divvy up. Many of them drank and gambled too much. They were under enormous pressure: for most of them, if they couldn't cut it in the big leagues, it meant trying to make ends meet by going back home to jobs in the fields or the mines or the factories. In Bob Ryan's pithy description, "[The dead-ball era's] system of justice was equal parts Old Testament, King Arthur's Court and Dodge City."

Many of us have a tendency to romanticize the past. That's especially true when it comes to extolling our national pastime. We see these immigrant sons and farm boys with gaunt cheeks and hollow eyes staring at us from sepia-tinted photographs and we want to put them on a pedestal, to believe that they embodied virtues superior to our own. There's no doubt it was a simpler time. There is much to admire about the intellect and courage and passion of these early practitioners of the game.

But then as now, baseball was a microcosm of the forces surging through society – the game back then, like virtually every American institution, was rife with labor acrimony, violence, bigotry, and corruption. Tris Speaker personified the best and worst of his times. The young Speaker was a man of infuriating contradictions, capable of genius and generosity one minute, ignorance and cruelty the next. On the field and in the dugout, he helped forge the magnificent game now played the world over. Off the field, darker forces drove him. The youngster from the Texas frontier lipped off to his manager and challenged teammates to fight on his very first day in professional baseball in 1906. He mellowed as the years went on, becoming a respected – even courtly – elder statesman, but that cowboy feistiness never left him.

Indeed, Tris Speaker's whole life is testament to William Faulkner's conviction that "the past is never dead – it's not even past."

CHAPTER 2

Texas Frontier Child

For every Southern boy fourteen-years-old, not once but whenever he
wants it, there is the instant when . . . the brigades are in position behind
the rail fence, the guns are laid and ready in the woods and the furled flags
are already loosened to break out . . . and it's all in the balance, it hasn't
happened yet, it hasn't even begun yet . . . we have come too far with too
much at stake and that moment doesn't need even a fourteen-year-old boy
to think: *This time. Maybe this time.* — William Faulkner, *Intruder in the
Dust*

Most Americans in the mid-nineteenth century had never witnessed anything even remotely approaching the brutality of the Civil War. But that
wasn't necessarily true on the Texas frontier. Texas pioneers had known
little but bloodshed from almost the moment they emigrated to what had
been Mexico's northeasternmost province. Many Texans saw the War
between the States as an extension of a bloody struggle for freedom that
had begun two generations before.

Texas's War of Independence against Mexico in 1836 lasted only a few
skirmishes. Innocents on both sides, however, were slaughtered before a
truce was declared. And the mythic battle that defined the insurrection –
the defense of the Alamo in San Antonio – was, in fact, a defeat for the
Texans.

A decade later, after the Texas Republic had joined the Union, its
citizens volunteered in droves to aid the U.S. war against Mexico. The
fact that every defender of the Alamo had perished was not lost on Texas
schoolboys in the years to come. Frontier youngsters could also recite
the stirring tale of the brave infantrymen who scaled the walls guarding
Chapultepec, the hilltop fort that was Mexico City's last line of defense.

Blood feuds and military heroics, then, were part of Texas folklore
long before two brothers named Speaker rode north of the Red River
in 1861 to fight Union-sympathizing Creeks and Seminoles in the In-

29

dian Territories. The Speaker boys, twenty-three-year-old Byron and nineteen-year-old James, had migrated to the northeast Texas village of Tarrant from Illinois a few years before. When news of the Confederate attack on Fort Sumter reached Hopkins County, the two young men immediately enlisted in the Texas militia. A carpenter by trade, Byron volunteered for artillery duty before being transferred to the same cavalry unit as James. Both enlisted as privates. Within a year, James was elected a second lieutenant and eventually earned a promotion to first lieutenant.

What became Capt. Lewis G. Harmon's Company D of the Eleventh Texas Cavalry Regiment was formed in late May of 1861. Byron and James could never have foreseen the adventures and heartache that awaited them. Through three theaters, their unit stayed in the thick of the fight.

After defeating the Indians at Chustenahlah and Hopo-eith-le-yo-ho-la in the winter of 1861–62, they joined Gen. Ben McCulloch's Army of Arkansas, battling Union troops at Bentonville and Pea Ridge in March. Later that spring they were ordered to Corinth, Mississippi, to help blunt the advance of Union general U. S. Grant. They served as dismounted cavalry throughout Grant's offensive in Tennessee. After the Battle of Chicamauga in September 1863, they were ordered to remount, joining the Eighth Texas Cavalry.

In late 1864 the Speakers and the Eighth Texas were part of Gen. John Bell Hood's doomed effort to contain the army of Union general William Tecumseh Sherman in the hills of north Georgia. On October 13, 1864, while his cavalry unit shielded Hood's host as it slipped across the Alabama line, Lt. James Speaker was captured by Sherman's troops outside the Georgia village of Rome. He was shipped to a dismal prisoner-of-war camp on the shores of Lake Michigan in Illinois. Named after the family of U.S. senator Stephen Douglas, the prison held some twenty-six thousand Confederate captives. Conditions were so bleak that roughly four thousand of the inmates died while imprisoned, most of them buried in unmarked paupers' graves in Chicago's City Cemetery.

James Speaker was fortunate. He survived the harsh winter of 1864–65 and was released from Camp Douglas two months after the surrender at Appomattox. Private Byron Speaker also defied the odds, escaping the war without serious injury and returning to Texas.

The Speakers suffered through four years of horrific combat. They saw "the Cause," for which they had sacrificed so much, disintegrate. They tried and failed to stop Billy Sherman's troops from pillaging the South. Young James spent the last half-year of the war watching hundreds of comrades-in-arms die of starvation and disease.

As they made their way back home at war's end, these hard-bitten soldiers would have been incredulous to learn that a half century later, the children and grandchildren of their enemies all over the North would pay good money to see their nephew play a child's game.

How much young Tristram knew about his uncles' exploits is unclear. But in the South of that era, as historian C. Vann Woodward has noted, a family's Confederate heritage was like a precious heirloom; it defined their sense of self-worth. Surely the valor and suffering of uncles James and Byron and the family's other Rebel heroes was a recurring theme in the Speaker household. We know this much: in later years, whether in a baseball clubhouse or a hotel lobby, Tris Speaker liked to hold forth on the War between the States, hectoring any Northerner within earshot. Maybe he couldn't help himself. Maybe he looked at certain Northerners and saw only his uncle's captors.

Tris Speaker grew up, literally, deep in the heart of Texas. As local historian and genealogist Cleo Davis proudly points out, Hill County is almost the exact geographic center of the state. Some time back, mapmakers changed their calculations and placed the midpoint of Texas a few miles west of the Hill County line – causing no small amount of consternation in and around the courthouse and chamber of commerce in Hillsboro. Speaker's hometown, known then as Hubbard City and now simply called Hubbard, sits roughly halfway between Waco to the south and Dallas and Fort Worth to the north.

It's an area known as Cross Timbers, a stretch of flat, scruffy terrain rich in moist black-soil farmland. Scrub and live oak, mesquite, cedar, cypress, and native pecan trees dot the broad landscape today just as they did a century ago.

Unlike its neighbors to the north, Hill County has only a handful of the huge Texas ranches of yore. The one ranch of historical note in Hill County is the Steiner Valley. It's been around since the nineteenth century, although the Steiner family is long gone. A big agribusiness in Houston now owns it. The mindset hasn't changed, though: Cleo Davis drove onto Steiner property a few years ago to explore a private cemetery and was met by a truckload of cowboys toting shotguns.

Hill County was formed in 1853 when Navarro County was divided into four smaller jurisdictions. For decades, the most important installations in Hill County were the military forts established to keep local Cherokees and Comanches in check. Hill County was named after George W. Hill, who served the Texas Republic as secretary of state. Hubbard City was named in honor of Richard Bennett Hubbard Jr., a Harvard-trained lawyer and intimate of President James Buchanan who later served as a Confederate officer, governor of Texas, and minister to Japan in the first Grover Cleveland administration.

The legend of the Old West is deeply rooted in Hill County. One of the branches of the fabled Chisholm Trail ran through its western edge. Until after the century turned, it was not uncommon along the Brazos River to see cowboys on horseback driving thousands of bleating Texas longhorns north to Kansas and the Indian Territories.

Before rail lines were linked, the Butterfield Overland Stagecoach used to stop in Hillsboro on its way from Springfield, Missouri, to Tombstone, Arizona, and other exotic outposts out West. Butterfield drivers and the brave souls "riding shotgun" had to keep a wary eye out; danger lurked around every bend – and not just from the Comanches and the Cherokees. Bandits roamed the Texas plains.

Originally a tiny crossroads known by the crude name Slap-out, Hubbard City wasn't laid out until 1881. According to Hubbard native Gene Fulton, the community's current justice of the peace, "Slap-out" was derived from the favorite phrase of the proprietor of "Tip-Top," the first general store to open in southeastern Hill County. When farmers would ask for a certain item that Tip-Top didn't have in stock, the owner would bang his knee and exclaim, "We're slap out of it!" Well into the next century, cows, chickens, pigs, horses, and mules wandered the erstwhile Slap-out's dusty streets.

In its day, Hubbard was a fairly bustling resort, railroad, lumber, and cotton town. The population grew as high as twenty-seven hundred in 1925. But the mineral waters that gave rise to a large sanitarium, a bathhouse, and two hospitals dried up. The supposed healing powers of the mineral waters brought a dozen or more physicians to town. They built magnificent Victorian homes along Magnolia Avenue and Bois d'Arc

Street. Today, a number of the manses have been beautifully restored – some as private homes, others as bed-and-breakfasts. The big bathhouse burned down many years ago, but the sanitarium still stands. It has been converted into Magnolia Manor, an apartment complex for seniors.

The St. Louis Southwestern Texas Railway, which built a depot in Hubbard seven years before Tris Speaker was born, eventually petered out, too. Much of the land used to raise cotton got farmed out; most farmers today have switched to growing grain. The majority of folks who live in the Hubbard area still work in businesses tied to the agriculture industry. Fewer than sixteen hundred people reside in Speaker's home-town today.

The heartache and rebelliousness of Willie Nelson's music has its ante-cedents in Hill County. Country music's renegade grew up in Abbott, a little town west of Hubbard, where his grandparents raised him after his dad died and his mother abandoned the family.

A couple years back, actor Dennis Quaid caused quite a stir when he stopped at Hubbard's Dairy Queen after visiting his grandparents' graves at Fairview Cemetery outside town. Dennis and Randy Quaid's maternal grandfather was a gentleman known as "Preacher" Jordan. Ex-actly why he was called "Preacher" remains a mystery to Billy Mack Waller, the owner of Hubbard's Country Kitchen restaurant, who has known the Jordan and Quaid families for decades. As far as anyone knows, the only creatures that old man Jordan ever proselytized were his farm animals. Nevertheless, his grandson D.Q.'s visit to the DQ made the *Hubbard City News*. Dennis's fondness for Hill County was later highlighted in *Texas Monthly*.

When Billy Mack Waller was a boy, he loved to pull up an apple box and sit next to Charlie Vaughn when Charlie came to visit the Wallers' service station in town. Charlie, a master storyteller, was for many years the caretaker of Tris Speaker's ranch outside town. Vaughn and Speaker were great hunting and fishing pals. After the ballplayer died, Charlie gave Billy Mack one of Speaker's fishing rods, a rare model crafted with Asian bamboo. It now proudly hangs on the wall of the Country Kitchen, near Billy Mack's collection of Speaker and Hubbard memorabilia.

Although Hill County was a quiet place in the early part of the twentieth century, it remained unbridled frontier country; violence was ingrained in the culture. Among the first armed robberies that landed Depression-era desperado Clyde Barrow in jail was committed in Hill County. A few years later the Bonnie and Clyde gang staged a dramatic "rescue" of fellow hoodlums Raymond Hamilton and Joe Palmer at nearby Eastham penitentiary, killing one guard and wounding another before careening through Hillsboro with the cops in hot but futile pursuit.

Hamilton was later accused – falsely, it turns out – of robbing and murdering Hillsboro jeweler John Bucher, who kept a cache of diamonds in his safe. Other members of the Barrow gang apparently did the dirty deed, since Bonnie, Clyde, and Raymond were otherwise occupied at that precise moment. As Raymond was being led to "Old Sparky," the electric chair at Huntsville penitentiary that saw plenty of action in the 1930s, he protested that he was innocent of Bucher's murder, but then allowed that he was guilty of so many other capital crimes that it didn't much matter for what he was being executed. Local folklore has it that the Barrow gang kept a hideout just across the Brazos River in Clifton.

Remarkably, the tiny village of Hubbard City produced three men of national prominence after the twentieth century turned. Fundamentalist Baptist preacher John Franklyn Norris spent a turbulent boyhood in Hubbard. In a life-altering moment straight out of a Hollywood Western, young Norris was shot three times by horse thieves seeking vengeance against his father for turning them over to lawmen. Norris vowed at that instant to devote the rest of his life to the Lord. He became such a spell-binding fire-and-brimstone orator that it was said he could draw a crowd of 5,000 to 10,000 anywhere he showed up in Texas – including a street corner. Throughout the 1920s and 1930s, his evangelical newsletters, the *Fundamentalist* and the *Searchlight*, were among the most popular religious pamphlets in the country. His circulars featured screeds against the evils of Catholicism and evolutionism. In the 1928 presidential election, Norris's denunciation of Catholic Al Smith was credited with helping Protestant Herbert Hoover carry Texas – an unheard-of feat for a Republican back then.

Xenophobia run amok propelled another son of Hubbard into the national spotlight. Hiram Wesley Evans served as an imperial wizard of the Ku Klux Klan from 1922 to 1939. His books, *The Menace of Modern Immigration, Alienism in the Democracy*, and *The Rising Storm*, warned of the apocalyptic dangers of immigration and miscegenation. Evans rose quickly through the ranks of the KKK when, in 1921, he and several accomplices used acid to burn the group's initials into the forehead of a young black bellhop who had somehow offended them. He helped preside over the Klan when it wielded formidable political, economic, and religious power – not only in the South but also throughout the country. It was a time when the KKK's parades in the nation's capital attracted thousands of white-hooded Klansmen proudly marching down Pennsylvania Avenue.

Today, the teachings of Norris and Evans would be dismissed as hateful bigotry or worse. Eight decades ago, however – especially on the Texas frontier – the ignorance they spewed was considered mainstream. How much interaction there may have been among the Norris, Evans, and Speaker households in Hubbard City is not known; Tris was eleven years younger than Norris and seven years younger than Evans. But in his early years, Speaker certainly subscribed to Norris's anti-Catholic bias. And for a time, the ballplayer told chronicler Fred Lieb, he belonged to Evans's KKK.

Not much is known about how the Speaker family came to settle in Texas. In many ways, Tris's paternal grandfather Henry was the quintessential restless American of the nineteenth century: constantly uprooting his family to find better land and a better way of life.

Census and cemetery records are murky at best, but from various sources it appears that Henry Speaker was born in Maryland in 1809 or 1810. He married a Pennsylvania woman three years his junior named Eliza and started a family in the 1830s, moving first to Ohio, where sons Byron, James, Melville, and Calvin were born, then to Illinois, where their last son, Archery Oscar, was born in 1852. Lured like other pioneers by promises of huge tracts of land, the Speakers relocated to Texas in the late 1850s, settling in Hopkins County. It was there that Byron and James, who had spent most of their lives in the North, volunteered to fight for the Confederacy.

At some point after the war, Henry moved most of his brood to the southeastern section of Hill County. Henry and Eliza's youngest son, Archery Oscar, or A.O., as he apparently preferred to be called, established roots in Hubbard City. He married a feisty transplanted Georgian named Nancy Jane "Jenny" Poer. Jenny's mother, Mary, by then a widow, lived next door.

Like the Speakers, the Poers had answered the Confederacy's call of duty. No fewer than ten Poers served in various Texas units. An R. B. Poer, believed to be Jenny's older brother Robert, enlisted in a cavalry regiment that distinguished itself on both sides of the Mississippi, earning plaudits for its spirited defense of Atlanta.

A.O. and Jenny eventually had seven children, six of whom survived infancy. Elsie, the first child, was born in 1879. Tristram, the youngest, was born nine years later. In between were daughters Maude, Pearl, and Gypsie and a son named Loyd, who was destined to die young.

We don't know what inspired A.O. and Jenny to bequeath such an unusual name to their lastborn, but "Tristram" might well have come from their fondness for the legend of King Arthur – a major source of inspiration for many Americans in the nineteenth century. The mythical "King of Lyonesse," Sir Tristram was among the most dashing and headstrong characters in Arthurian lore. Whether or not it was done by design, the name fit their offspring.

Unlike his famous younger sibling, Loyd apparently never found his niche in life. In Tris's eyes, his older brother must never have amounted to much. Later in life, Tris often told people that he was the only boy in a household full of women, conveniently skipping over the presence of his older brother. In later censuses, Loyd listed his occupation as "chauffeur," which in all probability meant he owned a horse-drawn rig that ferried passengers to and from the Hubbard train depot.

The Speaker siblings had plenty of playmates in town. A.O.'s brothers Calvin and James also lived in Hubbard with large families. And various Poers, including Rebel hero Robert, settled in town, too.

Like his father and his oldest brother, Byron, A.O. was a carpenter. The Speakers and Poers, like virtually everyone on the Texas frontier, helped make ends meet by farming. In addition to whatever crops they grew on their village property, they may have tilled other land in Hill County. One published account suggests that A.O. also had an interest in a dry goods shop in town. The A.O. Speakers appear to have been reasonably well-off – at least until A.O.'s untimely death in 1898. Records in the Hill County clerk's office show that on three occasions between 1884 and 1893, A.O. acquired property in the village of Hubbard. Exactly what the family did with those lots is unknown: records are incomplete.

In the years to come, Tris Speaker was frequently described in print as the "son" of a Confederate cavalryman. But his father, who was just nine when hostilities broke out, was too young to serve. Like a lot of sons who lose their fathers early in life, Tris may have fabricated a past to make his departed dad seem more heroic.

The Speaker homestead sat at the intersection of Third and Bois d'Arc, across the street from what today is the Wade Funeral Home. A.O. was only forty-six when he died of undisclosed causes. Losing the family breadwinner meant that the Speakers had to find revenue from other means. At the time the 1900 Census was taken, there were three nonfamily members boarding in the Speaker household. Between the mineral waters and the railroad, many transients came to town and must have kept the place buzzing. Jenny helped put food on the table by taking in boarders. An advertising flier from the town's glory days urged folks suffering from "Rheumatism, Malaria, Constipation, Blood and Skin Diseases" to avail themselves of "Hubbard's Hot Mineral Water Cures." Among the lodging options listed in the ad was a week's stay at "Mrs. Speaker's" for five dollars. Jenny charged a buck and a half more a week than the Magnolia Café, which must have rented out its back room. In a 1912 interview later reprinted in the *Cleveland Plain Dealer*, Jenny described their home as "a quiet little house" with sunflowers in the backyard and morning glories on the side porch.

Marlin, another central Texas village not too far off, was even more celebrated for the healing power of its mineral waters. The Falls County resort's notoriety was such that John McGraw – year after year – would bring his New York Giants there for spring training. We don't know for certain if young Tris Speaker jumped onto a freight train to watch the Giants work out in Marlin, but given his passion for the game and his penchant for gratis rail rides, it would be surprising if he didn't.

Between hopping freights, hollering at engineers, and – no doubt – heaving an occasional rock at the caboose, the trains that ran through Hubbard in the 1890s and 1900s must have provided Tris and his pals with plenty of entertainment. Tris and his gang loved to prowl around at night, "cooning melons," as Speaker put it in a 1920 interview. By all accounts, young Master Speaker was a handful. The world of the cowboy may have been dying all around him, but young Tris did what he could to keep the ideal alive.

"[He was] never bad, you understand, but wild," a childhood companion named Wiley Johnson remembered many years later in an interview with Gordon Cobbledick. "When he wasn't more than 12-years-old, he packed a 'six-shooter' as big as he was. Used to worry the town marshal, but I never heard of him getting into any real scrapes. Just a lot of mischief like kids stumble into when they've got more energy than they know what to do with." Later in life Johnson became a lumberman in Hill County.

When Tris was still in knickers, his father taught him the essentials of a Texas boyhood: how to ride, hunt, and fish. The youngster's knack for bareback riding caused some anxious moments in the Speaker household.

"Why, that young one used to ride high-spirited horses without a saddle or bridle when he wasn't much more than a baby," Tris's older sister Pearl Speaker Scott told Cobbledick. "I recall a time we missed him in the house and mother sent some of us girls out to look for him. Pretty soon we saw a horse galloping down the road with a tiny kid in skirts perched way up on its bare back, digging his heels into the horse's ribs to make it go faster. We managed to flag the brute down and pull Tris off. Mother gave him his spanking and then the whole family practically fainted."

Pearl and Tris remained close the remainder of their lives. She named her youngest daughter after her famous sibling. Miss Tris Speaker Scott, the ballplayer's niece, is now in her mid-eighties, a retired schoolteacher still living in Hubbard. She was recently honored for her lifetime of devotion to the schoolchildren of Hill County and is actively involved in the management of the Tris Speaker museum at Old Hubbard High School.

Exactly when and under what circumstance Tris Speaker was introduced to the game of baseball is not known. His uncles may well have learned the rudiments of the game during their war years, since "base" was popular in camps on both sides. Town and club teams began to spring up all over the frontier after the war.

The sandlot game to which Speaker was first exposed in the 1890s bore little resemblance to the sport to which he devoted his career. There may have been nine players to a side, but chances are, few if any of the fielders wore gloves; they couldn't afford them. Outfielders were perched just beyond the scruffy infield. Sandlot pitchers stood forty-five or fifty feet from home plate and flung the dirty, beat-up ball sidearmed or underhanded. Catchers often stood several feet behind the batter's box, attempting to corral the ball on one hop. Batters tried to slap the ball through the infield and race toward first base all in one motion.

Speaker's mother remembered in that 1912 interview the precise moment when she realized her young son had a yen for baseball. One Sunday morning Tris set out from the house "with a penny clutched in one hand and a Sunday school quarterly in the other. Three hours later he came home, minus the penny and quarterly. He was also minus his cap and coat: one shirtsleeve was slit from top to bottom, and blood was coloring a sock.

" 'I beat 'em, muvver!' [Tris] was shouting, wrinkling his scratched and grimy face into a grin. 'Two home runs and a single. I made 'em, an' we beat!' 'Well, you won't beat 'em again on Sunday, anyway,' said muvver. And forthwith she administered chastisement."

In a 1911 bylined article for the *Boston Post*, Speaker recalled that "All the ball fields around Hubbard City had skin diamonds, and the balls would get fuzzy after playing a while. This would give pitchers a better chance to curve the ball, and the average player was handicapped, but it never seemed to bother me." His sister Pearl was amazed that Tris was so taken with the game. "Not that he wasn't always good at it, but baseball just seemed to me to be too tame to hold him long. Not enough excitement, you know."

Excitement is what young Tris craved. Even before his father died, he ran wild. After his father's death, in his early teens, he may well have become something of a loner, developing an antisocial streak that dominated his early years. Maybe stalking Hubbard's streets with that six-shooter strapped around his waist was his way of compensating for the loss of his father.

Col. J. C. Mecklin, editor of the weekly *Hubbard City News* in the early 1900s, remembered that "[Speaker] may have been a little wild, but he wasn't a loafer. I guess he couldn't hold still long enough to loaf properly. Anyway, you never saw him hanging around the post office with the other town boys."

Anything resembling a baseball field, though, grabbed Tris's full attention. John Walker, later the manager of the village's only drugstore, was the first baseman on Hubbard's town nine. It was the first real team on which Speaker ever played. "All the other players were young men who wore long pants, but Tris was still in knickers. He was so small the other teams always kidded us about using a mascot in the lineup, but the kidding stopped about the first time he came to bat. His hitting won our championship game with Alamo," Walker told Cobbledick.

Like many youngsters in Hill County, Speaker fancied himself a rodeo cowboy. Later in life he became such a skilled horse-and-rope performer that Will Rogers prevailed upon him to join the Oklahoman's traveling show whenever Spoke's schedule would allow.

Right around the time his father died, Speaker, a natural right-hander, was thrown from a buckin' bronc and suffered multiple fractures of his lower right arm and a break of his upper right arm and collarbone. He refused to let the injury disrupt his ballplaying. Undaunted, he taught himself to throw and bat left-handed, which he continued to do for the remainder of his career. "I feared my days in athletics were over," Speaker wrote in a bylined article for the *Cleveland Press* in May 1916. "Even before the fractures healed, I was out practicing to peg with the left hand. I found I could throw left-handed even more accurately that I could with my right. Then I got back my job with the [Hubbard] team."

Speaker became essentially ambidextrous – indeed, he was that rare human being who could write legibly with both hands – a skill that later contributed to his genius in the outfield, where he stunned onlookers by making many an off-balance one-handed grab, some with his glove, some with his bare hand. He taught himself to throw so well with his left hand that he became a pretty fair country pitcher, developing a mean curve ball. Over time, even Speaker's throws from the outfield had a natural left-to-right break in them.

At Hubbard High School, Speaker starred in both football and baseball, graduating in 1904. In his spare time he worked at a cottonseed oil mill, "starting at the bottom and rising to the position of boss," Speaker recalled in the 1916 *Press* piece. He also strung telegraph wire around Hill County and toiled as a cowpuncher.

He was a good enough student to be accepted at Fort Worth Polytechnic, where his mother hoped he would sharpen his skills for a career in the cattle or oil business. Speaker also had big plans to play both football and baseball at Fort Worth Poly. But after he got knocked around on the gridiron, injuring his left arm, his alarmed mother persuaded him to concentrate on baseball. In later years, a story that the macho Speaker apparently never dispelled had him mangling the arm so badly that he developed blood poisoning; a surgeon supposedly urged amputation. The story gained such currency that upon Speaker's death in 1958 it made the wire service obituaries. It also appears in Speaker's write-up in the *Dictionary of American Biography*.

Whatever his football injury may have been, it wasn't serious enough to have disrupted his baseball career at Fort Worth Poly. Speaker's performance on the diamond at Fort Worth Poly has been lost to posterity. Regardless of how he fared, though, no scouts came calling.

CHAPTER 3

Texas Leaguer

Unlike such dead-ball luminaries as Ty Cobb and Honus Wagner, who lit up every league they played in as youngsters, Tris Speaker was not exactly a prodigy in his mid- to late teens. Had Speaker shown more promise, he would have been scouted while still playing ball for the Hubbard town nine. In the end he was "discovered" entirely by accident. Ironically, the day he was spotted for the first time, he was toeing the rubber on the pitcher's mound, not patrolling center field.

In the spring following his sophomore year at Fort Worth Poly, Speaker was playing semipro ball for a team sponsored by the Nicholson and Watson Department Store in Corsicana. One afternoon in May 1906, Doak Roberts, the owner of the Cleburne Railroaders in what was then known as the North Texas League, came to a Corsicana game intent on checking out a hard-hitting right-handed outfielder. Instead, Roberts found himself intrigued by Corsicana's starting left-handed pitcher, who not only used his curve ball to hurl a gritty game but also happened to slug two home runs.

After Speaker retired the last three batters, Roberts approached the eighteen-year-old and asked if he'd be interested in playing professional baseball. Decades later, in affectionate profiles by Gordon Cobbledick and Lee Greene of *Sport Magazine*, Speaker chuckled when recalling the moment; for once, apparently, the cocksure boy from Hubbard City was rendered speechless. Eventually, Tris remembered, he managed to stammer out a "yes."

Roberts replied, "All right. You'll hear from me in a week or two."

Spoke later admitted that "if I had fallen down in my ambition to become a professional ballplayer I presume I would have remained in Hubbard City – working as a night supervisor at the cottonseed oil mill."

True to his word, Roberts showed up at the Hubbard railroad station two weeks later. Roberts told the youngster he wanted him to join the

Cleburne club in time for its game in Waco against the Navigators the following day. They shook hands and Roberts gave Speaker what amounted to a "signing bonus" – one dollar – to offset his train fare.

Speaker knew how to play every angle along the St. Louis Southwestern Texas line. He certainly didn't need a buck to travel thirty miles south to Waco. The next morning, Speaker hopped a freight train and pocketed the cash. By his own account, he arrived just minutes before the ball game started, angering player-manager Benny Shelton, who'd been expecting him much earlier. Shelton, miffed, immediately scribbled Speaker's name into the starting lineup at pitcher.

Cleburne's Railroaders lost to the hometown Navigators 3–0 that day but Speaker acquitted himself well in his professional debut. The May 22 *Waco Times-Herald* reported, "Speaker, the pitcher for Cleburne, did fine work. His one trouble was in locating the plate, and as a consequence, he issued five passes." Tris struck out four and allowed only four hits but was tagged with the loss. At one point, noted the *Times-Herald*, Speaker and Railroader second baseman Mickey Coyle "executed the 'Gaston and Alphonse' act with professional perfection," allowing an easy pop-up to drop when they got their signals crossed. Speaker went 0-for-3 at the plate.

A day later Roberts rejoined his club and found Shelton and Coyle waiting for him as his train pulled into the Waco station. "You better get rid of that kid left-hander you sent up from Corsicana. He's cussed out Shelton and challenged everybody on the ballclub to fight, including me," Coyle supposedly told the owner.

Roberts immediately began searching Waco for his young charge. He found Speaker eating breakfast at a local hotel. As related to Cobbledick, this is Speaker's sprightly description of their tête-à-tête:

> "What's the idea of insulting Shelton?" Roberts asked [me]. "Who insulted him?" [I] replied. "All I said was that he was a splay-footed, butter-fingered tramp that ought to pay his way into the ballpark. He booted an easy grounder that made me lose my game yesterday. And that monkey-faced second baseman stuck his nose into it and I told him I could lick him. Which I can."

Stories tend to get exaggerated as the years wear on – especially anecdotes rooted in adolescent conflict, then relayed to writers not immune to hyperbole. The actual exchange between Speaker and Roberts may have been a tad less colorful. Still, Speaker's recollection of his first two days in professional baseball provides a glimpse into his take-no-prisoners personality, not to mention his tough-hombre manner of speaking. On the Texas frontier of a century ago, "splay-footed" and "butter-fingered" must have been serious trash talk.

"Son," Roberts said softly after Speaker finished his tirade. "Come upstairs with me. We've got some business to talk."

They reached an agreement: Speaker would sign a fifty-dollar-per-month contract and apologize to Shelton. The youngster's apology must have been somewhat less than heartfelt. In Cleburne's next game, the manager gave Speaker his comeuppance. Shelton started Speaker at pitcher and left him in for all nine innings of a twenty-two-run pasting. After Speaker had been battered for one extra-base knock after another, Shelton came out to the mound and sarcastically pointed out that the opposition had yet to record a "single" hit.

"That convinced everybody, including me, that I was an outfielder if I was anything," Speaker chortled to Cobbledick. The next day Shelton watched Speaker shag flies and told the Hubbard boy he was a natural outfielder. Nevertheless, Spoke told readers of the *Cleveland Press* eleven years later that he started seven games for Cleburne as a pitcher, losing them all. "I was beginning to weaken on the job when luck smiled on me one afternoon," he recalled. A right fielder known as "Dude" Ransom was beaned by a pitch. Spoke was sent to right field as a substitute. "I shall always be indebted to Ransom for stepping into the bean ball that put him on the bench and, thereby, gave me a chance. There's no telling what would have happened to me," he wrote.

"Gentleman Ben" Shelton, Speaker's manager, was a Texas League institution, having played for and/or skippered Galveston, Houston, Corsicana, Temple, Dallas, Waco, and Cleburne throughout the 1890s and early 1900s. He brought in old Texas League fly hawk James Maloney to teach the finer points of outfield play to the Hubbard youngster. Shelton's mentoring of Speaker ended up defining his life. When Ben died of paralysis in 1945 at age sixty-six, the wire service obituaries all saluted his work with Speaker in the summers of '06 and '07. For the remainder of his season with Shelton's Cleburne club, Speaker hit a quiet .268 but managed to steal thirty-three bases. The Railroaders chugged their way to the North Texas League pennant that year, Speaker was fond of pointing out later in life.

Speaker's skills as a pugilist must have been more refined than his skills as a pitcher. In his most memorable fight as a North Texas Leaguer, he allegedly knocked teammate Bill Powell, a big catcher, through a train coach window. "After that," Greene's profile wryly noted, "they left him alone."

The Texas League, North and South, was far from a top-rung operation at that point in its history. It had been around in one form or another since 1888, the year Speaker was born. Its track record was, to put it charitably, spotty. In some years all the franchises stayed intact, teams met payroll, and a champion was declared. In other years franchises folded in the middle of the season and players jumped willy-nilly from one team to the other. By 1906 North and South Texas Leagues had been formed. But the thinned-out union included too many small towns and shaky operators. Gate receipts for most franchises were tiny and had little prospect of getting bigger.

Cleburne was a fairly typical Texas League town from that era. It was situated in Johnson County some thirty miles north of Hubbard on the St. Louis Southwestern Texas line. Named after Confederate martyr Patrick Cleburne, an Irish-born major general killed at Franklin, Tennessee, the railroad junction prospered in the decades after the war in ways that Hubbard could only dream about. By the time the century turned, Cleburne's population was roughly five times that of Hubbard's. Cleburne proudly tapped land in its city park to create a ball yard for its North Texas League franchise.

Still, only a few thousand people lived in Cleburne – which made it tough for Roberts to sustain a professional club. At one point late in the 1906 season, Robert almost included Speaker in a trade with Shreveport, pulling Tris's name out of the deal only at the last second. Cleburne always occupied a soft spot in Speaker's heart. He developed friendships that summer of '06 that stayed with him the rest of his life.

The next season, 1907, the two leagues consolidated into one Texas League and sought to locate franchises in bigger population centers. Roberts transferred his franchise two hundred miles south to Houston. And he brought his pugnacious outfielder with him.

In 1907 Houston was bursting at the seams. Nearly sixty thousand people lived within its limits, with more arriving every day. It had become a major railroad hub in the late nineteenth century, its many tentacles serving the cotton, cattle, and timber industries throughout Texas and the Southwest. By the early 1900s city fathers were determined to make Houston a major port; their massive dredging project was ultimately completed in 1914. Six years before Roberts and Speaker arrived in Houston, Spindletop, the first well to strike oil in the state of Texas, came in big some one hundred miles east in Beaumont. All in all, Houston was a noisy boomtown, proudly flexing its muscles and its big-city trappings. It was also causing anguish among devout Texas Protestants, who viewed the city as a den of iniquity, full of grimy flophouses, gin joints, and brothels.

Houston's many temptations may have overwhelmed young Speaker, the country boy from the cow town up north. Unlike his experience as a student in Fort Worth, this time he had a few dollars burning a hole in his pocket.

Speaker was fortunate to have fallen under the tutelage of Benny Shelton and Doak Roberts. Roberts was a wily promoter with superb baseball instincts. He recognized talent and knew how to package and market it. In the decades to come, Roberts became a key figure in the expansion of the Texas League, helping to transform a once disparate string of franchises into one of America's most celebrated minor leagues. As the head of the league in the 1920s, he was instrumental in creating the Dixie Series, a postseason competition between the winner of the Texas League and the champion of the Southern League (later Association). For years, the Dixie Series captured the imagination of fans all over the South. Before dying young in 1929, Roberts watched such future immortals as Dizzy Dean, Al Simmons, and Joe "Ducky" Medwick hone their skills in the Texas League.

In a different bylined series, this one for the *Boston Post* in 1911, Speaker remembered the Texas League "spot bonuses" that a player could earn thanks to exuberant fans. "Many of the grounds in the Texas League were roomy and the players got the benefit of long drives. Homeruns were worth between $20 and $40 where the scores were close between the leading clubs. I have seen a shower of silver [thrown] at a player as he crossed the plate with a homerun." Speaker also recalled the contagious energy of the crowds in those tiny Lone Star ball yards. "The wild yells of cowboys and insane fans throwing their hats in the air had a telling effect on the young players. . . . I saw some great playing in that country."

That spring of 1907 Roberts arranged for his Houston club to play a series of exhibition games against the big league St. Louis Browns. Speaker's performance in that series grabbed the attention of Browns manager James McAleer – the same James McAleer who, five years later, parlayed his chummy association with American League president Ban Johnson into becoming the frontman for the new ownership syndicate that Johnson had created for the Boston Red Sox. "[Speaker] isn't ready yet," McAleer supposedly told Roberts. "But I'm asking you to wire me when he is."

The season was barely two months old when Roberts dispatched this telegram to McAleer: SPEAKER READY. STOP. YOU CAN HAVE HIM FOR FIF-TEEN HUNDRED. STOP.

No reply was forthcoming. Undeterred, Roberts upped the ante by wiring: I OWN TWO HUNDRED ACRES GOOD TEXAS BLACK LAND. STOP. WILL DEED TO YOU IF SPEAKER DOES NOT MAKE GOOD. STOP.

There was still no acknowledgment from the Browns' manager. Roberts next flagged the Pittsburgh Pirates. The Pirates expressed interest, Greene noted, "until their teetotaling owner, Barney Dreyfuss, learned that Tris smoked cigarettes. That was too much for Barney. Smoking cigars would have been bad enough, but cigarettes were considered a smoke for sissies in those days. 'No man who smokes cigarettes will ever be a big league ballplayer,' Dreyfuss rashly predicted."

Soon thereafter, a part-time scout for the newly christened Boston Red Sox named George Huff, who had been bird-dogging Speaker for weeks, bought his contract from Roberts. Huff was moonlighting from his job as athletic director (and intermittent baseball coach) at the University of Illinois, where he nurtured a number of future big leaguers, including Boston's Jake Stahl. In some accounts, Huff acquired Speaker for $750; in others, $800. Either way, Speaker came to the Sox cheap.

But the deal was far from done. As a minor, Speaker needed to obtain his mother's consent to sign a Major League contract. Jenny Speaker displayed the family recalcitrance by refusing to go along.

"I've never been so insulted in my life," Tris recalled her saying in

Greene's article. "I will not have my boy being sold around like a slave for so many dollars." (Revealing sidebar: In Cobbledick's account, Speaker quotes his mother as saying, "I will not have my boy being sold *like a longhorn steer*." Perhaps Speaker decided that a simile invoking a Texas bull was more flattering than likening himself to chattel.) Mrs. Speaker eventually came around, but only after Roberts and Huff had her cousin John Callicutt, a lawyer and old family confidante from Corsicana, intervene on Tris's behalf.

For years afterward, however, Mrs. Speaker never understood why her youngest child didn't go into the cattle or oil business as she had planned. In August of 1912, in fact, *Sporting Life* ascribed this quote to Mrs. Speaker: "His father died when Tris was nine years old and my boy has taken care of me since then. He always was a smart boy. Why, at 11, he ran an oil well all by himself. Now he is only 22 and I want him, my baby and my man, to come home. He should have been a mechanic."

On the afternoon of October 12, 1920, as his Cleveland Indians were cavorting on Dunn Field moments after clinching the World Series against the Brooklyn Robins, Speaker ran to his mother's box next to the Indians' dugout. Mother and son both choked back tears as he presented her with the game ball. "This is what I meant, Mom," Speaker said as he hugged and kissed her. "This was why I had to go away and play ball."

Cleveland fans witnessing the heartfelt embrace between mother and son stood and cheered for several minutes. Long-time newspaper columnist J. J. Lowman wrote, "This little tribute of Speaker's to his mother was the most impressive scene I ever witnessed in professional baseball."

The Red Sox elected to keep their new acquisition in Houston for most of 1907. Speaker led the Texas League in hitting that year, batting .315. Back then there was no limit on the number of farm leaguers who could be brought up to the big leagues late in the season. So along with a couple dozen other prospects, including Houston teammate George Whiteman, another outfielder, Speaker reported to Boston's six-year-old ball yard, the Huntington Avenue Grounds.

Boston was concluding another desultory season – its third year in a row of finishing in or near the cellar of the American League. The team was in such bad straits that it was already on its fourth manager that season. One of the Sox's '07 skippers was none other than George Huff, the scout who had signed Speaker earlier that summer. In seven games with Huff at the helm, the Sox dropped from fifth place to seventh. George quickly beat a retreat to Champaign-Urbana. Huff wasn't the only ill-starred manager for the Sox during that era. Boston's player-manager the previous year, Chick Stahl, was so despondent over a personal tragedy that he took his own life in midseason – the only time in big league history that's happened.

Here's how Greene describes Speaker's rude awakening to life in the big leagues:

> The 19-year-old Texan walked confidently into the [locker room] and approached Red Sox manager Jim (Deacon) McGuire. "I'm Speaker," he announced and held out his hand. McGuire took it mechanically and then asked, "You're who?"
>
> "Speaker, the new outfielder from Houston," Tris said, swallowing his surprise. Hadn't they heard that he was the Texas League batting champion? Apparently, they hadn't.

Tris did little to distinguish himself that fall. His Major League debut came as a substitute right fielder in Philadelphia on September 12, 1907. He went 0-for-2 in a 7–1 loss to the A's. According to research conducted by the Hall of Fame, the first pitcher Speaker faced in his big league career was the A's diminutive spitballer Jimmy Dygert. "[Speaker] failed to connect," Fred Lieb remembered many years later. In the autobiography he penned for the *Press* a decade later, Speaker said he played in only two games that fall. In truth, he appeared in seven games, hitting a paltry .167. One of the three safeties he collected that fall, however, came against the great Addie Joss, a Hall of Fame hurler for the Cleveland Naps. The other two singles came against "Long Tom" Hughes and Frank Oberlin, both of the Washington Nats. His defensive skills must not have stood out, either. Less than impressed, the Red Sox released him at the end of the season. In the winter of 1907–8, Tris Speaker was that rare commodity in the dead-ball era: a genuinely free agent.

His pal Whiteman was similarly frustrated. It took young George six more years to make it back into the Big Show, this time with the New York Highlanders.

Speaker dashed off telegrams all winter, desperately shopping himself around to other big league clubs. He couldn't find a taker. That March he showed up uninvited two days in a row at the Giants' spring training camp in Marlin, which was about thirty miles from Hubbard. Maybe he owned or borrowed a jalopy, but he could have hopped a freight train and walked the mile or so from the Marlin depot out to the Giants' practice field. Crusty John McGraw, the Giants' skipper, eyed the impudent youngster and told him he had no room in camp for another outfielder. Muggsy, who hated anyone or anything associated with his scorned rival, American League president Ban Johnson, had no use for a ballplayer who wasn't even good enough to make the roster of a last-place team in the "junior circuit." In the years to come McGraw would call his dismissal of Speaker the biggest mistake of his career.

Tris wasn't invited to the Red Sox camp in Little Rock, either, but at least his former club allowed him to train with them after Speaker showed up, hat in hand, a week or so after camp opened. It's impossible to know if the Sox gave Speaker a chance to prove his mettle that spring. Judging by the club's shoddy treatment of him, though, it doesn't appear he made much of an impression.

The Sox were leasing the facilities of the Little Rock Travelers of the Southern League, which were owned by a local businessman named Mickey Finn. As the Sox broke camp, Finn demanded that the Red Sox make good on their obligation. In arrears, the Sox offered Speaker as "ground rent," to use the phrase of columnist Joe Williams. Finn wasn't happy, but he reluctantly accepted, agreeing to sell Speaker back to Boston on the odd chance that the kid would make good.

So Tris Speaker's big break came because the Red Sox were short on cash and more than willing to divest themselves of a ballplayer for cynical, short-term financial gain. Thus, the club established a pattern that would be repeated over and over again in the history of the franchise – much to the chagrin of its rabid fans in New England.

Most mortals would have resigned themselves to fate and hung up the cleats. But Tris Speaker was too stubborn to quit. If winning a batting title weren't enough to impress the big leagues, then, by god, he'd do even better. "The turndown I received from Boston didn't discourage me," Spoke wrote in 1916. "I was determined to polish up the defects that caused the big leaguers to brand me green." In Greene's phrase, "He clamped his mouth shut and went to work."

The 1908 season is when all the stars aligned for Speaker. He won his second straight batting championship, hitting .350, the highest mark at that point in Southern League history. His defensive play, Greene wrote, "rocked the Ozarks." A young sportswriter from Atlanta named Grantland Rice happened to catch a Little Rock game against Nashville early that summer. Three decades later Rice wrote, "That day [Speaker] was all over the lot – six or seven put-outs and three hits. He was the smoothest-looking minor league outfielder I ever saw." After watching Speaker make one scintillating play after another, a big league scout supposedly raved, "There's the greatest outfielder that ever lived."

Just a few months earlier, Speaker couldn't get a big league club to answer his telegrams. Now, suddenly, the Giants, the Pirates, the Washington Senators, and others were tailing him. A few weeks after McGraw rebuffed Speaker, he saw him make a couple of nimble plays in an exhibition game between Muggsy's Giants and the Travelers in Little Rock. Muggsy offered Finn five thousand dollars in cold hard cash for Speaker, according to the *New York Journal-American*'s Sid Mercer. But to his credit, Little Rock owner Finn stuck to his commitment to the Red Sox. He sold Speaker back to the Sox for a mere five hundred dollars, the original bill for his park rental in spring training.

Once again, Speaker showed up at the Huntington Avenue Grounds for a late season call-up. Although his hitting was only marginally better this time around (he batted .220 in thirty-one games), his fielding grabbed the attention of certain people in the organization.

One Red Sox veteran smitten with Speaker's defensive promise was legendary pitcher "Cy" Young. Denton True Young was born on a farm in Tuscarawas County, Ohio, and eighty-eight years later, having seen the bright lights and the big cities, died on a farm in Tuscarawas County, Ohio.

Born two years after Appomattox, Young had seen with his own eyes professional baseball's humble origins on rustic sandlots and ramshackle ball yards. He was also an authority on club owners' slipshod financial dealings, having abruptly left St. Louis to sign with Boston in 1901 when he tired of the Cardinals' skinflint ways.

He was tagged with the nickname "Cy" in the late 1880s while a member of Canton in the Tri-State League when a couple of his practice pitches dented a wooden backstop. Someone watching the warmup said the damaged fence looked as if it had been "struck by a cyclone." There may have been a reason Young bonked that backstop. Legend has it that he liked to belt back a little medicinal moonshine before heading out to the mound.

Cleveland's Spiders of the National League signed Young for three hundred dollars. Cleveland fans were as nasty as any in the league; Chicago's legendary Cap Anson called them "hooligans." Visiting players at old National League Park learned to duck the fruit, vegetables, bottles, and garbage that the hooligans heaved their way.

To this day, Young holds more unassailable records than anyone in baseball history. No one will ever come close to his 511 wins, or his 315 losses, or his unfathomable 750 complete games.

In 1903 Young had been a mainstay in Boston's World Series triumph over Honus Wagner's Pittsburgh Pirates. Although the four runs Young gave up in the first inning of his losing effort in game one raised suspicions that he was kneading the Series' betting odds, he dominated the Pirates in his next two starts.

Young was already in his forties when he first encountered Speaker in the dressing room of the Huntington Avenue Grounds. He could see in Tris Speaker the qualities that separated great players like himself and Wagner from good ones: innate talent coupled with a burning desire to excel.

Speaker revealed his grit to readers of the 1916 *Press* series. "I was up in the big show to stick this time, however, and played my head off to make good. I studied every angle, absorbed every item of information available and practiced constantly until I became a regular."

Instead of letting those rats in Speaker's belly stew on the bench, Young would come to the ballpark early every day and hit dozens of fungoes to the young center fielder. Young had perfected the art of lacing a fly ball that required the fielder to race full tilt – then lunge to make the catch. In between lofting fly balls, Young would quiz Speaker about where to position himself for various hitters and how to react to different situations on the field. The more Speaker trained with Young in the late summer and fall of 1908, the more the youngster learned how a batted ball was likely to behave in the air – and what he should do with it once he caught it.

The veteran helped Speaker come to the realization that, in the dead-ball era, far more balls fell in front of center fielders than were hit over their heads. "I figured that 98 percent of all safe hits to the outfield drop in front of outfielders or between them," Speaker remembered years later. "That's why I played so close in."

"[Young] always hit the ball one step beyond my normal range, so I had to hustle," Speaker recalled in a *Baseball Digest* piece written by Morton Roth. "After awhile I knew just by the way he swung whether the ball would go to my right or left. If I could do that with a fungo hitter, I could do it in a ballgame. I watched each batter as he started his swing. Right then I knew if he'd hit it to my right or left and I was on my way."

A half century later, following Speaker's death, Tom Meany paid homage to both men when he wrote that "Few 'Texas Leaguers' ever fell safely when this Texas League alumnus was in center."

Young and Speaker shared much beyond a passion for the subtleties of the game. Twenty-nine years after Young gave Speaker a primer on outfield play, the two of them shared a platform in Cooperstown, New York. They were among the first inductees into the National Baseball Hall of Fame. For more than six decades, the plaques of the old fungo partners have hung next to each other.

Boston, 1908

The more the center of gravity of the nation shifted to the West, the more the Boston mind, thrown back upon itself, resumed its old Colonial allegiance. — Van Wyck Brooks, *Indian Summer in New England*

The Boston that Tris Speaker encountered in the fall of 1908 could not have been farther removed – geographically, culturally, or economically – from the plains of Texas. The young man who grew up riding bareback with a pistol strapped to his waist, mimicking cowboys as he spurred his horse on make-believe cattle drives, found himself in a city contemptuous of anything or anyone with roots west or south of the Charles River.

John Winthrop's "City on a Hill" was a profoundly changed place by the turn of the twentieth century. Boston was caught in a vise between its Puritan forebears and its immigrants – mainly Irish, but Italian, Portuguese, and eastern European as well – who crowded the city. The tenements that historian Oscar Handlin chronicled in *Boston's Immigrants* were like nothing Speaker had witnessed in Fort Worth or Houston. Nor had the Texan seen anything like the estates that had sprung up in suburbs such as Brookline and Chestnut Hill, as many of the Brahmins retreated from the flood of unsavory immigrants at their doorstep.

Ironically, the civil upheaval sparked in no small measure by Boston's abolitionists in the first half of the nineteenth century spelled its demise in the century's latter half. Unlike New York, Philadelphia, and Baltimore, which prospered by building an infrastructure to exploit trade with the West, Boston shunned the new America. As historian Doris Kearns Goodwin wrote in *The Fitzgeralds and the Kennedys*, "Refusing to follow the way the other parts of the country were hastening, Boston turned its mind backward and clung to the past."

Boston's "past," of course, was at complete loggerheads with the "past" that Tris Speaker had absorbed in central Texas. Everywhere the ballplayer looked were painful reminders that his uncles and the Confederacy had lost the war. The city was full of people that Speaker's upbringing had taught him to dislike and distrust – not only the smug heirs of white abolitionists, moneyed Northern intellectuals who looked down their noses at Southerners and Westerners, but immigrants who lived in squalor and worshiped the papacy in Rome, or even more appalling, renounced the New Testament altogether. To an unreconstructed Rebel, 1908 Boston must have seemed like Hades come to life.

The uneasy marriage between Speaker and the city of Boston lasted seven years. There were three different owners of the Red Sox during Speaker's tenure; Tris had a stormy relationship with all of them. Each time his contract came up for renewal, negotiations turned tough, especially when Speaker – to his credit – shrewdly used the upstart Federal League as a bargaining chip in 1914. Although he never forgave the Red Sox management for their shabby treatment of him early in his career, Speaker's hustle and spectacular defensive play made him the toast of every tavern and gentlemen's club in Beantown. The people of Boston took the feisty Texan to their hearts, a sentiment that was never quite reciprocated.

By 1910 Boston's immigrants had swollen its population to 670,000, the fifth-largest metropolis in the nation. Immigrant families were shoehorned into tenements all over the city. Those who settled in the South End found themselves within easy walking distance of the two ball yards that served Boston's franchises in the National and American leagues.

Professional ball in Boston dated all the way back to 1871, when brothers Harry and George Wright, refugees from the original Cincinnati Red Stockings, baseball's first truly professional franchise, established a Boston club in the National Association. Five years later the association dissolved and the National League was formed. Boston became a flagship franchise, dominating the league's first two decades of play. The Boston Nationals won twelve of the National League's first twenty-five pennants. Its roster included such fan favorites as Dan Brouthers, Hugh Duffy, "Cozy" Dolan, and Tommy McCarthy, all young men of Irish extraction.

The Nationals' biggest Irish American star in the late 1880s, however, was outfielder, catcher, occasional infielder, and matinee idol Michael Joseph "King" Kelly. After the Boston club acquired him from the Chicago White Stockings for the then-grandiose sum of ten thousand dollars, plus a five-thousand-dollar signing bonus, Kelly was dubbed "the 15,000 Beauty." His flamboyant base-running style inspired the popular song "Slide, Kelly, Slide." Kelly and his old Chicago teammate and manager, Cap Anson, are credited with inventing the hit-and-run, the double steal, the infield shift, and other on-field maneuvers. Part of Kelly's mystique was his capacity to manipulate the "rules" in his favor. According to legend, he was once sitting out a game when an opponent's foul pop-up drifted toward the White Stockings' bench. He supposedly leapt off the bench, hollered "Kelly now substituting!" and made the put-out. The rule forbidding such spontaneous substitution was adopted soon thereafter.

During the off-season, Kelly drew huge crowds to a Boston theatre to hear his dramatic rendition of the poem "Casey at the Bat." When asked if he ever imbibed while playing, Kelly deftly replied, "It depends on the length of the game." Like many larger-than-life characters, King Kelly exited the stage early, dying a month before his thirty-seventh birthday in 1894.

In 1888, the year after Kelly joined the club, the Nationals built a new park sporting six spires and a double-decked grandstand on the north side of Columbus Avenue, smack in the middle of an Irish working-class community known as "the Village." Viewed as an architectural masterpiece, it was named the South End Grounds. After a fire destroyed much of the wooden grandstand in 1894, a less ambitious single-decked structure emerged.

By the 1890s the National League had spawned a postseason tournament known as the Temple Cup. Boston lost the 1897 cup to the Orioles, the rugged Baltimore club of Wee Willie Keeler and Muggsy McGraw that made an art form out of rough play. The Nationals' toughness in going toe-to-toe with the fearsome Orioles won them the allegiance of Bostonians of every stripe, but none more than the Roxbury saloon-goers at McGreevey's.

McGreevey's beer joint was located just down the street from the South End Grounds. The sign over the door may have advertised M. T. McGreevey & Co. Importers, featuring fine teas, coffees, groceries, and a downstairs bowling alley, but everyone who walked into the saloon portion of the establishment knew what to expect: spirited gossip about politics and baseball, topped off with copious amounts of lager and ale. McGreevey's became *the* watering hole for every ballplayer, union leader, ward heeler, and business or political wannabe in the immigrant world of Boston. Nuf Ced McGreevey was so proud of his association with the Nationals that he renamed his pub Third Base, posting a sign that bragged it was "the last place you stop before going home." He began calling himself and his most rabid patrons the Royal Rooters, which humorously played off the contempt most Irishmen felt toward the British crown.

Relations between the Rooters and the Nationals became severely strained following Boston's loss of the 1899 pennant to the Brooklyn Superbas. Brooklyn's owner and manager, Ned Hanlon, had taken full advantage of the slippery rules of "syndicate baseball" to stock the Superbas with former Orioles. Syndicate baseball back then allowed the owner of one franchise to buy a large stake in other franchises. Thus, Hanlon simultaneously controlled a significant chunk of both the Baltimore and Brooklyn clubs. After the 1899 season began, he elected to break up the Orioles and forge a powerhouse in Brooklyn. The Rooters were outraged that Boston Nationals owner Arthur Soden not only failed to condemn the anticompetitive practices of syndicate baseball, but sanctioned them with his own wallet. Much to the Rooters' chagrin, Soden also owned a piece of the New York club. Soden, like most owners of his era, was a cheapskate. Such Boston Nationals stalwarts as third baseman Jimmy Collins, outfielder Chick Stahl, and pitcher Bill Dinneen were paid peanuts – and since they drowned their sorrows at McGreevey's, the Rooters knew it.

Equally upsetting to the Rooters was the exorbitant fee the Nationals were charging for admission to the South End Grounds. Tickets now cost an unheard-of fifty cents apiece – double the league average of two bits. In keeping with the spirit of an era dominated by the likes of Rockefeller and Carnegie, the National League was comporting itself like a monopoly. If there was one issue that united the crowd at McGreevey's and every other blue-collar tavern in town, it was fervor against monopolies of all kinds. Immigrant workers tended to be passionately pro–trade unionist; their sympathies lay with the poorly compensated ballplayers and against Hanlon, Soden, and their colluding ilk. The men who frequented McGreevey's, in the words of writer Peter Golenbock, "built Boston's roads, canals, railroads, and other public works, using their muscle and brawn. 'Those aren't cobblestones,' an Irishman once remarked. 'They are Irish hearts.'"

In the winter of 1900–1901, when Byron Bancroft "Ban" Johnson, the driving force behind the successful Western League, began exploring the prospect of establishing a new franchise in Boston, McGreevey and the other Rooter chieftains greeted him with open arms. Johnson, a veteran sportswriter for the *Cincinnati Commercial Gazette*, brought a messianic vision to professional baseball, coupled with an unshakable arrogance that it was his destiny to achieve it. An alumnus of Oberlin and Marietta Colleges, his girth and ego were as large as his ambitions for the newly relabeled "American League." The National League had gone out of its way to spurn Johnson at several points in the past; now he plotted revenge. He recruited a phalanx of deep-pocketed businessmen around the country, then devised a strategy to spread their money around to frontmen best equipped to run teams in each market.

One owner that Johnson didn't have to bully – at least not in the early days – was his great Western League ally and frequent drinking companion, Charles Comiskey of the Chicago White Sox. "Commy" had been the manager of the Cincinnati National League club when

Johnson had taken the Western League, a moribund group of minor league franchises in the Midwest, and turned it into a profit maker. He nursed the same dreams for the American League, demanding complete obeisance from his business partners and fellow "owners." Although his old columns in the *Commercial Gazette* had deplored the evils of syndicate baseball, Johnson one-upped his adversaries in the National League. Instead of stretching control of the syndicate among a dozen or more owners, the American League became in essence a one-man syndicate, with a bespectacled taskmaster calling almost all the shots. Cleveland millionaire Charles Somers became Johnson's sugar daddy, giving the nascent league financial muscle undreamed of by the National League. Johnson decided who would "own" his league's franchises, how they would be run, and how successful their win-loss record would be. If certain "owners" didn't respond to his beck and call, Johnson didn't hesitate to uproot them.

Johnson wrote for the local paper. In the mid-1890s, the two conspired to take over the Western League, eventually overhauling professional baseball. Later, they would have an ugly falling out, but in the early days of the American League, Commy, Johnson, and moneyman Somers were thick as thieves.

In Boston, Johnson commissioned a native of East Brookfield, Massachusetts, to find a suitable site for his new team's ballpark. Cornelius Alexander McGillicuddy, better known by his ballplaying name Connie Mack, had been a longtime catcher for the Washington and Philadelphia franchises of the National League. Recruiting Mack for the Western League and eventually his new venture had been quite a coup for Johnson. The American League founder promptly tabbed Mack as part owner and manager of a planned franchise in Milwaukee, and then transferred the enterprise to Philadelphia.

But first Johnson wanted to put Mack's popularity in Boston to work. The man destined to run the Philadelphia Athletics for a half century checked out several sites in Boston, finally settling – at Ned McGreevey's urgent prodding – on an area along Huntington Avenue across the railroad tracks from the South End Grounds. Over the years the property had hosted Buffalo Bill's Wild West Show, Barnum and Bailey's circus, and carnivals of all stripes. It was an easy stroll from the Irish enclave in the Village and just a few minutes by foot or streetcar to the Third Base saloon.

Boston's American League franchise became an overnight success for two other reasons. First, Ban Johnson and his handpicked owner, local businessman Henry Killilea, were determined by hook or crook to field a competitive team right away. The American League upstarts stunned the National League by luring Jimmy Collins, Chick Stahl, and Bill Dinneen from the Boston Nationals and signing the venerable Cy Young from the St. Louis Cardinals.

But most importantly, the team became, at least in the public's mind, linked to Boston's immigrant community. The two Irish pugs most responsible for this transformation were Nuf Ced McGreevey and his pal, whirlwind politico John Francis Fitzgerald.

Born two months after Lee embarrassed Burnside at Fredericksburg, Johnny was the third of nine surviving children of "Cocky Tom" Fitzgerald, a grocer and liquor merchant who set up shop in a hardscrabble neighborhood in the North End. The Fitzgeralds had escaped County Wexford during the grimmest days of the Great Famine of the 1840s. Somehow Tom and Rosanna scraped together enough money to send young Johnny to the prestigious Boston Latin School, which earned him admission to Harvard Medical School. When both parents died young, however, Fitzgerald had no choice but to leave school to feed and clothe his younger siblings.

At the urging of his late father's mentor, North End boss Matthew Keany, Fitzgerald entered ward politics – one of the few professions available to immigrant sons in an era when businesses all over town posted signs that read, "No Irish Need Apply." Fitzgerald maneuvered his way to the top of the Democratic machine. In 1892 he was elected to the state senate. Three years later he won a congressional seat, serving three terms in Washington. He returned to Boston in 1901, intent on winning the ultimate prize: the mayoralty. Since Fitzgerald's political base was in his native North End, he needed to burnish his ties to the heavily populated South End. Naturally, he gravitated toward the neighborhood's nerve center: the saloon inside McGreevey & Co. Importers. Fitzgerald and Ned McGreevey became business partners, political allies, and baseball soul mates. Along with Third Base fixture Arthur Dixwell, whose ballpark chant began with a shrill "Hi! Hi!" they headed up the Royal Rooters, which became an extension of Fitzgerald's political apparatus.

Fitzgerald's syrupy nickname derived from his sweet public disposition. "Honey Fitz" was a man of beguiling charm and bluster. While campaigning in a lavish open convertible – a sporty ride not often seen in Boston's poorer precincts – he would flash a toothy grin at bug-eyed kids and bellow, "If my car were as big as my heart, I'd give you all a ride!" As former *Boston Globe* editor Martin Nolan put it, "After a rousing speech, a skewering of his political enemies, and a farewell chorus of his signature song, 'Sweet Adeline,' Fitzgerald's roadster roared off to another ward."

His leprechaun blarney obscured a cutthroat approach to politics. Unlike two previous mayors of Irish descent who preached conciliation with the Yankee establishment, Fitzgerald took great delight in bloodying Brahmin noses. His recurring campaign slogan was "A Bigger, Better, Busier Boston" – and he certainly delivered on the first and third parts of that promise.

Honey Fitz's bride was never comfortable in the public spotlight, so his eldest daughter, Rose, accompanied the mayor to political functions – including outings to the Huntington Avenue Grounds for baseball games. A Harvard undergrad named Joseph Kennedy, the son of Fitzgerald's sometime ally, sometime adversary East Boston saloonkeeper Patrick Kennedy, began courting Rose over her father's strenuous objections. Joe and Rose were married in October 1914 – the same month Rabbit Maranville and Boston's "Miracle Braves" swept the World Series over Connie Mack's Philadelphia Athletics. A year earlier, in a scandal that cemented Boston's reputation for bare-knuckled politics, Rose's father was forced to give up the mayor's office when cronies of his bitter rival, James Michael Curley, exposed Fitz's dalliance with a cigarette girl named "Toodles."

In 1904, the year before he became mayor, Fitz nearly acquired Boston's American League franchise. Ban Johnson's frontman, Henry Killilea, reached an agreement with Fitzgerald to sell the defending world champions for $140,000. But Johnson, a stern Presbyterian, balked at an Irish Catholic politician running his prized Boston franchise. At the last minute, Johnson voided the deal, triggering accusations of bigotry from Fitzgerald and his supporters at the immigrant organ, the *Boston Post*. The following year, Johnson and Killilea sold the franchise to John Taylor, the scion of the Brahmin family that owned the *Boston Globe*.

From the first moment they took the field at the Huntington Avenue Grounds, Ban Johnson's Boston boys didn't disappoint. Thanks to the refugees from the National League, they were a solid club from day one. In 1901 player-manager Jimmy Collins, the slickest third baseman in either league, guided the team to a second-place finish behind Chicago, with Cy Young winning thirty-three games. The next year, they finished a respectable third behind Connie Mack's Philadelphia team and the St. Louis Browns, with Young once again winning more than thirty games.

Boston wasn't the only market that Johnson successfully invaded. By 1902 the high and mighty National League, tired of being raided by the upstart circuit, had begun negotiating a truce. In 1903 Collins's club finished 44 games over .500, a remarkable feat in a 138-game regular season. That was the year that, as part of the new rapprochement, the

National League champion Pittsburgh Pirates agreed to play the American League pennant winners in a postseason competition.

The first "World's Series," as it was tagged by newspapermen, was not professional baseball's finest hour. Players on both sides groused about the pittance they were being paid to extend the season an extra couple of weeks. In the Pittsburgh clubhouse, Honus Wagner and company made ominous noises about a possible strike; a couple of important Pirates feigned injuries. Bookies made Boston such a heavy favorite that Cy Young and his teammates may well have deliberately lost the first game of the Series at the Huntington Avenue Grounds just to make the odds more attractive for themselves and their betting brethren. Whatever their motivation, the Pilgrims quickly found themselves down three games to one.

That first Series lives on in lore because of the Royal Rooters' conspicuous presence and their alleged impact on the outcome. As related in Peter Golenbock's *Fenway: An Unexpurgated History of the Boston Red Sox*, "[The Rooters'] entrance into the [Huntington Avenue Grounds] was not easily forgotten. Novelist John R. Tunis was waiting in line to buy tickets to one of the games. In the distance, he heard the music signaling their arrival. When the Royal Rooters came into sight, they were wearing black suits with high white collars; blue rosettes pinned on their lapels. 'Each man had his ticket stuck jauntily in the hatband of his derby,' said Tunis, and 'at their head, was the leading spirit, Nuf Ced McGreevey.' "

Despite the Rooters' flashy support, their Pilgrims struggled. So when the Series shifted to Pittsburgh, McGreevey sent a piano-playing member of the Rooters out to a music store to see if he could find a catchy tune for the Rooters to sing in the stands. Nuf Ced settled on a lighthearted number called "Tessie" that could be easily spoofed.

The Rooters wheeled out their version of "Tessie" early in game five – *et voilà!* – Boston rallied for an 11–2 win. For the remaining three games of the Series – all Boston victories – the Rooters tormented the Pirates and their fans with a screeching more suited to an English soccer match than a big league baseball game.

Boston also won the American League pennant in 1904, although under somewhat dubious circumstances. The New York Highlanders had the title all but wrapped up until a suspicious late-season collapse. Some bizarre wild throws by ace Jack Chesbro in the last inning of the last day of the season capped off the Highlander tailspin and allowed the Pilgrims to sneak off with the flag.

There was no renewal of the "World's Series" that year, however. John Tomlinson "Tooth" Brush and Muggsy McGraw, respectively the owner and manager of the National League champion New York Giants, despised Ban Johnson for bringing an American League franchise into their city. When it looked like the hated Highlanders would win the rival crown and play in the Series, Brush and McGraw announced that they would not deign to play the "invaders." McGraw viewed Johnson as "an arrogant, overstuffed windbag"; the two had a stormy relationship stemming from Muggsy's unhappy season and a half managing Johnson's Baltimore franchise in 1901. "When we clinch the National League pennant, we'll be champions of the only real major league," Muggsy declared.

McGraw and Brush were no saints, but they were right about one thing: The early Highlander organization reeked from top to bottom. Chesbro's gaffes at the end of the '04 season didn't appear to unduly deflate his bosses, a pair of hustlers named Frank Farrell and Big Bill Devery, who had somehow wormed their way into Ban Johnson's orbit. The Highlanders were such heavy favorites to win the pennant that a killing could have been made betting the other way. Boston ended up winning its second successive crown. Once the Giants demurred, the *Sporting News* anointed the Boston Americans "World Champions by Default," delighting New England fans and reporters.

In 1905 a rookie first baseman named Hal Chase joined the Highlanders. Chase, a slick gloveman, looked at the skullduggery going on all around him and determined that an enterprising first baseman could make some nice spending cash with well-timed "errors." The player that Fred Lieb would label "the Corkscrew Brain" spent much of the next two decades booting balls at opportune moments, further corrupting every clubhouse he entered. Chase could apparently cheat at poker with the same panache he cheated with on the field. Joe Wood recalled fifty years later that, through fancy shuffling, Chase could deal himself or anyone around the table four "4's" whenever he felt the urge. "Hey, Hal, what are the odds?" fans liked to scream at Chase as he took his position on the field.

Like most Major League franchises in the early 1900s, Boston's American League team went by a number of different nicknames. In its first few years of existence, many fans referred to the team as the Pilgrims or the Puritans. In deference to Ban Johnson's financial angel Charles Somers, the team was known for a time as the Somersets. But no name stuck until 1907, when owner John Taylor decided to equip his charges with bright red hose and call them the "Red Sox."

Taylor was the consummate spoiled rich kid. He was something of a bon vivant, enjoying the company of ladies and more-than-occasional cocktails. At one point, his father, Civil War veteran Gen. Charles Taylor and the *Globe*'s publisher, insisted that young John try his hand at the family business, forcing him to labor in both the advertising and editorial departments. But neither job took.

General Taylor knew that Johnson had grown weary of the bad press that Killilea was getting in Boston following the Pilgrims' Series triumph. Certain writers were convinced that Killilea had made big bucks by scalping tickets during the Series. When Johnson spurned Honey Fitz's bid to buy Boston's American League franchise, General Taylor worked a deal with the AL czar, acquired the club, and handed the team over to his ne'er-do-well son, who had squandered many an afternoon at the South End and Huntington Avenue Grounds.

In the puckish phrase of Stout and Johnson, "[Taylor's] tenure at the helm of the team was easily the most unsuccessful of any Boston owner – no small accomplishment considering the competition." But Red Sox Nation fondly remembers Taylor's regime for three reasons: he gave the team its stylish nickname, he signed a number of outstanding players from faraway places out West, and he built a park so beautiful that, a half century later, novelist John Updike joined countless other writers in penning a paean to the "lyric, little bandbox of a ballpark."

The Taylors may not have known how to run a ball club, but they certainly knew how to increase their newspaper's circulation. The *Globe* had always been a reliable defender of the Brahmin GOP establishment. But upon taking the reins in 1873, old man Taylor looked around at Boston's changing demographics, counted noses, and concluded that there was merit to the political, social, and economic views of the immigrant community and its Democratic Party that he had heretofore not fully appreciated. Virtually overnight, the *Globe* changed its editorial stance and slashed its price to a far more working-man-friendly two cents a copy, dramatically improving sales.

Despite their business foresight, the Taylors nevertheless took a championship club and ran it into the ground. The franchise that had been so good so early became very bad very quickly. A series of disastrous front-office moves and clubhouse dissension sent the franchise into a downward spiral. The pennant-winning clubs of 1903 and 1904 quickly became cellar dwellers.

When he unpacked his gear for good in the Boston clubhouse in 1908, Tris Speaker found a kindred spirit and a pal for life in teammate Joe Wood. The Texan may have been raised on the periphery of the Wild West, but Wood was the genuine article.

Born in Kansas City in 1889, Wood grew up in southwestern Colorado just a short stagecoach ride from such primitive outposts as Lizard Head Pass and Slumgullion Gulch. Wood's dad was a noted trial lawyer, representing such high-profile clients as the Western Federation of Miners and the Missouri Pacific and Santa Fe railroads. But at heart Wood *père* was an adventurer; he sounds like a character straight out of a Bret Harte tale. Wood's old man couldn't resist the siren song of a gold rush, panhandling in Nevada and California and racing up to the Klondike in 1897. As Joe told Lawrence Ritter, his father returned from Alaska "with his legs frozen, Yukon diarrhea, and lots of great stories, but no gold." The old man was a compulsive risk taker, eventually blowing the family fortune on prairie land speculation in Kansas.

When Joe was in his midteens, the Woods moved in a covered wagon to Ness City, a town on the Kansas prairie not far from Dodge City. There, young Joe began playing for the Ness City town nine against such frontier villages as High Point, Ransom, Ellis, Bazine, Wa Keeney, and Scott City. "The ball game between two rival towns was a big event back then, with parades before the game and everything," Wood told Ritter. "The smaller the town the more important their ball club was. Boy, if you beat a bigger town, they'd practically hand you the key to the city. And if you lost a game by making an error in the ninth inning or something like that – well, the best thing to do was just pack your 'grip' and hit the road, 'cause they'd never let you forget it."

Young Wood was impossibly handsome. Photographers loved his dark choirboy features. He had brooding brown eyes, impeccably groomed black hair, and a sculpted chin and nose. His good looks helped him earn his first dollars as a professional ballplayer. In September 1906 one of the "Bloomer Girl" outfits came barnstorming through Kansas and lost a game to Ness City's young pitching prodigy. Some of the Bloomer Girls actually were of the distaff persuasion, but about half the squad consisted of young men dressed up as women. The Bloomer Girls' manager approached Wood about joining the team, telling Joe that with his baby face, he wouldn't need to wear a wig like the other fellows. "So I asked Dad if I could go," Wood remembered to Ritter. "He thought it was sort of unusual, but he didn't raise any objections. I guess it must have appealed to his sense of the absurd."

Young Joe spent that fall barnstorming with the Bloomer Girls, then was spotted by a scout for Cedar Rapids in the Three-I League and signed a ninety-dollar-a-month contract in January 1907. But before the Three-I season began, the Cedar Rapids owner transferred Wood's contract to the Hutchinson Salt Packers of the Western Association. He won twenty games for Hutchinson, unleashing the fastball that became his trademark. After the 1907 season, he was sold to the Kansas City Blues in the American Association. The Red Sox began bird-dogging Wood early in 1908, finally signing him that August. There he first met Speaker, who also had reported to the Huntington Avenue Grounds as a late-season call-up.

It's easy to see why Speaker and Wood became such fast friends. They were two Westerners caught in a town and a clubhouse a long way from the frontier. The roommates quickly developed such a close bond that some viewed the relationship as haughty; in the years to come, it caused teammates in two clubhouses to bristle. With their put-up-or-shut-up swagger, Wood and Speaker never let people forget that they hailed from a mythic part of the country. All the qualities traditionally associated with frontiersmen – orneriness, defiance, quick-trigger tempers – Speaker and Wood had in abundance, or at least pretended to. And they almost never hesitated to lord those qualities over people.

They also didn't hesitate to press their views on racial and religious superiority. Speaker and Wood were white Anglo-Saxon Protestants who deeply distrusted the papists who had come to dominate Boston politics and culture. They never felt welcomed in the South End's immigrant world, choosing to live miles away in a boardinghouse in the seaside village of Winthrop. It's instructive that given a choice between socializing in working-class taverns where they'd never have to buy a beer or in stodgy gentlemen's clubs where black or white tie was de rigueur, they chose the latter. "My mental image of Speaker and Wood back then is two guys dressed to the 'nines' going out to play snooker or bridge in some fancy club," says Richard Johnson.

Many a quarrel in the Sox clubhouse featured religious epithets being tossed back and forth between the Bill Carrigan–led Catholic contingent, nicknamed in press accounts the "K.C.s," or the Knights of Columbus, and the Speaker-Wood Protestant faction, which labeled themselves the "Masons." Speaker, especially, reveled in showing teammates and hangers-on just how tough he was. He and Carrigan were constantly at loggerheads.

Speaker and Wood, like many back then, also reveled in abusing people who had the misfortune of being born with a different skin color. A *Boston Globe* article from spring training one year related an episode where Speaker and Wood unmercifully hounded a young black busboy, taking great delight in humiliating him in a restaurant full of teammates and fans.

Wood's nickname came from a remark Paul Shannon of the *Boston Post* made while watching Joe's fastball blaze to the plate during spring training in 1909: "That fellow really throws smoke." Before Wood's shoulder and elbow were damaged, he threw as hard or harder than anyone before or since. Like most hurlers of his day, he whipped the ball sidearm after an abrupt leg kick, a motion that put enormous strain on his right elbow and shoulder.

His great rival Walter Johnson was once asked to compare his own velocity to Wood's. "Listen, my friend, there's no man alive who can throw harder than Smoky Joe Wood," the Big Train answered. But Johnson also observed early in Joe's career that Wood's "flick of the wrist motion" would make him susceptible to injury. Sadly, Johnson proved prophetic:

Joe's last pitching victory came at the too-young age of twenty-five. Grantland Rice saw Wood pitch near the end of the 1915 season and commented, "The smokeball appellation has been canned."

The ache in Wood's right arm and shoulder never left him. Former Red Sox scout and historian Ed Walton befriended Wood in the 1970s and 1980s. In a recent interview, Walton said he witnessed numerous instances of the aging Wood grimacing in pain while simply shaking a hand or putting on a blazer. In his *Red Sox Triumphs and Tragedies*, Walton writes that during Wood's epochal 1912 season, Joe often volunteered for extra duty. "If the game was close and a relief pitcher might be needed, his teammates would come and say, 'How about it, Woodie?' And usually manager Stahl would say, 'Okay, go down to the corner' (as they called the bullpen in those days). Joe would start throwing and throwing just in case he was needed."

It's a testament to Wood's character and natural athletic skills that once his arm soured, he turned himself into a creditable outfielder and batter. In 1921 he hit .366 in some two hundred at bats for the Indians. The next year, with more than five hundred at bats, he hit .297. His bullpen mate Charley Hall once said, "Show me anything athletically that involved working with the hands and body and ask me who I'd single out as the best, and I'd say without hesitation that I'd pit Joe Wood against the world. He was the most natural and talented of them all." That natural talent extended to the billiards table, where Joe routinely cleaned up.

After the Sox purchased him from Kansas City, Wood appeared in six games at the end of the 1908 season. Like Speaker, he showed a glimmer of greatness to come that fall, going 1-1 with an earned run average of 2.38. In 1909 he started nineteen games, appeared in five others, and compiled a record of 11-7, lowering his ERA to 2.21. In addition to his meteoric fastball, he developed a repertoire that included what Tim Murnane once described as "slow drops and dreamy curves." Joe liked to lather the ball with licorice and saliva. "If someone kicked about it," Joe told Ritter in 1963, "the umpire would throw it out." In short order, he became one of the most feared right-handers in the American League.

Although Taylor persisted in making dumb trades, the Red Sox had begun putting together the nucleus of a fine club in late 1908. Being platooned at catcher was the salty twenty-five-year-old Carrigan, the son of an Irish immigrant grocer from Lewiston, Maine, who somehow finagled enough money to attend Holy Cross College. Carrigan played with such ferocity that his peers nicknamed him "Old Rough" or just "Rough" – high praise, indeed, in the dead-ball era.

Rough Carrigan swung an adequate bat but it was his rugged presence behind the plate that earned him the reputation of being one of the better catchers of his generation. His forte was blocking runners off the plate. In his book *The Pitch That Killed*, writer Mike Sowell related this anecdote from a 1908 game between the Tigers and the Red Sox:

> Detroit's George Moriarty – who had three inches and thirty pounds on Carrigan – reached first base and yelled down to the Boston catcher, "Hey, you Irish S.O.B., I'm going to come around the bases and knock you on your arse." Sure enough, a few moments later, Moriarty rounded third base and went barreling into home plate. When he did, he was the one who ended up flat on his back. Standing over the fallen player, Carrigan shot a stream of tobacco juice into Moriarty's face and asked, "How do you like that, you Irish S.O.B.?"

Later, Rough and his chaw of tobacco became the only skipper in Red Sox history to win two World Series. Babe Ruth, a tough player to please, considered Carrigan the finest manager for whom he ever played. Rough's on-field persona belied a sentimental streak. With the help of a faithful fan, Carrigan and his wife kept a scrapbook of his Red Sox years, now housed at the Sports Museum of New England. The year-by-year booklets are crammed full of yellowed clippings from the *Globe*, *Journal*, and *Post* that document the Red Sox's glory years. Carrigan felt such loyalty to the franchise that he allowed himself to be talked out of retirement in 1927 to manage a dreadful Sox team that lost only seven fewer games than the Yankee juggernaut *won* that year. In the off-season he ran what had been his dad's cigar and liquor store in Lewiston. Eventually he acquired and ran a bank and a string of area movie theaters. He died at home along the Maine coast not far from where he had been born eighty-six years earlier.

Another immigrant son anchored the middle of the Sox infield. Like many Germans of his generation, Charles Wagner was tagged with the nickname "Heinie." A middle infielder, Wagner became a cog of the championship clubs in 1912 and 1915, earning the captaincy in 1912.

Heinie was never much of a hitter, but he flashed a good glove and could play multiple positions.

At first base was another future player-manager for the Sox, Midwesterner Jake Stahl, who had attended the University of Illinois. Arriving in a midseason trade with the New York Highlanders, Stahl's offensive numbers were mediocre. But he knew the game (at twenty-six the Washington club had made him player-manager) and helped solidify what had been a shaky infield.

A member of the Sox rotation in 1908 and for the next three seasons was scrappy right-hander Eddie Cicotte, who went 11-12 with an earned run average of 2.43. Cicotte was a steady pitcher for the Red Sox, but it was as a member of the Chicago White Sox that he earned both fame and infamy. He became a consistent big winner for Comiskey's club, perfecting a "shine" ball by rubbing the seams with forbidden paraffin. Joe Wood remembered to Ritter that umpires "couldn't see [Cicotte] put [paraffin] on there, though, so he kept throwing them. . . . He was a 'fixer,' you know." By plunking the Cincinnati Reds' lead-off man in the first game of the 1919 World Series, Cicotte "the fixer" signaled to Arnold Rothstein, Sport Sullivan, and a coast-to-coast gambling cabal that the Series was rigged.

By 1908 Sport Sullivan had figured out how to make a lot of money manipulating odds and controlling events. He was living in the lap of luxury in a sumptuous Milton, Massachusetts, home complete with servants. Owners, reporters, front-office executives, and ballplayers from both Boston's American and National League franchises – not to mention most saloon-goers in town – knew precisely who he was and what he represented. Yet he rarely lacked for public company when he socialized at McGreevey's and other sports-crazy taverns around town. " 'Touts 'n pints' were a huge part of the Anglo-Irish tradition," Glenn Stout said in a recent interview. "There was no stigma attached to [Sullivan] because practically everyone had some action going." In the years to come, Sport Sullivan and his cohorts would play an increasingly sinister role in professional baseball – not just in Boston but around the country.

CHAPTER 5

Early Years in Boston

The architects who designed the Huntington Avenue Grounds learned from their predecessors' mistakes at the South End Grounds. Across the railroad tracks, the Nationals had built an all-wooden structure. Although aesthetically pleasing – the original spires that adorned the rooftop gave it a distinctly European look – the Nationals' park was prone to fires.

So Boston's new American League franchise got a ballpark whose main grandstand was made largely of concrete. The design of the Huntington Avenue Grounds featured a single-tiered grandstand with a remarkable innovation: a covered lobby to shield fans during rainstorms. An even more wondrous amenity greeted players as they arrived in their dressing rooms: brand-new "shower baths."

The fact that the park had a place to dress, let alone a shower room, must have signaled to Speaker and Wood that they'd come a far piece from the bush leagues. When the two frontiersmen showed up at the intersection of Rogers and Huntington avenues, they beheld a park whose dimensions were otherworldly. It took a poke of 440 feet to traverse the left-field line – an impossible distance in the dead-ball era. Straightaway center was an eye-straining eighth of a mile from home plate: 635 feet! Down the right-field line, meanwhile, was a mere 280 feet, which must have given the Huntington Avenue Grounds a peculiarly misshapen feel: bloated in left and center, cramped in right. There was a reason the park had a slapdash feel to it – construction was completed in less than two months.

It was so immense that overflow crowds could easily be accommodated on the playing field. During the 1903 World Series, thousands of standing-room-only field tickets were sold. A single rope separated fan from outfielder. Policemen wielding rubber hoses and baseball bats kept unruly customers in line.

There was room to seat some nine thousand people in the main grandstand and the abbreviated bleachers (known back then as "bleacher boards") that ran down both lines. In the Grounds' early years, a huge sign on the interior center-field wall urged patrons to buy their clothes from Boyle Bros. haberdashers. Outside the park, next to the main entrance, a garish advertisement hawked C.M.C. "garters for men" with the slogan "Hoot Mon!"

The Pilgrims' world championship banner hung on a center-field flagpole next to pennants commemorating the 1903 and 1904 American League crowns – awkward reminders that the franchise had once been a perennial contender. But that had been a different era under different ownership.

An owner fond of late-night binge drinking now called the shots. Legend has it that in the middle of those benders John Irving Taylor was capable of firing anyone in the organization. In February 1909 Cy Young was lost to the franchise when Taylor, supposedly on a drunken spree with fellow owners at the league meeting in Chicago, traded Young to Cleveland for two middling pitchers and $12,500 in cash. The Royal Rooters, themselves no strangers to inebriated decision making, blamed Ban Johnson for the one-sided deal. Charles Somers, the Cleveland financier who had been Johnson's sugar daddy in the formative days of the league, now controlled the Ohio franchise. The gang at McGreevey's suspected that Taylor was doing Johnson's dirty work by bucking up the Cleveland club while bushwhacking his own. Struck by the circuslike atmosphere that surrounded the team, Boston newspapermen took to calling the owner "Phineas Taylor Barnum."

No doubt dispirited by the loss of baseball's most accomplished pitcher, the Red Sox gathered in Hot Springs, Arkansas, for spring training in 1909. They were led by manager Fred Lake, a genial Canadian who guided the Sox to a surprising third-place finish that year. Yet when Lake worked up the gumption to ask for a raise at the end of the season, Taylor dumped him.

Spring training back then was full of rituals that appear a bit bizarre today. In addition to drilling and scrimmaging, the players went on mandatory hikes through the woods. It was believed that long nature strolls would not only tone up players' legs and lungs but also serve as tonic for the soul. So visitors to big league spring training camps in that era witnessed the strange sight of several dozen young men decked out in full uniform and cleats clomping through the woods.

Nineteen nine was the first year the Sox trained in Hot Springs. The previous two seasons the Sox had done their late winter workouts up the road in Little Rock. But in Speaker's first full year with the club they retreated to a rustic resort town some fifty miles away in the pine forests of the Ozark Mountains.

Speaker knew all about the appeal of warm springs; natural waters that supposedly soothed the body and spirit, after all, had contributed to the coffers of his hometown and homestead. But the town fathers of Hot Springs put their counterparts in Hubbard City to shame, branding their area the "Valley of the Vapors," snaking three rail lines through the Ozarks, and trumpeting their resort's healing powers far and wide. By the turn of the century Hot Springs had become a booming tourist destination. Because the resort brought in folks not afraid to part with a few bucks, Hot Springs had the festive ambiance of a nonstop state fair. At one end of town, visitors could go on hot-air balloon rides. At the other, they could watch bicycle races or sit in the grandstands and take in shows or band concerts.

The Red Sox trained at Majestic Park at the south end of town. On one side of the park stood an ostrich ranch; on the other, presumably encircled by a sturdy fence, was an alligator farm and zoo. One of the few playful photographs that survives from Speaker's early career shows him "riding" a Hot Springs alligator equipped with a bit and harness. Speaker, sporting a bowler and a cigar clenched between his teeth, is mugging for the camera, giving the photographer the complete look-Ma-I'm-a-cowboy treatment.

Hot Springs also offered entertainment of a more salacious variety. On the outskirts of town was a "dance hall" known as the Black Orchid. More than a few ballplayers availed themselves of a dance or two with the Orchid's "hostesses." Those who sashayed with the wrong girls were said to have come down with "malaria" – that era's preferred euphemism for venereal disease, at least among sportswriters. Besides brothels, the Valley of the Vapors had racetracks, speakeasies, cockfights, and all manner of gambling dens – around which local authorities must have been well compensated to look the other way.

With all these prurient diversions, it's no surprise that ballplayers loved coming to Hot Springs. The first professional club to discover the resort was the Chicago White Stockings of Cap Anson and King Kelly. In 1886 owner Albert Spalding sent his White Stockings to the Ozarks for what is believed to be the first full-fledged spring training. Besides putting his charges through a regimen of twice-a-day drills, manager Anson insisted that they visit the bathhouses, hoping the warm waters would "boil out" their "alcoholic microbes." It was Anson who started the tradition of a long daily hike through the woods – a workout that other teams soon began to copy.

In *Harry Hooper: An American Baseball Life*, Paul J. Zingg notes that visitors to Majestic Park were occasionally treated to "the sight of an enormous ostrich harnessed to a cart dashing across the grounds." Hot Springs, it seemed, churned with the manic zaniness of the balloon departure scene in *The Wizard of Oz*. The Sox were so taken with Hot Springs that they trained there for twelve of the next thirteen springs.

Tris Speaker wasn't the only promising young outfielder in Hot Springs that February and March. Also trying to make the club was a college-trained railroad engineer from Northern California named Harry Bartholomew Hooper. Harry Hooper, like Speaker, moved with lithe and elegant efficiency. He had an exceptional throwing arm and excellent if untested instincts in the outfield. Over time Hooper became a reliable lead-off hitter, but in the spring of 1909 he was having trouble showing the Red Sox his potential at the plate. In baseball's time-honored tradition of letting the rookie know who was boss, Sox veterans were muscling Hooper out of the batting cage.

Harry Hooper's California childhood had little of the turbulence that marked Tris Speaker's upbringing on the plains of Texas. Unlike the Speakers, the War between the States had not traumatized the Hooper clan. Originally of English extraction, Harry's father, Joe, had grown up on Prince Edward Island in Canada's maritime provinces. Joe Hooper left the island in the decade following the American Civil War to find work as a jack-of-all-trades laborer in Portland, Maine. In 1876 he learned from two siblings who had already migrated to California of the opportunities that existed in the Bay Area. So he booked the least expensive fare on the Union Pacific–Central Pacific line – a ticket so cheap that his car was continually bumped for higher priority traffic.

It took Joe fifteen long days and more than one hundred station stops before he finally pulled into San Francisco.

He found work on a Santa Clara ranch, courted and married its German-born housekeeper, and eventually moved his young family to more affordable land near Volta in the San Joaquin Valley. There the Hoopers raised cattle and horses, plus enough alfalfa to keep young Harry and his three older siblings clothed and fed. To be sure, the Hoopers worked hard to make ends meet, but they had chosen a fortuitous time to run a ranch in Northern California. Each year brought new settlers to the area, increasing the demand for livestock and crops. Over time the Hoopers' ranch became reasonably prosperous – enough to send Harry off to college when the time came.

The childhood that Harry described to interviewers decades later sounds idyllic. He went to school in Volta's two-room schoolhouse, hunted, fished, and rode horseback around the valley with his siblings and cousins, and developed such a strong arm that he once pegged a rock and felled a small wildcat that was stalking the chicken house. Harry's chicken-yard heroics earned him the nickname "Cat."

While on a trip back East, an uncle took the ten-year-old Harry to New York to see the National League's Louisville Cyclones (one of the precursors to the Pittsburgh Pirates) play the Brooklyn Bridegrooms (forerunners of the Superbas, who in turn gave way to the Robins and Trolley Dodgers) at Brooklyn's Eastern Park. The Cyclones, led by two hits from their rookie infielder, Honus Wagner, dusted the Bridegrooms 16–8. Young Harry was hooked. When he got back to the San Joaquin Valley, he became a terror in schoolyard and town games.

Harry was such a promising student at the Volta schoolhouse that teachers urged his parents to extend his education. Dutiful Catholics, the Hoopers began looking into Saint Mary's College in nearby Oakland. They first elected to enroll Harry in a two-year program that cost $320 a year in tuition, then later allowed him to pursue a more advanced five-year degree that cost substantially more money.

Harry had just turned fifteen when, in his words, he "leapt at the chance" to go to Saint Mary's. Saint Mary's was a Christian Brothers school that served the Bay Area's burgeoning immigrant community – especially young men of Irish heritage. Morning prayers began promptly at 6:00; lights out was strictly enforced at 8:30 p.m. Harry immediately gravitated to engineering studies, with an eye toward becoming a rail-road surveyor – a profession always in demand out West.

Harry at first captained an intramural baseball team known as the Midgets, then worked his way onto the Phoenix varsity squad. Hooper grabbed the attention of professional scouts by hitting .371 and gunning down runners like they were wildcats prowling the family chicken yard.

Just as he was graduating in the spring of 1907, Harry played briefly for Alameda in the "outlaw" (e.g., not sanctioned by "organized baseball") California State League, then signed a contract with the CSL's Sacramento Sacts. The owner of the Sacts knew that the field engineer for the Western Pacific was a big baseball fan, so they worked out a twofer arrangement: Harry earned seventy-five dollars a month as a surveyor for the railroad and eighty-five dollars a month as a ballplayer for the Sacts.

In his debut for the Sacts, Harry ripped seven hits and scored three runs in what the *Sacramento Bee* termed "an impressive performance." He hit .328 for the remainder of the Sacts' 1907 season, stealing thirteen bases. The following season he hit a robust .347 and began developing a reputation up and down the Golden State for his quickness in the field and on the base paths. Toward the end of the 1908 season, Sacts manager Charles Graham startled Hooper by revealing that he was, *sub rosa*, a scout for Boston's American League franchise. Graham surprised Hooper even more by volunteering that he had written to Boston club owner John Taylor on several occasions about Harry's potential.

Harry agreed to meet with the Boston owner, who was due in North-ern California a week later on one of his periodic scouting trips out West. (Taylor may have been scouting more than ballplayers on his pilgrimage to the coast. At some point in this period he began courting San Fran-cisco society belle Dorothy Van Ness, eventually marrying her.)

Hooper and Taylor met, not surprisingly given the latter's predilec-tions, over a couple of pints of porter in a Sacramento saloon. At Gra-ham's direction, Harry agreed to sign for $2,800 – a full thousand dollars more than he was making in his dual role with the Sacts and the Western Pacific. Harry didn't know it at the time, of course, but the Sox gave him four times more to sign than they had given Tris Speaker two years earlier – a telling commentary on the club's assessment of the two ballplayers' potential.

"I wanted to be an engineer," Hooper remembered later, "but I went to Boston."

"Cat" Hooper was a cagey competitor who was especially tenacious in the clutch. "When the chips were down, that guy played like wildfire," Joe Wood once said of him.

But off the field Hooper had a wry smile and a disarming wit that drew people to him – unlike Speaker, whose bulldog persona tended to push people away.

In many ways, the two were obverse sides of the same coin. One was raised in an immigrant household with two devoted parents and schooled by celibate men wearing cassocks. The other lost his father early in life and was brought up in a frontier village pulsating with evangelical fundamentalism. One family was untouched by the ravages of the Civil War; the other permanently scarred by it. As Paul Zingg observed in a recent interview, because of the differences in their backgrounds, there was a lot more "give" in Hooper's personality. Between the lines, Hooper was all Germanic precision and seriousness. Away from the park, he could chuckle at himself and enjoy life and people in a way that was difficult for the young Speaker.

Hooper was a little longer-limbed than Speaker, not as thick in the chest or as world-weary in the face. Although Harry wasn't as classically handsome as Joe Wood, in his youth he had a pleasing combination of dark brown hair, bushy eyebrows, and dark eyes.

One trait Hooper shared with Speaker was a lethal arm. Speaker threw left-handed; by 1909 he had perfected the art of hurling the ball on a tight parabola to the infield, usually curving it slightly from left to right. Hooper's right arm was a Clemente buggy whip; his throws from the right-field corner to second base were said to crackle through the air. In the years to come, the two of them formed a Hall of Fame center-field–right-field combination that nearly a century later has never been bettered.

In spite of the religious tension that separated the K.C.s from the Masons in the Sox clubhouse, Hooper and Speaker became friends – not bosom buddies exactly, but at least occasional hunting and fishing companions.

For intrasquad games that spring, Red Sox manager Lake divided his men into the "Regulars" – a group comprised mainly of veterans – and the "Colts," or "Yannigans" (ragtime-era slang for newcomers), made up of rookies and second-year players. The Regulars enjoyed giving the Yannigans a hard time, especially the fresh-faced ranch kid from California. They shouldered him out of the way so obnoxiously that Harry and a couple of other rookies were reduced to pitching themselves batting practice on a distant field.

Boston sportswriters were equally cool. *Globe* reporter Harry Casey went out of his way to express skepticism about Taylor's Sacramento signee, suggesting that Hooper needed several more years of seasoning in the minors. "That made my blood boil," Harry recalled to Lawrence Ritter. "I *knew* I was good enough to make that team."

Harry also knew, after a few days of sizing up his new teammates, that Tris Speaker had a "stranglehold" on the center-field job. Speaker's skill and zeal for the game were apparent to Harry from his first day in camp.

There were all kinds of "Harrys" vying to join Speaker in the outfield in Hot Springs. Harry Niles, a Michigander, only lasted a couple of years in the big leagues but was getting most of the playing time that spring. Harry "Doc" Gessler, a western Pennsylvanian, bounced from team to team in a journeyman career that spanned eight years. And there were the two Harrys from the West Coast: Hooper and his constant companion in Hot Springs, a fellow Northern Californian from Monterey named Harry Wolter. Wolter doubled as a left-handed pitcher. Given the paucity of southpaws on the Sox, Wolter spent a good deal of his time in Hot Springs on the mound.

The fielding prowess of the Regular Harrys – Niles and Gessler – has been lost to history, but suffice it to say Speaker probably tracked down more than a few balls in the gaps. Another journeyman outfielder with pedestrian skills, Jack Thoney, was also getting playing time in the outfield in Hot Springs. If his diary entries are any indication, it drove Harry to distraction that he wasn't getting more of an opportunity to prove his mettle to Lake.

The Sox broke camp that year with a rotation led by Frankie Arellanes and Eddie Cicotte. Arellanes appeared in a remarkable forty-five games that season, winning seventeen and saving seven more. Cy Young had taken Cicotte under his wing the previous season, helping Eddie add a knuckler and spitter to his repertoire. Joe Wood, who was worked into the starting rotation as the season progressed, won eleven and saved two that year. A veteran lefty named Fred Burchell, who had posted a respectable 10–8 record the previous season, rounded out the starters. Hooper's pal Wolter made the club as a spot pitcher and substitute first baseman and outfielder.

The closest thing the Red Sox of 1909 had to a star was their prima donna third baseman and captain, the felicitously named Harry Lord. A Mainer like Carrigan, Lord was a steady batsman but a serious liability in the field. He was also, by most accounts, a clubhouse lawyer and a shady character. In Joe Wood's recollection, Lord picked up more than a trick or two by hanging around the grubby Hal Chase. Since John Taylor's judgment about people was as clouded as his judgment about ballplayers, the two naturally became drinking buddies. Taylor vowed to Lord's face never to trade him, then shipped him off to the White Sox for peanuts the following year after Lord got into a public spat with the manager.

Larry Gardner, a University of Vermont alum who could play third, short, and second, was trying to win a regular infield job. A Protestant, Gardner soon hooked up with the Masons in the Sox clubhouse. The only infield holdovers from 1908 were shortstop Heinie Wagner and catcher Rough Carrigan, a pair of K.C.s.

The weather in the Ozarks was so miserable in late March that Lake decided to head north a week early. Traveling by train, the Red Sox worked their way toward the season opener in Philadelphia by scheduling exhibition games against minor league teams in Memphis, Nashville, Indianapolis, Dayton, Buffalo, and Wilkes-Barre, plus a match-up in Cincinnati with the National League Reds. It must have been sweet vindication for Speaker to visit his old Southern League haunts in Memphis and Nashville as a starting big league center fielder. The bad weather continued to dog them: a number of exhibitions were canceled; they dodged snowflakes during their final workout before the regular season opened at Shibe Park in Philadelphia.

Opening day, 1909 – the first of many to come in the big leagues for Speaker, Hooper, and Wood – dawned bright and beautiful. A crowd of more than thirty thousand at Shibe Park enjoyed an unseasonably warm day. Both teams paraded out to center field for a special pregame ceremony. A flag with forty-six stars – one for each state in the Union – was unfurled; a band played a stirring rendition of "America." Philadelphia mayor John Reyburn threw out the first ball.

Then Boston's Yannigans warily eyed the A's Eddie Plank as he took the mound. "Gettysburg Eddie," born in the hallowed village twelve years after Pickett's Charge and a graduate of its college, was in the middle of a Hall of Fame career. The southpaw won his 170th career game that afternoon, 8–1, scattering six hits and baffling the young Sox with an assortment of off-speed pitches. Before Plank retired, he won another 157 games in the big leagues, all but 42 of them for Mr. Mack.

Speaker had earned the center-field job during spring training but was hard-pressed to find hits against such wily A's moundsmen as Plank, Chief Bender, Cy Morgan, and Hal Krause. Hooper not only didn't play in that opening series – he wasn't even in uniform. Harry's road uniform had been lent to substitute infielder Charlie French, who was pressed into duty when Heinie Wagner left the club to tend to a family emergency.

The Sox next traveled south to Washington DC for a series against the Senators. When manager Lake told Harry the morning of the series opener that Hooper would again be sitting the bench, the Californian took out his frustrations by pounding up the steps of the Washington Monument. Much to Harry's surprise, Lake was waiting for him with a package in his hands when Hooper arrived in the clubhouse of National Park, the Senators' seventeen-year-old ball yard near the campus of Howard University. Lake was holding Harry's uniform: Heinie Wagner had still not returned from his family crisis, so the manager had moved Niles to shortstop and had slated Hooper to fill the hole in left.

There was a runner in scoring position in the top of the second when Harry came to the plate for his first-ever at bat in the big leagues. Like Speaker, Hooper was a natural right-hander who taught himself to swing from the port side because it put him one step closer to first base. Unlike Spoke, however, Cat preferred a slightly open stance, his front foot closer to the right-hand edge of the batter's box than his rear foot. He bent somewhat at the waist, keeping his hands separated on the bat, as was fashionable at the time. Anticipating the pitch, his bat swayed back and forth like an upside-down metronome; as the pitcher wound up, Harry's hands came to rest about chest high. Befitting a player nick-named Cat, Hooper looked deceptively relaxed at the plate.

Staring at Harry from the hill was brawny left-hander Bill Burns. Harry caused war whoops to come from the Sox dugout when he drove in his first career run with a solid line drive. He banged out another sin-gle, handled three chances in left without incident, and threw a runner out at the plate. Despite Harry's best efforts, the Red Sox lost.

"That's the boy I signed out in California," Taylor crowed after the game to anyone who would listen. Manager Lake opined that "there is awful good material in that boy" and predicted that "he will make his mark in the big league just as Speaker is doing now." The Sox headed to their home opener in Boston with a 3-2 record and one complete Yannigan and one semi-Yannigan acquitting themselves nicely in the outfield.

It was practically snowing in Boston on April 21, but that didn't stop thousands of New Englanders from swarming the grandstand and the temporary bleachers that the Sox management had installed in the Grounds' yawning center field. Lake decided to reinsert Thoney in the lineup for the home opener against the A's, disappointing Hooper no end. The highlight of the Sox's 6–2 victory was a triple steal, flawlessly pulled off by Lord, Gessler, and Speaker. Tris also stole two other bases that day. The Texan was beginning to win over the South End crowd with his hustle.

As the year wore on, Tris grew more comfortable at the plate, ending at a .309 clip. Hooper played in only half the games in 1909, hitting .282 in 255 at bats. By midseason, though, Hooper became a certified big leaguer when his teammates stuck him with a new nickname: "Cat" devolved into "Pussy Foot" in the Sox clubhouse.

For much of the 1909 season, Speaker, Wood, Hooper, and virtually all the other bachelors on the Sox bunked at the Putnam Inn, a four-story combination apartment house, drugstore, and saloon just down Huntington Avenue from the Grounds. "The whole house is theirs," the *Boston Post* enthused. "On the second floor is a suite with plenty of windows so that the crowd can see everything of interest that passes on the avenue. Up stairs in the suite directly overhead, Heinie Wagner and Bill Carrigan fight it out over a game of pinochle. . . . They have few secrets from one another and the place, in fact, looks more like a boarding school than a place where ball players live."

Joe Wood recalled that in the late summer and fall of 1908, Cy Young spent a lot time sipping his famous medicinal moonshine in the little diner-pub on the ground floor of the Inn. Having experienced the joys of living the "boardinghouse" life in the immigrant-filled South End, Wood and Speaker decided to rent rooms in suburban Winthrop for most of the rest of their careers with the Red Sox.

The dominant team in the American League of that era was the Detroit Tigers. In 1909 Detroit was en route to its third successive pennant. The Tigers lost the 1907 and 1908 World Series to the Chicago Cubs and were destined to lose a classic seven-game series to Honus Wagner's Pittsburgh Pirates in 1909.

Hughie Jennings, a moon-faced eastern Pennsylvanian who'd escaped the coal mines of Pittston, managed the Tigers. Like his cohort John McGraw, Jennings learned his craft while a member of the rough-and-tumble Baltimore Orioles clubs of the 1890s. "Let me tell you, after you'd make a trip around the bases against [the Orioles] you knew you'd been somewhere," remembered one opponent. "They'd trip you, give you the hip, and who knows what else. Boy, it was rough. There was only one umpire in those days, see, and he couldn't be everywhere at once."

Whether in the dugout or in a coach's box, Jennings was fond of yipping at his charges. It became his signature. "Eh yah!" Jennings would shriek to get his players' attention. Hughie, despite his academic background at Saint Bonaventure and Cornell Law School, wasn't above squirrelly gamesmanship.

Whenever his Tigers faced the Athletics' left-handed ace Rube Waddell, Hughie would bring dime-store toys like a jack-in-the-box or a rubber snake out to the first base coach's box. One member of the Tigers recalled that Hughie would set them on the grass and yell, " 'Hey, Rube, look!' Rube would look over at the jack-in-the-box popping up and down and kind of grin, real slow-like." Grinning "real slow-like" was not an unusual happenstance for Waddell. The first of several pitchers in baseball history to be tagged with the epithet "$100,000 dollar arm and a 10-cent head," Rube was almost certainly mentally impaired; he may have been something of an idiot savant. Throughout his career, he was notorious for leaving the mound to go chase fire engines or showing up late at the ballpark because he was shooting marbles with some kids down the street.

Waddell wasn't the only ballplayer Jennings and the Tigers buffaloed. The whole league had trouble containing the Tigers at the plate and on the base paths. Detroit's lineup featured two future Hall of Famers: a slap-hitting slasher and a slugger who could also run.

Sam Crawford, the Tigers' center fielder, was one of the few dead-ball-era hitters known for his power. He led the American League twice in home runs and five times in triples. His record of 312 career three-baggers has stood for eight decades and may never be challenged.

Crawford was so proud of his tiny hometown – Wahoo, Nebraska – that he insisted it be inscribed on his Hall of Fame plaque. "Wahoo Sam's" parents had run the general store, arranging for their teenaged son to apprentice for the town barber. On Saturday nights, the youngster practiced his skills on the farmers who came to town for a thirty-five-cent haircut and shave before hitting the saloon.

Wahoo Sam was a thoughtful observer of the game and the people who played it. The remarks about Jennings, Waddell, and the old Orioles quoted above came from Sam's interview with Lawrence Ritter in *The Glory of Their Times*.

Sam shared Detroit's outfield for fifteen years with a belligerent Georgian who made Speaker's allegiance to the Confederate cause look weak-kneed. Tyrus Raymond Cobb, in Crawford's words, "came up [to the big leagues] with an antagonistic attitude, which in his mind turned any little razzing into a life-or-death struggle. He always figured everybody was ganging up against him. . . . He was still fighting the Civil War. As far as he was concerned, we were all damn Yankees before he even met us. Well, who knows, maybe if he hadn't had that persecution complex he never would have been the great ballplayer he was. He was always trying to prove he was the best, on the field and off."

Ty Cobb's persecution complex didn't happen by accident; its roots ran deep. His family life in Royston, a crossroads not far from the South Carolina border, had the gothic torment and loathing of a Tennessee

Williams play. Cobb's father, William Herschel Cobb, came from a family with a proud Confederate heritage: one Cobb served as Jefferson Davis's secretary of the treasury; another wrote a widely admired treatise defending slavery before being killed in the line of duty as a brigadier general at Fredericksburg.

W. H. Cobb was a stern schoolmaster who rarely spared the rod and took a dim view of his eldest son's yen for baseball. Known as "Professor" for his learned ways and imperious demeanor, he had wed one of his schoolhouse students, a lass named Amanda. It's believed that Amanda was all of twelve years old at the time of her nuptials to Professor Cobb. The couple may have waited some time to consummate the marriage. Their first child, named in honor of the city of Tyre's heroic fight against the armies of Alexander the Great, wasn't born until nearly four years after the wedding, in December of 1886. Another boy and a girl soon followed.

The Professor became a pillar of Royston society; the Cobbs a fixture at Baptist services every Sunday morning. As Ty grew into adolescence, though, his parents' marriage began stirring the rumor mill in staid little Royston. The still-fetching Mrs. Cobb was said to have certain needs that were not completely satisfied by her aging husband. As related in Charles Alexander's biography *Ty Cobb*, one stifling August evening when Ty was off playing ball for Augusta in the Sally League, Mrs. Cobb shot and killed Professor Cobb as he attempted to enter their home's master bedroom through a second floor porch window. Amanda told the sheriff that she had mistaken her husband for a prowler. The tongues that wagged all over Royston, however, suggested that Professor Cobb had deliberately entrapped his wife in the middle of a tryst – and that she knew exactly whom she was shooting and why. A small revolver was found in the victim's coat pocket. Neighbors reported hearing a long interval between the two blasts of Amanda Cobb's shotgun.

The local prosecutor didn't believe Amanda's story, indicting her for voluntary manslaughter. Mrs. Cobb's case became a cause celebre in northeastern Georgia, with the state's solicitor general leading a four-person prosecution team. Amanda countered by hiring five attorneys of her own. In what must have been a searing experience for Ty and his younger siblings, their mother was subjected to a very public – though mercifully brief – trial. An all-male jury ended up acquitting Mrs. Cobb.

Young Tyrus had always been thin-skinned and temperamental. But following the ghastly death of the man he tried desperately to please, he became a paranoiac. Cobb took out the fury of his family's humiliation on virtually everyone and everything he encountered. If fielders got in his way on the base paths, he spiked them. If teammates dared look at him cross-eyed, he defied them to fight. If fans booed him, he had to be restrained from going into the stands after them. And if black people had the temerity to give him "lip," as he once put it, he pummeled them.

While dining in Cleveland early in his career, Cobb somehow became convinced that an African American waiter was getting "uppity" with him. Ty grabbed a knife and stabbed the man, slipping away before the police arrived. Cobb then spent the next year and a half avoiding the state of Ohio, lest he get hit with an arrest warrant. Eventually, Fred Lieb related in *Baseball as I Have Known It*, the charge was dropped.

"[Baseball] is no pink tea, and mollycoddles had better stay out," Cobb once growled. Tris Speaker was no mollycoddle – and Cobb, inevitably called "the Georgia Peach," became the standard by which Spoke measured himself. From his first days on the Hubbard City sand-lots, Speaker had been a hard-nosed player. But after eyeballing Cobb, he raised the intensity level of his own game.

Spoke's take-no-prisoners base-running style and his newly honed ability to slap an outside pitch into left field became, in effect, homage to Cobb. Speaker's first full year in the big leagues, 1909, also marked Cobb's third consecutive year of leading the American League in hitting. Cobb batted .377 in 1909, the *lowest* average he would compile for the next five years. In 1911 Cobb led the league in every offensive category save one: Frank Baker's nine homers bested Cobb by one. Only once in a thirteen-year skein did Cobb fail to lead the American League in hitting – in 1916, when Speaker's .386 average in his first year with the Indians bettered Cobb by fifteen points.

Branch Rickey once said of Cobb, "[He] lived off the field as though he wished to live forever. He lived on the field as though it was his last day." Asked to size up Cobb and Ruth after both had retired, Speaker said, "The Babe was a great ballplayer, sure, but Cobb was even greater. Babe could knock your brains out, but Cobb would drive you crazy."

Toward the end of Cobb's life, Ty sat down with Smoky Joe Wood to reminisce about their playing days. Joe's son Bob was in the hotel room that afternoon as the two old-timers swapped stories. Bob remembers Smoky Joe paying the Georgia Peach the ultimate tribute, saying that Ty and Spoke were in a different league than all the rest of the players.

The Red Sox were twenty-five games above .500 in 1909, finishing nine games behind Detroit and five games behind Philadelphia in their best showing since 1904. Speaker made an immediate impression in center field, leading the league in put-outs, assists, and catch-and-throw double plays from the outfield. By midseason 1909, Jimmy McAleer, the skipper of the St. Louis Browns, was calling Speaker a better all-around player than Cobb.

The press corps became infatuated with Speaker during the Sox's postseason exhibition series with the Giants that October. Called the Inter-League Championship, the best of seven series was conducted by the National Commission and played – oddly enough – the same week as the World Series between the Pirates and the Tigers. "Had it not been for Speaker, there would have been no chance for the Boston Americans to have beaten the Giants in the post-season series," wrote the *Boston Post*. "Over on the other side of the river, they don't call it a victory for Boston. Talk to a base ball fan about it and he will insist that it was a victory of Speaker over the New York team; and hanged if it don't look pretty much that way. It is sure that all the season in the National League, the Giants never had one player who made such a fight against them as Speaker. Not even Hans Wagner." John McGraw must have been kicking himself as he watched the young man he rebuffed less than two years before buzz around the Polo Grounds. The Sox won the Series four games to one; Speaker collected six hits against Mathewson over two games and batted .600 for the series.

Around the time of the postseason match-up with the Giants, Taylor dumped manager Lake and replaced him with a skipper whom immigrant Boston could claim as one of its own: combative Irishman Patsy Donovan. An émigré from County Cork, Donovan had knocked around the big leagues in a journeyman career that saw him change uniforms nine different times. He'd been a player-manager for the Pirates and Cardinals, then guided the hapless Senators to a ninety-seven-loss season in 1904. His win-loss record as Brooklyn's field manager from 1906 to 1908 was mediocre, too, yet somehow he caught the Boston owner's eye, becoming a Sox scout and Taylor intimate in 1909. Donovan brooked no nonsense from his players; every clubhouse he ever ran chafed under his leadership.

With the volatile Donovan at the helm, the Sox finished a disappointing fourth in 1910, a distant twenty-four games behind Connie Mack's club, whose pitching once again dominated the league.

Harry Hooper finally had the chance to play every day in right field in 1910, since the Sox had also parted company with Doc Gessler early that spring. Although his hitting tapered off to .267, Hooper distinguished himself in the field, assuming the league leadership in assists from Speaker with thirty. American Leaguers learned their lesson that season: run on Hooper's arm at your own peril. Harry never again recorded that many assists in a season.

Speaker, meanwhile, increased his put-out total in center field and once again led the league. He also found his groove at the plate, hitting a formidable .340 with forty-one extra-base hits and seventy-seven runs-batted-in. Larry Gardner got a chance to play nearly every day at second, hitting .283. Joe Wood's earned run average was a sporty 1.68 in 1910, but lack of run support saddled him with a 12-13 record.

Unlike spring 1909, two-thirds of the outfield was set when the team arrived to train in Hot Springs the following year. Giving Harry Niles a run for his money for the third slot was a bow-legged but nimble-footed San Franciscan whose fondness for dapper clothes made him the constant butt of jokes. George "Duffy" Lewis had preceded Harry Hooper as an outfielder at Saint Mary's College during the 1903–4 school year – the only year Duffy attended the school. Lewis and Hooper played together briefly for Alameda in the California State League in 1907, then became CSL rivals when Harry joined the Sacramento Sacts.

Lewis came up the hard way. The Gay Nineties were anything but for the shanty Irish in San Francisco. Few places in America were rougher: the city lured more than its share of down-on-their-luck prospectors, railroaders, sailors, and longshoremen. Duffy had been schooled near those mean streets; he didn't take guff from anybody. His crooked smile couldn't hide a nasty Irish temper. After arriving in Hot Springs in February of 1910, he refused to accept the Regulars versus Yannigans folkways that governed life at Majestic Field. Unlike Hooper the previous spring, Lewis balked at giving up his time in the batting cage to the Regulars – an act of defiance that immediately put him at odds with Tris Speaker. The two developed an instant enmity that lasted much of the rest of their careers.

Duffy also butted heads with Patsy Donovan in Hot Springs. On more than one occasion, Duffy was fined for insubordination. But Duffy had other qualities besides his temper that distinguished him: He impressed Donovan and Taylor with his ability to cover ground in the outfield and slug the ball at the plate. Duffy's arm, although strong, wasn't quite as unerring as Speaker's or Hooper's.

With two second-year players manning the other outfield slots, Donovan was reluctant to start a Yannigan in left as the season opened. But on April 27, 1910, Patsy penciled Lewis's name into the starting lineup for the first time, thus giving rise to the most celebrated outfield of professional baseball's first half century.

Dubbed "the Golden Outfield," the trio of Speaker, Lewis, and Hooper would remain intact for nearly six full seasons, starting more than 90 percent of Boston's games from 1910 to 1915. During that stretch, the Sox's winning percentage was just under .600; Boston actually won two more games (but two fewer pennants) than the mighty Athletics during the six-year run of the Golden Outfield.

Along with the Chicago Cubs' double play combination of "Tinker to Evers to Chance" (immortalized in the verse of Franklin Pierce Adams) and the Philadelphia Athletics' "100,000 Infield," the Spoke-Duffy-Cat outfield became an emblem of the dead-ball era, its fame enduring well after the principals had retired – but not nearly as long as it should have. For sheer athletic verve and audacity, it remains among the finest outfields in history. Grantland Rice three decades later called them the "greatest defensive outfield I ever saw. . . . They were smart and fast. They covered every square yard of the park – and they were like three fine infielders on ground balls. They could move into another county, if the ball happened to fall there."

In a 1951 column saluting the game's best outfields, the *New York Times*' Arthur Daley placed four other trios on the same pedestal as the Sox's golden boys: the Bob Meusel–Earl Combs–Babe Ruth Yankees of the late '20s; the Al Simmons–Mule Haas–Bing Miller Athletics of the late '20s and early '30s; the Stan Musial–Terry Moore–Enos Slaughter Cardinals of the early '40s; and the Joe DiMaggio–Charlie Keller–Tommy Henrich Yankees of the late '40s and early '50s. As run producers in the lively ball era, these other triumvirates bettered Speaker-Lewis-Hooper. But taken collectively, none of those units could run, catch, and throw quite like the Sox of 1910–15. Nor did they play with Spoke, Cat, and Duffy's zeal or panache. Imagine a team with Willie Mays in center, Roberto Clemente in right, and Carl Yastrzemski in left – all at the peak of their defensive genius – and that's not far removed from the old Red Sox.

Unlike the Cubs' trio, the Sox's Golden Outfield wasn't the product of fawning journalism. Joe Tinker and Johnny Evers were adequate fielders but neither ranked among the best glovemen of their generation. It's true, they pulled off some clutch double plays against McGraw's Giants with Franklin Pierce Adams and other Gotham scribes in the press box, but their combined career statistics were hardly the stuff of legend. Maybe Tinker and Evers would have turned more double plays had they not turned each other's stomach. If accounts of contemporaries are to be believed, the feud between Tinker and Evers made the one between Speaker and Lewis seem tame. Evers's disposition was so nasty that his teammates referred to him as "the Human Crab." Had Adams not filed his famous doggerel, "Baseball's Sad Lexicon," for the *New York Evening Mail* in July of 1910, Joe Tinker and Johnny Evers would still be shrouded in obscurity.

Connie Mack's infield, on the other hand, was worthy of public adulation. It earned its handle when $100,000 was, to most Americans, an incalculable sum of money. Although their four salaries didn't add up to anything close to a hundred grand – it was not for nothing that Connie Mack was known as a skinflint – the A's infield of Jack Barry at shortstop, Frank "Home Run" Baker at third, Eddie Trowbridge Collins at second, and John Phalen "Stuffy" McGinnis at first slung leather as well as any quartet in history. Two of Mack's men were players for the ages: Baker, the third sacker with a penchant for dramatic home runs, and Collins, the heady second baseman who hit a lofty .333 for his career.

Duffy's outfield and Stuffy's infield went head to head scores of times in the second decade of the century. The A's won pennants in 1910, 1911,

1913, and 1914; the Red Sox took the AL crown in 1912 and 1915. In 1915, Speaker's final year with the Sox, the club engineered a midseason trade with the Athletics to acquire none other than Jack Barry to solidify their middle infield. Boston won the World Series that year and the year after with Barry alternating between short and second.

The Boston trio enjoyed a bravura debut in late April 1910. Among them, they had ten hits as the Sox routed the Senators 11–1. Boston went on to win four of the next five games.

Lewis, who consistently led the Red Sox in RBIs, carrying a career batting average of .284, was only a notch or two behind his more famous mates in terms of on-field productivity, mainly batting cleanup. He meticulously patrolled the mammoth left field at the Huntington Avenue Grounds, and then made the transition to the smaller but still daunting Fenway left field in 1912. Speaker gave Hooper at least some leeway in right center but annoyed Lewis by constantly poaching in left center.

Spoke and Duffy inhabited different worlds and weren't shy about letting those worlds collide. Lewis was not only an outspoken member of the K.C.s, he was their social ringleader, always looking for an excuse to don loud clothes for a night out on the town. After a big day at the plate, John Taylor liked to reward his left fielder by taking him out shopping for a thirty-five-dollar suit. Speaker and the other Masons certainly weren't averse to a cocktail or two but may have felt that working-class tavern hopping was beneath them. Certain Masons may also have looked down their nose at the crude burlesque acts that Lewis, Carrigan, Wagner, and the other K.C.s liked to take in.

Ironically, however, it wasn't cultural, social, or religious differences that finally caused the tension between Speaker and Lewis to erupt. It was a bad haircut. During a heat wave in July 1913, several of the Sox decided to get buzz cuts. A barber in St. Louis who clearly had not been trained at Sam Crawford's former shop gave Lewis a sloppy trim that didn't grow back quite right. For the next few weeks, Lewis made it a point to wear a hat in public. Speaker could never resist a cruel joke. One afternoon, with friends and hangers-on gathered on the field before a game, Tris made a big show of yanking Duffy's hat off his head. Lewis warned Speaker that if the Texan did it again, Duffy would "kill him." Sure enough, Tris snuck up from behind Duffy and struck again. Lewis retaliated by chucking a bat at Speaker, bruising the star's legs and putting him out of commission that day. Spoke was banged up so badly that fellow Masons Joe Wood and Larry Gardner had to help him off the field. After that episode, the Lewis-Speaker relationship, always icy, turned downright frigid. The two barely exchanged a civil word off the field. But "once a game started we forgot personal feelings. We helped each other as willingly as we helped anybody else in the line-up," Lewis remembered years later.

The formidable athletic skills of the Red Sox trio were showcased a month after they began playing as a unit. On May 30, 1910, Connie Mack organized a fundraising event at Shibe Park in Philadelphia to benefit the widow of former Athletics catcher Michael "Doc" Powers, who had succumbed to a mysterious stomach ailment the year before. In addition to an exhibition game between a group of AL all-stars and his A's, Mack arranged for a series of special skill competitions, with individual winners receiving "handsome Loving Cups."

Hooper, Speaker, and Lewis, in that order, swept the long-distance throwing competition. And Harry finished a close second to the High-landers' swift Jimmy Austin in the hundred-yard dash. Some twelve thousand people showed up at Doc Powers day at Shibe Park, raising seven thousand dollars for Mrs. Powers and her three children. The following year, Harry won an accuracy throwing competition at a similar event at Chicago's brand-new Comiskey Park and once again finished second in the sprint.

By the end of the 1910 season, Spoke was an established star. When he arrived in Dallas that November to begin his winter siesta in Texas, an enthusiastic crowd greeted him. Later that day, the *New York Times* noted, he drove on to Hubbard City, where the locals again turned out en masse to cheer their native son.

Despite their superstar outfield, the Red Sox finished just nine games above .500 in 1910, and then struggled to a 78-75 record in 1911. They had to win their final six games in 1911 just to stumble above .500.

Nineteen eleven was the only year the Golden Outfield–era Red Sox trained in someplace other than Hot Springs, Arkansas. That year, owner John Taylor insisted that the club train in Redondo Beach, California. He wanted to fatten his margins by playing a series of exhibition games up and down California. Not coincidentally, having his charges out on the coast also enabled him to impress his new in-laws, the socially prominent Van Ness family of San Francisco. Southern California was thrilled to have big leaguers in the neighborhood. The *Los Angeles Times* gave breathless coverage to every aspect of the Sox's training camp, no matter how mundane. Reporter Lou Guernsey's article on February 26 began with this hyped-up lead: "Tris Speaker, the star outfielder of the Sox, is the real honest-to-goodness Ike Walton, and when he isn't picking 'em out of the sky he is dangling a hook and line off Redondo pier. Tris landed several surf and a pompano yesterday and Judge Wells, the genial manager of the Redondo Hotel, served them at the evening meal for the great fielder and slugger."

In a passage that must have amused his counterparts from Boston, Guernsey asserted:

> The Red Sox family is a most peace-loving and happy one. A dozen college boys are on the squad, and the old-timers took them to the bosom of their family fireside without any delay. The boys are all willing workers and there isn't a booze-fighter on the squad, which is saying a great deal. Half of the boys don't indulge in joy water of any description, and the boys that do, drink nothing but beer. Donovan doesn't object if the boys knock over a glass of beer or ale now and then, but he won't stand for any lushing. He is very temperate in his habits, and wants the boys to be the same.

The local paper was so smitten with Speaker that it gave him his own bylined column, no doubt ghost written by the excitable Guernsey. Tris's column on March 1 offered this insight, which reads like a parody of early-twentieth-century sports writing (and, ironically, expressed a sentiment with which the "author" almost certainly didn't agree): "Anybody can catch a ball, but it takes a man with a keen eye to biff the pellet when the mounder is shootin' 'em down smaller than peas. Managers always try to pick out swatters for the outer garden positions."

The swatters, mounders, and outer gardeners moved up the coast to play their exhibition games in the Bay Area. In a March 14 game against the San Francisco Seals of the Pacific Coast League, Tris wowed the crowd with a home run, a triple, and two singles. Speaker was "full of ginger, and insisted upon backing up either right or left field whenever the chance presented itself," the wire services reported.

Ten straight days of rain put a damper on the exhibition tour, denying Taylor some hefty gate receipts. But on April 8, the day before the team was scheduled to depart California to head back east, the weather was good enough to allow the Sox and Saint Mary's College to play an extemporaneous exhibition. Brother Agnon, Harry Hooper's old mentor, commissioned a Saint Mary's student to ride through Berkeley and Oakland on a mule alerting folks via megaphone to the game on campus. A huge throng turned out, despite just a few minutes' notice. Saint Mary's pitcher Tiny Leonard threw beautifully, holding the Sox to a handful of hits in a 1–0 win for the college boys. The game ended on a sour note. Tris was on third with one out in the top of the ninth when he tried to score on a long fly out to foul ground in left field. A perfect peg nailed Speaker at the plate.

Speaker, for reasons not entirely clear, elected to blame Hooper for the loss, telling reporters that Harry had deliberately misplayed a ball hit to right field that plated his alma mater's only run. Paul Zingg writes that an agitated Hooper took immediate exception, telling the Oakland paper, "No, I did not let it go by. You know me and you know that I could not have done that." So in one exhibition in the Bay Area, Speaker made too big a show of backing up his outfield mates, which no doubt caused some teeth to grind. In the other, he blamed the best right fielder in baseball for losing a meaningless game. If Spoke was maturing, it wasn't on full display during Taylor's exhibition tour of California.

Maybe Spoke's barb in Oakland inspired Cat in 1911, because he raised his batting average forty-five points in 1911 to .311, while Speaker's dipped to .327 and Lewis batted .307 with eighty-six RBIs. Gardner, who switched to third base for the bulk of the season, hit a solid .285. Carrigan, meanwhile, batted .289 while fast developing a reputation around the league as a first-rate handler of pitchers.

Rough's tough-guy persona was further embellished that year when he supposedly licked Speaker in what must have been the clubhouse brawl to end all clubhouse brawls. The Speaker-Carrigan brouhaha may or may not have been sparked by "Papist vs. Prod" trash talk, although there's little doubt that religious tension contributed to the ill will between them. Rough and Spoke barely stayed on speaking terms for the next few years – yet it didn't seem to affect their on-field performance.

The Sox clubhouse's other leading Prod, Joe Wood, had another fine season in 1911, compiling an ERA of just 2.02, yet losing seventeen games against twenty-three wins. Bad luck seemed to plague Wood through his first three years in the big leagues. At Hot Springs in 1909, he injured his right foot while roughhousing with Speaker in their room at the Majestic. The following season, he was struck in the ankle by a Harry Hooper line drive during batting practice, an injury that sidelined him for six weeks and hampered him throughout the rest of the season.

On July 29, 1911, Wood pitched a gorgeous no-hitter against the St. Louis Browns, only the fifth ever recorded by a member of the Pilgrims or the Red Sox. Smoky Joe kayoed twelve Browns, walked only two, and allowed just three balls to leave the infield. Spoke's solo home run that day spurred his roommate to victory, 5–0.

How Wood, Speaker, Gardner, and the other Masons may have re-acted to the stormy Irish brogue of Patsy Donovan is not known. What is known is that the Sox Regulars – whether K.C. or Mason – viewed Patsy as Taylor's patsy. In all likelihood, there was much snickering and more than a few rolled eyeballs whenever Patsy threatened to get tough.

The dead-ball era took a turn toward offense in 1911. A slightly less dead dead-ball, made with a center composed of cork and rubber, replaced the truly dead dead-ball, which had been made with a soft rubber core. Hitting numbers went up appreciably, with Cobb batting a career-high .420 and a Cubbie named Frank "Wildfire" Schulte bashing an unheard-of twenty-one homers. Batting averages in the American League, in fact, rose a startling thirty points that year. The balls used for the remainder of the last decade of the dead-ball era supposedly lacked the hardness of the 1911 ball.

Toward the end of the 1911 season, owner Taylor began rumbling about wanting to move Speaker, by then hands-down the best center fielder in the American League, to first base. Ban Johnson had seen enough.

Taylor wasn't around as president of the club to sack Donovan at the end of the season. In September 1911 Johnson engineered a deal whereby Taylor gave up a 50 percent ownership stake in the club and all day-to-day responsibility in running the club.

Boston's new "owner" and president was none other than James Mc-

Aleer, the former St. Louis Browns executive who first spotted Tris Speaker's talent in the Texas League – then was short-sighted enough to reject him. McAleer was the consummate Ban Johnson company man. A native of eastern Ohio, Jimmy McAleer spent nine seasons laboring for Cleveland's National League franchise, the Spiders, as a good-glove, weak-stick outfielder. He was a nervous, beady-eyed sort. In 1901 he jumped aboard Johnson's new vessel, skippering Cleveland's American League franchise in its inaugural season. The next season, Johnson finagled a part-ownership stake in the St. Louis Browns for McAleer, where he stayed for eight mainly run-of-the-mill seasons as manager. In 1910 McAleer moved over to the even more hapless Washington Senators.

A year later Johnson decided to reward McAleer's years of dutiful service by setting him up as the Red Sox frontman. Virtually all the money in the deal came from Johnson. To ensure that McAleer carried out Johnson's wishes, the AL czar arranged for his personal secretary, a bean counter named Robert McRoy, to serve as McAleer's deputy.

By selling half of his stake back to Johnson, Taylor could finance his dream of becoming the Sox's landlord – and make a handsome profit to boot. In cahoots with his father, Taylor began scouting possible locations to build a new ballpark, finally settling on a parcel of marshy land in the Fens neighborhood of Boston. Taylor senior, the general, was a major investor in the Fenway Realty Company, which had acquired the area adjoining Frederick Law Olmsted's park and the Kenmore Square area. After the general bought the land and issued $275,000 worth of bonds to underwrite construction of the ballpark, Mayor Fitz and other city fathers saw fit to expand trolley lines out to the Fens. There was one slight holdup: members of a local Unitarian Church expressed trepidation about something as secular as a ballpark going up in the neighborhood. But once the Taylors provided the pastor with a lifetime pass, the Unitarians miraculously saw the light and dropped their objections.

As Glenn Stout and Richard Johnson put it, "John I. Taylor announced that he planned to call the new ballpark Fenway Park 'because it's in the Fenway, isn't it?' thereby insuring that no one would forget the name of his dad's real estate company, either. The cost of the ballpark

95

would be more than offset by the increase in land values in the surrounding area. There was backslapping all around."

The backslapping wouldn't stop for a while. Boston's American League franchise was poised to make history and gobs of money – some of which actually found its way to the three stars that manned its Golden Outfield.

CHAPTER 6

Championship Season

Connie Mack was not farwrong [*sic*] when he remarked that Boston was one of the greatest ball teams ever known to the game. This band of players has played its best game when forced by the leaders, and it can be counted on for brilliant work in the post-season. — T. H. Murnane, *The Sporting News*, September 12, 1912

A local architect named James McLaughlin was commissioned to design Boston's new ballpark in the Fens. The park's quirky asymmetry was born out of the curious order McLaughlin received from the Taylors: mimic the alignment of the Huntington Avenue Grounds, the architect was told.

So McLaughlin dutifully designed the third base line to point precisely north – just as it had in the old ball yard. In practical terms, that meant that barely three hundred feet from where McLaughlin was planning to put home plate, the third base line would run smack into Lansdowne Street. Since ballplayers in that era rarely hit the ball that far, it didn't seem necessary for McLaughlin and the Taylors to rejigger things. The architect did, however, incorporate a little flair into his design for left field by making its last ten feet slope sharply upward before meeting the fence.

Left fielder Lewis would soon become masterful at spearing balls that skittered up what reporters and cartoonists dubbed "Duffy's Cliff." A half century later Lewis shared the secret of playing his cliff with John Gillooly of the *Boston Record-American*. "At the crack of the bat you'd turn and run up it. Then you had to pick up the ball and decide whether to jump, go right or left, or rush down again. It took plenty of practice. They made a mountain goat out of me." A fence some twenty-five feet high was installed in left field to discourage fans from sneaking into the ballpark or watching the game from rooftops across the street. It wasn't until 1934, though, that Fenway's trademark, a monstrous left-field wall with a hand-operated scoreboard, was erected.

Taylor *père et fil* once again demonstrated that they knew how to make a buck: the seating capacity at the new park dwarfed the old one. Fenway's original design could accommodate some fifteen thousand fans in reserved seats, along with thirteen thousand unreserved and bleacher seats. Moreover, there was plenty of room in the outfield to put overflow crowds.

The two other members of Boston's Golden Outfield had their work cut out for them as well. Tris Speaker had acres to cover in center field: the distance from home plate to the flagpole that McLaughlin put in center field was a leg-wearying 550 feet! Harry Hooper, meanwhile, confronted a right field that was the mirror opposite of the Huntington Avenue Grounds. Although it was barely three hundred feet to the foul pole later named for Sox star Johnny Pesky's penchant for wraparound homers, the right-field wall curved radically away from home plate as it headed toward right center. The bullpens weren't moved into the right-field stands – thereby considerably reducing the distance to the fence – until 1940, and only then to exploit the prowess of a young left-handed slugger named Theodore Samuel Williams. Since Harry's eyes would gaze directly west while in the field, he also had to contend with a fierce late-afternoon sun. Harry soon became the first American League outfielder to wear flip-down sunglasses, a device pioneered by Pittsburgh's Fred Clarke. To tether his sunglasses, Harry punched two holes in the bill of his cap, then wormed a piece of string through them. Fenway's right field to this day remains one of the tougher sun fields in the big leagues.

McAleer, McRoy, and the Taylors knew their cash register would ring heavy with a new ballpark, but they weren't exactly keen to share much of it with their standout center fielder. Speaker seethed over the contract offer he received from management that winter. When the Sox gathered in Hot Springs that February for spring training, Speaker stayed home in Hubbard City, an unhappy holdout.

Tris's tough negotiating stance immediately put him at loggerheads with Ban Johnson and the new ownership syndicate. Speaker doubtless bore a grudge toward Jimmy McAleer, the man who had rebuffed him years before. Now that McAleer was signing his paycheck, Speaker may well have decided it was time to ply a little revenge. He hung out in Hubbard City through much of spring training before heading northeast to the Ozarks to sign a two-year deal at roughly nine thousand dollars per year.

McAleer and company succeeded that winter in persuading Garland "Jake" Stahl to leave his promising career as a banker in Chicago to manage the Sox and play first base. Although *The Baseball Encyclopedia* erroneously identifies the two as brothers, Stahl was in fact no relation to Chick Stahl, the former Sox skipper who had committed suicide under tragic circumstances five years before. In his two and a half seasons as a Sox first sacker and occasional outfielder, Jake had been a popular figure in the clubhouse. After the rocky tenure of Patsy Donovan, the club needed a calming influence; Stahl provided it.

Stahl knew that to overtake the Athletics, who had won the previous two AL pennants, the Sox would need a deep and strong pitching rotation. It was clear that Joe Wood, who had come into his own with twenty-three wins the year before, would anchor the staff. In Hot Springs, Stahl decided to give a job to rookie right-hander Hugh Bedient, a twenty-two-year-old fresh off his family's farm in Chautauqua County, New York. Sophomore right-hander Thomas Joseph "Buck" O'Brien also made the rotation. A spitballing immigrant kid from down the road in Brockton, O'Brien had shown promise in 1911 with a 5–1 record. Buck, a K.C., quickly became a thorny antagonist to Speaker and Wood. Charley "Sea Lion" Hall and Vermonter Ray Collins completed the staff. McAleer and Stahl were so confident of their mound depth that Eddie Cicotte, Cy Young's erstwhile pupil, was sold to Charles Comiskey's club in Chicago.

Californian Charley Hall was one of the dead-ball era's true characters. Born to parents of Mexican heritage and christened Carlos Clolo, he adopted an Anglo name in his late teens, well aware that few professional clubs would give a second look to a Latino. Charley was on his honeymoon in Ventura when he got word of Stahl's appointment as manager. He told the *Boston Post* that he hoped to help "Old Jake pull off that rag" – baseball slang for winning the pennant. Hall was one of big league baseball's first relief specialists, consistently coming through in

99

the clutch for the Sox that season out of the bullpen. Collins, too, flexed his muscles in 1912, winning fifteen games with a 2.53 ERA.

Stahl made one other decisive move in Hot Springs, shifting captain Heinie Wagner to shortstop and Steve Yerkes to second base. So Boston's everyday lineup in 1912 consisted of Wagner and Yerkes up the middle, Larry Gardner at third, Stahl at first, Rough Carrigan behind the plate (with Forrest "Hick" Cady, an Illinois farm boy, in reserve at catcher), and the three Golden Outfielders. Although McAleer and Stahl felt good about their prospects as the team headed north for its traditional preseason exhibition tour, no one could have predicted that Wood and Speaker were destined to have seasons for the ages – or that the Sox would go through the entire year with a new park as their talisman.

Unlike Boston and Detroit (which opened Navin Field that year), Connie Mack's men didn't have a new ballpark, but they felt confident about their chances of repeating as AL champs for a third consecutive year. Anchored by its brilliant infield, the A's also boasted the finest rotation in the game: Eddie Plank, Chief Bender, Jack Coombs, and Jersey native Carroll William "Boardwalk" Brown, who among them won seventy-three games that year. Mack's lineup also featured such steady stickmen as Baker and Collins in the infield and outfielders Rube Oldring and Amos Strunk, whose names seem to come from a dead-ball-era casting call. The Shibe Parkers ended up winning 90 games – a handsome total in a 152-game season – but didn't come close to the Sox machine, which set a league record with 105 wins against only 47 losses.

Joe Wood set the tone for the season by beating the New York Highlanders, 5–3, on opening day at Hilltop Park in the Washington Heights section of Manhattan. The Sox went on to win three of their next four games, all on the road. Although the formal unveiling of Fenway Park wasn't slated to take place for another week, the Sox played an exhibition game there against the Harvard University nine on April 9, winning 2–0 before a shivering crowd that withstood snowflakes all afternoon.

Even damper weather and an unreliable vendor disrupted the grand opening of Fenway, which had been scheduled for April 17. A couple of drizzly days turned the park's virginal infield into mud when a promised tarpaulin failed to arrive. The delay gave New Englanders plenty of time to kibitz about the sinking of the ss *Titanic* a couple of days before. Workers continued to pound away, as much of the new park remained incomplete that spring. The bleacher boards along both outfield foul lines wouldn't be finished for another few weeks.

Some twenty-four thousand folks crowded into Fenway on April 20 to witness history. Mayor Fitz threw out the first ball as the Sox renewed their rivalry with the Highlanders. To commemorate the occasion, the Red Sox arranged for a special panoramic photograph to be taken of both squads. The photographer positioned the Red Sox on his left, the Highlanders on his right. Given the photographic technology of the day, it took the rotary camera a couple of minutes to finish its left-to-right sweep. After the camera had moved past them, Speaker and Wood must have raced around the photographer's rear and jumped into line with the Highlanders. The final product shows Wood in the midst of the Highlanders, sporting a broad grin, with his arms folded. Speaker characteristically took the moment to the hilt. His arms are propped up on the shoulders of two Highlanders, his legs too-nonchalantly crossed, as if waiting for a bus. His impish grin suggests a schoolboy who knows he's getting away with something. Maybe their teammates were amused by Speaker and Wood's antics. But making light of a seminal moment in the history of the franchise may not have gone over too well with certain people in the organization.

Brockton's own prodigy, Buck O'Brien, started for the Sox but had trouble controlling his spitball, and gave way to relief specialist Sea Lion Hall after the Sox fell behind by four runs. The Red Sox capped a thrilling come-from-behind victory in the eleventh inning when Speaker, the line jumper, punched a single through the left side of the Highlander infield, plating Steve Yerkes to break a 6–6 tie.

Boston got off to a solid but not spectacular start that April and May, managing to avoid the early-season injuries that plagued them in previous seasons. They didn't seize first place until mid-June – but once firmly in hand, never gave it up. In deference to the Sox's quickness afield and on the base paths, the press corps revived an old franchise nickname that had long been a favorite of John Taylor's. For the next few seasons, the moniker "Speed Boys" would appear in innumerable headlines.

The Speed Boys attracted huge crowds to the new ball yard. A letter writer to *Baseball Magazine* noted in June that year that gamblers weren't subtle about plying their trade in Fenway's crowded stands. "To have gambling in the open, in the fifty-cent bleachers, within easy earshot of the grandstand and lady patrons, is a disgrace to Boston and the American League," he wrote. The correspondent's letter was featured in a commentary presciently titled "Gambling: Baseball's Greatest Danger."

Surprisingly, the Speed Boys' main competition in 1912 came not from Philadelphia but from Washington, a franchise so inept that the *San Francisco Chronicle*'s Charley Dryden had forever lampooned it as "First in war, first in peace – and last in the American League." Washington was led by its right-handed ace, the indomitable Walter Johnson, who was in his sixth year of pitching in the big leagues.

The highlight of the 1912 regular season for player and fan alike was the much-ballyhooed duel between Johnson and Smoky Joe Wood, both of whom were virtually untouchable that season. Johnson was a broad-shouldered Kansas farm boy with pronounced cheekbones and light coloring. Sportswriters glanced at his hulking Scandinavian features and the "son" at the end of his surname and tagged him "the Big Swede." As Shirley Povich, the longtime columnist of the *Washington Post*, loved to point out, however, there wasn't a drop of Swedish blood in Johnson's ancestry. But Walter was such a self-effacing soul that he couldn't bring himself to correct the misnomer. When Povich asked him why, Johnson replied, "There are a lot of Swedes I know who are nice people."

The Perrys, his mother's family, were of English descent. Johnson's maternal grandfather, who lived in the household through much of Walter's boyhood, rode with the heavily decorated Fourth Pennsylvania Cavalry during the Civil War. The family ran a farm near Humboldt, a village on the Neosho River in southeastern Kansas.

Born in 1887, a year before Speaker, Johnson was introduced to the mechanics of throwing a ball by playing the schoolyard game "one o' cat." In 1902 Johnson's uncle found work in the oil fields of Southern California and wrote home to Kansas urging relatives to join him.

Walter's father obliged, uprooting three generations of Johnsons and Perrys and moving them west to Olinda, a small company town of the Santa Fe oil and railroad conglomerate some twenty miles southeast of Los Angeles. There the rawboned teenager played for town and company teams, fast developing a reputation on Southern California's sand-lots as a speedballer. Future New York Giants center fielder Fred Snodgrass, a native of Ventura, went up against Johnson several times in semipro ball. "If people think Walter was fast later on, they should have seen him then. Whew! Most of the time you couldn't even see the ball!" Snodgrass recalled years later.

Young Walter was initially signed by Tacoma in the modest Northwestern League – then joined Weiser in the even humbler Southern Idaho League, an association with franchises in such Bitterroot Mountain metropolises as Nampy and Caldwell. Postmarked "Weiser," a letter praising Johnson's potential arrived unsolicited at National Park in Washington DC one day in 1906. "He knows where he's throwing because if he didn't," the correspondent drolly observed, "there would be dead bodies strewn all over Idaho."

Johnson's delivery was deceptively simple. Grantland Rice, who dubbed Johnson "the Big Train," would later call it "the finest motion in the game," lauding its deadly efficiency. "How do they know what Johnson's got?" Rice rhetorically asked readers upon witnessing Walter's fastball early in the Kansan's career. "Nobody's seen it yet!" Joe Wood marveled at the length of Johnson's arms: "Tremendous spread. About a foot past mine on either side."

As described by Henry W. Thomas, Johnson's grandson and the author of *Walter Johnson: Baseball's Big Train*, Johnson "had a short 'windmill' windup in which he rotated his arm in a circle while standing straight up on the mound, then swept the arm behind his back as far as it would go before whipping it forward in a smooth sidearm-underarm arc."

Johnson was never tormented by the demons that afflicted so many of his dead-ball contemporaries – Cobb, Speaker, and fellow hurler Grover Cleveland Alexander among them. The boy may have left Humboldt but Humboldt never left the boy: Johnson went through life pretty much unaffected by celebrity. He had the same aw-shucks demeanor the day he retired as he had on the Humboldt schoolyard. Even running for Congress in Maryland (albeit unsuccessfully: he was a Republican candidate in 1940, a big Democratic year) at age fifty-three didn't swell his head. The Big Train was probably the only real "friend" that the prickly Georgia Peach had in baseball. Through most of the first decade of their mano a mano confrontations, Johnson consistently got the better of Cobb. But after Walter accidentally beaned Ossie Vitt in 1915, Johnson began easing up on inside pitches – and Cobb began hitting him harder. So did the rest of the league.

The 1912 campaign was the third of seven successive seasons in which Johnson won twenty-five or more games – a record of enduring brilliance unmatched in big league history.

In July and August 1912 the two fireballers were scorching hot. Johnson had won sixteen consecutive games, breaking Jack Chesbro's record of fourteen straight, set eight years earlier for the Highlanders. By the time September approached, Wood's winning streak was thirteen and counting. With the Senators scheduled to come to Boston in early September, Washington manager Clark Griffith decided it was time to throw down the gauntlet. Probably egged on by his old cohort, Sox president McAleer, Griffith issued this public ultimatum to Wood: "We will consider him a coward if he doesn't pitch against Johnson. The race isn't over yet. Just wait until my team gets through wiping up the floor with the Red Sox and then you'll see we have a chance."

In truth, the Sox had the pennant all but wrapped up and Griffith knew it. But McAleer and McRoy, sniffing big ticket sales, played along, moving Wood's start in the rotation up one day so that the two stars could meet head to head.

It was among the most anticipated – and hyped – regular season baseball games in history. "The newspapers publicized us like prizefighters: giving statistics comparing our height, weight, biceps, triceps, arm span, and whatnot. 'The Champion, Walter Johnson, versus the Challenger,' Joe Wood," Wood remembered years later. "Standing room only" doesn't begin to describe the size of the crowd that showed up at Fenway on September 6. Tens of thousands of people were crammed into the outfield, including hundreds of patrons perched on Duffy's Cliff. For the first and only time in the history of the park, fans were allowed to stand along the first and third baselines during the course of a game. A classic photograph from that afternoon shows Smoky Joe warming up – or at least trying to – while practically engulfed by scores of men decked out in suits and straw boaters.

The forty thousand or so fans – McRoy bragged that it was the largest crowd in Boston baseball history to that point and he was no doubt correct – were treated to a terrific spectacle. Both pitchers were in brilliant form – as were the Royal Rooters. McGreevey, Dixwell, and company led the crowd in a series of ear-piercing screeches.

Neither team was able to get much going against the two maestros. "Wood was a bit nervous at the start," wrote Tim Murnane. "[Clyde] Milan led off with a hit. [Kid] Foster tried to sacrifice, but hit to Wood, and the ball was shot to second where Wagner turned in a double play and the boys were off." In the top of the third, Wood struck out Danny Moeller with the bases jammed to end a Nats threat.

With two outs in the bottom of the sixth, the Sox finally broke through when Speaker slashed a Johnson fastball down the left-field line and into the crowd that swarmed in front of Duffy's Cliff. Spoke was awarded a ground-rule double, then scored a moment later when Lewis's opposite-field flare eluded the dive of Senators right fielder Moeller.

The one run was all Smoky Joe needed; although runners got on base in the eighth and ninth, he shut the Senators down. Wood ended up striking out nine and giving up six hits; Johnson fanned five and allowed only five hits and the one run, but got stuck with the "L."

"The battle between these premier slabmen was staged in grand form and the two great pitchers gave the crowd a chance for a hundred thrills," Murnane told the readers of the *Sporting News* a week later. Clark Griffith was so pleased with his take of the gate receipts that he gave Johnson a five-hundred-dollar spot bonus. Smoky Joe went on to win his next two starts to tie Johnson's winning streak at sixteen before losing a game in late September to Hughie Jennings's Tigers, who had fallen on hard times.

Between them that season, Johnson and Wood won sixty-six games (just seven fewer combined wins than the A's *four-man* staff), struck out 561 batters, and hurled seventeen shutouts – all while ringing up earned run averages that require a magnifying glass to examine. In the modern era, no two pitchers have ever combined for such formidable numbers in the same year. Their respective sixteen-game winning streaks that season is still – nine decades later – the American League record for consecutive pitching victories.

Despite the superior play of center fielder Clyde Milan, who was consistently among the league leaders in stolen bases and assists, the Senators were not able to keep up the pace of the Sox and the A's in the years to come. Milan, a speedy center fielder whose defensive acumen was often compared to Spoke's, hailed from Tennessee. So four of the AL's star outfielders during the 1910s – Speaker, Cobb, Jackson, and Milan – were sons of the South.

It would take Johnson another decade to appear on the World Series stage – and by then he was almost too old to enjoy it.

Nineteen twelve was the year of big numbers: Almost all the Speed Boys had career seasons. Third baseman Larry Gardner hit .315 and became one of the better hotbox glovemen in the league. Left fielder Lewis drove in 109 runs. Rough Carrigan hit a clutch .263 and burnished his reputation as a great defensive catcher.

Buoyed by a strong offense, the Sox staff also exceeded expectations. Wood had as good a year as anyone in Major League history. Buck O'Brien had an erratic postseason but won twenty games. Hugh Bedient also won twenty games and matched that brilliance in the Series.

Alone among the starters, Harry Hooper had an off year. He batted a career low .242, a surprising average for a man later enshrined in the Hall of Fame. Although he became a solid hitter, it was never Harry's bat that distinguished him. His calling cards were his glove, arm, and feet – and there was no letdown in his fielding and base running in 1912.

Speaker's year was nothing short of sensational. Missing a big chunk of spring training didn't faze him. Spoke started off the year hot and stayed hot, threatening .400 much of the season before finishing at .383, collecting fifty-six more hits in 1912 than he had the previous season. Three times during the course of the year he had hitting streaks of twenty games or more – a feat not even the great DiMaggio could ever duplicate. Research recently conducted by dead-ball-era specialist Dan Holmes at the Hall of Fame suggests that Speaker came within an "eyelash or two," in Holmes's words, of a seventy-plus-game hitting streak that season. From May 27 through August 14 he played in seventy-eight games and got a hit in all but four of them. Speaker led the league in doubles with fifty-three and homers with ten – the only time in the pre-1920 era that he achieved double digits in round-trippers.

As impressive as his offensive numbers were, however, it was his defensive performance that earned Speaker that Chalmers "30" convertible as most valuable player. He established a record for outfield assists that season – thirty-five – that has never been equaled. Spoke also led the league by engineering nine catch-and-throw double plays that season. The mojo was so positive in Fenway that summer that, between innings, Speaker often led the crowd in group cheers, swinging his arms to keep the fans in rhythm.

The year 1912 also marked one of the most peculiar and disquieting episodes in the annals of the dead-ball era – no mean feat. On May 15 Ban Johnson suspended Detroit's Ty Cobb for leaping into the stands at Hilltop Park to assault a disabled Highlanders fan who'd accused Ty of being "half nigger." After exchanging insults with the fan for three innings, Cobb jumped off the Tigers bench and over the railing to pummel the man, who had lost one hand and three fingers of the other in an industrial accident the year before. Horrified fans sitting nearby tried to restrain Cobb by pointing out that the man had no hands to defend himself. "I don't care if he doesn't have any feet!" Ty supposedly snarled in the middle of the fracas. To protest Johnson's punishment, Cobb's teammates voted to boycott their May 18 game in Shibe Park against the Philadelphia Athletics.

Tigers skipper Hughie Jennings had no choice that afternoon but to field a ragtag team that included a local Catholic seminarian at pitcher, several other area amateurs, and a forty-eight-year-old coach, Deacon McGuire, behind the plate. The future priest, Aloysius Joseph Travers, hurled a complete game, giving up twenty-six hits in what was simultaneously his Major League debut and finale, a 24–2 drubbing. Jennings, who hadn't played regularly for a decade, even inserted himself into the lineup late in the game. Despite the presumed prayers of soon-to-be-Father Travers, Old "Eee-yah" went hitless in his only at bat.

The Sox officially clinched the pennant in mid-September, giving Stahl plenty of time to get his pitching rotation set for the postseason clash with the New York Giants. Their final margin of victory over the Senators was a hefty fourteen games. When the triumphant Speed Boys got off the train after nailing down the flag, there were tens of thousands of New Englanders at South Station to greet them. McGraw's minions also sewed up their race early, winning 103 games and coasting to the pennant ahead of the Pirates and the Cubs.

It was the Giants' second appearance in a row in the World Series. In the 1911 fall classic, the Giants had lost to Connie Mack's Athletics, four games to two. The A's third baseman hid clutch round-trippers in both the second and third games, earning him the sobriquet that stayed with him literally the rest of his life. No player in the game's history ever had a nickname as thoroughly embedded in his identity as Frank "Home Run" Baker. The Giants' ace, Christy Mathewson, pitched twenty-seven full innings in the '11 Series (impressive even by the sadomasochistic standards of the dead-ball era), holding the A's to a handful of earned runs, but was tagged with two losses when his mates couldn't get anything going against the A's pitching staff. "You have one of the greatest teams I've ever seen," McGraw told Mack as he shook his hand to congratulate him after the 1911 Series ended. "It must be. I have a great team, too, but you beat us."

From its earliest days in muddy cow pastures and scruffy city lots, organized baseball had benefited from the counsel of a succession of *shanachies* – wise men dedicated to the growth and betterment of the game. The heirs of Alexander Cartwright, the Johnny Appleseed of baseball who went from city to village in the nineteenth century teaching the rudiments of the game, included men such as "Father" Henry Chadwick, Alfred H. Spink and his son, J. G. Taylor Spink, and Fred Lieb. These historian-scribes devoted much of their lives to popularizing and chronicling the game. Sometimes they didn't get their facts straight – and sometimes they out-and-out fibbed – but their passion helped make baseball our national pastime.

No one among baseball's gray eminences, however, commanded more respect, cast a wider net, or left a larger legacy than New England's Tim Murnane. In a 1928 essay for the *Saturday Evening Post*, Hugh Fullerton, himself a baseball seer, identified Murnane as one of the game's most seminal influences. Even Murnane's nickname, "the Silver King," conveyed the high regard in which he was held by virtually everyone – owners, players, coaches, umpires, and fans.

By the second decade of the twentieth century, Murnane had a Rushmore-esque mane of gray hair, matched by a bushy moustache and thick silver eyebrows that partly concealed a pair of all-knowing eyes. By then he was approaching his sixties. Born in Naugatuck, Connecticut, nine years before Fort Sumter, Timothy Hayes Murnane had an even deeper appreciation for professional baseball's primitive roots than his friend Denton True Young, which is saying something. Murnane went *way back* to the earliest days of the National Association, so far back that at age twenty he played for the meteor that was the Middletown Mansfields. Alas, his home state club, a charter member of the National Association, folded in the middle of its inaugural season. Later in the 1870s he joined two different franchises in Philadelphia before returning to New England to toil for Boston's National Association franchise, as well as National League teams in the Hub and Providence. In 1884 Murnane managed Boston's franchise in the short-lived Union Association. The young Murnane is among those credited with "inventing" the bunt. Back when flat bats were legal, Murnane and his National Association cronies referred to the practice of deliberately deflecting a ball into the infield dirt as "butting."

The Silver King had seen and done it all – and he was determined to capture much of it in writing. Adopting the byline "T. H. Murnane," he wrote several rulebooks, counseled umpires and managers in the nuances of the game, served as de facto historian of the National Association, and became for three decades the baseball editor of the *Boston Globe* and a frequent contributor to the *Sporting News*. Somehow he also found time to serve as president of the New England League for twenty-four years. His articles were widely reprinted; his influence extended far beyond the readership of the *Globe* and *Sporting News*. He became something of a *consigliere* to all manner of executives, arbiters, and reporters.

In Bob Ryan's *When Boston Won the World Series*, the story of the Pilgrims' triumph over the Pirates in the 1903 World Series, Murnane is a pivotal figure, sizing up the relative strengths of the two teams and providing incisive commentary throughout. "Both teams are in the pink of condition, and a battle royale may be looked for," Murnane advised readers in typically brisk argot before the '03 Series began.

Murnane was so respected that when he died at age sixty-five in 1917, luminaries across the country organized a late September exhibition game and skills contest at Fenway to benefit his widow and children.

The Red Sox played an exhibition against an American League all-star team that included Speaker (alas, for Sox fans, by then an Indian), Cobb, and Joe Jackson – all at the peak of their skills. Will Rogers, with Spoke's mischievous help, put on a little rodeo show. Ziegfeld Follies songstress Fanny Brice chipped in by selling programs. Former heavyweight champion John L. Sullivan "coached" third for the Sox. Harry Hooper, Ty Cobb, and Rabbit Maranville of the National League Braves all tied a "world record time" of 3.15 seconds in going from home to first. Ray Chapman of the Indians circled the bases in fourteen seconds flat, besting Hooper by a tenth of a second. Babe Ruth pitched the first six innings and won the long-hitting contest. Shoeless Joe, meanwhile, won the long-throwing contest with a heave of 396 feet! The benefit raised some fourteen thousand dollars for Murnane's survivors.

The Silver King worshiped the game, but he was no naïf. He knew all too well that the outcome of certain games was preordained. No doubt he had been on the business end of an illicit wager or two as a player and manager. He also spent enough time in taverns to know that hard-core gamblers and bookies did more than just buy ballplayers and their bosses an occasional beer.

Murnane's practiced eye spotted the amount of cash changing hands in saloons and the conspicuous presence of high rollers hanging out in hotel foyers and surmised that there would be problems with the '12 Series before it even started. "There's more money that's been wagered on this Series than ever before," Murnane acknowledged before play began. Estimates on how much money had been wagered on the Series ran upwards of a million dollars. Some of the more outrageous bets found their way into the New York and Boston papers. Although most New York money stayed loyal to the Giants, McGraw chum George M. Cohan, the vaudeville tunesmith, told Jimmy McAleer that he had fifty thousand dollars to doodle on the Speed Boys. In today's world, Cohan's stash would equal at least a couple million dollars. Given his closeness to McGraw, Cohan's exorbitant wager must have raised some eyebrows.

The first game of the best-of-seven series was to be played at the Polo Grounds in Harlem. Honey Fitz and the Rooters traveled to New York in style, arriving in a well-appointed coach on a special train. Once they emerged from Grand Central Station, the Rooters, several hundred strong, proceeded to parade north through Manhattan, eliciting boos, catcalls, and random cheers as they sang the praises of the Red Sox.

New Yorkers, too, got caught up in the spirit of the occasion, countering with torchlight parades of their own and erecting a state-of-the-art electronic diamond scoreboard in Times Square. Some New Yorkers turned nasty. Joe Wood, the Sox's game one starter, received no fewer than six death threats via the mail, all of them allegedly postmarked "New York." One of them, scrawled in blood red ink, warned: "You'll never live to pitch against the Giants."

Despite the threats, Joe and his mates arrived unscathed at the Polo Grounds on the afternoon of October 8. There, McGraw stunned Giants partisans – not to mention the ink-stained wretches in the press box – by warming up rookie right-hander Jeff Tesreau instead of Matty. To some observers, it was almost as if Muggsy were conceding game one to Wood and the Sox. McGraw's reasoning, however, was sound: He wanted to save Matty for the following day at Fenway, where a hostile crowd figured to make things rough for the Giants' starter. Muggsy's gamble almost paid off big time when Tesreau, a beefy Missourian who had won sixteen games during the regular season, out-pitched Smoky Joe for most of the afternoon. Wood gave up two early runs while the Speed Boys struggled against Tesreau. In the sixth inning, though, Speaker finally got a pitch he could handle and deposited it over Fred Snodgrass's head in the Polo Grounds' gaping center field. Speaker's triple led to one run. In the next inning, second baseman Larry Doyle's boot of an easy double play grounder led to a big three-run inning for the Sox, keyed by Harry Hooper's double down the first base line and Steve Yerkes's clutch single.

The gritty Giants rallied in the ninth, scoring a run against Wood when, with one out, Fred Merkle, Buck Herzog, and Chief Meyers poked consecutive singles. Right fielder Harry Hooper prevented another run from scoring by scooping up Meyers's hit on one hop and firing a Hooperian strike to Hick Cady at the plate. McGraw, coaching third, had to hustle Herzog back to the bag after Buck had rounded third at full force. Wood then proved his mettle by rearing back and striking out Art Fletcher and Doc Crandall to preserve a 4–3 win. A few minutes later in the Sox dressing room, Wood supposedly uttered his memorable line: "I threw so hard I thought my arm would fly right off my body."

One interested spectator in the Polo Grounds' press box that afternoon was Smoky Joe's great rival, Walter Johnson, who was being paid by the *Boston Herald* and *Washington Times* to share his observations on the Series. Johnson opined before game one that the Giants would be hard pressed to get anything going against Wood – hardly an earth-shattering prophecy. Nevertheless, the next day's headlines shrieked: "Johnson Predicted that Wood Would Win the Game!"

A series of cabs whisked both teams from Coogan's Bluff to Grand Central for the ride to Boston. Although the day dawned gray and dreary, the Rooters and their ilk were out in full force. Thousands of fans milled around the Fens, hoping to sneak or scalp their way into the park. All the folks crammed into standing-room-only sections in the outfield, coupled with the three rows of temporary box seats that McAleer horseshoed around the infield and sold for five bucks a pop, gave Fenway a claustrophobic feel. Fitz, McGreevey, and Dixwell led the usual Rooter pregame parade around the park, waving pennants and leading choruses of "Tessie," "Sweet Adeline," and even "The Star-Spangled Banner" as the crowd impatiently waited for game two to begin. When it did, the quality of play was surprisingly patchy. The game seesawed back and forth as neither pitcher proved effective.

Mathewson made a couple of out-of-character mental and physical mistakes, allowing the Sox to score three early runs with only one hit leaving the infield. Duffy Lewis botched an easy fly ball in the eighth that led to two runs for the Giants. Stahl replaced Sox starter Ray Collins in the eighth with Sea Lion Hall, who was promptly touched up by Buck Herzog's double that put the Giants back ahead. McGraw hung tough with Matty even when the game stretched into extra innings. In the bottom of the ninth, with the Giants nursing a one-run lead and one out from victory, shortstop Art Fletcher let Matty down by allowing Larry Gardner's grounder to dribble past him into left field, scoring Duffy Lewis to tie the game at five.

The not-so-boneheaded Merkle tripled in the top of the tenth, eventually scoring on a sacrifice fly to give the Giants a 6–5 advantage. Darkness was rapidly descending when, with one out, Tris Speaker strode to the plate, the Fenway crowd chanting his name. For the second time in two days, Speaker delivered in the clutch, pounding a line drive over Snodgrass's head and flying around the bases at breakneck speed for his inexorable collision with Buck Herzog.

Irritated at Art Fletcher's miscue the previous inning, McGraw had put backup Arthur Joseph "Tillie" Shafer in at short. Ironically, the utility infielder let Muggsy down, too, dropping Snodgrass's relay as Speaker was racing around third, hellbent on an inside-the-park homer. Knowing that umpire Silk O'Laughlin and his partners had their eyes focused elsewhere, third baseman Herzog reprised Muggsy's infamous maneuver from years gone by, subtly tossing his hip into Speaker as Spoke sprinted past.

Despite being tripped up, Speaker kept his wits about him, instantly changing directions once he and third base coach Stahl realized that Shafer had muffed the relay. Ty Cobb never came into home plate with his spikes flashing any higher or heavier than Speaker did an instant later, crashing into catcher Art Wilson with such force that the Giant fumbled the throw from Shafer. The game was once again tied as the hometown crowd roared its appreciation of Speaker's hustle. Most fans probably stayed on their feet to watch the fireworks that followed. Spoke retagged home plate, then stormed back up the third base line to even the score with Herzog. Accounts vary as to the rock 'em, sock 'em nature of the scuffle that ensued. Some reports have Speaker and Herzog exchanging blows; others claim they just squared off and yapped toe-to-toe, with a couple of shoves thrown in for good measure. Either way, with precious daylight fading by the minute, both benches emptied, and it took Silk O'Laughlin quite a while to get the combatants settled down. The Sox finished the inning without plating another runner, so the game headed into the eleventh as darkness began to envelop the field.

Sox manager Stahl called on rookie Hugh Bedient to take the mound. The western New York kid, all of twenty-two, came out skittish, hitting lead-off batter Fred Snodgrass and then walking journeyman outfielder Beals Becker. But Muggsy was too anxious to end the game: Sox catcher Rough Carrigan rubbed out both runners attempting to steal. When Matty got the Sox out in the bottom half of the inning, O'Laughlin, a veteran who tolerated little backchat, huddled with the two managers and declared the game a tie – to be replayed in its entirety. (The longtime arbiter may have been irascible, but he was something of a wag. When questioned once about a call, Silk allegedly snapped, "[The Pope] is for religion. O'Loughlin's for baseball. Both are infallible.") Christy Mathewson always called the tied contest "the hardest ballgame I ever went through."

There was no Marvin Miller around to represent the players the next day when the National Commission, baseball's "governing" body, convened in a Boston hotel to figure out what to do with the proceeds from the game. According to the rules the owners and players had jointly adopted, the players were supposed to get a share of the gate from each of the first four games of the Series. But the rules didn't account for a "tie" – or the extra game necessitated by such.

Much to the players' chagrin, the chairman of the commission gave every penny of the gate receipts to the owners. For a decade, ever since the World Series began, players had complained – sometimes bitterly – that they weren't getting their fair share. Now the grousing in the two clubhouses must have reached a fever pitch. Both teams had played their guts out and had nothing to show for it. One can only imagine the barbed conversations that went on as the players contemplated the thousands of dollars that had been denied them and shamelessly pocketed by the owners. The seeds of whatever disquieting actions may have happened later in the Series were no doubt planted at that instant.

The suddenly bad karma surrounding the Series got worse later that afternoon during the third game. Instead of heading back to New York, the tied game forced the two teams to stay at Fenway. As if to match the players' moods, dank skies once again hung over the Fens.

Bucky O'Brien hooked up against the flamboyant Giants pitcher Rube Marquard, star of stage and slab. Both hurlers distinguished themselves, giving up only a few harmless hits. The part-time vaudevillian took a 2–1 lead over the full-time spitballer into the bottom of the ninth inning. With two outs and two runners on base, Boston's reserve catcher, Hick Cady, scorched a line drive into right field. Giants right fielder Josh Devore raced back and speared the ball before sprawling onto the turf. But hundreds of Red Sox fans couldn't see through the gloom and assumed the ball had gotten over Devore's head and that the Sox had plated the

1. The Cleburne Railroader, age 18. The first known portrait of Tris Speaker in a baseball uniform. He proudly posed during the summer of 1906 while playing for his first professional team, pennant-winning Cleburne in the North Texas League. His "signing bonus" consisted of one dollar to offset the cost of a train ride from Hubbard to Waco. He pocketed the cash and hopped a freight instead, angering his manager by arriving late for his first game. Courtesy of National Baseball Hall of Fame Library, Cooperstown NY.

2. Beantown prodigy. It took Speaker two tries to stick with the Boston club,
but he won the center-field job for good in 1909. The Tigers' Donie Bush said
Speaker's arm was so strong and accurate he could throw a strike across the plate
from any spot in the outfield. Speaker still holds a passel of career and single-
season defensive records, including the most *unassisted* double plays from the
outfield. Courtesy of National Baseball Hall of Fame Library, Cooperstown NY.

3. After leading the league in putouts and assists in 1909, Speaker garnered considerable attention from the press corps during a postseason exhibition series between the Red Sox and the Giants. He would go on to find his hitting groove in 1910, hitting .340 with forty-one extra-base hits and seventy-seven RBIs. Courtesy of Transcendental Graphics.

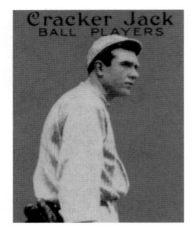

4. Cracker Jack kid: Speaker's vintage Cracker Jack baseball card, as one of the "Boston Americans," circa 1910 – well before his hair turned gray. Courtesy of Transcendental Graphics.

5. Never a proper Bostonian: The young Speaker's piercing dark eyes missed nothing on or off the field. Note the flat nose, which suggests that it had been on the business end of more than one punch. His scowl here is classic early Speaker: he didn't suffer fools gladly. Courtesy of Transcendental Graphics.

6. Roommates and compadres for life. Smoky
Joe Wood (*upper right*) and Tris Speaker (*center*) pose with neighborhood kids on the steps
of their boardinghouse outside Boston. Wood
and Speaker played together for fourteen years.
Their cowboy swagger caused certain teammates to bristle. Courtesy of Cleveland State
University Library.

BOSTON AMERICAN Baseball Team 1912

7. The 1912 Red Sox (Speaker is at middle left) began the season with a new stadium, the charmingly asymmetrical Fenway Park. They went on to defeat a New York Giants squad managed by the legendary John McGraw in the World Series. In the deciding eighth game, Speaker drove in the tying run off future Hall of Famer Christy Mathewson. Courtesy of Transcendental Graphics.

8. Boston's "Golden Outfield" plays pepper:
(*left to right*) Duffy Lewis, Harry Hooper, and Tris
Speaker taking part in a spring training drill.
Grantland Rice said they were so fast, "they could
move into another county, if the ball happened to
fall there." All three had exceptional arms. Lewis
and Speaker, bitter clubhouse rivals, put aside their
personal differences on the field. Ty Cobb and
Babe Ruth agreed that the Lewis-Speaker-Hooper
combination was the best outfield they'd ever seen.
Courtesy of Transcendental Graphics.

9. Conquerors of the Phillies. Babe Ruth always called the 1915 Red Sox the finest defensive team he'd ever seen and ranked Speaker his all-time center fielder. Ruth, in his first full year in the big leagues, is in the top row, second from right. Speaker sits in the front row, second from left. Spoke and the Babe had, at best, a prickly relationship. Player-manager Bill "Rough" Carrigan, another Speaker rival, sits in the middle row, third from right. Courtesy of Cleveland State University Library.

10. Hazardous duty. In the fall of 1918, Speaker volunteered for an elite naval aviation unit that trained at MIT. Spoke and fellow trainees used the Charles River for seaplane landings and take-offs. World War I ended before his unit was called up, but Lieutenant Speaker earned his pilot's wings. He continued to astound teammates and fans by piloting biplanes well into the 1920s. Courtesy of Cleveland State University Library.

11. Tragedy and triumph: the 1920 Cleveland Indians. Speaker's brilliant performance that season following teammate Ray Chapman's tragic death has to be considered among the most inspired in baseball history. Speaker is in the back row, standing third from right. Courtesy of Cleveland State University Library.

12. Chief of the Tribe. Arguably the best and most resourceful manager of his generation, Speaker led the Indians to the 1920 World
Series championship and came within three games of the mighty
Yankees in 1926. After the Cobb-Leonard scandal surfaced, Tris
was blackballed from ever running a big league team again. Courtesy of National Baseball Hall of Fame Library, Cooperstown NY.

13. Seer and student at rest: Speaker's affection for Cy Young (*left*) was genuine. Young saw Speaker's defensive potential early on and worked tirelessly with him to sharpen his skills. Joe Wood remembered Young at the end of his tenure with the Red Sox, sipping alcohol in the little pub on the ground floor of the Putnam Inn. Courtesy of Transcendental Graphics.

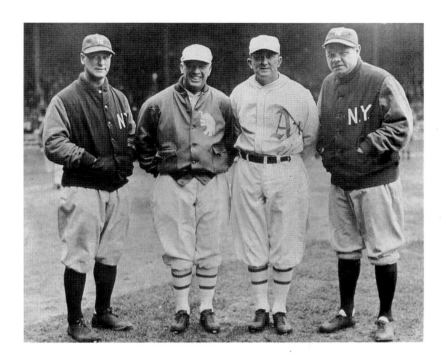

14. Top left: Thundering into third. Speaker flashes his spikes at Giants third baseman Heinie Groh during an exhibition game in the early 1920s. Later in life Speaker
enjoyed pointing out that he had stolen more bases in one year than Joe DiMaggio
had in his entire career. Courtesy of National Baseball Hall of Fame Library,
Cooperstown NY.

15. Bottom left: Teammates and co-conspirators: Ty Cobb (*left*) and Tris Speaker.
Speaker modeled his inside-out swing and aggressive base running after the nonpareil Cobb, who was already an established star by the time Speaker made the big
leagues. Cobb could "beat your brains out," Speaker said later in life. After Dutch
Leonard leveled his cheating allegations against the two stars, they were forced to
leave their respective clubs. They ended up in Philadelphia together playing a final
frustrating year for Connie Mack's A's. Courtesy of Transcendental Graphics.

16. Above: Cooperstown quartet: (*left to right*) Lou Gehrig, Tris Speaker, Ty Cobb,
and Babe Ruth, posing before a Yankees-A's game in 1928. Teammates on the old
Red Sox, Speaker and Ruth were able to overcome at least part of their enmity later
in life. Speaker admired Gehrig's skills but still named George Sisler his all-time
first baseman. Speaker had many friends in baseball; Cobb practically none. Courtesy of Transcendental Graphics.

17. Two legends celebrate their merger. After being banished
from Cleveland and Washington, Speaker spent an unhappy
year at the end of his career playing for Connie Mack – and
with Ty Cobb – in Philadelphia. Here Speaker, fresh from the
links, greets Mack at spring training. Ty and Tris's big salaries caused resentment within the A's clubhouse. Courtesy of
National Baseball Hall of Fame Library, Cooperstown NY.

18. Hardscrabble Texas boys make good. Ben Hogan *(left)* and Tris Speaker during 1951 induction ceremonies for the brand-new Texas Sports Hall of Fame. Speaker was the Texas Hall's first inductee; Hogan soon followed. A generation apart, Tris and Ben shared much in common: Both lost fathers early in life and both were consumed by ambition. Neither cared about winning popularity contests. Courtesy of Cleveland State University Library.

19. The Gray Eagle meets the Say Hey Kid. The day
after Willie Mays made his spectacular catch against
Vic Wertz in the 1954 World Series, photographers
arranged for the two standout center fielders to be
pictured together at the Polo Grounds. Speaker's
spirited play in that same park forty-five years earlier
during the Red Sox–Giants Inter-League Championship wowed the New York press corps. Courtesy of
Cleveland State University Library.

two runners to win the game. Many Sox partisans left the park convinced that their Olde Towne Team had won. Instead, the Series was knotted at one game each.

"Rest" was an alien concept in the dead-ball era. The two clubs hopped a train to the Big Apple that night and squared off the following afternoon at the Polo Grounds. Tesreau and Wood, the two studs from game one, were back on the track with just two days' rest. In spite of tired arms, the two right-handers pitched gutty games. Wood gave up nine hits but allowed only one runner to cross the plate. Tesreau hung in for seven innings, allowing three runs on nine hits.

Heinie Wagner, a native New Yorker, saved Smoky Joe several times that afternoon by pulling off spectacular plays at short. Speaker, who was "writing" a column for the *Boston Post* that week, proffered that "Wagner never played more brilliantly than today and he never will, because that would not be humanely [*sic*] possible." Whether the sentiment was human or humane, certain observers were worried about Joe Wood. Tim Murnane and others noticed that Wood was throwing more curves than normal, giving rise to suspicions that something was wrong with his arm.

Once again there was no rest for the weary. And once again the Boston weather refused to cooperate. Yet another cold and miserable day greeted the ballplayers as they arrived at Fenway. Conditions were so unpleasant that some players wrapped blankets around themselves on the bench; others donned thick wool mackinaws to ward off the chill.

Mathewson, the northeastern Pennsylvanian from the farming hamlet of Factoryville, took on Bedient, the southwestern New Yorker from the village of Gerry. Despite the similarities in their background, there was a slight discrepancy in their experience. Bedient was in his first year in the bigs and had twenty wins to his credit. Matty had been pitching in the big leagues since Bedient was twelve and had nearly three hundred career victories.

It had all the trappings of a classic mismatch. The odds were heavily in Matty's favor, even with the game at Fenway. A ton of money must have been wagered on the Giants to knot the Series that day. Matty didn't disappoint, pitching a brilliant five-hitter and allowing only two scratch runs to score. It wasn't enough, however. Young Hugh was magnificent, throwing a three-hitter and limiting the Giants to one lone run.

Speaker, the part-time scribe, was once again a prime-time hero, albeit in less dramatic fashion. Following back-to-back windblown triples by Harry Hooper and Steve Yerkes in the third, Speaker dug in for yet another confrontation with Mathewson. Unlike game two, this time Matty dominated Speaker, forcing the Texan to top a little grounder toward Larry Doyle at second. Doyle charged the ball but couldn't make the play as the Speed Boys lived up to their billing, with Yerkes chugging home and Speaker sprinting down the first base line. That extra run was all young Hugh needed. Suddenly the Sox were up three games to one over McGraw's mighty Giants.

The Red Sox were ecstatic as they mobbed Bedient on the Fenway mound. The next day was a Sunday, which meant that the teams would finally get a much-needed day of rest. With that extra day, Smoky Joe would be primed and ready to go to clinch the Series for the Sox in game six back at the Polo Grounds.

"There was jubilation in the two Pullman cars occupied by Red Sox personnel on the leisurely Sunday daytime trip to New York," Fred Lieb remembered. "They could smell the sweet scent of victory and those fat World Series checks." Some of the Sox were literally calculating their winnings on scraps of paper – and gossiping about what they'd do with the cash.

Boston's moneymen, McAleer and McRoy, were calculating, too – but arriving at a much different conclusion. Eyeing the prospect of another busy day at Fenway's turnstiles, they decided to save Wood for a seventh game back in Boston – and pitch young Bucky O'Brien in game six. Did the Red Sox frontmen act unilaterally – or was a higher power involved? Given the hands-on control that Ban Johnson exercised over the Boston franchise – and the scratch he stood to make from an additional game in the Fens – it's highly improbable that McAleer and McRoy would have made a decision of that import without the AL czar's blessing.

Whether or not it was done in collusion with Johnson, his bosses' peremptory greed triggered a strong reaction from Sox skipper Jake Stahl. Accounts differ as to how McAleer broke the news to Jake. Fred Lieb, who often took liberties with the truth, claimed that McAleer sat down with Stahl as the train neared New York that Sunday afternoon. Others, including Glenn Stout and Richard Johnson, maintain that McAleer and Stahl met in an after-midnight parley that Sunday evening in Stahl's hotel room in New York. Either way, Jake begged McAleer to reconsider but McAleer would hear none of it. Whether or not his manager liked it, Buck would get the nod the next day.

If indeed McAleer broke the news late Sunday night, the timing of his meeting with Stahl probably wasn't coincidental. It should have occurred to someone in the organization to inform the Brockton spitballer right away that he would be called into duty the next afternoon. But by the time McAleer left Stahl's hotel room, it was well after midnight; Jake was so annoyed that he probably wasn't thinking too clearly. It may have been too late, anyway: Buck may have already been out on the town.

Part of the legend of the '12 Series is the incessant pounding Buck O'Brien would take over the next forty-eight hours, first from his own carousing, second from the Giants, third from Boston fans and reporters, and finally the worst beating of all, the literal one inflicted by the brothers Wood. First Paul, then Joe, may have taken turns pummeling Buck, as if somehow McAleer's heavy-handedness had been O'Brien's fault.

It's a shame no tape recorder was available to capture the reaction of Speaker and Wood when Stahl relayed the news, probably in the still of the night. Word spread quickly among the Speed Boys. By the time the players reached the hotel dining room for breakfast, the jubilation of the train ride the day before had turned into bitterness.

According to certain accounts, O'Brien didn't get word of his impending start until he arrived, hung over to beat the band, in the dressing room at the Polo Grounds. Whatever his condition, the Giants roughed him up for five quick runs in the first on a balk, a double steal, and back-to-back doubles by Merkle and Herzog. Speaker's sparring partner was having a terrific Series. He ended up leading both teams in hits with twelve, batting a sparkling .400.

The train ride back to Boston following the Sox's 5–2 defeat must have been every bit as gloomy as the ride down to New York had been giddy. Rumors about McAleer, McRoy, and Johnson gilding their pocketbooks must have run rampant. By the time the train pulled into South Station, the whole team must have been in a very black mood indeed.

Who knows what the Sox plotted that night and the next morning? This much is certain: the team with the best hurler in baseball, pitching on plenty of rest, buttressed by perhaps the finest defensive squad of the dead-ball era, went out and threw up all over themselves in the top of the first inning – and kept the hijinks going well into the second. All of this happened against the backdrop of the pandemonium that went on before the ballgame started, with an ugly battle being fought in the outfield between the Royal Rooters and mounted police. The Speed Boys' black moods must have gotten even blacker as cops wielding billy clubs herded the crowd behind the outfield barrier.

If the Sox's gaffes weren't done by design, then they were almost comically inept. Tim Murnane characterized Wood's pitching as "a clear case of cutting the ball over the heart of the plate." Joe wasn't smoking; he was lobbing.

The burlesque began with the Giants' Josh Devore dribbling an easy grounder to Heinie Wagner at short, who promptly booted it. Hooper, who almost never made errors of either commission or omission, muffed a line drive hit just a few steps away. With runners manning first and second, Wood pitched from the windup instead of the stretch, permitting the Giants to pull off an effortless double steal – a mental mistake that earned a rebuke from Christy Mathewson in a bylined article that appeared in the next day's papers. Duffy Lewis failed to make a play on a pop-up to left, then lazed an ill-advised throw to the wrong base. After Wood had "thrown" a dozen pitches, giving up seven hits and six runs, the top of the first came to a merciful close. No one will ever know if first baseman Stahl sanctioned the sloppy play, but it should be noted that the one grounder hit the skipper's way that inning was handled without incident.

Stahl relieved Wood with Sea Lion Hall to begin the top of the second with the Sox down 6–0. Any hopes that Hall would key a Boston comeback were quickly dashed. He hit Larry Doyle, walked the next Giants hitter, and then tried to pick Doyle off second. Captain Wagner wasn't able to get leather on Hall's pick-off attempt and Speaker somehow couldn't come up with the bouncing pill, either. Harry Hooper had to come all the way over from right to corral the ball and heave it back to the infield. By then, of course, Doyle had cruised home and the other Giant was encamped at third. Laughing Larry must have been chuckling pretty hard as he rejoined his mates on the bench. He'd been on base

118

twice in the first two innings and had advanced, respectively, on a double steal when the pitcher failed to use the stretch and when a pick-off throw somehow got through both the shortstop and the center fielder on the best-fielding team in baseball. The Giants slapped Sea Lion around for nine more hits and five more runs.

At least for one afternoon, the Speed Boys turned into the Keystone Kops. Virtually all the money – but perhaps not their own – was riding on them. It was almost too easy: anybody who bet the Giants that day fattened their wallets. Hugh Fullerton's column a few days later argued that Wood was embarrassed because he had urged brother Paul and certain pals to bet heavy on the Sox in game six. "For a comparatively trifling bet, Wood risked Boston's title and the wealth that accrued to the winner," Fullerton scoffed.

Maybe the players allowed themselves to be coaxed into something by Sport Sullivan; surely Sullivan and other hustlers knew all about the disaffection on the train ride home from Gotham. Or maybe the whole episode was just a curious coincidence of slapdash baseball. Whatever may have occurred, the Sox's 11–4 loss that afternoon doesn't pass the smell test.

In his bylined column in the *Boston Post*, almost assuredly ghostwritten by Paul Shannon, Spoke admitted that the Sox played their poorest game of the season. "Looking at the game from every angle, one can find there was not a redeeming feature in it from a Boston viewpoint," he wrote the next day.

Red Sox fans couldn't find a redeeming feature, either. The Boston management's off-field betrayal and the club's on-field collapse that day led to the most impassioned fan anger and disillusionment in baseball history. How many times has a team's most rabid fans gathered outside the home ballpark in the middle of a championship series and denounced the club, as Fitz and the Rooters – many of them drunk – did that night? How many times has there been an active grassroots boycott of the deciding game of a championship series?

The irony that all this unsavory intrigue was unfolding in Boston, the cradle of American liberty, certainly wasn't lost on two unabashed Rebels. If indeed they had "arranged" a rough outing, Speaker and Wood probably figured that Stahl would turn around and start Wood the next day in game eight, since Wood hadn't exactly exhausted himself that afternoon.

From a distance of nine decades, the Speaker–Wood–Speed Boys' gambit that day looks like a "butterfly" move in a modern arbitrage deal: on the one hand, they may have profited from some well-timed bets; and on the other, they were still in good shape to win four grand each for the winner's share of the Series. All they had to do was score a couple of runs on Christy Mathewson the next day, which they had already done twice in the Series. Speaker had always hit Mathewson hard. And Smoky Joe was raring to go.

Jake Stahl, a decent man, must have been on the horns of a dilemma. He was every bit as angry as his players about being denied the second-game money and about being forced to throw O'Brien to the wolves in the sixth game. Joe Wood's behavior in the past twenty-four hours certainly must have caused Stahl some serious consternation. Smoky Joe not only had gotten beat up by the Giants, but he may have tried to beat up a teammate when he should have been concentrating on getting ready for the game. Wood's head and heart were clearly elsewhere, Stahl may have reckoned, while Bedient had pitched great in his head-to-head confrontation with Matty in game five. Or maybe McAleer and Johnson dictated that Stahl give Bedient the nod.

One element of the drama that surrounds the last game of the '12 Series is that Speaker had a couple of marginal defensive moments that led to Giants runs, triggering speculation in some quarters that the previous day's fix was still in place. That's not likely: both plays came about because of Speaker's shallow positioning and hustle. In the third inning, Red Murray's double was blasted well over Speaker's head. In the tenth, he dove in a futile effort to snare Fred Merkle's line drive, then bobbled the ball momentarily, allowing Murray to score from second. But Spoke had made a superb play just to cut the ball off.

The standout defensive play that afternoon, Harry Hooper's bare-handed grab in the sixth off of Doyle's long smash to right, may have been the product of divine intervention. As related in Paul Zingg's book, Hooper had scooped up a piece of paper in right field as he assumed his defensive position in the top of the first. To his surprise, it turned out to be a Catholic prayer card – a rendering of the Sacred Heart of Jesus with an inspirational message. "Thinking the card had been left by a fan who intended for him to find it, Harry recited the prayer to himself and stuck the card in his pants pocket. As the magnitude of his catch grew with the years, so, too, did Harry's wonderment at a connection between his discovery and the good fortune that followed," Zingg wrote.

By all accounts, it was one of the most spectacular catches in baseball history. Speaker called it the greatest play he'd ever witnessed. William Phelon, the editor of *Baseball Magazine*, described it as "unequaled, unexampled." Eyewitnesses reported that Harry turned first one way, then the other, as he raced to catch up with the ball as it headed toward the three-foot-high standing-room-only cordon in right field. The ball and Harry plunged into the crowd at precisely the same instant. Hooper came out of the horde with the ball in his bare hand and a dozen fans thumping him on the back. McGraw charged out onto the field to confront umpire Bill Klem, claiming that Hooper had made the catch off the field of play, but Klem didn't budge.

After Steve Yerkes crossed the plate in the tenth inning with the winning run, "insane enthusiasm went thundering around Fenway Park," Murnane wrote. Even though the park was only half full, "men hugged each other, women became hysterical, youths threw their caps in the air, one man in the bleachers fell in a dead faint, strong hearts lost a beat and started off again at double time."

Speaker batted .300 and had nine hits during the Series – all of them clutch. He scored four runs and drove in two others. His tenth-inning smash to center and mad dash around the bases saved the second game and enabled the Sox to maintain control of the Series. Smoky Joe won three games; despite his disputed performance in the first inning of the seventh game, he rang up a respectable ERA of 3.68. Harry Hooper also had nine hits, scoring three times and driving in two.

In the aftermath of Boston's first World Series triumph in nine years, all was forgiven. Well, maybe not all – a lot of wallets were thinner – but enough so that Honey Fitz was able to put on a parade the next day that remains one of the biggest in Hub history. The people who balked at showing up at Fenway for the deciding game the day before turned out in massive numbers to salute the new champions. A *Globe* cartoon that week joshed that the whole city had a hangover.

Mayor Fitz arranged for the ballplayers to brave the autumnal chill and ride in open convertibles. Jake Stahl, Smoky Joe, and Larry Gardner rode with His Honor. The *Globe* described the scene at Faneuil Hall as a "seething whirlpool of humanity. . . . The police used all their power to control the throng, but their efforts were like those of ants trying to push back a landslide." At one point, things got so out of control that plain-clothed policemen were forced to hurl unwanted well-wishers off the stage.

A day or two later Murnane decided he wanted to dispel certain "wild yarns" that had bounced around Beantown during what "was by all odds the most stubborn contest for the post-season honors I ever witnessed." In a remarkable column headlined "Stories of Put-Up Job Decried," Murnane speculated that certain ugly rumors had been circulated for the effect it would have on wagering. O'Brien hadn't been out carousing that Sunday evening before the sixth game in New York, Murnane said, although his article conceded that he hadn't actually seen the spitballer close the door to his hotel room. And Joe Wood hadn't fought with Buck on the train ride home to Boston that Monday night, Murnane maintained, without acknowledging that others had reported that it was Wood's brother who had socked O'Brien on the train, not Joe. Oddly, Murnane's post-Series analysis didn't address the biggest issue of all: the bizarre goings-on in the top of the first and second innings of the controversial seventh game.

Murnane was far more forthright than most commentators about the influence gambling had on the game. Still, he was part of baseball's cabal – an incestuous group whose duty was to ignore unpleasant truths and perpetuate myths about the game and its players. "The King is dead," T.H.'s piece concluded. "Long live the King."

At that moment, King Tris and the Boston Red Sox sat on top of baseball's throne. But the perch proved precarious. All the internecine issues that the Sox managed to overcome that season – clubhouse dissension, deceitful ownership, a thin rotation – came back to haunt them. It should have been the cusp of a Boston dynasty in the American League. Instead, the organization would have to endure much upheaval and two mediocre seasons before they recaptured the glory of 1912.

Speaker, too, would experience much frustration over the next couple of years. Spoke no doubt had big plans to add future Chalmers automobiles to his collection as the league's most valuable player. But it wasn't meant to be.

CHAPTER 7

Last Years in Boston

The purpose of the trip was twofold – to prove to the foreign element that baseball is better than cricket, roulette, hopscotch, baccarat, Parcheesi or any of the other sports in vogue abroad, and to convince Herman Schaefer and the rest of the heathen included on the roster of the two clubs that Ireland, one of the stopping points, is the greatest country in the atlas.
— Ring Lardner

The spell of good fortune that the new ballpark seemed to cast over Tris Speaker and the Red Sox disappeared in a hurry. The year 1913 quickly dissipated into a nightmare of freakish injuries and Steinbrennerian infighting. Just as they'd done nine years previously, Boston's newspapers spent most of the winter skewering the team's owners for blatant profiteering during the Series the previous fall. The karma stayed bad all year.

Once his shiner wore off, Buck O'Brien hit the vaudeville circuit that winter, forming a singing group called the "Red Sox Quartette" that toured small towns throughout New England. The climax of Buck's act was a tune called "The Ballad of Buck O'Brien, the Spit Ball Artist." It's unknown whether the Brockton youngster actually expectorated on stage. What is known is that young Buck's spitter only garnered him four more wins in a career that ended – ingloriously – that year after a midseason trade to the Pale Hose. Bucky showed up at Hot Springs pasty and out of shape. All those rubber chicken dinners and late nights closing down taverns in backwoods Vermont and Maine had inflicted their damage on "the Spit Ball Artist."

Boston's injury bug even hit player-manager Jake Stahl, who was hampered with a groin pull all spring, a happenstance that couldn't have helped his testy relationship with McAleer. The worst of Boston's injuries, though, happened to Speaker's roommate and closest pal, Smoky Joe Wood. Joe's whole year was dogged by misfortune. Wood severely sprained an ankle during spring training – an injury that Tim Murnane in the *Globe* accurately predicted would hamper his pitching motion. Then, in early July, Wood tried to trap Wahoo Sam Crawford in a rundown and slipped on slick turf at Navin Field. Wood fell awkwardly, breaking his right thumb as he braced himself. Joe never pitched again without severe pain in his right shoulder, according to Joe's son Bob, now in his mid-eighties. Perhaps his father had tried to come back too soon, Bob conjectures.

Given the severity of Smoky Joe's discomfort, Stout and Johnson speculate that perhaps Wood had damaged his rotator cuff. In all probability, he needed surgery that wasn't available in baseball's early days. Wood, just twenty-three, was close to being washed up as a pitcher. He won only twenty-four more games in the big leagues before making himself into an outfielder – and a darned good one.

By 1913 Speaker was seen by many writers and fans as part of the American League's holy trinity of outfielders. Just as spring training camps were breaking in late March, the *Cleveland Leader*'s Gordon Mackay saluted Ty Cobb, Shoeless Joe Jackson, and Spoke by poking fun in verse at skeptics who said they couldn't possibly be as good as advertised. Entitled "When the Dope Went Afield," his doggerel for Speaker read in part:

> Tales that blazed the wires from southland came a-buzzing to the north,
> Of a wizard that the Red Sox had discovered and so forth.
> Wires they sang their merry ditties, told about his splendid skill,
> And they kept the threads a-humming telling how he hit the pill.

But the Sox did not begin the season "a-humming": Opening day 1913 was a harbinger of the next two seasons. Smoky Joe got thumped in a 10–9 loss to the Athletics. Joining Hooper and Lewis on the Sox that season was left-hander Hubert Benjamin "Dutch" Leonard.

Dutch, a battler, became a steady presence on the mound throughout the midteens. But he proved to be, at least from the players' perspective, an unsteady personality off of it. Out of spite years later, he broke the dead-ball era's sacred code by ratting on Speaker, Wood, and Ty Cobb, accusing them of misconduct that forever altered their careers in big league baseball. Even worse from the players' point of view is that Dutch wasn't man enough to show up at a hearing to press his charges. But that ugly episode was more than a decade off: Dutch, all of twenty-one, was a welcome addition to the staff, especially given Wood's woes later in the year. Dutch had decimated hitters in the Rocky Mountain League in 1912, winning twenty-nine games for Denver.

Stahl tabbed another rookie to join Leonard on the staff: a slight Oklahoman named George "Rube" Foster. Young Rube only reached five foot seven on his tippytoes yet became a consistent winner for the Sox. Vermont southpaw Ray Collins turned in another fine season, winning twenty games. Try as they might, however, the Sox moundsmen couldn't compete with Connie Mack's mighty fivesome of Eddie Plank, Chief Bender, Boardwalk Brown, and the Minnesota "twins," Byron "Duke" Houck and "Bullet Joe" Bush, a rookie right-hander with a fastball that crackled. In 1913 the five combined for an astounding eighty-four of the A's ninety-six wins.

The A's and the Red Sox, more than most ball clubs of that era, discovered that college campuses served as fertile sources of talent. Connie Mack, an Irish Catholic, was no fool: he forged an "agreement" with Brother Agnon at Saint Mary's, Harry Hooper's mentor, to keep the A's pipeline full.

Today "Connie Mack" conjures up the image of Ichabod Crane, an Adam's-appled anachronism sadly out of sync with the world around him. The funereal garb, the stiff collars, the straw boaters, and the silver hair stubbornly parted down the middle all conspired to project the mien of a small-town preacher – the perfect rube. He was anything but.

Nobody in baseball knew how to count a buck like the man born Cornelius Alexander McGillicuddy. Raised in East Brookfield, Massachusetts, he was the son of immigrant parents who had fled Ireland's privations for the New World. For a fellow who later prided himself on being a conservative tightwad, Mack was something of a firebrand as a player, jumping from the National League's Washington franchise to join Buffalo in the short-lived Players' League in 1890. When the Players' League disintegrated after one season, Mack signed with Pittsburgh's National League franchise. Three years later, he became Pittsburgh's player-manager, leading the team to respectable finishes in 1894 and 1895 before being fired near the end of the '96 season. He was one of the better catchers of the '80s and '90s, a good receiver behind the plate who never did much standing by it with a bat in his hands. Mack first crossed paths in 1897 with the man who would become his benefactor, Ban Johnson, when he managed Johnson's Milwaukee franchise in the still-minor Western League.

Four years later Johnson gave Mack a 25 percent interest in the Philadelphia club in the freshly minted American League, hooking him up with sporting goods magnate Benjamin Franklin Shibe. Among other things, Shibe invented and patented the cork-center baseball. In 1909 Mack and the Shibe brothers built a park with a beautiful French Renaissance brick facade at the intersection of Twenty-first and Lehigh. It drove Mack to distraction that people who lived in the row houses along Twentieth Street could sit on their rooftops and watch games for free or, even worse, charge friends and passers-by a couple of bits that didn't end up in the A's coffers. Mack took the row houses to court and lost. Years later, Mack and the Shibes finally succeeded in erecting a "spite fence" to obstruct the sight lines from the rooftops along Twentieth Street.

As Philadelphia native Wilfrid Sheed put it in a marvelous essay on Connie in *The Ultimate Baseball Book*, "Mack served up two kinds of teams: unbeatable and lousy." Championships, Mack was fond of pointing out, cost money. His métier was building a team from scratch, wreaking havoc for a few years, then scrapping it, selling off the parts, and starting over from square one. The A's lean years – and there were a lot of them; Mack won nine pennants but finished dead last no fewer than sixteen times – Sheed likened to "biblical plagues." Sheed compared Mack's aura in the dugout to that of a "renaissance cardinal. He wagged his scorecard as if it were a papal bull, and lesser men went running." In his twilight years, the aging Mack took forever to signal to "lesser men" – his frustrated coaches and players – what he wanted done on the ball field.

Unlike so many of his contemporaries, Mack refrained from smoking, drinking, or cursing. His vices ran to greed and perhaps an unduly generous view of himself as a baseball Pygmalion. He genuinely thought he could take mediocre talent and make it good – and on occasion, he did.

The 1905, 1911, and 1913 World Series brought together two beautifully book-ended Irish American egos: Mack and John McGraw. One was lanky and austere, the other stumpy and shrill. Each was a cutthroat competitor. And each was convinced the baseball gods had bestowed supernatural powers on him – and him alone. Mack got the better of McGraw in two of their three postseason dustups. Only in 1905 did McGraw's Giants beat the Athletics. Connie's ace Rube Waddell supposedly "injured" himself on the eve of the '05 Series opener while foolishly wrestling a teammate over a straw hat. Certain commentators over the years have given Waddell's "accident" a more sinister interpretation, suggesting that the erratic left-hander from Elk County, Pennsylvania, fell prey to gamblers and took a dive. No matter, there was no beating the Giants that year, not with Matty operating at full throttle.

After his heavily favored 1914 club tanked – many believe deliberately – against the "Miracle" Boston Braves in the Series, Mack broke it up out of bitterness and/or gluttony, pocketing fifty thousand dollars for the A's ownership syndicate in peddling Eddie Collins to Charles Comiskey's club. Connie so thoroughly dismantled the A's that Home Run Baker quit in disgust, sitting out the 1915 season at home on the eastern shore of Maryland rather than play for Mack. The next year Mack sold Baker to the Yankees.

It wasn't until the mid-1920s that the A's recovered from Mack's 1914–15 fire sale. But by then "the Tall Tactician" had begun to assemble the parts to challenge the dynastic Yankees of Ruth and Gehrig. Starting in 1929, Mack's men beat the mighty Yanks three years in a row for the American League pennant, capturing the World Series twice – a stunning achievement given the Yanks' breadth of talent.

Mack and Ben Shibe were partners for four decades. When old man Shibe died in 1940, Mack became the controlling partner in the A's ownership group with 58 percent of the holdings. He could have hung up the high-button shoes – or at least moved them to the front office. Yet Mack and his cadaverous wardrobe soldiered on in the dugout for another decade of mainly horrific baseball. When he finally retired in 1950, President Truman feted him at the White House and the people of Manhattan gave him a ticker-tape parade. He ended his managerial career with 3,731 wins – just 217 games short of his career loss total.

Baseball in the early part of the twentieth century "needed class," Sheed mused, "but it couldn't have handled a real saint. Mack was the perfect compromise."

Mack's men got off to a solid start and were never headed in 1913. Stahl's men got off to a bumpy start that got even bumpier as the weeks wore on. So bumpy, in fact, that Stahl was fired by McAleer in early July when the Sox were two games below .500. The dismissal incensed Ban Johnson, who began worrying anew about the steadiness of McAleer's hand on the till of his prized franchise. McAleer made a pile of mistakes running the Red Sox, but his choice to replace Stahl was inspired: Rough Carrigan. The tough but even-keeled Carrigan was exactly what the ball club needed. Boston responded to Rough's leadership, winning forty of the remaining seventy games and salvaging a decent season.

Carrigan's ascension to manager must have been brutally tough for Speaker to swallow. Not only was a teammate getting the nod instead of Speaker, but it was no ordinary teammate. Rough, after all, was Spoke's longtime clubhouse rival. There's a good chance that Speaker and Carrigan eventually figured out why they had such trouble getting along: they were too much alike. Both were hardheaded and obstreperous – neither backed down from a fight. It's a testament to both men that they were able to put their differences aside on the field while barely remaining civil off of it.

Although he didn't lead the league in any offensive category, Speaker had another exceptional season in 1913 – but not quite up to the spectacular pace of his 1912 campaign. He ended up finishing fourth in both the Chalmers Award race – Walter Johnson, whose numbers were otherworldly, won it – and AL batting average, once again trailing Cobb and Jackson, plus Eddie Collins. Some nagging injuries caused Spoke to miss a few games that season. His doubles total decreased from fifty-three in '12 to thirty-five in '13. His triples, however, increased from twelve to a stout twenty-two. Amazingly, though, his three-baggers didn't lead the league. Wahoo Sam, who played his home games in a then-classic triples park, Navin Field, did Spoke one better.

In early July 1913 the Red Sox visited League Park in Cleveland for a series against Napoleon Lajoie's club, the Naps. Ed Bang, sports editor of the *Cleveland News*, watched Speaker several afternoons in a row and came away infatuated. "What a wonderful ball player Speaker is," Bang wrote on July 2.

Not satisfied with driving in the Red Sox's first run with a long sacrifice fly, he also produced the single that scored the winning run. But that's not all. Not even half. He had nine putouts in center field, and you can believe it or not, but seven of those nine were really difficult chances. Tris robbed [Steve] O'Neill of a double and a triple, [Ray] Chapman of a triple, [Joe] Jackson of a triple, [Larry] Lajoie of a double, and [Terry] Turner of a triple and on down the line. Without Speaker, the Red Sox would have been beaten by an overwhelming score.

Bang's slight hyperbole aside, his column is typical of the kind of press that Speaker was receiving all over the country. The boys in the press box ran out of superlatives to describe his all-around brilliance. The phrase "Where triples go to die" was originally written of Tris Speaker's glove. Later, curiously, it somehow got ascribed to Joe Jackson's.

After the Sox finished a disappointing fourth, despite their strong showing under Carrigan, Spoke decided at the last minute not to go home to Hubbard for his usual winter of hunting, fishing, and hanging around the fire station and the feed store. It no doubt upset his mother that her son accepted Charles Comiskey's invitation to join the first leg of what would be the "Tour to End All Tours" – the Chicago White Sox–New York Giants exhibition tour of the world.

The world tour was the brainchild of two of baseball's colossal egos and pocketbooks, Charles Comiskey and John McGraw. In December 1912 Commy and Muggsy met for cocktails one night in the back room of "Smiley" Mike Corbett's tavern in Chicago. Their drinking session went well into the morning while they tried to figure out ways to increase the profitability of their respective clubs by creating new fans and bringing baseball to new markets. Commy pointed out that the twenty-fifth anniversary of the 1889–90 "world" tour that Albert Spalding spawned for his Chicago White Stockings was fast approaching. Why not celebrate the milestone with a White Sox–Giants tour of Asia, Australia, and Europe as a way to fatten their wallets – and increase baseball's popularity worldwide? The notoriously cheap Comiskey dug deep and obtained a $100,000+ line of credit to meet the tour's expenses. But for Commy, it was money well invested; he more than recouped it in the end. The other two principal investors, McGraw and minor league impresario Ted Sullivan, also made out handsomely.

Baseball's potentates soon realized that not all their subjects would be able to spend nearly half a year encircling the globe. So they decided to augment their regular lineups with a group of standout players from other clubs. Two and a half decades before, Spalding had passed off a bunch of mediocre players as "all-stars." This time around, McGraw and Comiskey wanted to show the world the genuine article. Ty Cobb and Napoleon Lajoie demurred, but Speaker and Wahoo Sam Crawford accepted, as did Herman "Germany" Schaefer of the Senators. Schaefer, a weak-hitting utility fielder, was an endearing clown so funny that teammate Davy Jones thought he was more entertaining than Charlie Chaplin. As related in James E. Elfers's *The Tour to End All Tours*, Comiskey and company "understood the need for a comedian to keep everybody loose on such a grueling road trip. For Germany, the tour represented an opportunity no clown could resist, the chance to make the world his stage."

Regular members of the White Sox along for the tour included third baseman George "Buck" Weaver, first baseman "Prince Hal" Chase (who no doubt tried to manipulate whatever action he could on the exhibition games), and catcher Ray Schalk. Like Speaker, however, Chase and Schalk would only commit to the transcontinental phase of the tour.

The Giants' troupe included the revered Christy Mathewson and wife, first baseman Fred Merkle, hurler Jeff Tesreau, second sacker Larry Doyle, center fielder Fred Snodgrass, and catcher Chief Meyers. Phillies third baseman Hans Lobert also joined the fun. Mathewson, Snodgrass, Tesreau, and Meyers were scheduled to leave the tour once the last exhibition had been played in Seattle, the jumping-off point for Asia. Also along were Mr. and Mrs. James McAleer.

The pilgrimage began with a grueling twenty-seven-city exhibition tour of the Midwest and West. To pay homage to baseball's first professional franchise, the 1869 Red Stockings, Comiskey and McGraw chose Redland Field in Cincinnati for the October 18 inaugural game. The tour then bounced its way west and south for another month. Ted Sullivan had helped found the Texas League years before and made certain that the tour made a big footprint on the Lone Star State. On October 30 the tour reached Bonham, Texas, quite literally shutting the little burg down. Schools and businesses closed early as an overflow crowd of four thousand crammed into the town's tiny ball yard.

When the tour reached Dallas, pandemonium broke loose when fans got a glimpse of their favorite son, Tris Speaker. The excitement started the night before in Denison, when a thousand Texans showed up at the depot just to see the players' train get sidetracked for the evening. The next day, Matty and Merkle got to play a little golf before the entourage was due at Gaston Park at the Texas State Fairgrounds in Dallas. Five thousand folks ringed the field as the White Sox roughed up Matty, who'd probably left most of his energy back on the links, 10–3. Spoke then left the tour for a few days to visit his mother at home in Hubbard, plus do a little hunting with his pals.

Speaker rejoined the gang in Marlin. McGraw, to his credit, had insisted on a game in the Falls County resort town that his Giants had helped put on the map. Thousands of central Texans crowded into the tiny field on which the Giants had trained for so many years. Since the "Giants" were defending home turf, the "White Sox" may have decided to go easy on them. Jeff Tesreau gave up just four hits in blistering the Pale Hose all-stars, 11–1.

Tris had proudly brought with him the fruits of several days' labor in the wilds of Hill County: a bevy of duck and quail. A big postgame spread was planned; Tris had his stash of game bird stuffed and steaming as the game ended. But the players were running so far behind schedule that afternoon that they had to leave the delicacies behind as they dashed for the train.

At Abilene, their next stop, the game was rained out, so the red-blooded men familiar with Texas folkways organized a badger fight. "The way it worked was simple yet repulsive," Elfers writes. "A dog and a badger were released at the same instant into a ring. Whoever placed bets on the surviving animal would collect." Over the years, McGraw had witnessed a few badger-dog tussles and wanted to be sure that others on tour could experience the same macabre spectacle. Muggsy, always looking to gain a betting edge, ensured that the badger was famished. Umpire Bill Klem, one of two arbiters along for the tour, was nominated to pull the badger's cage door. But as reported in the *Abilene Daily Record*, Klem refused, declaring "in a stentorian voice with a guttural twang: 'No, you ain't going to get Mr. Klem to pull no badger.'" The crowd packed into the barn howled.

Finally, a brave Abilenian was pressed into duty. The starved badger pounced out of his cage, quickly making mincemeat of the overmatched dog. McGraw, no fool he, must have been grinning fiendishly as he collected money from those naive saps who wagered on the dog.

The tour wound its way to the West Coast, heading north through California and into Oregon. Medford's weather on "Apple Day," November 18, was so miserable that fans could hardly see the players on the field. But twenty-five hundred folks showed up anyhow, clamoring to see their "two dollars' worth." The players obliged them, conducting the game in a downpour. That day, Speaker waxed machismo to the *Portland Evening Telegram*, telling a reporter, "When you see a bunch of people ready to stand out in the rain just to see their National game played by big leaguers, a man would be willing to go out and court rheumatism just to gratify them."

As the tour's train pulled into each community, Germany Schaefer would be called upon to exchange public pleasantries with the welcoming committee that would inevitably gather at the depot platform. Sometimes Germany would deliver the remarks as himself; at other venues he'd pretend to be one of the big names on tour. In those days before radio and perpetual wire service photos, the vast majority of folks around the country wouldn't have been able to distinguish Germany Schaefer from Tris Speaker on sight. The only celebrity on board who would have been instantly recognizable was Matty – and then only because of the commercial endorsements in which his likeness had been used.

So Schaefer, a great mimic, would do dead-on impersonations of various ballplayers, all the while tossing out bromides about the magnificent town, its stunning scenery, its inspired leadership, its beautiful children, and its God-fearing citizens that would have made Honey Fitz envious. People from the Ohio to the Columbia ate it up. The players loved to hang just out of public view, grabbing their sides in laughter, as Germany piled it on for the umpteenth time.

By the time the troupe reached Seattle, the tour had taken in a cool $100,000 in gate receipts. Instead of sharing the wealth, though, Commy insulted the players by giving them a meager $250 bonus apiece. Earlier that year, regular members of the White Sox had made a bigger bonus for a mere three-game exhibition series against the crosstown Cubs. There was much grumbling as Matty, Meyers, Snodgrass, Tesreau, and others took their leave before the *Empress of Japan* sailed from Puget Sound.

Speaker, too, had promised his mother that he'd be back in Texas by December. But at the last second he decided to explore the globe, no doubt upsetting Jenny when she received his wire. Since formal attire was de rigueur aboard ship and for many of the places they would visit abroad, it can only be assumed that Speaker must have hurriedly visited Seattle or Victoria haberdasheries, unless he'd had the foresight to pack white and black tie. The Comiskeys alone brought seven trunkloads of clothes. Speaker, a tenderfoot who had barely gotten out of the state of Texas in his first nineteen years of life was, at twenty-five, off to see the world.

Spoke and his compatriots eventually visited thirteen nations on four continents, traveling some thirty thousand miles over four months. The ensemble entertained such luminaries as King George V of England, Sir Thomas Lipton, the tea magnate, and Abbas II, the last khedive of Egypt. And in Rome, a certain rabid antipapist, surrounded by reverent Catholic teammates and their spouses, came face to face with the Holy See.

Ironically, the most famous athlete aboard ship played baseball as a side-light. He was the Giants' Jim Thorpe, the only man ever to win the pentathlon and the decathlon in the same Olympiad. As King Gustav V of Sweden presented Thorpe with his gold medals at the 1912 Olympic Games in Stockholm, he gushed, "You, sir, are the greatest athlete in the world!" The story may be apocryphal, but Thorpe supposedly replied, "Thanks, King."

Thorpe's father was an English fur trapper who had married the daughter of Chief Thunder, a leader of the Sac and Fox Tribe in the former Indian Territories – the place where Speaker's uncles had gone to fight Union-backed tribes two generations before. In his youth, Jim came east to study at the Carlisle Indian School at Dickinson College in Pennsylvania, where he excelled in every game he attempted. At the Stockholm Olympiad, he represented two "countries" – the Sac and Fox Tribe and the United States. But in truth, given the awkward conventions of the day, he didn't become a full-fledged American citizen until 1917. Sports came almost too easily to Thorpe. He picked up a bowling ball and soon began breaking two hundred. He picked up golf clubs and quickly broke eighty. As Elfers put it, "Thorpe was the living personification of his Sac tribal name, Wa-tho-huc, which means 'Bright Path.'"

In January 1913 the United States Olympic Committee abruptly bumped Thorpe off his bright path. He was stripped of his medals when it came to light that he had played bush league baseball for a few dollars – a violation of the Olympics' strict amateur code. In the summers of 1909 and 1910 Thorpe had earned the princely sum of thirty dollars a month playing for the Rocky Mount Railroaders of the Eastern Carolina League. Like most college kids of the day, he needed the extra money. Thorpe's mistake was not using a pseudonym while playing pro or semipro ball, like countless other college athletes of that era did, including Lou Gehrig and Mickey Cochrane. After being forced to relinquish his medals, Thorpe signed a three-year contract to play for McGraw's Giants at the heady clip of six thousand dollars a year. Muggsy knew that even if the Olympic champion didn't pan out as a baseball player, he'd be a serious gate attraction for a couple of seasons. Thorpe, the best lacrosse and football player of his generation, backed down from nobody. He and McGraw would butt heads more than occasionally.

Easily the most recognizable athlete on the planet, Thorpe and his wife, Iva, were mobbed virtually everywhere they went on the trip. As the *Empress* pulled into the harbor at Shanghai, thousands of Chinese admirers began chanting, "Thorpe! Thorpe! Thorpe!" The exquisite Mrs. Thorpe, a Caucasian, also stirred passions on tour. She was exceedingly photogenic, never shy about putting herself in front of cameras or making herself the center of attention. Jim and Iva had just gotten married a few months before. Like Mr. and Mrs. Sam Crawford, they were essentially honeymooning; the miscegenation the Thorpes represented, though, heightened the world's interest in them, no doubt setting tongues to wag aboard ship, too. As the tour wore on, American newspapers kept readers abreast of every twist and turn, running front-page accounts complete with photographs of the ballplayers visiting exotic locales and mingling with wide-eyed locals.

The tour was not without its harrowing moments. As the *Empress of Japan* neared home waters, the ship was wracked by a late-season typhoon. Waves fully sixty feet high threatened to capsize her. Prairie boys like Nebraska's Sam Crawford and Texas's Tris Speaker must have wondered why they ever left home. The storm was so intense that the *Empress* actually lost her bearings for a time.

It only took a day or two on the bright blue Pacific for Speaker to discover he suffered from violent seasickness. He took to his bed almost immediately. Had Spoke known that Matty, too, suffered from the same malady, he might have gotten on the train back to Texas. But Matty never let on that the real reason he didn't want to join the world tour was that he turned green at the mere sight of an ocean. Instead, Matty told McGraw and his tour mates that he had family obligations in California.

Spoke wasn't alone. Comiskey and others were seasick, too. In fact, Commy was so sick for so long on the voyage that the newspapermen on board the *Empress* competed with one another to see who could have the most fun in print at "the Old Roman's" expense. John O. Seys of the *Chicago Daily News* wrote a sprightly poem called "Aboard the Good Ship *Empress of Japan*," which read in part:

> We were crowded in the cabin.
> Not a player was asleep.
> There was breakfast on the waters,
> There was luncheon on the deep.
> 'Tis a fearful thing in winter
> To be shuttered by the blast
> And be forced to give up dinner –
> Or whatever went down last.

Even the players concocted verse to while away the time. In late December, White Sox player John Burns, who'd stayed home in the Windy City, received a ditty from his teammates aboard the *Empress*. As reprinted in the *Chicago Record-Herald*, it went something like this:

> If we ever get back to the Loop again,
> We'll never sail a day;
> Tho' we had fun the world around
> We —— all the way.

Since the *Record-Herald* was a family newspaper, and this was, after all, 1913, it chose to delete the bodily function in the last line, although readers certainly had no trouble inserting "retched" or "puked" or whatever the euphemism of the day was for "vomited."

Finally, the retching stopped and the sightseeing started. The conquering heroes' reception as the *Empress* steamed into Yokohama Harbor with Mount Fuji off the stern bow was something that they would never forget. Since the rough seas had delayed the *Empress*'s arrival, only three games – all of them in Tokyo – could be played in Japan. A combined Giants-Sox squad overwhelmed the Keio University team in the first game; the following day, they played a doubleheader exhibition against one another. Tens of thousands of Japanese jammed into Keio's tiny ballpark.

As only he could, Speaker put on a spectacular show. Despite the lingering effects of seasickness, he slugged two home runs in the first game of the doubleheader. In the finale, with the White Sox leading the Giants 12–9 with two outs in the ninth, Speaker threw Mike Donlin out at the plate from a distance that everyone who witnessed the play – journalists included – swore was more than 480 feet. Catcher Ivy Wingo didn't have to budge as Spoke's prodigious peg came winging in from deepest center field. McGraw thought Speaker's throw defied belief; Muggsy always listed it at the top of the best plays he'd ever seen.

Along the way there were more than a few boys-will-be-boys moments. Naturally, Spoke was in the thick of the action. The tour's bachelors – Speaker, Merkle, Donlin, and Schaefer among them – liked to go out and christen each of the cities they visited. In Nagasaki, an all-day spree concluded at a pool hall near the pier, where one of the Americans managed to rip the cue ball so far off the table that it couldn't immediately be located. Since the ball was made out of real ivory, authorities were summoned as the players beat a retreat to the *Empress*, which was poised to leave Nagasaki's harbor at any instant. Maybe the boys had paid the bar tab – maybe they hadn't. They were so drunk they couldn't remember. At any rate, the *Empress*'s departure was held up as Nagasaki's finest responded to the pool hall's complaint. Germany Schaefer was sent out to the dock to smooth things over. Just then, word came that the missing cue ball had been miraculously found, thus averting what could have been a major diplomatic crisis. When word of the escapade reached the newspapermen on board, they roared, agreeing to keep the incident – and its perpetrators – under wraps.

In Shanghai the bachelors slipped away from the rest of the tour long enough to visit forbidden "Chinatown," a dusky section of town that was literally walled off from the rest of the city. Its brothels and opium dens were said to be Asia's most notorious. When they turned up late at the hotel, almost causing the rest of the troupe to miss the next leg of the trip, Speaker and his chums claimed to have "gotten lost" – which no doubt was at least partly accurate.

Fears of a smallpox epidemic and other disease outbreaks forced many of the travelers to receive primitively administered inoculations while in Asia. Spoke was among those confined to his cabin when he had an adverse reaction to a shot from what may have been a dirty needle.

The weather and the group's spirits improved considerably as the *Empress* headed toward Australia. On New Year's Eve, as they entered Brisbane's harbor, a felicitously named reporter, F. Z. Eager, pulled an ingenious stunt: he went to Brisbane's post office and grabbed several burlap sacks' worth of mail that was awaiting the troupe's arrival. Eager then commissioned a tugboat to meet the *Empress* as it entered the channel, hollering up to those on board that he wanted an exclusive interview in exchange for the mail. The Americans hadn't received mail of any kind since leaving Puget Sound six weeks before, so they eagerly snapped up Eager's quid pro quo.

The problem was that there was no easy way for Eager to get the satchels up from the tugboat to the homesick Americans. Speaker characteristically took charge, forming a makeshift "bucket brigade" and taking on the toughest responsibility himself: two guys grabbed Speaker's ankles and lowered him headfirst from the *Empress*'s bottom-most deck down toward Eager's tugboat. The reporter then stood on his tiptoes and handed the burlap sacks one by one to the Texan. In Tris's sure hands, not a single sack or envelope splashed into Brisbane harbor.

Speaker was greeted as a hero when he was hauled back on deck. An impromptu party broke out as weary travelers read letters from loved ones back home.

A few days before, Spoke had impressed his traveling companions with the kindness he had shown a group of Russian immigrant children who were sharing space on the schooner that was transporting the troupe down China's interior rivers. The Russian kids were scared to be on a strange ship in a strange country. Without knowing a word of Russian, Spoke and several other players and wives kept the kids entertained for several days. Speaker clearly had a soft spot in his heart for kids, making it all the more puzzling that he waited so long to get married and didn't have any children himself.

Almost every evening aboard ship turned into a party. Speaker and three of the other bachelors on board – Schaefer, Merkle, and Buck Weaver – kept themselves so busy dancing with unattached young ladies that they dubbed themselves "the Tango Four." As their new vessel, the RMS *Orantes*, steamed toward the British tea plantation of Ceylon in the Indian Ocean, the Tango Four decided that the troupe needed to invest in a record player so that they could dance all day long. They created "the Onion Club," a fraternity of fun lovers on board that was named after the dozens of crates of onions that had been loaded onto the *Orantes* in Fremantle, Australia. The Onion Club's little phonograph became so popular that on many evenings the regular band was banished to one of the decks below. At each stop, the travelers would buy the latest records of fox trot and tango music, spending hours perfecting their steps. Jim and Iva Thorpe regularly wowed passengers with their mastery of each new dance.

By the time the entourage reached Egypt, nerves were getting a tad frayed. The National Leaguers got so tired of the American Leaguers' barbs about Fred Merkle being a "bonehead" that a near-brawl developed on a dusty soccer field. With the ancient pyramids clearly visible in the distance, cooler heads had to prevail to avoid what would have been an embarrassing international incident that not even *those* reporters, as pliable as they were, could have kept out of the papers. Poor Merkle could never get away from his late-season gaffes in 1908 and 1912. In China earlier in the trip, an American sailor mistook one of the other players for Merkle on a Shanghai street, harassing the fellow about why he'd failed to touch second in that big game against the Cubs five years before. If the American Leaguers were sympathetic toward their pal Fred, they sure didn't show it in Egypt.

As the troupe was nearing Europe, however, a much different issue began percolating: a new baseball league was coming into being in America. One of its first victims would be the man on board who had known Speaker the longest: shipmate Jimmy McAleer.

American League czar Ban Johnson was appalled that McAleer had dismissed Jake Stahl the previous summer. Johnson and Stahl had been pals and confidantes for a long time. (In fact, when Jake died much too young in 1922, Johnson served as one of his pallbearers.) Moreover, McAleer's money-grubbing during the '12 series – done, no doubt, at Johnson's direction – had generated sufficiently bad press in Beantown that Johnson wanted him gone.

Without ever letting Jimmy in on his plan, Johnson found a new combination frontman and sugar daddy – one sure to be deeper-pocketed than McAleer and hopefully more compliant. His name was Joseph Lannin, a native of Quebec who had made millions in New England real estate. Among Lannin's many holdings was the Boston hotel that had employed him as a bellhop when he first emigrated to the United States years before.

The American League needed Lannin's reserves of cash. Suddenly a new threat had emerged to the market dominance of the two major leagues. Industrialist James Gilmore and oilman Harry Sinclair joined other prominent tycoons in bankrolling the Federal League, the only creditable attempt in the last century to establish a third major U.S. league. Johnson needed Lannin's checkbook to keep his stars from jumping to the new outlaw circuit. So Lannin rid himself of his minority piece in the senior circuit's Braves and plunked $200,000 down for a controlling interest in the Red Sox.

McAleer got the news that he was no longer the Red Sox's president in quintessential Ban Johnson fashion: via a tersely worded telegram. Jimmy, who had served Johnson loyally – some would say subserviently – for fourteen years, was completely blindsided; his days as a club owner were finished. The chronically nervous McAleer spent the remaining fifteen years of his life battling what today would probably be diagnosed as alcoholism and clinical depression. In 1931 he committed suicide by shooting himself in the temple.

The Federal League began life as the unassuming Midwestern Federal League, a union with franchises in midsized burgs up and down America's breadbasket. Using Johnson's reformation of the old Western

League as a template, Gilmore, Sinclair, and the other Federal League financiers pursued their no-holds-barred strategy with a vengeance. They knew that ballplayers were fed up with the monopolistic and often devious practices of owners in both leagues. Certain ballplayers couldn't wait to stick it to owners who had treated them with such disdain.

One of the most outspoken critics of baseball's status quo was Tris Speaker. Many an evening on the *Empress* and the *Orantes* – and later the *Lusitania* – had featured Spoke's harangues against the owners' penny-pinching ways – and his hopes that this new league would change all that. Speaker was such a champion of free enterprise in baseball that when the tour reached Paris, he felt obliged to release a statement denying that he was acting as an agent of the Federal League. His buddy Sam Crawford was also said to be one of the Feds' main targets.

Cincinnati's Joe Tinker was the incipient league's first prize, agreeing to join the Chicago Wales as shortstop-manager. The Wales immediately set out to build a state-of-the-art ballpark on the North Side of Chicago. After the Federal League collapsed in 1915, the Cubs took it over and eventually renamed it Wrigley Field. Mordecai Centennial "Three-Finger" Brown, also of the Reds at the time, was the next big name to jump, joining the Federals' St. Louis franchise. Brown was followed quickly by the likes of Hugh Bedient of the Red Sox, who went back home to western New York to pitch for the Buffalo Buffeds. Johnny Evers and Al Bridwell of the Cubs also jumped. Cleveland's Joe Jackson allegedly turned down a Federal League contract of twenty-five thousand dollars per year – more than four times what he was making with the Indians. But that didn't discourage the moneymen from chasing the American League's big triumvirate: Ty Cobb, Walter Johnson, and Tris Speaker.

The Big Train, coming off perhaps his most dominating season – thirty-six wins and a microscopic ERA of 1.09 – supposedly agreed in principle that winter to jump to the Chicago Wales when his contract ended after the 1914 season. But at the eleventh hour, Walter reneged, but only after Clark Griffith received ten thousand dollars in emergency beneficence from Charles Comiskey. Detroit also had to sweeten the ante to keep Cobb from jumping.

The European leg of the global journey was almost anticlimactic. Everyone was exhausted and eager for the trip to end. And the players were anxious to get home to negotiate in earnest to get some of the Federal League's lucre. Besides playing before royalty, the highlight of the European visit came on February 11, when the group was granted an audience with Pope Pius X at the Vatican.

Although their meeting was scheduled at 11:00 a.m., the group decided to don formal evening wear for the occasion. Here's how Elfers describes their attire: "The men wore morning coats and white vests with matching white bow ties. If they had a stovepipe hat, they wore one; others donned black bowlers. To conform to protocol the men were supposed to wear matching headgear, but apparently no two of them had the same taste in chapeaus off the diamond. Instead, most of the men greeted His Holiness bareheaded."

Bareheaded or not, Speaker and the other Protestants who went to the Vatican that day – Sam Crawford among them – came away impressed. Later, they told journalists that their visit to the Vatican was one of the most vivid memories they had of the tour. Most of the Americans with them were Catholic – including all three of the tour's leading lights, Comiskey, McGraw, and Sullivan. The troupe could have heard a pin drop as Pius X assured them that he would bless their future endeavors and travels.

As the ensemble headed west, White Sox manager Jimmy Callahan led a group on a quick side trip to the Emerald Isle. For twenty-five thousand miles around the world, Callahan had been contemptuous of anything that smacked of the despised British – until the gang played in London, when suddenly, to the amusement of his charges, he became awestruck in the presence of royalty. It's doubtful that any of the Protestant "heathen" that Ring Lardner wrote about made the trip to Ireland because that would have involved missing Paris.

The group's sojourn to the City of Lights was full of so much "ooo la la" that virtually no one went to sleep for four days. Grantland Rice was among the American reporters covering the tour's European leg. Rice's "In Gay Paree" serves as a telling glimpse of how the Fourth Estate protected celebrities back in the good old days. It ended:

They told us of London, of gulping down tea.

142

Of royalty there without stint:
They told us what happened in Paris as well –
But I'm not gonna put it in print.

In London, they played before King George V at the Stamford Bridge Grounds in front of some twenty thousand curious Brits. Not all of the exhibitions on tour featured the all-stars playing at their best, but this one did. The "White Sox" won a sparkling 5–4 game that include several outstanding defensive plays. Substitute "Giants" outfielder Lee Magee robbed Speaker of what would have been a homer late in the game. Speaker stared in disbelief when Magee snagged his line drive, then snapped in his harsh Texas baritone: "Yes, you lucky stiff. You tried that grandstand play eleven times on this trip without making it and now you pulled it off before the King!"

On March 6, 1914, the Cunard liner *Lusitania* at last steamed into New York harbor to conclude the final lap of Commy and Muggsy's global adventure. Everyone was happy to be home after five months of touring, but no one was happier than Spoke, because he knew exactly what was going to happen: he would benefit big time from a bidding war between the new Sox ownership and the Federal League. Spoke had promised Commy, Callahan, and the other American League domos on the tour that he wouldn't sign with the Federals until he entertained a competing offer from the Red Sox.

New majority owner Lannin and team vice president John I. Taylor were there with bells on as the boat approached the Hudson River docks. Rumor had it that the Federal League was sending a party of its own to greet the *Lusitania*. The Red Sox syndicate wanted to beat Gilmore and Sinclair to the punch. So they commandeered a customs vessel that was heading toward the *Lusitania* – probably slipping the skipper a few dollars for his trouble. Their gambit worked. The Federal Leaguers were left on the pier as Taylor and Lannin spirited Speaker away. Fingering a contract, Lannin told Speaker he could write his own ticket as long as the terms were "within reason." Speaker shrewdly declined to sign until he had a chance to sit down with the Federal League fellows.

Eventually, Gilmore caught up with Speaker in a suite at New York's Knickerbocker Hotel. A classic dead-ball-era moment thus ensued –

143

about as subtle as a Walter Johnson fastball. Legend has it that Gilmore put fifteen thousand dollars in cold cash in a suitcase and flipped it open. There's more where that came from, Tris was told. The Feds promised a three-year deal with their planned Brooklyn franchise at fifteen thousand dollars per year, plus the largesse in the suitcase as a bonus. Speaker listened politely, made no promises, and then headed off to dinner with Lannin and Taylor. Years later, Speaker confided to Lee Greene that he would have signed with the Feds had they been able to guarantee a multiyear deal. But they couldn't. That night at dinner Spoke must have been the happiest man in Manhattan as he signed a new two-year deal with the Sox for literally double what he had been making. His new salary was a stratospheric eighteen thousand dollars a year – easily the highest in baseball.

"I'm glad to be back in the USA and delighted to be on the Boston payroll again. President Lannin and Vice President Taylor have treated me with great generosity and I would be ungrateful had I not decided to meet them halfway. The Red Sox are a great team, Boston is a great ball town, and it goes without saying that Manager Carrigan will surely have the best that is in me at all times," Speaker said in a statement released to the press that night, sounding perhaps a tad *too* magnanimous. It's instructive that the club felt obliged to add the "it goes without saying" line about Spoke playing his "best" for Carrigan. Maybe word about the Rough-Spoke rivalry was so widespread – not only in Boston but throughout baseball – that Johnson, Lannin, and Taylor wanted to knock down rumors that the two hardheads couldn't coexist.

Spoke wasn't the only Speed Boy smiling that off-season. Virtually overnight, Lannin and Taylor, acting on orders from above, were forced to nearly double the team's payroll. No doubt it made them grind their teeth.

The five-month whirlwind finally came to a close in Chicago in March, where Commy and company were honored with a big parade and banquet.

Spoke must have been exhausted. In the previous twelve months he had played in some two hundred games. The last thing he needed was to work the kinks out. But after an all-too-brief respite in Hubbard, he headed to the Ozarks to do just that.

Speaker's dalliance with the Federal League allowed him to sign a fat contract that made him the envy of every ballplayer in the bigs. But it turned out to be a double-edged sword. Yes, he got his money, but Johnson, Lannin, and Taylor – and probably Carrigan, too – developed a quick case of buyers' remorse, resenting their now-worldly superstar all the more, especially when it became clear in a few months that the Federal League probably wasn't going to survive. Spoke didn't know it, but by inking that contract, he was signing his walking papers with the Red Sox.

It was Rough Carrigan's first spring training as player-manager, and he made some substantial changes. Eliminated was the bizarre daily stroll through the woods, which the players hated. Instead of long workouts, Carrigan put in shorter and crisper sessions that stressed fundamentals. To keep everyone on their toes, Carrigan brought in youngsters from throughout the country. One of them, a rookie named Everett Scott who'd played for St. Paul in 1913, won the shortstop's job. He soon became the most durable middle infielder in the league. Before Lou Gehrig put together his iron man streak, Scott held the Major League record for consecutive games played. The Sox, full of veterans with fat and happy contracts, were definitely playing sharper than they had the year before.

Lack of pitching depth was once again the club's Achilles' heel. Despite the addition of promising rookie right-hander Rankin Johnson, who dueled with and beat Walter Johnson that April, the Sox rotation once again wasn't stout enough to compete with Connie Mack's men. Smoky Joe tried to join the regular rotation but was thwarted by his damaged shoulder.

By midseason the Sox were well behind the A's, struggling to get more than a few games above .500. Their sluggish start was the best thing that could have happened to the Red Sox, because it forced Lannin and Carrigan to look for new sources of pitching. They found a couple of promising young hurlers playing for Jack Dunn, the owner of the International League franchise in Baltimore. Dunn needed a quick infusion of cash because the Federal League had moved a franchise into Baltimore and located it literally across the street from his Orioles. His gate receipts had plummeted. So he was auctioning his two prized pitching prospects – a right-hander from North Carolina named Ernie Shore and a left-hander from Baltimore named George Herman Ruth – to the highest bidder. It took some twenty-five thousand dollars of the former hotel bellhop's cash to consummate the deal.

Shore was considered the big prize – a broad-shouldered, beefy right-hander who could help the Sox right away. Ruth was a lesser-known quantity; Lannin and Carrigan considered him something of a gamble. Dunn had originally approached Connie Mack about acquiring Ruth. Mack didn't want to spend that kind of money on an unproven kid. The Sox immediately put Shore into the rotation and gave Ruth a start or two before sending him down to Providence for some more seasoning.

On July 11, 1914, the man destined to forever change baseball – and with it, the *zeitgeist* of popular culture in the twentieth century – walked into Fenway Park for the first time. Babe Ruth started against the Indians that day, holding them to five meager hits through six innings before tiring in the seventh and giving way to Dutch Leonard. T. H. Murnane captured the Babe's debut in the *Globe*: "The giant left-hander, who proved a natural ballplayer and went through his act like a veteran of many wars. He has a natural delivery, fine control and a curveball that bothers the batsmen, but has room for improvement and will undoubtedly become a fine pitcher under the care of manager Carrigan."

There was also room for improvement in Ruth's clubhouse deportment. He was a brash and cocksure teenager "only lightly brushed by the social veneer we call civilization," in Harry Hooper's wonderful phrase. Ruth wasn't about to defer to the crusty veterans on the Sox. He insisted on taking batting practice before games – a luxury not usually accorded a rookie pitcher. Speaker, Wood, and company gave the wild child plenty of lip – and the Baltimore prodigy lipped right back.

Behind his back, they sniggered that Ruth was a "big baboon." When the clubhouse hazing got more confrontational, Ruth challenged everybody to put up or shut up. His teammates took a look at Ruth's strapping body and – wisely – chose the latter course. Eventually, the worst of the hazing stopped. But the Masons in the Sox clubhouse were appalled at Ruth's personal hygiene and a lifestyle that careened from saloon to cathouse and back again. "[Ruth] would go after a snake if he thought it was female," Joe Wood chuckled in 1963.

Ernie Shore roomed with Ruth for a time in 1915 and complained to the skipper about Ruth's crude behavior. "Mr. Carrigan, I can't live with that man Ruth," George Sullivan relates in his history of the Sox.

"I thought you were friends," Carrigan responded.

"We are," Shore replied, "but there's a place where friendship stops. A man wants some privacy in the bathroom. Just this morning, I told him he was using my toothbrush, and he said, 'That's o.k. I'm not particular.'"

Speaker had run wild on Hubbard's streets as a kid. But "wild" doesn't begin to describe Ruth's upbringing on the far meaner streets of Baltimore. His parents ran a saloon near the wharves that attracted a rough clientele. They didn't have a clue about how to raise their wayward son. He was sneaking smokes at age eight and guzzling beer and whiskey not long after. Baltimore's other street urchins loved him because he could steal money from his folks' till and show them a good time.

Ruth loved being called "Jidge," which was New England shorthand for "George." Not even the presence of other ballplayers' wives, though, could get Jidge to behave. He was partying with some teammates and their spouses one afternoon in a restaurant early in his career when he abruptly stood up and announced, "I've got to take a piss." As Ruth made his way down the hallway, a horrified teammate grabbed him and admonished, "My God, Jidge! You don't use a word like that when there's women around." "What word?" Ruth queried. "'Piss,' for Christ's sake. If you have to say that, say 'urinate.'"

As writer Robert Smith recounts in *Baseball in the Afternoon*, "In due time, suitably schooled, Babe returned [to the restaurant table], penitent, and declared, 'Jeez, I'm sorry! I oughtn't to have said that. I ought to have said urinate!'"

Almost everything about him offended Speaker and Wood – and they weren't alone. The Babe was, in a word, porcine. His culinary habits in Hot Springs or Beantown or anyplace else didn't always require him to use actual eating utensils. Ruth's decadent ways got so bad that Carrigan had no choice but to take Ruth on as a roommate and put him on a daily stipend that Ruth routinely blew through.

Jealousy was surely one of the reasons that Wood and Speaker took an instant dislike to Babe. Even at Ruth's precocious age, perceptive baseball men like Smoky Joe and Spoke could see Jidge's preternatural talent. Although his pitching mechanics were still unrefined, his fastball crackled and his curve snapped. Back then, his hitting was erratic, but every now and again he'd catch one during batting practice or a game, sending the ball into Fenway crannies not normally visited by mortals. One afternoon early in the '15 season, after insisting on a long session in the batting cage, Ruth returned to the clubhouse to find all of his bats sawed in half. He suspected but couldn't prove that Speaker was the culprit. Ruth must have irked Speaker no end. Spoke prided himself on having the best all-around skills of anyone in the game. And now this snot-nosed kid from Baltimore was threatening to usurp all that. Even years later, when it became evident to *everyone* who followed the game that Ruth needed to play every day, Spoke refused to acknowledge Ruth's hitting prowess. Upon Babe's trade to New York, Spoke offered his infamous analysis that the Yankees were making a big mistake in taking Ruth off the mound.

Wood, too, felt threatened by Ruth. Babe, after all, was competing for a spot in what was fast becoming a crowded rotation for the Sox. It must have annoyed Wood to see this rubber-armed kid effortlessly throwing fastballs and curves when Smoky Joe's shoulder throbbed every time he drew his arm back. While warming up before a game in 1915, Wood asked Ruth to toss him a ball that had gotten loose. Instead, the Babe played the clown, allowing the ball to roll through his bowed legs. For some reason, that moment caused Wood to snap. Carrigan had to intervene to keep the two from coming to blows. Smoky Joe and the Babe ceased speaking. To show solidarity with his roommate, Spoke basically gave Ruth the silent treatment, too. The Speaker-Ruth relationship remained chilly over the decades and never thawed completely. In later years, Ruth was always quick to acknowledge Spoke's greatness. But Spoke was reticent about praising Ruth too much.

The future phenom did well at Providence, helping the Grays secure the International League pennant. With just a few days left in the regular season, Ruth was brought back up to the Sox, along with another player destined to dog Speaker, a prickly right-handed pitching prospect named Carl Mays.

Skipper Carrigan got the ship righted during 1914 – but still couldn't stop it from being swamped by the A's. Connie's men won 99 games in a 152-game season. Rough's boys won 91, but finished well ahead of the third-place Senators. Ernie Shore vindicated Lannin and Carrigan's faith in him by going 9-4 after arriving from Baltimore in midseason. Dutch Leonard's ERA of 1.01 remains the lowest in Major League history for any pitcher with a minimum of 150 innings.

Spoke had another solid season in 1914, despite what must have been his exhaustion from the world tour. As almost always, he led the league in put-outs and double plays from the outfield. But his batting average "dipped" to .338 – a statistic not lost on Lannin and his bean counters, two of whom happened to be Lannin's sons. Spoke's forty-six doubles still led the league, however. In all, he had sixty-four extra-base hits – a handsome number in the dead-ball era. Still, the perception in the owner's box was that Spoke had slipped from his 1912 pedestal.

His fellow Golden Outfielders, Hooper and Lewis, had less than spectacular seasons by their standards. Duffy hit .279 with 79 RBIs and Harry batted an indifferent .258.

Ed Walton and other Red Sox historians believe that, by 1914, Speaker's abrasive personality had taken its toll. Speaker was never the easiest guy to get along with. Tris was a "showman" in center field who loved to get the crowd riled up, Harry Hooper's son John said in a 2004 interview. After making a running catch in right center to end an inning, Spoke would flip the ball to Hooper – a gesture that Mrs. Hooper always thought arrogant, John told Peter Golenbock years ago. Harry's son, now in his eighties, also told Golenbock that, with his dad at first base, Speaker would deliberately swing at bad pitches to spoil what would have been easy steals of second for Harry. "Another time, I remember Pop saying that the team got into a slump, and the manager changed the batting order, and put Pop in third place and batted Speaker first. After the first game, Speaker said, 'That will be all of that stuff, or else,' " recalled John. Historian Harold Seymour suggests that the Golden Outfield was rife with dissension – not only between Lewis and Speaker, but between Spoke and Cat, too.

What made 1914 difficult for the Sox to swallow was the astonishing success of their crosstown rival, the "Miracle Braves" of Rabbit Maranville. The Braves' second-half surge brought them from last to first in less than two months. They won a remarkable fifty-two of their final sixty-six games. And they did much of their damage in the friendly confines of Fenway Park. Lannin agreed to lend the National League club his park the final six weeks of the regular season, plus the World Series against the A's, making a few extra shekels for both clubs.

For the second time in three years, Fenway hosted a World Series. And once again, the Series was plagued by allegations of corruption and gambling run amok. The heavily favored A's, with one of the finest pitching staffs in history, went down in four straight. Chief Bender, who'd had a brilliant regular season, winning seventeen games against only three losses, got hammered so badly in the first game – à la Joe Wood in 1912's seventh game – that it may have propelled Connie Mack to break up the A's after the season ended. The A's potent bats also went suspiciously quiet against the Braves. Their Athletics had appeared in four of the previous five World Series, but that didn't stop Mack and the Shibe brothers from thoroughly dismantling them.

The Braves continued to rent Fenway for another half season until their new field was completed. The extra revenue helped Lannin compensate for the losses inflicted by the Federal League. Despite the extra cash, it must have rankled Carrigan and Lannin to see Boston's pedestrian "other franchise" become the toast of New England. They vowed to make 1915 different.

Like their predecessors three years earlier, the 1915 Red Sox started indifferently but got much tougher as the year progressed. They had to, because hot on their heels were the rejuvenated Tigers of Hughie Jennings, plus Commy's Pale Hose, which had begun to establish the nucleus that would secure two World Series berths in future years. The White Sox dominated the first half of the schedule before fading a bit in August and September.

Carrigan's club won 101 games that year, fighting Hughie, Ty, and Wahoo Sam tooth and nail for the pennant. Pitching was the key. The new acquisitions – Shore, Mays, and Ruth – won a combined forty-one games. Bantamweight Rube Foster won nineteen games, four more than Dutch Leonard. Throwing through excruciating pain, Joe Wood won fifteen games that season. Wood was so desperate to cure his shoulder ailment that he was willing to listen to anyone – whether or not they had a legitimate degree to practice medicine. One "doctor" would urge him to throw as hard as he could; the next would prescribe long rest. That season, Smoky Joe often had to wait so long between pitches to let the pain subside that fans would audibly count off the time. Harry Hooper always called Wood's performance in 1915 the grittiest he'd ever seen.

In late May Lannin picked up future Hall of Fame pitcher Herb Pennock on waivers from the penny-pinching A's, solidifying an already formidable staff. Speaker suffered the worst beaning of his career that spring, which caused him to miss several games. Shortstop Everett Scott was spiked by Cobb and missed some games. And Heinie Wagner, moved to second to accommodate Scott, battled a sore arm most of the season. Around the first of July, though, Lannin and Carrigan again took advantage of Connie Mack's fire sale, acquiring Jack Barry from the A's for eight thousand dollars. Barry was a popular Boston native who had starred in both baseball and basketball at Holy Cross. After Carrigan installed him at second in place of Wagner, the club swept three straight doubleheaders in as many days.

That summer, Spoke made a play at League Park in Cleveland so spectacular that it dazed denizens of the bleachers and the press box. A Boston paper recounted that:

> It was the eighth inning Tuesday at Cleveland. The score stood three all and [Joe] Jackson, the speed man of the Naps, was on second base. Griggs singled to centre and the game seemed sure. Then 'Spoke' Speaker dashed in, grabbed the ball on the run and made a perfect throw to Catcher Cady, cutting off Jackson. For a moment there was silence. Then suddenly appreciation surged like a wave over a thousand fans, and the stands rang with cheers for an alien player.

In July the Sox won thirteen out of twenty on a long road trip. Wood won the gutty first game of a big four-game match-up against the White Sox in Chicago. But the real highlight of the trip was an enormous home run smacked by Babe Ruth in St. Louis. Ruth's towering shot defined all of his mammoth homers to come, departing Sportsman's Park before bouncing onto Grand Avenue, leaving Browns fans dumbfounded. It would be years before the Grand Avenue feat would be duplicated again in St. Louis.

In late August Jennings and Cobb hosted the Red Sox for a crucial series at Navin Field. Even by his loathsome standards, Cobb behaved obnoxiously in Detroit, trying to provoke a fight after being thrown out on the base paths and deliberately inciting the crowd. At one point he planted a young man wearing a straw boater directly behind home plate and ordered him to wave his hat to distract Boston's pitchers. Carrigan's men didn't allow themselves to be intimidated. They lost only five of their last twenty-nine games.

The pivotal game for the Sox came on September 20 before nearly forty thousand frenzied fans at Fenway. Ernie Shore and Tiger ace Harry Coveleskie hooked up in a twelve-inning shutout thriller that wasn't decided until Detroit's Sam Crawford and Marty Kavanaugh made base-running gaffes in extra innings. In the bottom of the twelfth, manager Carrigan inserted pinch hitter Carrigan, who singled sharply, plating Duffy Lewis with the winning run. The Boston papers described it as "the greatest game of ball ever played in this city."

Earlier in that same series, Cobb again incited an overflow crowd, drawing taunts from Boston fans. A photograph taken at the end of the game shows Cobb engulfed by hostile fans in center field as he navigated his way to the visitors' clubhouse. Baseball narrowly averted a Fenway riot that could have been as disastrous as the one three years before.

In the postseason, the Sox would play the Philadelphia Phillies, who had won their first-ever National League pennant with a late-season surge over the defending champion Braves. So for the second year in a row, squads from Philadelphia and Boston would appear in the Series – but this time, the league affiliations were flip-flopped. And for the second year running, Boston's teams would flip stadiums. Lannin arranged for the Sox to borrow the larger and brand-new Braves Field for the postseason. The park's more spacious proportions were said to favor the Sox's Golden Outfield.

Philly was led by its slugging right-fielder, another dead-ball-era player whose name was so evocative it sounds made up. Clifford Carlton "Gavvy" Cravath, the pride of Escondido, California, bashed an unheard-of twenty-four home runs that season, muscling his way to a hefty 115 RBIs. Sweet-swinging first sacker Fred Luderus and his .315 batting average anchored an otherwise undistinguished infield. Dead-ball stalwart Dode Paskert manned center, with journeyman Beals Becker in left. Georgian Erskine Mayer was one of two aces in the Phillies rotation, winning twenty-one games that year. The Phillies' other ace, though, bested Mayer by ten games, the first of three consecutive years he would win thirty or more games. His name was Grover Cleveland Alexander and he would go on to lead the National League in victories six times in a twenty-year career that landed him in Cooperstown.

"Pete" Alexander was, like Sam Crawford, a product of the Nebraska prairie. But Alexander's upbringing lacked the stability of Sam's family life in Wahoo. Pete's parents weren't the genial proprietors of a general store. They were hardscrabble farmers barely able to make ends meet. His dad was a hard drinker – as was his father before him.

Pete wasn't exactly a prodigy in the low minors. While playing for Galesburg in the Central Association in 1909, he took a relay throw directly to the noggin while trying to break up a double play. He didn't regain consciousness for two full days, awaking with severe double vision that didn't go away for weeks. The Syracuse Chiefs of the International League eventually took a chance on Pete once his vision cleared. Their gamble paid off – and Syracuse sold him to the Phillies for $750.

He first arrived in Philadelphia in 1911, where he made his presence known by winning twenty-eight games his rookie season. By 1915 he had replaced Christy Mathewson as the dominant right-hander in the senior circuit. He led the league that year in both ERA and winning percentage. In fact, his 1.22 ERA that year has been surpassed in NL history only by Bob Gibson's 1.12 in 1968 and the otherwise obscure Freddie Schupp's 0.90 in 1916. In 1917 Pete joined Matty as the only pitcher in the twentieth century to have won thirty games or more three years in a row. The next year, 1916, he shut teams out no fewer than sixteen times, which will remain a Major League record well into perpetuity. All told, he threw ninety shutouts in his career, another mark not likely to be challenged in any immediate lifetime to come. For a guy who squandered so much energy off the field, he never wasted any of it on the field. He had an efficient and effortless windup. A three-quarter delivery followed a short stride: "The ball seemed to emerge from his shirtfront," one observer said. He could change speeds on both his fastball and his curve and could hit the outside corner at will.

What makes Alexander's achievements all the more remarkable is that he pitched half his games in the tiny Baker Bowl, a ball yard whose right-field porch was a mere 272 feet away from hitters. Alexander battled alcoholism his whole life and epilepsy most of it. His drinking problems were so well chronicled that even Hollywood felt comfortable in depicting them. Actor Ronald Reagan's portrayal of Alexander in *The Winning Team* (with a comely Doris Day as his love interest) was mainly hokum, because Pete didn't triumph over his problems in the end. Instead, his dependence on gin worsened and his life after the Cardinals and Phillies cut him adrift in 1931 bordered on the pathetic. He bounced around in lesser leagues and then grew a beard to pitch for a House of David team and a couple of other barnstorming outfits. He kept on pitching into his fifties.

The '15 Series triggered excitement up and down the East Coast. Scalpers were selling three-dollar tickets for as much as forty bucks a throw – almost the clip of the classic '12 Series. Some three hundred Royal Rooters trained down from Boston – not quite the showing three years earlier when they paraded through Manhattan, but still a fine turnout, considering the increased distance. Megaphones and pennants in hand, McGreevey and mates made an incredible racket in the tiny Baker Bowl. Inclement weather delayed the start of the Series for several days. Nervous officials dictated that a game would be played on October 8, no matter what. So the grounds crew at the Baker Bowl elected to "dry" the field by dousing it with gasoline and setting it ablaze. Fans arriving early for the game were treated to the noxious smell of smoke. Despite the crew's best efforts, the field remained a muddy mess for most of the Series.

Temporary stands were erected in left and center in the Baker Bowl, making an already cozy park even smaller. The Sox and the Phils agreed to an unprecedented ground rule: any hit ball that bounced into the crowd gathered in temporary seating or standing areas would be counted as a home run. Three years earlier, the Giants and the Sox had deemed such plays ground-rule doubles.

Alexander, of course, got the nod for the Phillies in game one, hooking up with Ernie Shore. The Phils drew first blood when Dode Paskert's flare fell in front of Harry Hooper, who was vainly trying to gain some traction through the muck. A bunt and a scratch infield hit later and the Phillies led, 1–0.

It stayed that way until the top of the eighth when Spoke walked, advanced to second on an error, and was driven home by Duffy's clutch single. Dode Paskert then speared Larry Gardner's long drive to center, which kept the Sox from having a big inning.

Gavvy Cravath drove in the Phillies' go-ahead run in the eighth with a smash up the middle that Scott was able to glove, but Milt Stock scored. It would prove to be Gavvy's only RBI of the Series. Babe Ruth was put into the game as a pinch hitter in the ninth but lined out. Cat Hooper followed Ruth with a fly out and the game was over. Not-so-Old Pete had scattered eight hits and allowed only Speaker to score.

In the overwrought language of the day, *Boston American* reporter N. J. Flatley crafted this lead for his account of game one:

> While a genial sun beamed down on a soggy field, while 20,000 fans – you couldn't get any more into that tiny Philly park with a shoe horn – howled every time the great Grover Cleveland Alexander lifted his mighty right arm, while the Boston Royal Rooters shook high heaven with their yelling as Ernie Shore, stout hearted as a lion, turned back the champions of the National League inning after inning, the world series of 1915 was initiated today. The goddess of fortune smiles, in fact she must have laughed, on the cause of the Morans, and the Red Sox were beaten 3 to 1, to the everlasting delight of the Philadelphia part of the assembled 20,000, more or less.

The actual turnstile count was 19,343, generating receipts in excess of fifty thousand dollars – good money for a tiny ballpark.

Game two, October 9, 1915, was also in Philadelphia and also played under overcast skies. President Woodrow Wilson, nicely turned out in a navy greatcoat, threw out the first pitch. He and his soon-to-be-bride, Edith Galt, a baseball devotee, enjoyed the entire game from box seats next to the Phillies' dugout that had been "nattily decked out" in bunting and small silk flags. "The President was a little bit late appearing on the scene," Flatley reported, "and the game had to be held up for five minutes while the guests of honor were being seated and responding to the roaring salute of the 20,000 watchers."

Wilson, the first sitting president ever to witness a World Series game, watched Carrigan send little Rube Foster to the mound – and the Oklahoman proceeded to pitch the game of his life, facing only three batters more than the minimum. The Sox jumped on Phillies starter Erskine

Mayer in the top of the first. Hooper coaxed a walk, then ended up on third when Speaker singled. The two Speed Boys attempted a little base-running larceny, with Speaker luring a throw from the catcher down to second to allow Cat to race home. The ploy almost backfired when Speaker was tagged out by Phils second baseman Bert Niehoff and Niehoff's throw back to the dish beat Hooper's slide. Catcher Ed Burns "dropped the sphere," Flatley noted, "and thereby started a storm of Boston cheering."

The score remained 1–0 until the fifth, when Cravath doubled between Lewis and Speaker. Gavvy scored a moment later when Fred Luderus followed with his own double to right-center. Rough elected to keep Rube in the game, which proved fortuitous: Foster's two-out single in the top of the ninth plated Larry Gardner with what proved to be the winning run.

Speaker made a nice running catch earlier in the game that probably induced polite applause from the president's box. But that grab paled in comparison to the one Spoke made to save the game – and with it, the Series. With Foster still on the mound and the Sox protecting a 2–1 lead, the Phillies got a runner to second with two outs. It could have been two base runners for the Phils after Foster hit Milt Stock with a pitch. But to his credit, home plate umpire Cy Rigler ruled that Stock had failed to make a legitimate effort to get out the way and was not entitled to a free base. The next Phillie to dig in at the plate was George Henry Paskert, a classic dead-ball journeyman who toiled for four different clubs in a fifteen-year career. "Dode," as he was universally known, was a dangerous right-handed hitter who had learned to drive a ball the opposite way at Baker Bowl, the better to take advantage of the short right-field porch. Paskert sent a Foster pitch exactly that direction. It looked for all the world like Paskert had hit a game-winning two-run homer that even today would be celebrated as one of the clutch postseason clouts in Major League history. Speaker had other ideas.

As recounted in George Sullivan's *Picture History of the Boston Red Sox*, "Paskert stroked a screecher that appeared ticketed for the temporary bleachers in center. But Tris Speaker galloped back and lunged desperately at the last instant to snare the ball before it went into the customers' laps" – an account corroborated by Flatley, the *New York Times*' John Foster, and other reporters. It must have been a surreal moment, with the crowd roaring, then groaning, then stunned into silence, then politely applauding out of respect for both the catch and for the presence of the president of the United States, who himself was standing to acknowledge the play as the Sox pounded Speaker on the back on their way off the field.

Flatley went with the political motif for his lead that day:

> President Woodrow Wilson was out this afternoon watching the series and naturally Bill Carrigan's Democrats had to win the battle for the greater honor and glory of the dear old party. The Carrigan Democrats defeated the Republican Philadelphians 2 to 1 in a game that was full of flight and fireworks. . . . George [Foster] did enough in the course of the hectic afternoon to make him forever loved and respected by the Democrats in the broad land. Of course, his name will be anathema in Pennsylvania, but that's Republican anyhow, so it doesn't make much difference.

For game three, the teams moved to Boston and Braves Field. Unlike 1912, there was actually a rest day. Dutch Leonard started for the Bosox while Pete Alexander handled pitching duties on just two days' rest for the Phillies. The Phils broke through against Leonard with a run in the third when Dave Bancroft drove home Ed Burns. That was it for the Phils: Leonard held them hitless the rest of the way, retiring the last twenty batters in a row.

Speaker, whose World Series legacy is steeped in clutch triples, did it again in the fourth, when he bashed an Alexander offering into the distant reaches of Braves Field. A sacrifice fly drove Spoke home.

The game stayed knotted, 1–1, until the bottom of the ninth. Hooper started the rally with a lead-off single. Scott sacrificed him to second, then Alexander intentionally walked Speaker. Duffy Lewis now dug in against Old Pete. Lewis had Alexander's number: he'd already had four hits against him in the Series. The fifth instantly followed, a solid line drive into center that easily scored Cat with the winning run. It was the seminal moment of Duffy's career. "The crowd came out of the stands, over the fences and they carried me off. They were so excited that they almost broke my back," Duffy recalled years later.

Carrigan ticked off Ruth by sending Ernie Shore to the mound for game four. "What about me, Bill?" the Babe supposedly wailed to Carrigan, according to George Sullivan. "What does a guy have to do to get a chance to pitch a World Series game for your club?" But Rough knew what he was doing: Shore pitched beautifully, holding the Phils to one run. Lewis was again the Sox's hero, doubling in the deciding run in the bottom of the sixth. The Phils' only run in another 2–1 loss came when, in glaring sunshine, Cravath's gap shot took an odd hop and skipped past Speaker for a triple.

The weary players piled onto a train to whisk them back to Philadelphia that evening. They were due back at the Baker Bowl the next day, with Foster and Mayer set to reprise their match-up in game two. Another one-run gem emerged that afternoon – but this one with more offensive action. The stars were Spoke's mates in the Golden Outfield: Duffy and Cat. Hooper, hardly a power hitter, became the first player in history to hit two homers in the same World Series game. Each of Harry's round-trippers were ground-rule jobs – line drives that bounced into the temporary field boxes in center. Harry's second homer came in the top of the ninth and broke a 4–4 tie. It marked the first time in Series history that the eventual winning run was scored by a homer. His pal Duffy had hit an equally clutch homer in the top of the eighth that tied the score. Duffy's homer, unlike Cat's, actually cleared the traditional fence in the outfield.

Years later Fred Lieb decided to cheapen Hooper's accomplishments, calling his two long balls in the deciding game "Chinese home runs" and deriding the notion of Hooper as the game's hero. It's true, neither of Harry's shots was titanic. But it hadn't been Hooper's idea to change the ground rules. All Harry could do was put the ball in play and try to hit 'em where they weren't. The fact that his balls happened to carry into the temporary bleachers surely wasn't calculated on Harry's part. Harry deserved the hero's mantle.

As the emotional Flatley put it, "Harry's drive was just what was needed to break up a 4–4 tie that had resulted from the widest and woolliest game of ball ever seen in a world series and win the fray that made each Red Sox some $3779 richer. The title snatched by the Braves a year ago remains in Boston, though the Morans made a valiant effort to bring back to the sacred haunts of Old Bill Penn the big honors of the national game."

The ghost of old Bill Penn didn't care about the 1915 World Series. But the tender ego of young Babe Ruth did. The prodigy from Baltimore only appeared in the Series once as a pinch hitter. Spoke and Smoky Joe must have taken not inconsiderable satisfaction from Ruth's frustrations – because Babe let Carrigan and anyone else who would listen know just how unhappy he was. Boston's pitching rotation was so deep that the left-handed kid wasn't needed.

The Golden Outfield had never been more lustrous. Hooper hit .350 for the Series – scoring four of the Sox's total of twelve runs. Duffy hit .444, driving in five runs. "He and I," Duffy said later, referring to Hooper, "we had a hell of a Series." Speaker, for his part, hit a clutch .294 and made several outstanding plays in center.

Connie Mack declared the '15 edition of the Sox to be superior to the '12 team. Many years later, while being jointly interviewed, Ty Cobb and Babe Ruth agreed that the 1915 Red Sox were the finest defensive team they'd ever seen. Ruth marveled that the pitching staff never needed more than a "run or two" to win a game. And Cobb volunteered, "On defense, I don't believe that club ever had an equal. [They'd] get off to a 2–1 lead and hold on like grim death. Time after time, we'd think we had a rally going in the late innings only to have 'Scottie' [Everett Scott, the shortstop] or Gardner come up with great stops, or Spoke, or Duffy, or Hooper pull one of those circus catches in the outfield."

The fact that the Sox won the World Series relatively easily without using Ruth, Wood, or Herb Pennock in their rotation wasn't lost on Ban Johnson or Joe Lannin. Johnson, never reticent about moving players from franchise to franchise to reward loyalty and fatten his own wallet, concluded that the Sox were so loaded that they could afford to lose a star or two. And Lannin, like all owners before or since, was looking to cut payroll.

Tris Speaker didn't know it, but when he walked off the Baker Bowl field, gamboling with Duffy and Cat, it was his last official moment in the uniform of the Boston Red Sox.

Early Years in Cleveland

His coming has given a number of other members of the team the one thing they lacked, confidence. Speaker is as necessary to the Cleveland club as a spark plug to an automobile. — Fielder Jones, *Cleveland Press*

Like many divorces, Tris Speaker's separation from the Boston Red Sox in 1916 turned ugly. As his salary talks stalled, Spoke, at least in public, handled himself with a modicum of dignity – which is more than can be said of Red Sox majority owner Joseph Lannin, whose public utterances got nastier as the stalemate wore on.

Now that the threat of the Federal League had disappeared, Ban Johnson and his skinflint owners wanted to return to the shameless old days when players were paid a pittance. Stars like Speaker, who'd gotten big money because of competition from the new league, were told to take a big haircut or hit the highway. Speaker, to his credit, fought back and tried to negotiate a decent wage – but the Sox wanted none of it.

Acting on orders from Johnson, Lannin that winter demanded in writing that Speaker take a 50 percent salary cut. When Speaker, in Hubbard for the off-season, initially received the contract proposal, he wrote back to the club and asked if the nine-thousand-dollar figure were a typographical error. It wasn't. Lannin was soon saying in private and public that such a drastic reduction was justified because Speaker's offensive production had waned. His batting average, Lannin pointed out, had dipped from .365 in 1913 to .338 in 1914 to .322 in 1915. In response, Speaker pointed out there was no drop-off in the number of runs he was scoring, nor had there been any decline in the quality of his defensive play, where he continued to lead the league in put-outs and double plays and near the top in assists. Spoke countered by asking for a salary of fifteen thousand dollars per year – still a 17 percent cut from his 1914 and 1915 pay but more than he'd earned prior to 1914. According to certain published accounts, Speaker reduced his demand to twelve thousand dollars as spring neared.

Johnson and Lannin wouldn't budge – so Speaker conducted a hold-out, repeating his strategy of four years earlier. The Red Sox team that assembled in Hot Springs in March 1916 was flush, with more genuine stars top to bottom than any team of that generation. Johnson and Lannin knew it – and more importantly, they knew that Speaker knew it. The potentates not only wanted to save a few bucks, they wanted to cuff Speaker around. Johnson and Lannin resented the way Speaker had manipulated the Federal League offer two years before and wanted to knock him down a few pegs.

Slimy misrepresentation wasn't beneath Lannin, either. Journalist Mike Sowell asserts that the Red Sox organization began spreading innuendo that Spoke had adopted a "baseball age" and was in fact five years older – a player not in the prime of his career at twenty-seven or twenty-eight, but someone approaching the twilight of his career at thirty-two or thirty-three. It's unknown whether the prematurely gray ballplayer ever felt obliged to produce his birth certificate or a census record to prove his 1888 birth date. Lannin's canard wormed its way into more than a few articles about Speaker over the years – and is still the subject of Internet chatter today.

Carrigan may also have grown weary of Speaker's confrontational demeanor in the clubhouse. Publicly, Rough said all the right things about wanting Speaker back in the fold. But his deliberations with Lannin behind closed doors may have been different. Rough had the luxury of two other great outfielders. If needed, Harry Hooper certainly had the moxie to play center.

Lannin that winter was, probably not coincidentally, also squeezing Speaker's best pal and fellow Mason, Joe Wood. The Sox owner wanted Wood to take the same 50 percent cut he was offering Speaker. When Wood told the press that he wouldn't play "for such a measly salary" (five thousand dollars), Lannin retorted that he was paying only for "Wood's measly victories in 1914 and 1915" – coldly ignoring the fact that Wood had pitched through excruciating pain. Smoky Joe retreated to his farm in the Pocono Mountains and spent the year plotting his future in the game.

At the American League owners' meeting in New York that February, rumors began to circulate that Lannin was in serious negotiations with Col. Jacob Ruppert and Col. Tillinghast L'Hommedieu Huston of the New York Yankees to sell or trade the Sox's star "centre" fielder, as it was often spelled back then. The speculation was reported in the press, reaching a crescendo a week or so before Opening Day. "Tris Speaker to Yankees if Magnates Agree as to Terms," a *Washington Post* headline blared on April 7.

By the time the *Post* article appeared, Tris had been back with the Sox for two weeks. Without signing a contract, he agreed to report to Hot Springs on March 24. Not many ballplayers in history have been compensated on a per diem arrangement, but Tris Speaker essentially was in late March and early April of 1916. Carrigan told Speaker to hang in until the team reached Boston for the start of the regular season. A compromise with Lannin could be reached then, Rough told Spoke, no doubt at the behest of the Sox owner. Speaker's second holdout in four years irritated certain members of the club. In *Red Sox Triumphs and Tragedies*, Ed Walton suggests that a faction of teammates had tired of Speaker's arrogance and was openly rooting for the team to unload him.

The trade talks with the Yankees must have disintegrated, because Lannin issued a statement the next day denying that they were ever serious. What Lannin didn't volunteer to the press on April 8 is that he had been secretly meeting with none other than Robert McRoy, the Ban Johnson sycophant and former Red Sox treasurer who now had taken over as general manager for the new ownership syndicate of the Cleveland Indians. McRoy, the man who sold the Royal Rooters' seats out from under them in the 1912 Series, was now dickering to bring the game's best center fielder to the lowly Cleveland franchise – undoubtedly with Ban Johnson's assent. Johnson almost certainly manipulated the whole scenario – including the "collapse" of trade discussions with the Yankees. The AL czar a few weeks before had arranged for Chicago contractor James Dunn to purchase the Cleveland club when Ban's financial angel, Charles Somers, ran into cash-flow difficulties. Johnson helped Dunn secure $200,000 in loans to acquire the franchise. Now he wanted to reward Dunn for his troubles. Ban had long sought to make Cleveland one of the stronger franchises in the league and was upset that it had hit rock bottom.

Speaker knew nothing about the Johnson-Lannin-McRoy Cleveland machinations. In fact, certain things Lannin told Spoke privately on April 8 encouraged him to think that a deal could be worked out to keep him in Boston. His uncertain contractual status didn't hurt Spoke's performance on the field. On April 9, in the last exhibition game of the season at Ebbets Field in Brooklyn, Tris smashed a ninth-inning home run off of Rube Marquard to win the game for the Sox. As Lee Greene told the story in his posthumous (1960) profile of Speaker in *Sport Magazine*: "Lannin was waiting in the clubhouse. He threw his arms around Speaker's shoulders. 'Great stuff, Spoke!' he shouted. 'You win. We'll sign when we get to Boston tomorrow.' "

Tris returned to his hotel room in Brooklyn convinced that the stalemate had finally been broken and that he'd stay with the Sox. When the phone in his room rang and Robert McRoy of the Cleveland club was at the other end, asking to come up to see him, Tris didn't understand what it meant. According to Greene, when McRoy opened the conversation by asking Spoke if he'd like to come and play for Cleveland, Speaker "looked him straight in the eye and said, 'Frankly, I wouldn't. Not under any circumstances. You've got a bad ball club and you're in a bad baseball town. I played on a pennant winner last year. Why would I want to come to a seventh-place club?' "

When McRoy countered by informing Speaker that he was now the property of the Cleveland franchise, Spoke supposedly snapped, "That's crazy! I talked to Lannin only a few hours ago and he told me he was ready to sign a contract!" McRoy told Speaker that Jim Dunn had consummated the deal with Lannin over the telephone minutes after the Sox-Dodger game had ended. The Sox were receiving two players and some fifty-five thousand dollars in cash from Cleveland, McRoy explained.

Spoke then pleaded with McRoy not to announce the deal or everyone would look foolish if he refused to report to Cleveland. A few moments later, Speaker heard the afternoon newsboys shouting from the street below that the great Tris Speaker had been sent to Cleveland in a blockbuster deal: "Speaker traded to Cleveland! Read all about it!" Somehow Lannin had gotten the news out to the wires in time for late afternoon deadlines, which suggests that the owner was either dishonest when he greeted Speaker in the clubhouse, or that Ban Johnson had done

Lannin's dirty work while the Sox owner had been at Ebbets Field, or most likely a combination of the two scenarios.

Greene maintains that Spoke immediately told McRoy that he wanted ten thousand dollars of the purchase price or he wouldn't report to Cleveland. Other reports suggest that Speaker didn't begin negotiating for a percentage of the purchase price until he arrived in Cleveland a couple of days later.

Either way, Spoke moved swiftly to get his side of the story out. The next day's *New York Times* had a story headlined: "Speaker Has Not Agreed – May Not Go to Cleveland: Seeks Explanation from Lannin." The star "centre" fielder gave reporters a thoughtful and measured statement:

> There is no need of my stating that this deal was a complete surprise to me. As I understood it, Mr. Lannin and I had practically agreed upon terms. I shall see Mr. Lannin tomorrow forenoon and look for an explanation. I have not signed any contract with the Cleveland Club yet, although I believe that as far as I am concerned, the Boston Club no longer has me on its list. Whether I shall go to Cleveland remains to be seen. Everything depends upon my interview with Mr. Lannin.

Oh, to have been a fly on the wall when the hotheaded Texan sat down with the man who had flung his arms around him the day before, then betrayed him minutes later! Speaker emerged looking "downcast," according to the *Times*. He matter-of-factly announced that he would be leaving for Cleveland on the 11:15 train that evening. "I will talk terms with the Cleveland owners when I get there tomorrow afternoon. If I am a hold-up or holdout as things are now I don't know it," Tris said to a corridor full of reporters.

One of the writers asked how his departure would affect the Boston club. "Don't worry about these Red Sox," Tris replied. "Carrigan has a great team with or without me." He then went on to say how much he'd miss his mates on the club and conceded that it "bothered" him to leave a team as gifted as the Speed Boys. It's a shame Lannin didn't display the same magnanimity as his former star.

The owner's initial statement that day was neutral, if misleading. Lannin told reporters that there were no differences between himself and Speaker – that the ballplayer hadn't asked for "a cent" of the purchase price, and that the trade was strictly a business transaction. Only the last assertion in that trifecta had any basis in fact.

With Opening Day just two days away, things turned nasty. Newspapers reported on the morning of April 12 that Speaker wouldn't sign with Cleveland unless and until he got five thousand dollars of the purchase price. Later that day Speaker did sign. Reports out of Cleveland suggest he received at least a few thousand dollars of his purchase price; other accounts say no. When asked if the Red Sox had contributed toward Speaker's signing, Lannin issued this brusque statement: "If Tris Speaker received a bonus for signing with the Cleveland Club, you may be certain that none of it came from the Red Sox. Speaker has been well paid for his work for me, and I will do absolutely nothing more for him." Any pretense that the situation between Lannin and Speaker hadn't turned bitter and personal disappeared with the owner's barrage. Years later, Speaker was still seeking revenge against Lannin. He told Gordon Cobbledick of the *Cleveland Plain Dealer* in the 1950s that he adamantly refused to sign until Ban Johnson personally guaranteed him that Lannin would fork over ten thousand dollars of the purchase price. Who paid what to whom and when will forever remain a mystery.

Bill Carrigan's reaction to the trade was recounted in George Sullivan's volume:

> I had nothing to do with the deal. It was Lannin's idea. He never told me why. He owned the club and he didn't have to give reasons. Anybody who thinks I suggested the trade doesn't know me. My only goal as manager was to win. I might hate a player's guts, but if he could help us win games I wanted him. If I were to get rid of a player because he and I didn't see eye-to-eye, I'd be cutting off my nose to spite my face. It wasn't a secret that Speaker wasn't one of my favorite persons and neither was I one of his. But I recognized his talent and was delighted to have him on our side. I hated to lose him.

In that same interview, Carrigan speculated that Lannin's hotel operation needed a quick infusion of cash – and that's why Lannin was so keen to unload Speaker. Tris Speaker's tumultuous tenure in Boston ended the way it started: with heartache, ambiguity, and more than a touch of recrimination. Toss in Lannin and Johnson's lack of appreciation for Tris's contributions to two World Series championships, and it adds up to one of the most acrimonious breakups in baseball history. There's little doubt that Spoke could be a pain in the clubhouse and a blowhard on a train ride. But there's also little doubt that he was the best all-around player in the game. Although they must have known it was coming, fans in New England were nevertheless aghast. Indeed, as Stout and Johnson point out, the fan reaction to the Speaker trade was far more visceral than the one following the sale of Ruth three years later. Red Sox partisans had no way of knowing that a precedent had been established: Speaker would be far from the last Boston immortal to depart town under a cloud.

Cleveland sent two players to Boston in the deal: pitcher "Sad Sam" Jones who, over time, became a solid hurler, especially while wearing a Yankee uniform, and journeyman catcher Fred Thomas. Fred appeared in all of forty-four games in a Boston uniform, hitting a punchless .257.

Cleveland was only five hundred miles away from Boston, but to Tris Speaker it must have seemed like light years. Boston was consumed by it own hubris on one hand and ethnic strife on the other. Cleveland had little of Boston's history or culture. By the time Speaker arrived, however, its reputation as a manufacturing, oil, and transportation hub was secure. Immigrants had also settled in Cleveland in huge numbers – by 1910 it was the sixth largest city in the country with more than 560,000 people, a third of whom were foreign-born – but new arrivals hadn't yet begun to flex their political muscles as Honey Fitz and his cohorts had done in Boston. Politics in Cleveland wasn't quite the Prod vs. Papist blood sport it had been in Beantown.

Reform mayor Tom Johnson was responsible for much of Cleveland's genteel politics and its image as a progressive city. Throughout the 1870s and 1880s Johnson was a railroad and steel monopolist, living on "Millionaire's Row" and cozying up to the likes of Mark Hanna. But in 1885 Johnson read Henry George's *Social Problems*, took its nostrums to heart, and resolved to dedicate the rest of his life to public service. He served two terms in the U.S. House and then was elected Cleveland's mayor for four consecutive terms beginning in 1901.

Much as Honey Fitz was doing in Boston at almost precisely the same time, Mayor Johnson overhauled Cleveland's infrastructure, building roads, parks, swimming pools, hospitals, and a new city hall. By the time he left office in 1909, Cleveland was known as "the Forest City," with more than twenty-two hundred acres of parkland. The city's system of public recreation and transportation, moreover, was a model for the rest of the country. Cleveland also benefited from the (at least occasional) philanthropic largesse of its local boys made good, Hanna, John D. Rockefeller, and Charles F. Brush, the inventor of the arc light, among them. The town had grown so rapidly in the past generation that locals proudly claimed to hold the "long-jump population record."

It was, in sum, a much different place than Boston. Its elite welcomed Speaker as the savior of their baseball franchise, the successor to the great Napoleon Lajoie. Spoke was embraced as one of their own. Almost immediately, he felt at home in Cleveland in a way that he never experienced in Boston. It's good that Speaker felt that way about the city and its leadership, because the baseball team for which he had come to play was still mired in mediocrity.

Seventeen years before Speaker arrived, Cleveland hosted what is without question the worst Major League team in history, the 1899 Spiders of the National League. The excesses of syndicate baseball had ravaged the franchise, as it had several other teams around the country, including the Boston Nationals and the Baltimore Orioles. When Spiders owner Frank Robison acquired a controlling interest in St. Louis's National League franchise in the winter of 1898–99, he transferred all of Cleveland's best players to the Cardinals. Cy Young was among those Spiders sent packing to St. Louis, leaving the good people of Cleveland with dregs. The '99 Spiders, tagged "the Misfits" by disdainful fans, finished eighty games out of first place with a 30–122 win-loss record. It was the death knell for the franchise. Western League magnate Ban Johnson immediately began eyeing Cleveland as a place to put a new outpost for his planned major league, particularly since his lead moneyman, Charles Somers, was a pillar of the local business community.

Cleveland's 1901 American League entrant was known as the "Blues" because the players inherited the Spiders' old uniforms of that color. Under the direction of manager Jimmy McAleer, a former Spider, the team finished a blues-inducing next-to-last in their inaugural season. Things got a little better the following season, when skipper McAleer moved on to the St. Louis Browns and the relabeled Cleveland "Broncos" finished two games above .500.

In 1902 Connie Mack presented his benefactor Charles Somers with a "gift" that no doubt had been arranged by the then-omnipotent Ban Johnson: Mack sold his second baseman to the Cleveland franchise. Napoleon Lajoie had been Mack's best player since the Tall Tactician had wrested him away from the crosstown Phillies two years before. But the Phillies had obtained a court injunction prohibiting their former star from playing for a rival franchise in the same city. Mack wanted to get some value for Nappy before the courts forced Connie to give him up. Lajoie became a Cleveland fixture, won the 1903 and 1904 batting crowns, and was worshiped along Lake Erie with such ardor that the team became known as the "Naps." Three years later he became player-manager, leading his namesakes to respectable finishes but unable to beat Chicago, Detroit, or Philadelphia out for a pennant. He stayed in Cleveland for twelve years before returning to the Athletics to finish his career.

By 1914, Nappy's last season in Cleveland, it was the Misfits redux. The Indians finished dead last that year; only Mack's breakup of his pennant-winning A's the following year prevented Cleveland from a repeat.

Nineteen fourteen was also the last full year in Cleveland for another superstar who'd been "given" to the franchise by Connie Mack: a South Carolinian named Joseph Jefferson Jackson. All Jackson did in his four full seasons in a Naps uniform was average .378 at the plate, lead the league in triples one season with twenty-six, and in total hits and doubles the next. His record for hits in a rookie season lasted nine decades before being broken by Ichiro Suzuki of the Seattle Mariners. The .408 batting average Jackson compiled as a rookie is – like Cy Young's records – unapproachable. Still, the cash-poor Somers peddled him to Comiskey's White Sox in the middle of the 1915 season.

The news that the Indians had acquired Speaker hit Cleveland like an earthquake. The *Plain Dealer*'s headline, "Tris Speaker Comes to Cleveland!" dwarfed the other front-page news: a boast by the Germans that their U-boats had sunk four more commercial ships in the North Atlantic. A drawing accompanying the trade story showed Speaker in three dramatic poses. The rest of the paper was crammed full of other articles eagerly reporting everything there was to know about the trade and the history of their new center fielder.

Two days later the *Plain Dealer*'s front-page cartoon showed a cigar-smoking James Dunn literally painting "Cleveland" on a "Base Ball" map of the United States. Indians beat reporter Henry P. Edwards used the same metaphor to describe the excitement and pageantry surrounding Opening Day. The mayor threw out the first ball, to the delight of the eighteen thousand folks who crammed into the tiny park. "By signing Tris Speaker, Cleveland has gone far toward restoring the city as a baseball power," Edwards wrote. He also saluted Dunn for signing newcomer Arnold "Chick" Gandil, a first sacker.

More banner headers followed the next day, none of which acknowledged that the lowly Browns had scuffed up the Tribe, 6–1, in the season opener. "Speaker and Indians Stir Old Time Joy," spouted one headline. A cartoon depicted enraptured fans muttering, "$55,000 . . . $55,000 . . . $55,000" – pinching themselves that their team had actually spent that amount of money to bring a superstar to Cleveland. Even a second loss to the Browns, 4–2, didn't dampen the fans' enthusiasm.

Speaker's new team wasn't a contender, but it wasn't completely dysfunctional, either. Cleveland's new owner had with Ban Johnson's backing the wherewithal to put real money into the franchise to make it a winner. "The purchase of Speaker will, I believe, show fans that I am making good on my promise to give them good baseball," Dunn declared. Speaker's acquisition was seen as the centerpiece of Dunn's strategy to overhaul the team. Manager Lee Fohl guided the team to a 77–77 season in 1916. A competent if uninspiring skipper, Fohl would go on to guide two other franchises in an eleven-year career.

Spoke had much different ground to cover in Cleveland. League Park, Cleveland's twenty-five-year-old baseball home at East Sixty-sixth and Lexington Avenue, had been completely refurbished into a steel-and-concrete facility six years earlier. Despite a few extra seats and amenities, it remained one of the most intimate baseball settings in either league. Only twenty-one thousand people could be seated in the park, which meant that on Sundays and holidays, extra bleacher boards would be installed in the outfield to accommodate overflow crowds. It was originally known as "National League Park" but once Cleveland's National League franchise abandoned the city the "National" was dropped. From 1916 to 1927 – the full breadth of Speaker's tenure in Cleveland, plus one year – it was renamed Dunn Field in deference to the club's owner. Cleveland's ball yard was located where two major streetcar lines merged. Not coincidentally, the business tycoon who built the park also happened to own the streetcar lines.

Because it was originally shoehorned around a saloon that refused to sell to the developer, League Park/Dunn Field had classically quirky dimensions, "more rectangular than square," one observer said. The left-field wall down the line was a hefty 375 feet from home plate; the "corner" in center field was 420 feet; the right-field wall down the line a cozy 290 feet – and it didn't get much deeper than that as it headed toward center. Spoke took a long look at the park's configuration and decided he'd tried to pull the occasional inside pitch instead of instinctively inside-outing the ball. Once the ball got livelier four years hence, he began hitting homers over the fence with greater regularity.

Tris had acres to patrol in left-center, whereas right-center was minuscule. When the old wooden right-field fence had been replaced in the 1910 renovation, club president Ernest S. "Barney" Barnard had installed a twenty-foot-high concrete wall in right, then ordered workers to erect some twenty feet of wire screen on top of that. Barnard wanted to cut down on the number of balls hit out onto Lexington Avenue. So Dunn Field's right-field wall cast the same shadow over its park as Fenway's "Green Monster" ultimately would in Boston. The wall had three different surfaces: concrete at the bottom, chicken wire at the top, and steel support posts – each of which would cause a deflected ball to behave differently. Some balls would drop straight down; others would careen wildly one way or the other. Many a well-struck line drive caromed off Barney's big screen, holding the frustrated runner to a long single. Spoke mastered the art and science of anticipating where the deflections would end up, whirling and throwing strikes to second, third, and home to nab shocked base runners. If the outfielders weren't alert, the second baseman would have to come out to play the caroms.

Mike Sowell, author of *The Pitch That Killed*, writes that "when Detroit slugger Wahoo Sam Crawford first saw the [right field] screen, he defiantly proclaimed: 'So that's Barney's dream. I'll show him.'" Crawford drove a ball over the fence in one of his first appearances in the remodeled park.

Speaker's new outfield mates – right fielder Robert "Braggo" Roth and left fielder Jack Graney – were respectable, but they sure weren't Lewis and Hooper. No one was going to baptize this outfield as "golden." Spoke could not always rely on Braggo, especially, to track down balls in the left-center gap, so he began positioning himself a couple of steps closer to the left side.

"It was a left-handed park, one of the greatest in the country for fans," remembered right-hander George Uhle, who spent eleven years in a Cleveland uniform, leading the league twice in wins. "You'd try to throw your best stuff away from [left-handed hitters]." In the 1910 renovation, the stands became double-decked and the old 1890s clubhouse got a much-needed facelift. A wide-open press box was perched over home plate, which meant that Ed Bang of the *News*, Henry Edwards of the *Plain Dealer*, and later the young Franklin Lewis of the *Press* and Gordon Cobbledick of the *Plain Dealer* had to duck many a foul ball. Loose-limbed kids who couldn't afford a ticket could squat down and watch a game through the tiny "window" that existed between the ground and the bottom of the right-field fence. Cleveland may not have been all that great a baseball town up to that point in its history. But it was about to become one. For nearly four decades, four different franchises had called Cleveland home. None of them had won a recognized "championship."

After Lajoie departed for Philadelphia in 1915, the Naps had to adopt a new nickname. So it revived a moniker that Cleveland's National League franchise had used for a time when Native American Louis Sockalexis joined the club in 1897: "Indians." Baseball savants like John McGraw and Ed Barrow described Sockalexis as the greatest talent they'd ever seen. While he was playing for Holy Cross, two Harvard professors measured a Sockalexis throw at 414 feet. One of his collegiate home runs supposedly shattered a fourth-floor window in the chapel at Brown University.

In his first sixty games with the Spiders/Indians, Sockalexis batted .338 with eight triples and sixteen stolen bases. He seemed destined to achieve the greatness that McGraw, Barrow, and others predicted for him. But he could never get a handle on demon rum. Halfway through his rookie year, Sockalexis, drunk and apparently acting on a dare, leapt from the second-story window of a brothel, severely injuring an ankle. It never healed properly. Louis played only sporadically before being forced to retire two years later. For the rest of his life, he carried around newspaper clippings to prove to people what a talent he'd been. When he died of heart failure at age forty-two, he was buried in an unmarked grave. It took twenty years to arrange a stone marker for Sockalexis's grave.

In January 1915, when "Indians" was officially adopted, the *Plain Dealer* wrote, "There will be no real Indians on the roster, but the name will recall fine traditions. It is looking backward to a time when Cleveland had one of the most popular teams of the United States. It also serves to revive the memory of a single great player who has been gathered to his fathers in the happy hunting ground."

Just as he had when McAleer had taken over the Red Sox in 1912, Ban Johnson installed his former secretary, Robert McRoy, to serve as his eyes and ears and provide some seasoning to the new owner. Dunn, McRoy, and Fohl had begun assembling a decent team in 1916 but it had a ways to go. Manager Fohl had Chick Gandil, a solid gloveman but not much of a stick at first, light-hitting Ivan Howard at second, Bill Wambsganss playing out of position at short, and swingman Terry Turner at third, another light hitter. Strong but sometimes erratic-armed (he led AL receivers that year in errors with twenty-one) Steve O'Neill handled catching duties. Speaker later called O'Neill the best caller of pitchers with whom he'd ever played. The Irishman's arm was so lethal that Ty Cobb rarely tried to test it. Braggo Roth made up for at least some of his defensive deficiencies by hitting .286 in 1916. Right fielder Jack Graney batted a powerless .241.

All of which makes Speaker's 1916 season even more remarkable. The only regular in the Cleveland lineup whose batting average came within *one hundred points* of Tris's was Roth's, at .286. Tris that year led the league not only in batting average (.386) but in slugging average (.502), hits (211), and doubles (41). He stole thirty-five bases and drove in eighty-three runs. Those numbers would have been standout in any batting order, but they were phenomenal given Cleveland's pedestrian lineup. With lackluster hitters in front of and behind him, Speaker must have been hacking at a lot of pitches off the plate. Tris had such a brilliant season that Red Sox owner Lannin must have wondered if Speaker didn't do it out of spite – and maybe he did.

On May 10, 1916, the *Cleveland Press* printed a poem by Grantland Rice that captured Speaker's impact on the club:

> Before Speaker –
> We were nothing but talented jokes
> A bunch of bums who were mostly blokes
> We had no speed and we had no steam,
> We had no hitters to bat in runs.
> After Speaker –
> "But how do we look for a bunch of dubs
> Up there in the Standings of the Clubs?"

The Indians' staff in 1916 wasn't a bunch of dubs, but it posed no immediate threat to the Leonard-Mays-Ruth-Shore-Pennock Red Sox. Cleveland had three solid starters. Jim "Sarge" Bagby was becoming one of the most respected right-handers in either league. He would go on to win 162 games in seven seasons in a Cleveland uniform, including a thirty-one-win season in 1920. Sarge had a nasty fadeaway and could apply foreign substances to the ball with the best of them. Ty Cobb always called Bagby the smartest pitcher he'd ever faced. Future Hall of Famer Stanley Coveleskie, the spitballing right-handed younger brother of Detroit southpaw Harry, won fifteen games in 1916. Between 1916 and 1924 Stan would go on to win 168 games for the Tribe. Alabamian Guy Morton won twelve games in 1916, typical production in a career that would last eight more seasons, all in an Indians uniform. The rest of the staff was rounded out by journeyman right-hander "Big Ed" Klepfer, lefty spot starter Fritz Coumbe, rookie right-hander Al Gould, and the itinerant Fred Beebe, who was mopping up a seven-year career for five different clubs.

There weren't a lot of exceptional players on the Indians' 1916 roster, but there were some affable guys who made Speaker feel good about his move to Cleveland. Right fielder Jack Graney, a native of St. Thomas, Ontario, wore a perpetually goofy grin and could keep a clubhouse cracked up with his clowning. His pals called him "Three and Two Jack," because he liked to work a pitcher deep into the count, groveling for a walk. For a guy with undistinguished career numbers, Graney achieved some historic "firsts": the first batter in history to get a hit off of a young pitcher named Babe Ruth and the first player to wear a uniform number in a big league game. Graney was so beloved in Cleveland that he spent his entire career there. Later, he became one of the first ballplayers to make the transition to broadcasting games on radio. Two generations of Clevelanders grew up listening to Jack's witticisms over the airwaves.

William Adolph Wambsganss, or "Wamby" as it was often abbreviated in game accounts and box scores, was another agreeable character that spent a decade in a Cleveland uniform. Wamby was a native northeastern Ohioan who enjoyed an enormous following in the city. Catcher Steve O'Neill was, like Rough Carrigan in the Boston clubhouse, a stubborn Irishman who backed down from no one. Although O'Neill and Speaker clashed on occasion, there was little of the enmity that plagued Spoke's relationship with Rough. Speaker and O'Neill ran in more or less the same crowd. The religious tribalism that dogged the Boston clubhouse was much less of an issue in Cleveland.

The Cleveland teammate with whom Speaker felt an immediate kinship, though, was a middle infielder from backwoods Kentucky named Raymond Johnson Chapman. With Joe Wood still holed up in the Poconos, Spoke needed a compadre – a fellow Southerner who loved to talk ball and hunt and fish. Ray Chapman was three years younger than Speaker and became, in many ways, the little brother that Tris never had.

Chappie's origins were even humbler than Spoke's. He grew up on a small farm in northwestern Kentucky, outside a coal-mining village called Beaver Dam. When Ray was fourteen, his father moved the family west to a downstate Illinois mining hamlet called Herrin. When not working in the mines, Ray's dad added to the family income by doubling as Herrin's constable.

Ray delivered groceries for the Herrin general store as a kid. Later, in his teens, he joined his dad in the mines, earning membership in Local 986 of the United Mine Workers. To remind himself of his roots, Chapman carried his union card with him throughout his days in the big leagues. He also played ball for the Herrin town nine. In the spring of 1910, a scout for the Springfield, Illinois, club in the Three-I League spotted him. By then, Chappie was nineteen and had grown to his adult height and weight – five foot ten and roughly 160 pounds. He had solid fielding and hitting skills but it was his speed that distinguished him.

Sowell's book notes that Springfield's hard-boiled manager was "affected by the youngster's unfailing cheerfulness. 'You know, kid,' [he] told Chapman one day, 'even if you never played a game, you'd earn your pay just by sitting on the bench and being such a cheerleader.' "

Despite Chappie's ebullience, he was sold to Davenport when the Springfield owner needed some extra cash. With a chance to play full-time in 1911, Chappie hit .293 for Davenport, stealing fifty bases and scoring seventy-five runs. The president of the Toledo Mud Hens of the American Association saw a Davenport series in August and thought enough of Chapman's potential to wire the big boss about him. His employer happened to be one Charles F. Somers, who then owned a controlling interest in both the Toledo club and the Cleveland AL franchise. Chappie played the final month of the '11 season for Toledo, then spent the bulk of the 1912 campaign there. He was hitting .310 with 49 steals and 101 runs scored when the big club called him up.

Chappie became a good Major League player but never quite a star. A wrenched knee caused him to miss significant games in a couple of different seasons. Moreover, it took the Indians too long a time to establish him as their everyday shortstop. In 1916, Speaker's first year with the club, Bill Wamby, a natural second baseman, was playing short and Chappie was rotating through the infield. Once given a chance the next season to settle in at short, Chappie became a steady contributor, leading both leagues in assists and put-outs. He was an accomplished bunter, setting a then–Major League record in 1917 for sacrifices. *Baseball Magazine*'s F. C. Lane called him the finest defensive shortstop since Honus Wagner.

Having spent his boyhood in Appalachia, Chappie knew how to tell a story. He was a brilliant raconteur, able to keep a room full of people in stitches as his high-pitched drawl wove one story into the next. His singing voice was good enough to allow him, Jack Graney, Steve O'Neill, and another teammate to form a quartet that entertained not only teammates but all kinds of people in and around Cleveland.

For a guy who grew up with next to nothing, Chappie became quite a sporty dresser and man about town. Cleveland society found him charming and irresistible. In the words of Ed Bang, Chappie was "his 100 percent self all the time, no frills or furbelows, and it was this trait that won him fast friends among the heads of manufacturing, industrial and mercantile concerns as well as among the newsies on the street corner."

One afternoon in the summer of 1916, a prominent Cleveland oilman named Martin B. Daly, a protégé of Standard Oil's John D. Rockefeller, happened to attend a game at Dunn Field in the company of his twenty-two-year-old daughter, Kathleen. Miss Daly must have been carrying something of a torch for the Kentuckian "without furbelows" because her father asked a team official to introduce them. The opulent homes along Millionaire's Row on Euclid Avenue were far removed from the shanties of Beaver Dam, Kentucky, or Herrin, Illinois, yet somehow they clicked. Kathleen's dad arranged for Ray to become the secretary-treasurer of the Pioneer Alloys Company and wanted him to retire from the game.

Speaker served as best man at Ray's 1919 wedding. Kathleen's brides-maid was Jane McMahon, her first cousin and best friend. For a time, Tris and Jane were an item – but their relationship, like all of Tris's romances back then, didn't stick. The other two members of the Tribe present at Chappie's nuptials were fellow quartet members Graney and O'Neill, who regaled folks at the reception with their favorite Chapman stories. O'Neill, in Sowell's words, was "the perfect straight man for Chapman's pranks." During spring training one year, Ray snookered O'Neill, a devoted golfer, into a long-drive contest at New Orleans's Pelican Park. With wild wagering and braggadocio going on all around, Ray snuck an exploding ball onto Steve's tee when O'Neill was looking the other way. When O'Neill lashed into the ball, it disintegrated, sparking howls of laughter from the crowd, all of whom, of course, had been tipped off about Chappie's scam.

Ray and Kathleen's reception was at the Hotel Winton, the downtown quarters where Spoke and Chapman shared a seven-room apartment. It was viewed as Cleveland's social event of the year. "[Chapman] was as much at home in the ballroom as on the ball diamond," Ed Bang once remarked.

Speaker's impact on the Indians' esprit de corps was immediate. It wasn't just his hitting and fielding – his aggressive base running was also contagious. According to research compiled by Speaker buff Fred Schuld, on August 25, 1916, Speaker scored from second on a ten-foot bunt by Bill Wamby. Spoke rounded third and was never headed. Another time, trailing Dutch Leonard and the Red Sox by one run with two outs in the bottom of the ninth, Speaker was on third and Wamby occupied second. As Leonard began his pitch Speaker broke for home. The rattled Leonard threw the ball away, the Sox catcher had trouble corralling it at the backstop, and Wamby ended up scoring, too, clinching a wild win for the Indians.

Just a few weeks after Spoke arrived in Cleveland, he had a chance encounter with Morris Ackerman, the hunting and fishing columnist of the *Cleveland News*. The two bumped into each other in a sporting goods store on Superior Avenue. "Thus was the beginning of a warm and constant friendship," Ackerman wrote. When it came to hunting or fishing, the two of them were just grown-up kids, Ackerman liked to say. Over the years, the two shared many an expedition into the woods, several of which Ackerman recounted to his readers.

"There has never been any work too hard or unpleasant on any trip that Speaker has not tackled with a whim to a satisfactory conclusion," Ackerman wrote in July 1920. "He will cook for nine men and have a lot of fun at the job. At washing dishes he is a bear and at diggin' bait and at cuttin' wood he only asks the chance. Last fall, he helped the carpenters build on our fish tug, when the wind, snow, and ice were making the natives scramble for cover." Henry Edwards once wrote that Speaker was a "true sportsman" who has "hunted everything from snipe and rabbits to grizzly bear, mountain goats, panthers, and moose. He enjoys fishing for anything from minnows to tarpon or sword fish." Spoke once "all but thrashed a man," Edwards noted, who took aim at ducks that had not left the lake's surface.

Spoke's friendship with pals like Ackerman and Chappie helped him get acclimated to Cleveland in a way he never did in Boston. At least some of the chip on Speaker's shoulder was beginning to dissolve.

Ban Johnson and Joe Lannin were proven right: the Red Sox were so good they *could* win without Speaker and Wood. With Ruth leading the league with a 1.75 ERA, the Red Sox won the pennant again, engaging in a spirited race with the White Sox most of the season. Thanks to some clutch pitching performances late in the season from Ruth, Dutch Leonard, and Carl Mays, Boston held off hard-charging Chicago by two games. The Red Sox dispatched the Brooklyn Robins in five games in the best-of-seven Series, with Shore, Ruth, and Leonard all pitching brilliantly.

For only the second time in his career, Speaker wouldn't be driving northeast for spring training. Instead, in late February of 1917 he pointed his car southeast. The Indians did their spring workouts in the bacchanalian world of New Orleans. New Orleans's big-city allure was much different than the small-town-gone-to-Sodom feel of Hot Springs, but Bourbon Street and the French Quarter offered Spoke and his pals plenty of distractions.

Spoke convinced Fohl and Dunn to give Joe Wood a tryout with the club. In a bylined article for the *News* on April 1, 1917, Spoke wrote, "I think we have the makings of a championship team. Much, of course, will depend upon what sort of shape our pitchers are in, and whether Joe Wood can successfully stage a comeback. Speaking of 'Woody,' however, I will say that it looks as if he had never had the least bit of trouble with his arm. If he doesn't pitch great ball for us, I'll miss my guess."

Tris missed his guess. Joe's shoulder was still so heavily damaged that he was a full year away from coming back full-time.

The Indians made huge strides in 1917, going from .500 the previous year to twenty-two games above break-even the next. Bagby and Coveleskie each had ERAs under 2.00, with Jim winning twenty-two games and Stan nineteen. Pennsylvanian Big Ed Klepfer had a career year, going 13–4 with a 2.37 ERA.

Spoke's teammates began to lend a hand in 1917 on the offensive side as well. Chapman hit .300 for the season, as did the new regular first baseman, a journeyman named Joseph "Moon" Harris. Harris got the job when Chick Gandil was sent packing to the White Sox during the off-season – no doubt with Speaker's encouragement. The two didn't get along. Braggo Roth turned in another solid season, batting .285. Chappie and Wamby became a superb double play combination, one of the most effective in either league.

Braggo, Spoke, and Old Three and Two combined for fifty-five assists, which suggests that they had begun to work well together. Certainly Graney and Roth had fewer objections to Spoke's penchant for poaching in their territories than his previous mates.

In the considered opinion of baseball writer Irwin M. Howe, who covered the game for four decades, Tris pulled one of the great ruses of all time against the White Sox in a regular season game early in 1917. The Indians were trailing the White Sox by one run with two outs in the inning. Speaker was on second and a teammate on third. The Cleveland hitter lifted an easy pop-up between short and third; White Sox third baseman Buck Weaver gathered underneath it. As Speaker ran past Weaver he rasped, "I'll take it, Buck!" Weaver, thinking the command had come from shortstop Swede Risberg, backed away. The pop-up fell untouched. The Indians scored two runs and went on to win the game.

Despite making headway, the Indians were no match for either of the Soxes. For the second year in a row, the White Sox and the Red Sox conducted a down-to-the-wire pennant race. This time the Speed Boys came up short. Jack Barry had taken over for Rough Carrigan at the beginning of the 1917 season, allowing Rough to return to his business empire along the Maine coast.

Allegations of impropriety dog the '17 White Sox almost as much as their infamous squad of two years later. The future Black Soxers may have altered the pennant race by rewarding illicit cash to the pitchers and catchers of the Detroit Tigers for service above and beyond the call of duty in laying down against the White Sox but hanging tough against the Red Sox (more about that in the "Scandal" chapter). Those revelations, however, were almost a decade away from surfacing. The 1917 edition of the Pale Hose won one hundred games and beat up on McGraw's hard-luck Giants four games to two in the Series.

Spoke relished confrontations with umpires, never backing down from a rhubarb. Teammates marveled at his capacity to yell so hard his face would turn blue. Then he would return to center field or the dugout without missing a beat.

In his first couple of years with the Indians, Spoke had two memorable dustups with arbiters. The first occurred on April 30, 1917, at Dunn Field in a game against the Browns. In the second inning, the Browns' Armando Marsans stole second and took off for third when Steve O'Neill's throw got past Chapman into shallow center field. Spoke speared the ball and fired to third basement Doc Evans, who slapped a tag on the sliding Marsans. Umpire George Hildebrand called the runner safe.

Spoke raced in from center to protest the call. Tris had barely reached the infield when Hildebrand (whom Henry Edwards the next day – in a fit of Great War jingoism – described as "the Teutonic umpire") thumbed Speaker out of the game. That didn't deter Spoke from continuing his furious dash toward third. When he finally reached Hildebrand, Spoke's cleats somehow failed to catch as he launched into his protest; he barged into the ump, knocking Hildebrand to the ground. Hildebrand's crewmates immediately banished Spoke from the playing field, "shooing" him, in Ed Bang's phrase, to the clubhouse. AL president Johnson suspended Spoke indefinitely but lifted the ban after three games, with the Tribe poised to begin a series against Detroit. On May 5 a *Press* wag known as "Lavery" waxed poetic on Speaker's run-in with Hildebrand:

> Hey, shoot this word along to Cobb –
> Tris Speaker's back upon the job:
> Hereafter Tris will save his bumps
> For someone else besides the umps

The next year, Spoke's belligerence toward umps took an even uglier turn. On August 27, 1918, in the waning days of the fractious season shortened by the war, Spoke was suspended from the final few games when he threw a punch at home plate umpire Tommy Connolly over a disputed "out" call at Shibe Park in Philadelphia. Spoke had tried to score from second on a short single that first baseman "Tioga" George Burns corralled in shallow right and gunned to the plate.

Enraged, Spoke popped up and threw an uppercut at Connolly. Only the quick intervention of crew member Dick Nallin "kept the fiery Texan from messing up the diminutive Tommy," the *News* reported the next day. Throwing a punch at an umpire in any circumstance is bad enough; doing it in the middle of a pennant chase – with the first- and second-place money still unresolved – was unconscionable. The Indians ended up finishing two games behind Boston but a game ahead of Washington.

America's entry into Europe's Great War injected much uncertainty into baseball in 1917–18. No one was absolutely sure if the games would go on or if dozens of players would end up being pressed into service.

Chappie joined the Naval Reserves and was assigned to a unit that patrolled Lake Erie. Speaker, typically, sought the most dangerous duty available. If racecar driver Eddie Rickenbacker could be an ace fighter pilot, why not a rodeo cowboy turned baseball star? Tris was awarded a coveted spot in a naval aviation unit that had been formed a year earlier at the Massachusetts Institute of Technology (MIT) in Cambridge. He reported for training in early fall 1918, after the National Commission and the Wilson administration's War Department agreed to end the season on September 1.

Although the Navy had actively recruited other "famous" trainees, Speaker and several hundred fellow cadets didn't have a cakewalk in Cambridge. They took classes in observation, boating, gunnery, navigation, aeronautical engineering, aerography, rigging, seamanship, signaling, and the theory of flight.

The Navy-MIT program had available to it five seaplanes that used the Charles River, one flying boat, and some fifteen other conventional biplanes. In the two years of the MIT program, some thirty-six hundred pilots graduated. Aviation duty back then was hazardous: twenty-four navy pilots died at MIT, many of them killed in training accidents. Watching those seaplanes buzz up and down the Charles must have thrilled Bostonians. Spoke and other celebrity trainees at MIT also prided themselves on raising money for war bonds. "Technology's War Record," a summary of MIT's contributions to the Great War, spotlights the fundraising prowess of the navy unit.

When the war ended less than two months after Speaker arrived at MIT, he chose to hang on long enough to get his pilot's wings. Remarkably, he continued to take crates up for a number of years, wowing fellow players and pals like Will Rogers with stories of near-crashes. At a time when many Americans had never even seen an airplane, let alone been in one, Tris Speaker was piloting them.

CHAPTER 9

World Champion Manager

If Cleveland should fly a pennant and world's championship flag to the winds, who among us will ever gaze with admiration on the coveted buntings and not give a thought to that man who gave his all, who died for the Indians' cause, Ray Chapman. — Ed Bang, Cleveland News

Instability over the war notwithstanding, the Indians finally became a contender in 1918, finishing just two wins short of the Red Sox. Roommates Chappie and Spoke led the league in put-outs at their respective positions. Smoky Joe became the Tribe's everyday left fielder, no doubt making Spoke breathe a little bit easier on balls hit to the left-center gap. Joe proved his mettle as a big league hitter, batting .296 in 422 at bats. The less agile Braggo Roth was moved to right, where he had less ground to cover in Dunn Field. Old Three and Two Graney joined Terry Turner that season as a utility player. The rotation was beginning to solidify: Coveleskie and Bagby between them won thirty-nine games in the shortened 1918 season and Morton and Coumbe won twenty-seven more.

During the 1918–19 off-season, the Indians, at Speaker's urging, obtained the services of Larry Gardner, his great pal and fellow Mason from the Red Sox clubhouse. Gardner had been traded to the woeful Athletics at the beginning of 1918 and was delighted to rejoin his buddies Woody and Spoke in Cleveland. Larry manned third for Cleveland every day the next four years – and played part-time in '23 and '24. He spent seventeen years in the big leagues – all but three of them as a teammate of Speaker's.

Gardner was a Vermonter who had studied at the state university. A decade earlier, the Red Sox had tried to make him a second baseman, flip-flopping him around the infield before settling him at third. He succeeded Home Run Baker as the steadiest third baseman in the American League. He was economical, not flashy, but teammates marveled at his coolness afield. Like his old pal Harry Hooper, Gardner had the reputation of being a great clutch hitter.

Spoke had never gotten along with the lippy Chick Gandil; the feeling was mutual. In the spring of 1919 they allowed their animosity to get the better of them. First at Comiskey Park, then at Dunn Field, the two of them came to blows. Their first brawl took place in late May at Comiskey during a 5–2 White Sox victory. Gandil accused Speaker of trying to deliberately spike him while attempting to leg out a single. Insults were exchanged; soon they were pummeling each other while rolling around in the infield dirt. The South Side crowd got so riled up that they later heaved pop bottles at Jack Graney, a convenient target in left field. Ban Johnson was so irate that he suspended Speaker and Gandil for a couple of weeks each – almost unheard-of in that era.

In their three years together, manager Lee Fohl and Speaker had developed a decent working relationship, although owner Dunn and Fohl were apparently on the outs. Dunn had come to believe that Fohl had lost the respect of players in the clubhouse.

Pitcher George Uhle, a rookie in 1919, was interviewed five decades later for Eugene Murdock's *Baseball Players and Their Times*. Uhle remembered the stormy events of July 18, 1919, with remarkable clarity. The Indians, although just eleven games over .500 at that point in the season, were in the thick of a pennant chase with the White Sox and the Yankees. Murdock's book cites Cleveland writer Franklin Lewis's contention that manager Fohl relied heavily – perhaps too heavily – on the counsel of his center fielder, particularly on changing pitchers during a game.

Cleveland happened to be playing Babe Ruth and the Red Sox the pivotal afternoon of July 18. Thanks to the perspicacity of Sox manager Ed Barrow, Ruth was finally beginning to play almost every day in the outfield and pitching only on a spot basis. Early in the game, Babe planted one over the right-center screen in Dunn Field. But the Tribe countered with four runs in the bottom of the eighth to take a 7–3 lead.

When Boston scored one run in the top of the ninth, then loaded the bases for Ruth, Speaker signaled to Fohl for a certain hurler to be brought in from the bullpen. But Fohl misread Speaker's sign and instead ushered Fritz Coumbe into the game. Speaker tried to get Fohl's attention, but then realized it would look like he was undermining his manager, so Speaker stayed mum. All of which was ironic, because earlier in the game Coumbe had been bragging to Uhle and Guy Morton in the bullpen about how he had Ruth's number. "I know how to pitch to that big monkey," Fritz swore.

When Coumbe got into the game, Morton turned to Uhle and said, "Now we'll see whether he can pitch to Ruth or not." As related by Gordon Cobbledick years later, Coumbe hung a curve on his first offering, which Babe took a rip at – but missed. "Catcher Steve O'Neill called time and went into earnest conference with his pitcher," Cobbledick wrote. " 'Don't,' [O'Neill] begged, 'throw another one like that. Keep it low and away. Walk him if you have to. Force in a run, but don't give him another one like that.' " Alas, Fritz spun a similar curve ball on pitch number two, which Ruth deposited onto the rooftop of a taxicab idling on the far side of Lexington Avenue. The Indians lost, 8–7.

The *Sporting News* reported that Coumbe cried like a baby in the clubhouse after the game and was soon released. Lee Fohl didn't sob, but he also didn't care for Dunn's icy stare or the chorus of boos sent his way at the end of the game. When the owner learned that Coumbe had come into the game as a result of a miscommunication between Speaker and Fohl, he must have erupted. Fohl was forced into resigning as manager that evening.

The only real surprise, Henry Edwards observed a few days later, would have been if Speaker were not named the Tribe's new skipper. "There is no doubt of Speaker being more aggressive than Fohl," Edwards told readers of the *Plain Dealer*. "He is more of a fighter than his predecessor. Possessing more ginger, he may speed up the 'Redskins' more than Fohl could. Fohl is of the phlegmatic type. [Speaker] is conceded to be the greatest outfielder the game has ever known. It is also admitted that he is one of the smartest men who ever wore spiked shoes."

Spoke's ascension to manager was well received everywhere: in the clubhouse, in the press box, and in the bleachers. Fans believed that Speaker's hustle would prove infectious to his new charges. They were right. The Tribe won thirty-nine of their final sixty games that season, finishing twenty-nine games above .500, and winning just four fewer contests than the White Sox. The press loved to refer to Speaker as "boy manager." Spoke, at thirty-one, was by far the youngest pilot in the big leagues.

In that 1973 interview, Uhle went to great lengths to praise Speaker as both a manager and a player, marveling at how he caught everything "with two hands" no matter how challenging the play. With the added pressure of managing, Spoke's batting average dipped below .300 for the first time in his career. But he once again led the American League in put-outs and had twenty-five assists. Smoky Joe battled injuries and illness most of the year, hitting .255 in fewer than two hundred at bats. Larry Gardner hit an even .300 and wowed Cleveland fans all year long with his play around the hot corner. Coveleskie and Bagby combined for forty wins.

As a manager, Spoke immediately instituted a substitution system that had been rattling around his head for years. Speaker was convinced that players should be platooned to take advantage of individual skills and match-ups. He also believed in using every player on the roster – a view not shared by all managers back then, many of whom tended to stick with the same lineup day in and day out. Columnist Henry Edwards saluted Speaker's first year as manager by writing, "He combines the gray matter of a thinking veteran with the effervescence of a college boy. He is the carefree rookie one moment, the critical manager the next. He is the happy-go-lucky practical joker one moment, the stern disciplinarian the next."

Spoke effectively used five different outfielders during 1920, weaving them in and out of the lineup depending on pitching match-ups and who was swinging a hot bat. Statistics maven Bill James, in his *Historical Baseball Abstract*, gives credit to Speaker for making such an aggressive platoon system work. Speaker's shuttle method became a model for many managers to come, Casey Stengel and Sparky Anderson among them.

The only teammate who was around on the afternoon of September 24, 1919, when Spoke met Ty Cobb and Dutch Leonard under the stands at Navin Field in Detroit was Joe Wood. Speaker had been player-manager of the Indians for just nine weeks when he and his crony Joe felt the need to consult with their rivals in the midst of a season-ending series. The White Sox had wrapped up the pennant by then and the Indians had clinched second-place money. But the Tigers were in a feisty race with the Yankees for third-place cash. The Navin Field parley only lasted a few minutes. But when it came to light seven years later, it would inflict permanent damage on Tris Speaker's life in baseball and the legacy he left in Cleveland.

Carl Mays had the disposition, one teammate remembered, of a man with a constant toothache. He was dour and abrasive, befitting the son of an evangelical Missouri preacher who was rarely at home to take care of Carl and his seven siblings. Preacher Mays contracted pneumonia while out on the circuit during a stretch of inclement weather. He died when Carl was twelve.

When Carl was fourteen, his mother moved the family to Kingfisher, Oklahoma, to be closer to relatives. A cousin arranged for Carl to make a few bucks by playing on the semipro Kingfisher town nine. Carl got an object lesson in the slippery ways of dollar-driven baseball after he beat archrival Hennessey. Hennessy offered Carl a salary of twenty-five dollars a month, plus living expenses, to come play for them. Carl didn't hesitate, jumping to Hennessy and leading them to the state championship in Enid by pitching five games in five days.

The next summer Mays grabbed a better-paying gig in Mulvane, Kansas. That winter Mays and a Mulvane teammate hopped a freight heading west, trying to get to California to hook up with a minor league team. But in Price, Utah, a local sheriff nabbed them for trespassing. When he learned that the vagrants played ball, the constable gave them two options: go to the lockup or sling some leather for the Price town team. Not surprisingly, they chose the latter. Mays, pitching under an assumed name, again came through in the clutch, hurling the Price squad to a victory over the hated nine from down the pike in Kennelsworth.

They spent the remainder of the winter in Price, then bolted on another freight to Boise, Idaho, where Mays caught on with a team in the Class D Western Tri-State League, earning ninety dollars a month. After a decent showing that season, he was sold to Portland in the Northwest League, the same union that had given Walter Johnson his start a decade earlier. Portland eventually sold Mays and a promising outfielder from Northern California named Harry Heilmann to the Detroit Tigers. Mays was sent to the Providence club in the International League for seasoning.

Tigers owner Frank Navin also had a controlling interest in the Providence club. It was right in the middle of the Federal League's flirtation with star players, and Navin was cash poor, having to part with so much scratch to keep Crawford, Cobb, and his other stars in the fold. So Navin sold his interests in the Providence club – including the rights to the submarine hurler – to Joe Lannin of the Red Sox.

Carl stayed in Providence for the bulk of the season, joining Babe Ruth in the rotation. Ruth and Mays comprised one of the great odd couples in baseball history. One was a saloonkeeper's kid; the other was the son of a fire-and-brimstone preacher. One was the life of the party; the other wore a perpetual scowl. One pitched left-handed, with a pronounced leg kick and an eye-pleasing three-quarter delivery; the other pitched right-handed with an underhand motion that, even by the dead-ball era's herky-jerky standards, was painful to watch. The odd couple came up to the Red Sox together late in the 1914 season.

Mays, like many pitchers back then, had originally thrown sidearmed. But as he got deeper into professional ball, he learned to whip the ball underhanded, to the point where his right knuckles almost brushed the dirt. His peculiar mechanics made it very difficult for hitters to follow his pitches – and even tougher to dive out of the way of his inside brush-backs. Batters called underhanded pitches "shoots."

He made no pretense about the fact that he enjoyed dusting hitters. It was part of Mays's primitively Calvinist worldview: hitters were sinners in Carl's angry hands. Over the years, Mays and Cobb developed what is probably the bloodiest pitcher-hitter rivalry in baseball history. On several occasions the two had fisticuffs over Mays's bean balls. Cobb once had the pleasure of spiking Mays when the pitcher had to cover first on a bunt attempt.

Speaker and Mays were teammates for a full season on the Sox, but that didn't preclude them from coming to blows years later when Carl's high hard one got too close to Speaker's head. In a 1918 game at Fenway Park, a Mays fastball grazed the top of Speaker's skull. Both benches emptied as Spoke had to be restrained from going after Mays. Mays also wasn't shy about directing verbal bean balls toward any club or league officials who crossed him. In 1919 Mays abruptly quit the Red Sox, refusing to play for owner Harry Frazee after the Broadway producer had destroyed the roster. Ban Johnson threatened all kinds of sanctions against Mays for vacating the Boston club, but in the end Carl got his wish: he landed with the rapidly improving Yankees. Speaker may have admired

Mays for the chutzpah he displayed in his showdown with Frazee and Johnson, but he despised the man.

Yankees owner Colonel Ruppert's acquisition of Mays infuriated the rest of the league, including the Indians. Had they known that Mays could be bought for a certain price, owner Dunn would have dickered with Frazee. But Ban Johnson had told Dunn and other AL owners that Mays was going to be taught a lesson – that the league wouldn't allow him to spurn the Sox and sign with a different club. But somehow Ruppert beat the rest of the league to him, the same way he had signed Duffy Lewis and all the other refugees from Frazee's world. Johnson had always wanted a strong franchise in the nation's biggest city – and he was about to get one, big-time.

As Sowell notes, Ray Chapman once confided to family and friends that Mays's submarine ball was hard to detect. Chappie also conceded that Mays liked to intimidate batsmen but assured his listeners that he was quick enough to duck out of the way. Chapman's sister Margaret remembered that a "dark look" came over Ray's face when he discussed Mays. "Carl Mays throws it so he'll dust you off the plate," Margaret recalled Ray saying. "But I'll be right up there. He doesn't bother me."

On August 29, 1915, T. H. Murnane's account in the *Boston Globe* of a 1–0 Red Sox victory over the Indians at League Park spotlighted a play in the fourth inning. Speaker, then still with the Sox, hit a hard grounder to shortstop Chapman, whose momentary bobble allowed Spoke to beat the throw to first "by an eyelash." The Sox took advantage of Chappie's slight miscue to push across the only run of the game – a shame, Murnane noted, because the Tribe's shortstop had made several outstanding plays. The article was eerily headlined, "Chapman Brilliant, But His Slip is Fatal."

The 1920 Indians benefited greatly from Frazee's implosion of the Red Sox and the late-season disharmony that plagued the White Sox. All the pieces fell into place for Cleveland that year: taking advantage of the somewhat livelier ball, every regular had a career year, save Wambsganss, who hit just .244. Spoke hit .388, led the league in doubles with fifty, knocked eight home runs, and drove in 107 runs – the first time in his career he had passed the century mark in RBIS. Beginning with a doubleheader against the Senators on July 8 that season, Spoke went eleven for eleven over a four-game stretch, breaking the big league record for successive hits and prompting the *Cleveland News* to declare, "Tris Speaker swung an immortal bat Saturday."

Tris's platoon system functioned like clockwork in 1920. Against right-handed pitchers, he played Doc Johnston at first, Elmer Smith in right, and Charlie Jamieson or Jack Graney in left. Against lefties, he was likely to start George Burns at first, Joe Wood in right, and Doc Evans in left.

A year later, H. G. Salsinger of the *Detroit News* facetiously wrote, "Should Tris Speaker ever hear of a player that can hit left- and right-handed pitchers, he will refuse to sign him, for a bird like that would wreck the 'Speaker system.'"

Gardner led AL third sackers in put-outs and assists and batted a smooth .310. Tennessean Doc Johnston, the first baseman who had taken over for journeyman Moon Harris the year before, batted .292. Well-traveled outfielder Elmer Smith, back for a second stint with the Tribe, hit .316 while patrolling right. Little Chappie hit .303. Even Steve O'Neill, formerly a feeble hitter, got into the act, batting a career-high .321.

Sarge Bagby had a memorable year, appearing in no fewer than forty-eight games and winning thirty-one of them, with an ERA under 3.00. Even with a spunkier ball, Stan Coveleskie's spitter held batters to a 2.40 ERA.

Veteran right-hander Ray "Slim" Caldwell, whom Cleveland had acquired from the Red Sox in a late-season trade the year before, won twenty games. Slim, a knuckleballer, was something of a knucklehead – at least when it came to carousing. His reputation as a drunkard preceded him in Boston and before that, in New York, where Slim's tavern hopping drove manager Miller Huggins to distraction. When Speaker signed him, he insisted that an unusual clause be added to Slim's contract. It read: "After each game he pitches, Ray Caldwell must get drunk. He is not to report to the clubhouse the next day. The second day he is to report to Manager Speaker and run around the ballpark as many times as Manager Speaker stipulates. The third day he is to pitch batting practice, and the fourth day he is to pitch in a championship game."

Gordon Cobbledick in the years to come loved to tell the story of Slim squinting at the contract language, thinking that the club's stenographer had left out a "not" in the phrase "get drunk." Nope, replied Speaker, the contract means what it says. Spoke's bizarre alcohol cessation method worked: Slim never showed up drunk on the days he was scheduled to pitch – at least not that year. "To say that [Caldwell] became a model of deportment would be to exaggerate," Cobbledick recalled two decades later. "[But] it was suspected that he sometimes violated his agreement by going home and curling up with a good book." In a separate 1948 interview with Cobbledick, Speaker recalled that "it got to be more and more of a chore for [Caldwell] to drink because it was in his contract that he had to. The further the season wore along the less of the stuff he guzzled. By the time he had won his 20th game he was showing up clear-eyed at the ballpark every day and I conveniently forgot about that clause in the contract.

"I happened to bump into him a year ago," Spoke continued in Cobbledick's piece. "He was running a little tavern in New York State and tending bar himself. I asked him how he was getting along with the liquor and he said, 'Oh, I haven't had a drink in years. A glass o' beer now and then, but no whiskey. That cure you gimme done the trick.' "

In Caldwell's first start at Dunn Field, a thunderstorm swept over the ballpark. Terrified fans and teammates watched as a lightning bolt struck Caldwell dead-on while he stood on the mound, knocking him flat. After a few agonizing moments, Slim stood back up, checked to make sure he still had all of his extremities, and resumed pitching. "As best as anyone could figure," Sowell writes, "the lightning had hit the metal button at the top of his cap, surged through his body, and exited through his metal spikes, leaving him only with a slight burn on his chest." Slim pitched a complete game victory that afternoon, earning the undying admiration of his teammates, who were convinced his knuckler now had lightning in it. So were the Yankees, whom he no-hit late in the 1919 season.

In 1920 baseball finally decided to move against the spitball. At the winter meetings in Chicago, the owners had voted to ban not only the spitter but any pitch that was aided by a foreign substance, whether saliva, licorice, emery, talcum powder, or anything else. But to protect hurlers who still earned their keep from throwing a spitter, the owners adopted "grandfather" exceptions that allowed each club to designate two incumbent pitchers who would be exempted from the ban. The owners abolished the spitter for the same reason they introduced the lively ball – to stimulate hitting. The fans wanted offensive fireworks for the top dollar they were paying to get into a ballpark. One of the many ironies of Tris Speaker's life is that the year that his beloved "inside baseball" was beginning to get wrung out of the game, he guided a team to a World Series championship – the only one he would win as a skipper.

As the 1920 season got underway, Speaker wasn't shy about predicting a great season if the Tribe's pitching depth held together. "[Speaker's] in a position right where he can reach right into his pitching grab bag and yank any one of [them] and feel certain that he is going to have a well-pitched game," Ed Bang of the *News* wrote on April 14. Bang's article was accompanied by a caricature of Speaker reaching into his "magic bag" to pull out the likes of Coveleskie, Uhle, Caldwell, and Bagby.

The Indians, the White Sox, and the Yankees, with Babe Ruth busting fifty-four homers (almost as many as the entire combined lineup of the Indians and White Sox!), tussled back and forth all season in a race that came down to the last week. Kid Gleason's White Sox no doubt were distracted when stories began to seep out that their play in the previous year's World Series was not on the level. By the time fall had rolled around, innuendo about a possible grand jury being empaneled had played out on front pages across the country.

Nevertheless, it took a heroic effort from Spoke and his charges to win ninety-eight games in an ultracompetitive environment. Speaker's macho genius was on full display early in year. In a play that set the tone for his club all season, Speaker made a catch in a mid-May game against the White Sox that Cleveland fans and reporters said was the greatest in League Park's history. White Sox slugger Joe Jackson blasted a line drive into center field that Spoke immediately began tracking at full speed. He never stopped as he speared the ball the instant before crashing into the wall, knocking himself out. The umpire, who had run out to center to signal "out," discovered the ball still clasped in the glove of the unconscious Speaker. Joe Wood always considered that catch the finest of the scores of brilliant plays he'd seen Spoke make over the years.

Speaker's slight concussion proved to be the least of the Indians' worries that year. Two weeks after Spoke robbed Shoeless Joe, Stan Coveleskie's wife died after a long illness. Dunn Field's flags flew at half-staff during a victory over the White Sox. Coveleskie was given a long bereavement leave.

Steve O'Neill, too, had to rush home when his wife developed complications after giving birth to twins. Jack Graney, a longtime favorite of Cleveland fans, developed tonsillitis in early June and had to be hospitalized. In his place Speaker inserted Charlie Jamieson, late of Paterson, New Jersey, who was batting a cool .380 in a part-time role. Charlie went on to play eleven more years for the Tribe.

For his part, Tris was hitting .397 in early June. He flirted with .400 on numerous occasions in his career and would come agonizingly close in 1920 – just six hits short. By mid-June Ruth's Yankees had gone on a tear and pulled even with the Indians in the standings.

Also in 1920 big league baseball finally bid adieu to the dead ball. A much livelier sphere was now in use in both leagues. Spoke's teammates on the Indians marveled at how shallow Speaker continued to play in center field despite the more resilient ball. Speaker might have backed off a couple of steps – but his prescient feel for how a batted ball would behave in the air enabled him to play much shallower than every other outfielder. Remembered one Indian: "You know how an infielder gets down for the pitch? Well, you'd get down and the ball would be hit – a shot. You'd turn, and in all that time I never did see him turn. He'd be turned and gone with his back to the plate, the ball, the infield, and when he'd turn around again, there would be the ball." Three years into the lively ball era, he still led AL outfielders in assists with twenty-six.

Despite the legacy of the old Spiders hooligans, Cleveland's fans had heretofore not been nearly as vocal or rabid as Boston's Royal Rooters. But a group that called itself the Stick-to-the-Finish Club was about to change all that. When Ruth and the Yankees came to town in mid-June, the Stick-to-the-Finish boys razzed them unmercifully, loudly deriding the Yankees as "bushers." The carnival atmosphere wasn't restricted to the stands; there was excitement in the skies, too. After earning his wings two years before, Spoke had joined an aviators' club in Cleveland, counting several pilots among his good friends. Biplanes buzzed Dunn Field before the first game of the Yankee series, causing the crowd to crane their necks. In the middle of the game they reappeared, circling overhead to pay tribute to the fellow aviator grounded in center field.

The airmen should have paid their way into the park; they missed several disputed calls and a near-brawl. The city of Cleveland had never experienced anything like it; the Stick-to-the-Finish Club was at full throat. A 4–4 tie was snapped in the bottom of the eighth when Chappie led off with a walk, Spoke advanced him to second after shortstop Roger Peckinpaugh speared a hot hit-and-run grounder, and Larry Gardner solidified his reputation as a great clutch hitter with a two-out poke that plated Chapman. Clear-headed Slim Caldwell snuffed out a Yankee rally in top of the ninth to send twenty-five thousand very happy Clevelanders home. An even bigger crowd the next day watched Ruth and the Yankees pound the Tribe, 14–0.

The Yankees moved past the Indians into first place by the narrowest of margins on July 1, with Chicago also nipping at their heels. Four days later, New York's new slugger nearly bought the farm when a car Ruth was driving crashed in Wawa, Pennsylvania, at 3:00 in the morning. The Babe and three other passengers, including his wife, Helen, miraculously emerged unscathed. Alcohol was surely to blame: the merry troupe apparently stopped for bootleg liquor at a couple of speakeasies en route from Washington to New York. Some nervous headlines the next day screamed: "Ruth Reported Killed in Car Crash."

By early August Spoke's Indians had opened up a four-and-a-half-game lead on the Yanks and a five-game lead on the White Sox. The Yanks came to Cleveland for a four-game series that Edwards and other scribes billed as the "little world series." Dunn could have sold upwards of thirty thousand tickets for each game, but he did a shrewd thing. Rather than roping off standing room in left and center, he turned down the extra revenue and made the New Yorkers play the park to its full breadth. In the previous series against the Yanks at Dunn Field, the opposition had laced several balls into the standing-room areas, earning extra-base hits on liners that Speaker and company normally would have tracked down. Somewhere, John Taylor, Jimmy McAleer, Joe Lannin, and their pocketbooks must have been frowning.

It was supposedly the fiftieth anniversary of Cleveland's first professional game. Dunn arranged for special "Golden Year" ceremonies. Amid the pomp, Indians fans presented Babe Ruth with a floral bat to salute the now-staggering number of homers – forty-one – he had whacked during the course of the season. Despite all the commemorative hoopla, the Yankees won, 6–3.

The next day the red-hot Carl Mays started for the Yankees. Mays had won ten of his last eleven starts but found himself in a bases-loaded jam with two outs in the third inning when Jamieson and Speaker both worked walks after an O'Neill single. Elmer Smith fouled off Mays's first offering, an underhanded change-up, then clobbered the next pitch over the right-field screen and onto Lexington Avenue. Smith's grand slam set off the wildest celebration in a half century of Cleveland baseball. Fans tossed thousands of straw boaters onto the field. Speaker and the other Tribesmen mobbed Smith at home plate, lifting him onto their shoulders for a ride back to the dugout worthy of a Roman emperor.

There was just one problem: six innings were left to play. By the sixth, the Yankees had knotted the score at four. Mays stayed in the game, settled down, and began doing what he did best – intimidating batsmen. In the bottom of the fourth, Mays sent Doc Johnston sprawling with a high hard one. Johnston flung his arm up to protect his head; the pitch glanced off his shoulder. Jack Graney and other Indians stormed to the top of the dugout steps, loudly accusing Mays of deliberately trying to hurt Johnston. Mays glared back, smirking. The Indians' little parade after Smith's slam wasn't lost on Mays; now he was gaining his revenge. A late error by Bill Wambsganss allowed the Yanks to escape with a 7–4 win. The Indians' lead had been reduced by two games.

The next day a still-grieving Stan Coveleskie saw the Yankees bop his spitter early and often in a 5–1 loss. Suddenly the Indians' lead was down to a game and a half. The Stick-to-the-Finish Club and other fans treated Wamby roughly when the second baseman continued to struggle both at the plate and in the field. In the following day's *Cleveland News*, manager Speaker wrote a defiant article that took the naysayers to task: "We haven't quit, as some few fans may have surmised. My boys don't know the meaning of that word."

Even with Spoke's stirring pep talk, the Indians lost the fourth and final game of the "little world series" the next day, 4–3. Ironically, the contest ended with Carl Mays called out of the bullpen to save the game and Tris Speaker at the plate with the tying run in scoring position. The submariner got the best of Spoke, whizzing a fastball past him for strike three. "As [Mays] left the field, he looked in the direction of the Cleveland writers, who earlier in the summer had been so quick to gloat over his demise," Sowell writes. "Mays seemed to be mocking his tormentors as he smiled briefly before disappearing from sight."

There was no respite for the Indians. The next weekend they were due at the Polo Grounds to renew their rivalry with the Yankees. Before leaving for the train station, Sowell relates, Jack Graney tagged along as Ray Chapman and his bride looked over the new home that Kathleen's father was building for them. "What are you going to do with all these rooms?" Graney winked at Ray. "Fill them up," Chappie winked back. Kathleen was expecting their first child; the Chapmans wanted a big family.

It was oppressively muggy in New York when the Indians arrived for the first game of the Yankee series. As the players took the elevated train from the Hotel Ansonia to the Polo Grounds, Chappie decided to break the tension by singing "Dear Old Pal o' Mine." Soon quartet members Graney, O'Neill, and Johnston joined in, followed by the whole club. "Mays is pitching for the Yankees today," Chappie announced with his usual theatrical flair as they entered the clubhouse. "So I'll do the fielding and you fellows do the hitting." His teammates chuckled. It was the most fun they'd had in a while. They put on their gray pinstriped visitors uniforms and took the field at the Polo Grounds.

Chappie's effervescence carried over to the game: the Indians got to Mays early for three quick runs. They were still leading 3–0 when Chapman came to the plate to lead off the top of the fifth. "Chapman was a 'crowder,' " columnist Joe Williams wrote years later. "He would lean over the plate, obscure the pitcher's target, then pull back as the ball was thrown. This made him a difficult man to pitch to. He was always getting the pitcher in a hole and drawing what the ball players call the fat ball to hit."

Spoke, the next batter, was waiting on deck. As Mays went into his elongated windup for the first pitch, the submariner noticed that Chapman's back foot shifted, as if Chappie were going to bunt down the first base line. Mays in that millisecond decided to throw one high and inside to discourage the bunt attempt. Chappie never moved as Mays's fastball gunned straight for his head. It crashed into Chappie's left temple with such force that fans assumed the loud *thwack*! was caused by the bat – not

Chappie's skull. Mays, too, thought that the ball had struck Chappie's bat. When the ball dribbled out toward the mound, Mays fielded it and threw to first baseman Wally Pipp.

Chappie fell in excruciating slow motion. Umpire Muddy Ruel and Speaker were the first to reach him. By now, blood was oozing out of Chappie's left ear. Ruel immediately shouted for medical assistance. Chappie tried to sit up as Speaker knelt beside him. Tris, assuming his friend was getting up to retaliate against Mays, restrained him. The Yankee physician and a doctor who had come out of the stands applied ice to the wound.

"After several minutes," Sowell writes, "Chapman was revived sufficiently to be helped to his feet. When he stood, there was an outburst of applause from the relieved fans." The clubhouse in the old Polo Grounds was located in center field. Chappie made it as far as second base before collapsing again. He ended up being carried into the locker room by teammates. In the immediate aftermath of the incident, Speaker stayed calm, but according to one account, Graney and O'Neill, Chappie's other great pals, had to be held back from going after Mays.

Tribe pitcher Stan Coveleskie had seen too much tragedy that summer, but he hung tough against the Yankees after the fifth-inning delay to tend to Chapman. Covey was nursing a 4–3 lead with two outs in the bottom of the ninth when Speaker jogged in from center to pass on encouragement. Sure enough, Covey induced a rookie named Lefty O'Doul to ground into a force-out.

With modern medical care, Chappie would have survived and probably recovered to have lived something approaching a normal life. But in the Coogan's Bluff of 1920, they lacked the equipment and know-how. After much too long a delay, he was taken by ambulance to Saint Lawrence Hospital, where doctors decided, after some six hours of consultation, to operate on him since his pulse rate was alarmingly low. Speaker left for the hospital immediately after the game ended. He released a statement to the press that attempted to alleviate people's fears. "I was badly scared when I saw Ray try to talk this afternoon, but he was able to talk tonight, so that worry is over. I am inclined to believe that if there is a fracture, it is not a severe one." Speaker's statement proved too sanguine. Chappie's condition worsened as the night wore on.

Kathleen rushed to New York on the overnight train. An old family friend, a priest, met her at the train station. Speaker's room at the Ansonia was full of grief-stricken men as Kathleen and the priest arrived. Kathleen took one look at the somber scene and said to Speaker, "He's dead, isn't he?" Spoke, white as a ghost, nodded. Kathleen fainted.

"Ray Chapman Is Dead," headlined that afternoon's late edition of the *Cleveland Plain Dealer*. In a letter to the people of Cleveland, Mayor William FitzGerald wrote that Chapman represented the "American ideal of a baseball player. He was a clean, high-principled sportsman." Tris called him "the best friend I ever had."

Yankees owner Colonel Huston indefinitely postponed that day's Indians-Yankees game and then sat down with Speaker to ensure that there would be no recrimination between the two clubs. Huston later that day released a statement that said Speaker had exonerated Mays of all blame in Chappie's death. But Speaker forced Huston to retract the statement the day after, saying he had never given the New York owner that blanket assurance. Huston countered with this clarification: "[What] Speaker did say to me was this, 'Nobody has a right to think it was other than an accident.' Speaker's attitude in the matter was splendid, and I would not misquote him for the world. He is a fine fellow, and I think too much of him." Maybe Huston's affection for Speaker was genuine. Or maybe the New York owner was hoping his flattery might discourage an ugly lawsuit.

Some three thousand people filed past Chappie's casket at McGowan's Funeral Home on 153rd Street in Manhattan before it was taken to Grand Central Station. Kathleen, Tris, Joe Wood, and Kathleen's friend (and Tris's sometime best girl) Jane McMahon accompanied the body on the awful train ride back to Cleveland.

The next day, O'Neill and Graney were so distraught that they both collapsed at the Daly home where Chappie's casket was taken before the memorial service. Graney was so inconsolable that Napoleon Lajoie drove him out to the country. O'Neill pulled himself together well enough to serve as a pallbearer. Speaker, too, was supposed to carry the casket, but after suffering what was described as a "nervous breakdown," he stayed in bed under the care of a physician.

At least that's the story that got told to the press and public. As Sowell puts it, "Among themselves, the Cleveland ballplayers were telling a far different story." Speaker, Graney, and O'Neill had apparently gotten into a row over the appropriate church for Chappie's funeral. Kathleen, of course, wanted a Catholic ceremony, which suited Graney and O'Neill. His widow confided to Chappie's friends that Ray had quietly planned to convert to Catholicism, which came as a harsh jolt to Speaker and to Ray's parents. After much discussion, it was determined that Ray's service would be held in a Catholic church but that he'd be buried in a "Protestant plot" in Lake View Cemetery, not the Daly family plot at Calvary. There were so many mourners that Ray's requiem mass was switched from St. Philomene's in East Cleveland to the Cathedral of Saint John the Evangelist, the largest Catholic church in Cleveland. Even at the cathedral, three thousand people were turned away.

The Catholic-Protestant compromise may have been reached *after* Speaker had come to blows with Graney and O'Neill. An occupant of the boardinghouse where many of the Indians lived claimed to have been an eyewitness to the Speaker-O'Neill fracas. "I saw the fight. Speaker picked O'Neill to pieces. With all the facial punishment Steve took, I was surprised he could catch the next day," Sowell quotes the bystander as saying. Sure enough, O'Neill was bothered the next few days by what got reported to the newspapers as "a slightly bruised right hand."

Bill Wambsganss many years later confirmed that Speaker had fisti-cuffs with Graney and O'Neill. "Speaker was a very bigoted man at the time," Wamby said. "He was a 32nd degree Mason of the South. And he couldn't see the idea of Chapman being buried in the Cathedral. I think there was quite an argument about it between him and Graney and O'Neill. And they really knocked the hell out of him. [Speaker] couldn't see to play ball – didn't show up for one day on account of the marks on his face.

"I asked Jack Graney about it point blank one time. He looked at me, and he kind of laughed and said, 'No Bill, that never happened.' But I know damn well it did."

No one knew damn well what to do about Carl Mays. Ban Johnson already hated Mays because of the pitcher's refusal the previous year to play for the Red Sox. Even though it was generally acknowledged that Mays was a headhunter, no one could prove beyond a reasonable doubt that he had deliberately tried to hurt Chapman. The day after Chapman died, Mays was summoned to the office of the Manhattan district attorney. The DA listened to Mays's tearful story and concluded there was no "intent," absolving him of blame.

Ty Cobb, not surprisingly, was Mays's most impassioned detractor. "That Mays has been pitching like that since he came into the league. . . . He killed a great little guy and a wonderful ballplayer. Give the man a taste of his own medicine, I say."

Cobb's Tigers joined the Browns, Senators, White Sox, and Red Sox in threatening a boycott of all games pitched by Mays. The *Cleveland Press* called for Mays's dismissal from the game. Johnson convened an emergency meeting of American League owners where various sanctions were discussed, but none imposed.

Mays characteristically blamed everyone but himself for the accident – from the umpires who missed the fact that the ball had a rough spot and should have been thrown out of play, to Chapman, who should have ducked out of the way instead of into the pitch.

After weeks of *sturm und drang*, no reprisals were taken against Mays. It was deemed an accident.

Speaker was in dreadful shape in the days immediately following Ray's burial. Unable to eat or sleep, he'd lost some fifteen pounds. His physician urged him not to travel with the team to its next series in Boston that weekend. Joe Wood was appointed interim manager. After the heartache of an all-night train ride, Joe guided the club to a loss against the Red Sox. Tris finally joined the club two days later in Boston, where they were scheduled to play a doubleheader at Fenway.

The first game had already started when Speaker arrived. When the Fenway crowd glimpsed their grieving hero as he emerged from the clubhouse, still dressed in a suit and tie, they rose to give him an ovation. One of the first plays Spoke witnessed was a routine fly to left-center that left fielder Jack Graney nearly butchered. Speaker immediately replaced Graney with Joe Wood. Tris then went back to the dressing room and changed into his uniform. An inning or two later he replaced O'Neill with Les Nunamaker. So in his first game after rejoining the team, Speaker benched the two guys with whom he'd fought. Maybe he did it out of spite, but more likely he did it out of compassion. He knew they were as exhausted as he was. Tris put himself into the game as a pinch hitter in the ninth with Cleveland nursing a 2–1 lead. He hit a weak pop-up to Stuffy McInnis. Slim Caldwell got three more outs in the bottom of the ninth to preserve a sorely needed Cleveland victory.

Cleveland lost a 4–3 heartbreaker in extra innings in the second game. Spoke had Jamieson play center and kept Wood in left. In the middle of the game, Spoke put himself into the game as Smoky Joe's replacement. He went hitless in two at bats.

In the series finale at Fenway, Spoke complained to Wood that he felt light-headed. Again, he kept himself out of the starting lineup, only serving as pinch hitter in the ninth inning of a 7–2 loss. Melville Webb of the *Boston Globe* wrote, "Without Speaker going in the lineup, the club surely is all at sea."

They all seemed at sea. One week to the day since Chappie died, the Indians were in Philadelphia for the first game of a series against the last-place Athletics. The Tribe was trailing 2–1 in the top of the ninth when Spoke worked a walk. He then signaled from first for the next batter, Elmer Smith, to lay down a bunt. Smith's bunt attempt down the third base line rolled foul – or at least that's what it looked like to Elmer, who remained in the batter's box. Hearing no "foul" call from umpire George Hildebrand, A's catcher Cy Perkins grabbed the ball and threw to second to force Speaker. The A's relay to first doubled up Smith.

Speaker went ballistic, racing in from second base to confront Hildebrand. "For a full ten minutes he shouted at the umpire in a violent fit of rage," Sowell writes. "Wood rushed to Speaker's side to join in if a fight broke out, but Hildebrand refused to react to the outburst. Knowing the strain Speaker had been under since Chapman's death, he stood by patiently while fellow umpire George Moriarity attempted to calm the Cleveland manager."

His charges gave Speaker a wide berth when he returned to the bench. They'd seen Tris turn blue arguing with an umpire. But they'd never seen a tantrum quite like that. The next day the Indians lost yet another one-run decision – their seventh loss in nine games. Fortunately, the White Sox were also in a tailspin, having lost six of seven to relinquish first place. When the Indians rebounded during a series against the Nats in Washington, they regained the top spot.

Still, Speaker was worried about the psyche of this team and feared the Tribe's pitching depth wouldn't hold up. He told Cobbledick years later that he "badgered the front office for help. 'Get me someone. Get me anyone who wasn't here when Chappie got it. Get me that big Mails from Portland!' "

By signing one John Walter Mails, Speaker betrayed his true gambling instincts. A Californian who bragged that he was raised within the shadows of San Quentin penitentiary, the left-hander's erratic behavior on and off the mound earned him the handle "Duster." But Duster had delusions of grandeur; he preferred being called "the Great Mails" – vanity that must have caused guffaws in the Cleveland clubhouse. The Great Mails loved to regale teammates and hangers-on with stories of playing hardball inside the prison yard at San Quentin. Ironically, Mails had been a bonus baby of the Brooklyn Robins but hadn't panned out. He spent five years in the minors and had two brief cups of coffee with the big club. Brooklyn let him go; Cleveland rolled the dice and signed him for a hefty thirty-five thousand dollars. When Speaker watched him warm up for his Indians' debut in Washington, the Great One's fastball was crackling; his curve was falling off a table. Speaker told Mails, "Forget the hitters. Just throw the ball over the plate and you'll never lose a game."

For that one memorable late summer, Spoke proved prophetic. Nobody touched the Great Mails that September. In nine appearances, he went 7-0 with a 1.85 ERA. It was the San Quentin prodigy's moment in the sun – and the cocky youngster soaked it up for all it was worth. Without the Great Mails, the Indians would never have won the pennant. He also pitched brilliantly in the postseason.

As August turned to September, Spoke wrote a bylined article for the *Cleveland News* that must have dampened thousands of eyes in northeastern Ohio:

> The boys had a tough time of it getting squared away following Chapman's death. It was the hardest battle I ever had in my life to overcome my grief and all of the boys felt the same way about it. But we realized that all our tears and heartaches couldn't bring dear Ray back, and we just pulled

ourselves together with that which was uppermost in Chappie's mind – the pennant and the world's championship – as our goal.

The deeper the Indians got into September, the more they responded to Spoke's admonition. It began with the Tigers game on September 3, which was declared Ray Chapman Memorial Day in Cleveland. Jim Dunn arranged for a lone bugler from Chappie's navy reserve outfit to play "Taps." In a message printed in the program, Ray's widow urged everyone to keep "a brave heart and a smile, for Ray loved both."

The Stick-to-the-Finish Club handed out miniaturized "Tris Speaker bats" and used them to beat a rhythm for their chanting. Cobb and the Tigers won a thrilling 1–0 game that wasn't determined until the final out. On Labor Day weekend, the three combatants – the Yankees, the White Sox, and the Indians – were within percentage points of one another. Chappie's replacement, utility man Harry Lunte, had performed yeoman service in the ten games after Ray's death. That weekend, however, Lunte pulled a leg muscle. Spoke and the Indians had no choice but to gamble a second time by calling up a shortstop from New Orleans in the Southern Association. Only five foot six, the twenty-one-year-old Joe Sewell was hitting .289 when he got the telegram from the big club.

Speaker was reluctant to put a raw kid into such a tough spot – but his options were limited. Inserting the unproven Sewell into the lineup was one of those fortuitous moments in baseball history. It was the start of a Hall of Fame career for the youngster and the beginning of friendship that lasted until the day Spoke died.

As a substitute, Sewell got off to ragged start, throwing away the first ball hit to him. But in his first start, the Indians won 5–3, with Sewell recording seven put-outs and five assists. Each time he fielded a grounder, the thirty-five-year-old Larry Gardner would shout from third, "Take your time now! Steady up!" Wamby also helped show the kid the ropes. At the end of the game, Steve O'Neill walked up to Sewell, smiled, and said, "Chappie's looking down on you, Joe. He's proud of you." Joe remained shaky in the field, making fifteen errors in his first twenty-two games, but he made up for it by batting almost .330. The Indians went on a tear and the Yankees, with Ruth in a slump, began to falter.

Just as Sewell was getting settled in the big leagues, a firestorm began sweeping over baseball. Amid much public outcry that the 1919 Series had been a fraud, Illinois state attorney general Maclay Hoyne called a grand jury. White Sox domo Charles Comiskey was Hoyne's first witness. Instead of unearthing the truth, Commy lobbed grenades. The White Sox owner conceded that he'd heard rumors about his own players dumping games in the Series, but said that he'd gone to Ban Johnson with the information and that the AL president had adamantly refused to investigate. Johnson then rebutted Commy by accusing the White Sox owner of having been in league with gamblers for years.

Comiskey then fumed that his former friend Johnson had financial interests in the Cleveland club and was trying to intimidate the White Sox before their big series with the Indians. Commy's contention was at least half right: Johnson did indeed have a pecuniary interest in the Cleveland club. But as Commy knew better than anyone, Johnson had similar stakes in almost every other franchise in the league – but not, apparently, Chicago's. Once bosom buddies, Commy and Johnson's friendship frayed after they disagreed in 1918 about how and when to shorten the season to accommodate the War Department. Commy was also incensed that Johnson the previous year had ruled against the White Sox and in favor of the hated Yankees on a sticky personnel matter.

As a guest correspondent for the *Boston Post* and *Cleveland Plain Dealer* at the 1919 World Series, Speaker had been outspoken in his criticism of the White Sox's spotty performance in game one against the Cincinnati Reds. "If the White Sox played smart ball today I am going to recruit the Indians for next season from some place over in Europe, where they never saw our national game played," he sarcastically penned in an article ghostwritten for him by Henry Edwards.

Many years later, Edwards confessed that as the '19 Series progressed, he and Speaker did exactly what Hugh Fullerton of the *Chicago Daily Tribune* and Christy Mathewson were doing at another spot in the same press box: dissecting suspicious plays down to their roots. But like Fullerton and Mathewson, they kept their darkest suspicions out of the newspaper in October 1919. As he was leaving the press box at the end of game one, Speaker turned to Edwards and said, "I saw some queer baseball today."

After the fourth game of the '19 Series, which featured Eddie Cicotte cutting off a couple of throws that would have nailed Cincinnati runners at the plate, along with some sluggish play by Joe Jackson in left field, Tris told Edwards, "[There's] something phony about it all but I don't know what it is."

Throughout 1920 Spoke had heard, like everyone else in baseball, rumblings that the press was on the verge of popping the fix story wide open. Yet when reporters on the eve of the big White Sox–Indians three-gamer in September 1920 queried him about the 1919 Series, Spoke volleyed the question back with the practiced ease of a politician:

> Such reports are entirely new to me, and I don't take any stock in them. In this series here, two great ball teams are fighting as hard as they know how, the honor of getting into the World Series as their stake. But the thing to do is to root out all the baseball gambling that is responsible for all these stories. Suppress this evil and you'll kill off the thing that is now besmirching our great national game.

Reporters lapped it up, playing it high in their stories. Spoke's statement had a crackling combination of righteous indignation on the one hand and a clarion call to action on the other. Gambling was indeed besmirching the great national game. And nobody knew it better than the man who gambled big money almost every day of his life, Tris Speaker.

The White Sox took two of three from the Indians in the series, closing to within a half a game of Cleveland, but that was Chicago's last push of the season. They got no closer as nasty stories continued to reverberate nearly every day about the probe into the '19 Series. Chicago's late-season troubles may not have been a coincidence. According to Joe Wood's original interview with Larry Ritter, Eddie Cicotte had confided to Wood that, after the debacle the previous fall, the White Sox did not want to put themselves through the wringer of another postseason. "We don't dare win," Cicotte told Wood in a hotel lobby early in the '20 campaign. "I got to admit that it wasn't exactly just on the 'up and up,'" Wood told Ritter forty-three years after the fact. "Well, a few of the fellows from the Detroit club let it be known that they weren't going to beat their heads off to beat us, see? If everything was on the 'up and up' they would rather have seen us win, anyway, put it like that."

Wood never hinted that the Yankees rolled over in September 1920, but the New York club's stretch of mediocre ball continued. Ruth finally snapped out of his slump by slugging his fiftieth and fifty-first home runs as New York lost to Washington.

Speaker, who had been hovering around .400 all year long, also went into a late-season swoon as the Tribe traveled to St. Louis to begin the last week of the season with a series against the Browns. George Sisler of the Browns finally overtook Spoke in the race for the American League batting crown in late August. In statistics printed August 29 in the *Sunday News-Leader*, Sisler was batting .401 (on his way to a league-leading .407 average for the season), with Speaker behind him at .393. Ty Cobb's average dropped a full fifty points that year to .334, his lowest average since 1908. The Peach would never again lead the league in hitting as Sisler and Cobb's fellow Detroiter Harry Heilmann assumed dominance. As the Indians-Browns series began, Spoke broke out of a 0-for-18 slump. The Indians hung tough against the Browns, winning a wild 7–5 game. In mid-September the Tribe somehow scraped together a seven-game winning streak.

Tris, fortunately for the Indians, wasn't the only one slumping. Charles Comiskey suspended the six players still with the club whose names had been linked in newspaper accounts to the 1919 Series fix: Joe Jackson, Buck Weaver, Swede Risberg, Happy Felsch, Lefty Williams, and Eddie Cicotte. The depleted White Sox could win only one game in the season's final week. All three teams were stumbling toward the finish line. But the Indians got there first, winning ninety-eight games to the White Sox's ninety-six and the Yankees' ninety-five. The honor of pinning the flag down fell to Jim Bagby. His complete game victory over Cobb and the Bengals in Detroit on October 2 clinched the pennant. Spoke had three hits that afternoon and scored twice, as did Bill Wamby. Smoky Joe had a triple and a single and also scored twice. Little Joe Sewell had a hit and fielded his position flawlessly.

The news from Detroit set off a celebration the likes of which pennant-starved Cleveland had never experienced. It had only been six weeks since the unspeakable tragedy with Chappie. The whole city rejoiced in what must have been massive relief for everyone. A front-page cartoon two days later in the *Plain Dealer* depicted Ray Chapman looking down from heaven, urging his former mates to "Carry on!" The caption at the bottom of the drawing – "It pays to play clean" – was both a tribute to

Chappie's integrity and a pointed commentary on the news coming out of Chicago.

It was after midnight, but that didn't stop thousands of Clevelanders from jamming Union Station when their boys returned from Detroit two days after Bagby's win cinched the pennant. It took Speaker and his squad a long time to work their way through the adoring masses. Reporters shouted above the din to ask Tris his plans for the Tribe's pitching rotation in the upcoming World Series. "I don't know who I'll pitch! We'll be able to tell more about that tomorrow!" Speaker hollered back.

"The greeting between the pennant-winning manager and Owner Jim Dunn in Dunn's rooms at The Hollendon Hotel was undemonstrative but affectionate, born of their close association during the past season in their strenuous effort to bring a championship to Cleveland," the *Plain Dealer* commented. " 'How do you feel, Tris?' the portly Dunn asked his skipper. 'Tired,' Speaker told the boss."

Exhausted or not, Speaker had to get his team ready for the Series. He had somehow found the courage to get himself and his club through the trauma of Chappie's death. Since Spoke had taken over the team in July of the previous year, the Tribe's record had been a sparkling 137-77. He not only did a great job working newcomers Uhle and Mails into the rotation, but also late in the season had to train a rookie to take over the most demanding position on the field. Speaker managed at the same time to keep everyone on the bench happy, operating his platoon system at crisp efficiency. Tris generally was the only left-handed hitter in Cleveland's lineup who stayed in the game against southpaw pitching.

On top of all that, he came within a handful of hits of batting .400, leading the league in doubles with 50, scorching 19 other extra-base hits, scoring a career-high 137 runs, and driving in more than 100 runs. Plus his play in center field remained nonpareil; at age thirty-two, he could still run with the best of them. All in all, Tris Speaker's 1920 season has to be considered one of most inspired performances in baseball history.

Before the club departed for Brooklyn that week, the Indians invited fans to join them at Dunn Field to celebrate the pennant and wish the club luck in the Series. "[We're] sharpening the tomahawks and I am sure we will scalp the Dodgers," Dunn told the press. Fans packed the old ball yard to the gills. Stick-to-the-Finish Club members and everyone else rejoiced when Cleveland's business leaders presented their gritty player-manager with the gift of a white horse. No ballplayer in history was as beloved by a community as Tris Speaker was in Cleveland in 1920. He was the alpha and the omega – the miracle worker who overcame tragedy to turn a pedestrian team into a pennant winner.

Speaker would be facing another wily manager in October, Wilbert Robinson of Brooklyn's National League club. Like the Washington club in the junior circuit, which was alternately known as the "Senators" or the "Nats" (Nationals), depending on who was writing the head-lines, Brooklyn also had two nicknames. They had been known as the "Robins" for most of the decade. But now many writers and fans were calling them the "Dodgers," short for "Trolley Dodgers" – a reference to the hundreds of trolleys that crisscrossed the crowded borough, causing pedestrians to bob and weave.

Uncle Wilbert, a no-nonsense catcher in his playing days, had done plenty of bobbing and weaving in a career that began two years before Speaker was born. The Hall of Famer careened from Philadelphia to Baltimore to St. Louis and back to Baltimore again for a brief stint with the city's ill-fated American League entry. In 1892 Robbie signed up with Baltimore's scrappy Orioles, where he became fast friends with third baseman John McGraw. Muggsy and Robbie stayed in baseball together for almost all of the next three decades. Robbie was a player-coach (and briefly, after McGraw quit, interim manager) for McGraw's Baltimore club in the brand-new American League, an experience that left Muggsy and Robbie at loggerheads with Ban Johnson – a feud that literally never went away. Johnson never forgave the two for abandoning his league. For their part, McGraw and Robinson never forgave Johnson for his broken promises and arrogant meddling.

Much like his contemporary Connie Mack, Robbie was considered a solid receiver. Unlike Connie, however, he was more of a threat as a hitter, batting over .300 four times as an Oriole in the 1890s. Famous for fractured quips and malapropisms that would have done Yogi Berra proud, he sometimes played good cop to Muggsy's bad in the clubhouse – then reversed roles to make McGraw look good. In 1914 Robinson moved a few miles east to take the job of skipper with the Brooklyn club.

Robbie wasn't afraid to laugh at himself, often playing the clown to the amusement of his charges. During spring training in Florida in 1915, Robbie agreed to a publicity stunt with aviatrix Ruth Law: he'd try to catch a baseball that was to be dropped from Law's biplane circling overhead. When word of Robbie's planned heroics reached his players, they secretly substituted a grapefruit for the ball, insisting that everyone for miles around come to witness the death-defying drama. Robbie, no spring chicken at fifty-two, gave the moment his all, staggering under the projectile as it came hurtling to earth from a distance of several hundred feet. The citrus exploded into Robbie's catcher's mitt with such force that it almost drowned him in juice and pulp. His players laughed so hard they had to be scraped off the ground.

Clown or no clown, Robbie took over what had largely been a moribund Brooklyn franchise in 1914. Two years later he had his Robins/Dodgers in the World Series. But there was no beating Boston's Leonard-Mays-Ruth-Shore-Pennock rotation. Robbie's boys went down in a best-of-nine series, five games to one.

Now it was four years later, and Robbie was back in the Series again – this time with a deeper and stronger team. He had six pitchers with double-digit wins: spitballer Burleigh Grimes led the way with twenty-three; righty Leon Cadore had fifteen; righty Edward "Jeff" Pfefer had sixteen; righty Albert Mamaux had twelve; lefty Sherry Smith had eleven, and the oft-injured, soon-to-be-former husband of vaudeville starlet Blossom Seely, lefty Rube Marquard, had ten.

Robbie's lineup boasted three .300 hitters. First baseman "Big Ed" Konetchy, the pride of LaCrosse, Wisconsin, hit .308; center fielder Henry "Hy" Myers hit .304; and left-fielder Zach Wheat, a Brooklyn perennial since the Superba days of the early 1900s, hit .328. Catcher Lowell Otto "Moonie" Miller hit a solid .289 and led the National League in put-outs and fielding percentage at his position. Second baseman Pete Kilduff, a Kansas farm boy, was considered one of the better-fielding second sackers in the league, as was the .291-hitting third baseman, Jimmy Johnston, the younger brother of the Tribe's first baseman, Doc Johnston. The Dodgers had cruised to the National League title, winning ninety-three games as Robbie bested his former boss McGraw by seven wins.

Like the ill-starred 1919 Series, the '20 championship was slated to be a best-of-nine affair (the 1921 Series was also best of nine; after that, the Series became best of seven). The first three games of the '20 Series were scheduled for Brooklyn's Ebbets Field. The next four games would be played at Dunn Field in Cleveland. If necessary, the Series would move back to Brooklyn for the final two games. Fans of both clubs were not exactly spoiled by a surfeit of postseason appearances. And given the depressing news coming out of Chicago that questioned the integrity of the previous World Series, the country was ready for an honest-to-goodness fall classic, set in two great baseball towns. America was treated to one of the wildest, wooliest, and ultimately, most satisfying World Series in history.

Future Hall of Fame hurlers spearheaded both staffs. Each ace, ironically, employed a now-illegal pitch, the spitter – but each was protected by the grandfather provision baseball adopted earlier in the year. "Ol' Stubblebeard," Burleigh Grimes, was in the middle of a nineteen-year career that would see him win 270 games for practically every team in the National League at one time or another. He would lead the senior circuit in wins twice and losses once. Grimes's spitter was heavily lacquered with saliva, tobacco juice, and anything else Grimes could slip onto the ball. Grimes was the last of the "legal" spitballers, finally giving his salivary glands a rest a full fourteen years after the pitch had been banned.

"Covey," Stan Coveleskie, also loaded his pitches with foreign substances so heavy that batters complained their hands would sting for hours after they made contact.

Robbie gambled that Marquard could recapture his former greatness and pitched him in game one. Spoke countered with Covey. The spitballer bested the stylish lefty 3–1, although neither team could get much offense going. Like the Robins, the Indians were held to five hits but managed to squeeze a pair of runs off Marquard in the second. Speaker made a couple of nice running catches in blustery wind conditions to snuff out Brooklyn threats. They were tough plays, but as always, Tris made them look routine.

The ineffable Damon Runyon was in the press box at Ebbets Field that afternoon. He filed his story as the players and fans were vacating the field. It was a brisk day, "much too cold for baseball," Runyon's lead observed in a wire service piece published in the *Plain Dealer*. Even in their new blue uniforms, at the end of the game the Indians seemed to "be moving sluggishly, like ants on a cold day," Runyon wrote.

> Stanley Coveleskie, a burly Pole, who is the victorious Cleveland pitcher, can be seen shoving through a knot of men and boys. Let Coveleskie go back and thank the prematurely gray-haired man who brings up the rear of the scattered Cleveland band. . . . Speaker is the greatest outfielder that has ever lived. . . . You have to go to the animal kingdom to find similes for further description. He has the speed of a greyhound. He has eyes like an antelope, which can see very far. His judgment of a fly ball corresponds in keenness to the sense of smell of a deer.

The combination greyhound-antelope-deer was up in the Series one game to none, but fearful that the other side's spitballer would shut his team down the next day. Ol' Stubblebeard did just that, holding the Tribe scoreless in a complete game shutout. Jim Bagby pitched well for Cleveland, limiting the Robins to just seven hits, but losing 3–0.

The next day Spoke crossed his fingers and sent the hard-living Slim Caldwell to the mound. Tris's worst fears were realized when the Robins chased Slim with two quick runs in the bottom of the first. Slim was able to record only one out before giving way to the Great Mails, who pitched six and two-thirds innings of gritty ball in relief. Robbie's men didn't score another run, but left-hander Sherry Smith made it hold up, winning 2–1. Brooklyn now assumed command of the Series, two games to one.

If Spoke were panicking, he certainly didn't share it with Runyon, Edwards, and the other newshounds covering the Series. " 'We have just begun to fight,' declared Manager Tris Speaker of the Indians last night on the eve of the first world's series game ever played in Cleveland," Edwards wrote, "and thus unconsciously repeating the famous remark of an American patriot in the days when the United States was becoming accustomed to its swaddling clothes."

The Series would not return to Brooklyn, Speaker vowed to the press boys. Cleveland would sweep the four games at Dunn Field, he promised, and clinch before the home fans.

Tris's words were balm to the tens of thousands of Cleveland fans who had waited decades to host a championship game. Covey again baffled the Brooklyns with his spitter, allowing only five hits as the Indians knocked Leon Cadore out of the box early in a 5–1 win. The Series was now knotted at two.

The fifth game remains eight decades later one of the most bizarre and sensational World Series games ever played. Whatever prospects Robbie's boys had of coming back in the Series were dashed in the first inning. Elmer Smith for the second time that season sent waves of delirium sweeping through Dunn Field by whacking a grand slam onto Lexington Avenue. It came in the bottom of the first against the previously untouchable Burleigh Grimes, triggering a deafening roar that reporters swore could be heard in Toledo. Jamieson, Wambsganss, and Speaker were all aboard and gave Elmer an escort back to the dugout that caused more delirium.

But Cleveland's joy had just begun. With the Tribe holding a comfortable lead with no outs in the top of the fifth, the Dodgers' Pete Kildruff was on second and Moonie Miller on first. Relief pitcher Clarence Mitchell, who replaced starter Grimes in the fourth inning, was at the plate. He scorched a line drive that looked to Kildruff and Miller like it was destined to land in right-center for extra bases. Second baseman Bill Wambsganss timed his leap perfectly, snagging the lower half of the ball with a snap of his glove, then having the presence of mind to outrace Kildruff to the bag at second. Moonie Miller, a lumbering catcher not known for his dexterity afoot, was flummoxed. He stood paralyzed, two-thirds of the way between first and second, stunned that Wambsganss was now coming toward him with the ball in his glove. Wamby applied the tag, nonchalantly tossed the ball at the pitcher's mound, and jogged toward the Cleveland dugout.

Virtually no one in the ballpark had ever witnessed an unassisted triple play at any level of baseball; it was only the second one in recorded big league history. It took folks a few seconds to do the arithmetic and absorb what had occurred. Then fans sent another full-throated cry across Lake Erie. After the game, photographers arranged for the accursed Brooklyn trio – Kildruff, Miller, and Mitchell – to pose with Wamby. They good-naturedly went along.

All the commentary that evening and the next morning centered on the two miraculous events – a grand slam and an unassisted triple play – *happening in the same game*! What were the chances? Everyone in northeastern Ohio was convinced that Ray Chapman was up in heaven, manipulating things with the Almighty.

Now an Indians triumph had the feel of destiny. Divine intervention seemed at play once again the next afternoon when Duster Mails, with all of seven games under his belt as an American Leaguer, went out and beat Sherry Smith, 1–0, in a duel of left-handers. The Great Mails held Brooklyn to three harmless singles. Spoke scored the only run with two outs in the sixth when he singled, then hustled all the way around from first on Burns's double off the right-center screen.

Cleveland was in a frenzy over the prospect of clinching the next afternoon, which, to add to the atmosphere, happened to be Columbus Day – a coincidence not lost on Henry Edwards. Casting large for historic if slightly fatuous parallels, Edwards's lead following Cleveland's 3–0 victory was "The better the day, the better the deed. On Oct. 12, 1492, Christopher Columbus discovered America, and thus paved the way for the organization of the American Baseball League. On Oct. 12, 1920, the Cleveland Indians, no relation to those discovered by Columbus 428 years ago, won the world's baseball championship. . . . Columbus Day from now on should be a Cleveland civic holiday."

Covey and Spoke were the heroes. Stan pitched a shutout for his third win of the Series, allowing only five harmless hits. His earned run average for the postseason was a Koufaxian 0.67. Speaker's triple – his last in a brilliant World Series career – keyed the Indians' big rally. Tris had eight hits and scored six runs in the seven games, batting .320 against a rugged Brooklyn pitching staff in cold weather. His fielding drew raves not only from Runyon, but from all the scribes in the press box.

Joe Sewell, Chappie's surrogate, fittingly had a hand in the final out. At precisely 3:57 p.m., Little Joe fielded a two-hopper from the Dodgers' Big Ed Konetchy and tossed it over to Triple Play Wambsganss, who stepped on second to retire Hy Myers, ending the Series. Wamby instantly flipped the game ball to Speaker rushing in from center as the Indians began somersaulting on top of one another with the hometown crowd roaring. Charlie Jamieson made a beeline for Speaker, intending to leap into his arms – but Spoke knew exactly where he wanted to go: to the box seats where his mother was sitting.

Spoke leapt over the railing and embraced Jenny for a good five minutes before joining the celebration on the field. He handed her the ball, hugging and kissing her over and over again, thanking her for letting him leave Hubbard to pursue his dream. To add to the sense of wonderment, October 12 happened to be Jenny's seventy-third birthday.

"No city that ever held a world's series had retained its interest in the event as long as Cleveland," mused Runyon, clearly taken with the way Clevelanders had embraced the games. "Cleveland, with three days of furious baseball, was still red hot yesterday. People again waited up all last night to get through the bleacher gates. Long before noon, the bleachers were packed again," he observed.

Runyon's piece humorously mentioned that Rube Marquard, one of his favorites since they hung in the same fast crowd, had been brought to justice before a Cleveland court. Rube had been caught in a Cleveland hotel lobby trying to scalp six tickets for three hundred bucks earlier in the week. On the morning of the final game, the vaudevillian-cum-hustler was fined one dollar for scalping.

It may have made for an amusing bon mot to Runyon, but Rube's little run-in with the law steamed his manager. Marquard's appearance before the judge caused him to arrive late at the ballpark for the seventh game. With Brooklyn facing do-or-die elimination, Robbie wanted to use Rube in case Grimes faltered early. But after Marquard showed up late, Robbie kept him on the bench. Rube's encounter with the judge was the least of his problems. Within a week of the Series finale, Blossom would file for divorce against her erstwhile song-and-dance partner.

"I knew the boys would come through and grab a world's championship for Cleveland. I knew they had the power to whip Brooklyn – and they knew it, too. Those two defeats in a row in Brooklyn did not discourage us at all," Spoke hollered in the raucous Indians' clubhouse.

Speaker's old running mates, Joe Wood and Larry Gardner, played bit roles in the Series, between them collecting only seven hits. But Gardner's ironlike presence at third helped steady the nerves of young Sewell. Wood, moreover, was an ardent supporter of Spoke's platoon system, never complaining about lack of playing time.

Mayor FitzGerald immediately organized a torchlight victory rally to be held at Wade Park. There weren't enough cops in the state of Ohio to keep the crowd under control. The tens of thousands of people who crammed into the park got overly exuberant when the mayor and Mr.

Dunn led the ballplayers onto a hastily constructed dais. The small stage was separated from the crowd only by a restraining rope that quickly got trampled. Speaker and his players had to get up out of their chairs and run for cover as the hordes descended on them. The people of Cleveland were so excited – and so new at this – that they couldn't contain themselves. Fortunately, no one was seriously hurt.

Before the rally was abruptly shut down, a telegram written to Spoke from a certain admirer at 1600 Pennsylvania Avenue in Washington DC was read to the crowd. In an oblique reference to the travails in Chicago, President Wilson commended Spoke and the Indians for their "honest and sincere" effort. The two Ohioans competing to succeed Wilson that fall, Senator Warren G. Harding, a Republican, and Governor James Cox, a Democrat, also sent congratulations to Dunn and Speaker.

Despite the ordeal with Chappie – or maybe, ironically, because of it – it was a magical year. Dunn and Speaker no doubt looked at their roster and thought there would be more World Series triumphs to come. But they couldn't anticipate just how dominant the Yankees were going to become – and how badly the Red Sox and White Sox were imploding. They also couldn't anticipate that Dunn wouldn't be around much longer. In June 1922 the rotund Dunn succumbed to the influenza epidemic that plagued America throughout the early 1920s.

Three months after the Indians captured the Series, Dunn awarded Spoke a batch of equity in the Cleveland Baseball Club and made him a director. On January 12, 1921, Dunn announced that Speaker was "without exception" the highest-paid principal in the big leagues. The salary wasn't disclosed, but when taken with his stock holdings, it made for what should have been a comfortable life for Spoke. But especially in those bachelor years, he spent too much time at the track.

Tris would have many fine moments to come as the Indians' player-manager. The Indians came close a couple of times, but they never appeared in the postseason on Speaker's watch again. It would take twenty-eight long years before another Cleveland player-manager, this time Lou Boudreau, would lead the Tribe to a world's championship.

Kathleen Daly Chapman gave birth to a little girl six months after her husband was killed. She named the baby Rae hoping the child would somehow come to embody her late husband's spirit. Kathleen remarried and moved with Rae and her new husband to California. But she was never able to shake the horrible depression caused by Ray's death. Six years later, she committed suicide by ingesting cleaning fluid. In 1928 little Rae contracted measles and died. Mother and daughter were buried next to each other in a Cleveland graveyard. But their remains were interred in the Catholic cemetery, Calvary, not the Protestant cemetery, Lake View, where the gravestone of "Raymond Johnson Chapman" rests alone.

At some point in the early 1920s, Tris Speaker, man about town, aviator, horseman, tango enthusiast, and confirmed bachelor, ended his relationship with Kathleen Daly's friend Jane McMahon and began dating a Cleveland woman in her early thirties named Mary Frances Cudahy. (Curiously, the name was spelled "Cuddihy" so often that it's unclear which version the family preferred). Miss Cudahy, called Fran, was an acquaintance of Mrs. Dunn, the owner's wife. Mrs. Dunn introduced the pair in 1919, although it doesn't appear that they began dating seriously until several years later.

A devoted Catholic, Fran was descended from a clan whose roots were in County Kilkenny in the southeast of Ireland. Exactly when her parents or grandparents emigrated from the Emerald Isle is not known. She did have brothers not far off in age from Spoke who shared his passion for sports and basement tinkering. Unlike the Daly clan, the Cudahys were not a socially prominent family. Fran was a workingwoman, employed at the Union Trust Company and later its successor, the Union Commerce Bank. Like the Dalys, however, the Cudahys worshiped at St. Philomene's parish.

How Speaker was able to square a lifetime of antipapist prejudice with romancing young ladies of Irish Catholic extraction is a puzzler. When he was playing in Boston, a dalliance with an immigrant girl would probably have been unthinkable, given the raft of guff he would have taken in the Red Sox clubhouse. But Cleveland was a less divisive place. Plus hanging around the ebullient Chappie all those years seemed to open Tris up. Maybe in the wake of his fistfight with Steve O'Neill and Jack Grady after Chappie's death he started to rethink certain convictions. Chappie, a fellow Southerner, had found happiness with an Irish Catholic lass. Why not him?

The first of many Yankee dynasties to come over the next eighty-plus years began in 1921. Miller Huggins's men won ninety-eight games. Anchoring the staff was the man many fans wanted to see locked up behind bars, or at least forced to give up the game: Carl Mays. Mays had a career year in '21, leading the league in wins with twenty-seven and saving seven other games. Bob Shawkey won eighteen contests and Waite Hoyt won nineteen. All Jidge did was hit fifty-nine homers and knock in 171 runs.

Speaker's defending world champions had a more than respectable year, battling the Yankees most of the season before finishing in second-place money with four fewer wins. Covey had another superb season, winning twenty-three games. George Uhle won sixteen games. The Great Mails reached the apogee of his career with fourteen wins. Jim Bagby, however, had by his standards a mediocre season, going 14-12 with a 4.70 ERA.

Smoky Joe had the offensive year of his dreams in '21, hitting .366 in a limited platoon role. Young Joe Sewell was nothing short of sensational at the plate that year, hitting .318 and driving in ninety-one runs. He was a little less than sensational in the field, making forty-seven errors. Spoke led AL center fielders in fielding percentage and doubles, compiling only two fewer extra-base hits than he'd had the previous season. The Tribe's old field boss, Lee Fohl, had taken over the St. Louis Browns, guiding them to a third-place finish. The next year, Fohl would skipper the Browns to within one game of the mighty Yankees when his first baseman, George Sisler, hit a scorching .420, tying Cobb for the highest American League average in history.

The 1921 season got off to a curious start when Tris Speaker, inveterate bettor, announced in late March that, to "baffle gamblers," he would no longer announce his starting pitchers in advance. Spoke's new policy was abandoned a few weeks into the season when he realized that he was not only baffling gamblers but also confusing his own staff. Plus the information was leaking out through other means.

In June 1921 the Ontario cabin that Spoke had purchased a couple of years earlier at Idylwyld Island on Price Lake was ransacked. The robbers took everything – literally including the kitchen sink, Spoke wryly told reporters. That fall, the local Hiawatha Indian tribe in the area surrounding Price Lake honored Speaker and his hunting and fishing buddy, second-string catcher Les Nunamaker, with a special dinner.

Idylwyld Island wasn't the only place that Tris and Les did their hunting and fishing. Tris was a longtime member of the Port Bay (Texas) Hunting Club, a preserve located not far from the Gulf of Mexico. In the fall of 1921 Speaker and Nunamaker invited columnist Tom Marshall to join them for a little duck shooting and socializing.

As printed in the *Los Angeles Times*, Marshall produced a column as laudatory about Speaker's skills in the great outdoors as anything written by Spoke's pal Morris Ackerman in the *Cleveland News*. Not only was Speaker an expert marksman, Marshall wrote, he could speak a duck's language! Spoke's duck calling seemed to hypnotize the birds, enticing grounded ducks to take wing and luring distant fowl to venture near the hunters' blind.

It wasn't just Speaker's mastery of duck language that impressed Marshall. "Speaker's home is near the Mexican border [which has] brought [him] in contact with those 'dusky hombres' who populate the 'land of the cactus,' " the columnist wrote, betraying the casual racism of the day. "Speaker acquired a knowledge of both Spanish and 'Greaser,' which he fluently speaks. Vicissitudes of a varied character are encountered in the baseball arena, necessitating artistic handling and concise enunciation of that common language, usually classed profane." All of which was Marshall's ornate way of saying that Speaker could swear like a sailor in "Greaser," which sounds like a strange combination of backwoods Texas-ese and Spanish.

"A noted darkey chef" known to Port Bay members as "Nigger Howard" prepared meals, Marshall wrote. Between Spoke's superb duck calling and Howard's culinary delights, everyone had a great time. The group had no trouble bagging its legal limit. Marshall ended his column by quipping, "Speaker is certainly the speaker of many languages."

In '22 the multilinguist's Tribe fell back to earth. Not even the acquisition of Speaker's old rival Stuffy McInnis could prevent a slide toward mediocrity. They finished a distant fourth, just two games above .500. Uhle had a solid season with twenty-two wins, but Bagby was hurt much of the year and ineffective when he did throw. Covey also struggled much of the season, finishing with just seventeen wins. Alas, the Great Mails was pitching himself out of the big leagues, with just four wins and an ERA of 5.28.

As revealed that June, Mr. Dunn's will specified that his wife remain majority owner, that longtime minority owner and president "Barney" Barnard be elevated to the boss of the club, and that Tris Speaker remain as manager. There's no way that the Tribe's new brain trust could compete with the bottomless fortunes of the team in New York, which was building its own ballpark and had a fan base that dwarfed Cleveland and everyone else's.

In mid-September 1922 Speaker announced plans to completely overhaul the Tribe's pitching staff, which except for George Uhle had aged and become less reliable.

In many ways, 1923 turned out to be Speaker's most impressive individual year. He broke not only his own American League record for doubles in a single season, but Big Ed Delahanty's twenty-four-year-old Major League record for two-baggers as well. Spoke finished the season with 59 doubles, 11 triples, 17 homers, 130 RBIs, and a remarkable 133 runs scored. Once again, he flirted with .400 before closing the year at .380. Not a bad season for a thirty-five-year-old. Spoke had figured out how to pull the lively ball over the inviting right-field screen at Dunn Field. His runs-batted-in total tied his old foe Jidge for the league lead, which must have given Spoke enormous satisfaction. Over the years, he led the league in more than a dozen different offensive categories and scores of different defensive statistics. But 1923 was the only time in his career that he led the league in RBIs.

Still, the Tribe was no match for the Yankees, who won ninety-eight games en route to their first-ever world title. For the third consecutive year, Huggins's men met McGraw's boys in a subway Series. But this time, the boys from the new ball yard in the Bronx prevailed, four games to two.

Spoke's club finished eleven games above .500 that season. Not bad, but squarely in third place behind the Bombers and the Bengals. George Uhle's twenty-six wins led the AL in wins that year. Ty's second-place finish in 1923 would turn out to be the best result manager Cobb ever achieved in Detroit. The next year, Cobb would again finish twenty games over .500, but Speaker's club descended into the second division, ending the season twenty-one games under .500. Spoke again was saddled with an overmatched staff.

In October 1923 Speaker gave his best girl what by all accounts was a huge diamond ring. Yet in classic Speaker fashion, he denied that he and Miss Cudahy were engaged. It was just a token of friendship, he told reporters – a public sentiment that must have caused a few sleepless nights in the Cudahy household. Fran would have to wait two years before she walked down the aisle – but their ceremony was such that there was no aisle down which to walk.

Spoke was never satisfied with the spring training facilities available to the Indians. Always in the market for the best deal and a better environment, he shifted their training camp from New Orleans to Dallas for a couple of years, then to Lakeland, Florida, for the last years of his tenure with the club. As a young ballplayer, Spoke had reveled in the spring training decadence of first Hot Springs, then New Orleans. But once he became a manager, he took a dimmer view of late-night diversions. Dallas wasn't exactly Hot Springs and Lakeland was a far cry from Bourbon Street.

Speaker continued to appear at rodeos around the country, often as part of Will Rogers's traveling troupe but sometimes as a solo performer. "Here's a guy who can twirl a rope better than I can," Rogers was fond of saying as he called Speaker down from the stands. On December 2, 1922, folks in Hillsboro, Texas, marveled when part-time cowpoke Tris came within three seconds of a "world's record" in calf roping. Speaker easily defeated "crack roper" Tommy Kirnan that evening, 21 seconds to 29 seconds. Rogers still loved to surprise audiences by bringing Speaker out of the crowd, decked out in either his baseball uniform or street clothes, and have him perform rope tricks or do a little fancy riding.

When the "manliest of men" decided to get married, he caught the whole world by surprise, including his seventy-eight-year-old mother and certain members of the family of the bride. In mid-January 1925 Speaker arrived in Cleveland ostensibly to take care of some personnel-related matters with the ball club after an extended hunting vacation. But he stunned everyone on January 15 by getting married to his long-time girl-friend/fiancée in a whirlwind ceremony.

Here's how the *Plain Dealer*'s Stuart M. Bell covered the event in a marvelous front-page story full of tongue-in-cheek baseball allusions:

> Tristram Speaker of Hubbard City, Tex., pulled the delayed steal of his life yesterday, when, without giving anybody a hit-and-run signal, he made Miss Mary Frances Cudahy of Cleveland his lifelong mascot. The manager of the Cleveland Indians was married to Miss Cudahy in the parish house of St. John's Catholic cathedral by Msgr. Joseph Smith, vicar general of the Cleveland diocese and pastor of St. Philomene's church. The rite was performed in the presence of Msgr. T. C. O'Reilly, pastor of St. John's. Immediately after the game, beg pardon, the ceremony, Mr. and Mrs. Speaker left for Akron, O., to board a Florida special of the Pennsylvania railroad. The bride and groom will spend two weeks in Lakeland, Fla., training city of the Indians, and then proceed to Hubbard City, where Mrs. Jennie Speaker, Tristram's mother, is waiting to give the couple her blessing. Speaker, known among baseball writers as "poor copy" because stories of the diamond are hard to worm from him, did not give out any three-sheet posters about the new contract he was signing.

Speaker not only didn't put up posters, he didn't tell anybody in the organization that he was getting hitched, save Indians' business manager Walter McNichols, who stood in for Tris as best man. The same held true for Fran's brothers, none of whom had a clue of their sister's impending nuptials. Fran did tell her sister Claire, who served as her bridesmaid. And Fran's mother, Mrs. Margaret Cudahy, was also among the few in attendance at the parish house.

Even by the Texas cowboy's round-'em-up standards, his nuptials were brutally quick. At 3:00 p.m., the *Plain Dealer* reported, he obtained the marriage license. At 3:15 he darkened the door of the parish house. By 3:30 he and Fran were in a cab headed for the train station to catch the train for Florida.

Why the bizarre approach to what should have been the most joyous day of his life? Maybe it was a spur-of-the-moment decision. Maybe Fran had delivered, to borrow reporter Bell's metaphorical device, the "play-me-or-trade-me ultimatum" and Tris had to move in a hurry or risk losing her. She had, after all, been wearing his diamond "nonengagement" ring for upwards of two years.

But the likeliest scenario is that the "Mason of the South" had trouble reconciling his marriage to an immigrant daughter in a papist ceremony.

It was no ordinary Catholic church in which Tris and Fran were married. The Cathedral of Saint John the Evangelist was back then – and remains today – the epicenter of Catholic activity in Cleveland. It's the place to which Ray Chapman's requiem mass was moved once his in-laws' church was pronounced too small. It's interesting that Tris chose the parish house, not an altar in the cathedral, in which to take his vows. In his reckoning, perhaps that made the ceremony less Catholic – not unlike his insistence that Chappie be buried in a Protestant cemetery. Or maybe it wasn't his call; maybe the monsignors deemed it inappropriate for a Methodist to be wed inside the cathedral.

No matter how it happened, Tris Speaker, prickly son of the Confederacy, was married in a Catholic ceremony in a Catholic dwelling in the presence of not one but two monsignors of Irish descent. When the news reached Lewiston, Maine, Rough Carrigan must have had himself a real good chuckle.

Nineteen twenty-five was another frustrating year for the Indians' club. Fans were so restless by midseason that a small drumbeat developed to replace Speaker as manager. Their pitching went from mediocre to bad, as Uhle fell off his pedestal and there were no quality youngsters to replace Bagby and Covey.

But 1925 proved to be yet another splendid individual season for Spoke. Perhaps married life agreed with him. In early May he eclipsed Cleveland icon Larry Lajoie's record for career doubles. On July 19 he was hitting .401. As late as September 20 he was hitting .398, only dropping to .389 in the last week of the season. At age thirty-seven, he lost the AL batting crown to Harry Heilmann by four measly points. Spoke once again led AL center fielders in catch-and-throw double plays with nine that season.

Yet it must have been difficult for him to see the Tribe remain well below .500 and finish third from the bottom. Oddly, that was also the year Huggins's Yankees fell from grace, dropping to 69-85. The difference was that Colonel Ruppert could dip into his personal treasury and rectify things in a hurry. Barney Barnard and Mrs. Dunn didn't have pockets quite that deep.

Joe's little brother, James Luther "Luke" Sewell, was signed by the Tribe soon after Joe made the big club in 1920. Like his older brother, Luke played shortstop for the University of Alabama. One day when Alabama was playing Oglethorpe College in Atlanta, the Crimson Tide's regular catcher was hurt, so Luke filled in behind the plate. Indians scout Patsy Flaherty happened to be in the stands and watched Luke gun down two runners. After the game, Flaherty told Luke that the Indians wanted to sign him as a catcher. "But I don't even own a catcher's mitt," Luke protested. "You will," Flaherty replied. Luke was planning on entering Alabama's medical school in the fall of 1921, but Speaker wanted him around as insurance in case O'Neill or Nunamaker got hurt. "If you'll just stay here and not go back to school, you'll make yourself a minimum of two or three thousand dollars," Speaker told young Sewell. "Now, that was a lot of money in those days," Luke recalled in Donald Honig's *Man in the Dugout*. "Well, that kept me out of school. But when the race was over, we hadn't won it, and by that time is was too late in the season to go back to school." Luke ended up becoming a baseball lifer, not a physician.

He spent the bulk of his first five years doing what he did in the fall of '21 – sitting on the bench. Luke wasn't happy with his substitute status, developing a much different perspective on Spoke's managerial skills than the worshipful view often expressed by his older brother. "Tris Speaker was a great ballplayer, just great, but I never thought he was an outstanding manager," Sewell told Honig. "He didn't seem to have much patience with a young player. That was the way it was in those days. A young player had to take his place on the sidelines until he had a chance to prove himself. . . . I didn't get to take batting practice in spring training until my third year. That's right. They knew I wasn't going to play, so they didn't want to waste any time with me."

The contradictory impulses of Tris Speaker were on full display in his treatment of the Sewell brothers. With one, he was patient and supportive. With the other, he was distant and unhelpful. Luke went on to manage ten seasons for the St. Louis Browns and the Cincinnati Reds. In 1944 he guided the traditionally wretched Browns to the AL pennant, taking the crosstown Cardinals to six games in a subway Series.

The 1926 Yankees were at least 95 percent as good as their more celebrated counterparts a year later. Lou Gehrig, in just his second full season, wasn't quite the RBI machine that he would become, but he still drove in 107 runs and hit .313. Tony Lazzeri drove in 114 runs and the Bambino swatted in 145 with 47 homers. Throw in Mark Koenig, Jumpin' Joe Dugan, Earl Combs, and the still potent Bob Meusel (.315 and 81 RBIs) and it was a very formidable lineup, particularly when coupled to a rotation that included Herb Pennock, Sam Jones, Waite Hoyt, and the man born sixty years too soon, the graphically named Urban Shocker.

Now take a look at the lineup that Speaker fielded every day in 1926: Burns, Spurgeon, Sewell, Lutzke, Summa, Jamieson, and Sewell, with Uhle, Levsen, Shaute, and Smith on the slab. How in the world did that team ever stay with the Yankees? The Tribe went from fourteen games below .500 in '25 to twenty-two games above it in '26. But the Yankees did Spoke a couple of games better. It's a testament to Speaker's savvy in the dugout that his Tribesmen dogged the Yankees all year – and won five more games than the at-long-last-improved Mackmen.

Speaker finally showed signs of age in what turned out to be his last year with the Indians. He batted just .304 and actually benched himself at several points in the season because of lackluster play in the field. His thirty-eight-year-old legs were betraying him; he couldn't go get it the way he used to. It was time to begin thinking of life beyond his playing days.

If Speaker told anyone the disquieting news he'd gotten from Ban Johnson that spring, they respected his confidence. His life was about to take a dramatic turn. And it wasn't for the better.

CHAPTER 10

Scandal

Judge Kenesaw Mountain Landis looked like something out of the Old Testament, or at least the Old Testament as produced and directed by Cecil B. DeMille. With his silver mane and stern visage, the pictures of Landis throwing out a first ball – his body painfully erect, his right arm cocked at a fierce angle – always made him look a little like Moses about to smite one of the Philistines.

It was this biblical image that got him the job in the first place. The league presidents and club owners picked him to be the first commissioner of organized baseball not because they wanted him to exercise power, but because they wanted him to *look like* he was exercising power. Landis was installed in the commissionership because he had a reputation – much of it undeserved – as a tough and uncompromising judge. Five years earlier, he had issued a surprisingly strong ruling that spanked the upstart Federal League in its suit against the National and American leagues. The owners never forgot the judge whose selective interpretation of antitrust law had gilded their pocketbooks.

He was named after a Civil War battle in which his father had been badly wounded. In the words of Robert Smith, author of *Baseball in the Afternoon: Tales from a Bygone Era*, "Landis tried to live up to his name by playing the part of a firm dispenser of rock-solid justice. Unfortunately, both in his courtroom and during his term as commissioner, he sometimes seemed more bent on the playing than the dispensing."

Landis reveled in theatrics. As a federal judge, he once allowed a young man who admitted he had embezzled $750,000 in government bonds to escape unpunished. The youngster was contrite, Landis asserted, and besides, his employer wasn't paying him enough. But woe be unto any apologist for the Kaiser, or instigator of unions, or defender of Bolsheviks who came before his bench. They were all "anti-American scum" – to use a favorite Landis-ism. He didn't just fan the flames of xenophobia that swept across America during World War I and its after-

224

math – he dumped kerosene all around and threw a torch. At one moment during the war, he opined from the bench that the Kaiser and his crew should all be rounded up and executed. At other times, the good judge referred to socialists and labor leaders as "filth" and "slimy rats."

Many of Landis's landmark rulings, including the stiff fine of $29 million he imposed on Standard Oil for extracting rebates from railroads, were overturned on appeal. In the judicial orbit, he was considered a grandstander – and an erratic one at that. But after the Black Sox revelations began to rock baseball, the league presidents and club owners felt like they had no choice but to put a high voltage personage in charge. Landis fit the bill – and besides, he was a fan. Humorist Will Rogers said Landis was appointed because "somebody said, 'Get that old boy who sits behind first base all the time. He's out there every day anyhow.' So they offered him a season's pass and he jumped at it."

The relationship between Ban Johnson and Kenesaw Landis got off to a rocky start and went downhill in a hurry. Johnson felt that Landis wasn't doing enough to shape the grand jury's investigation of the Black Sox scandal. Landis, though, was craftily playing politics and the percentages. He knew he had been handed a can of worms with the Black Sox – he just wasn't sure how rotten the can was. Plus the old judge knew a kangaroo court when he saw one. Rather than weigh in publicly as the farcical trial of the White Sox Eight progressed, he bided his time. When the prosecution failed to produce any evidence against the Black Sox and the jury voted for acquittal (allowing a triumphant Chick Gandil to tell reporters, "I guess that will learn Ban Johnson that he can't frame an honest bunch of players!"), Landis went into theatrical mode, assuming "the role of avenging angel," in Smith's phrase. The commissioner abruptly – and arbitrarily – announced that all eight of the Black Sox would be banned from organized baseball for life, despite the fact that certain players were clearly "dirtier" than others. It was the consummate public relations move for Landis. It made baseball's leadership look like it was taking charge of the effort to expunge cheating from the game, when in fact it was doing just about everything it could to avoid confronting uncomfortable truths.

We'll never know precisely what transpired in the Speaker-Cobb-Wood-

Leonard controversy anymore than we'll know exactly what happened in the Black Sox affair, Teapot Dome, Crédit Mobilier, or any one of a half dozen other "scandals" that plagued America during the Gilded Age and the supposedly Progressive Era that followed. Any examination of the Black Sox and Speaker-Cobb situations, though, yields an inescapable conclusion: the "gilded age" never really stopped in baseball. And if a "progressive era" ever happened, it certainly wasn't ushered in on Ban Johnson's watch. Big league baseball was almost as scummy on the day Johnson left office as it was on the day he formed the American League three decades before.

Landis and the leadership of the National League hardly deserve hosannas, either. Instead of rooting out the corruption that threatened the integrity of baseball throughout those years – mischief that began in the owners' boxes and wormed its way down to the clubhouses – the game's leadership elected to sweep its problems under first one rug, then the next. Ban Johnson almost never blew the whistle on cheaters because he knew the whistle could have been blown a lot louder on him.

The Black Sox scandal wasn't some isolated ethical lapse that, once unearthed and (in a half-assed way) rectified, wrung gambling forever out of the game. That scenario has as much basis in fact as the fable that General Abner Doubleday invented the game while a sprite in Cooperstown, New York. Landis and Johnson perpetuated the "myth of baseball's single sin," in historian David Q. Voigt's cutting phrase, for the same reason that Albert Spalding created the yarn about Doubleday: it served their cynical purposes. Fans in the early part of the twentieth century loved to wager on baseball games with the same relish they bet on prizefighting, horseracing, sculling, and anything else that moved. But if they knew just how susceptible to corruption their national pastime had been – for decades on end – it could well have destroyed the game.

Looking back from a distance of eight or nine decades, what's remarkable is that more "scandals" didn't come to the fore. The players back then showed amazing solidarity: it's as if they all took a vow of *omertà* – and maybe they did. It's now evident that what went on in the 1919 World Series was just the jagged tip of a lethal iceberg.

F. Scott Fitzgerald's celebrated line from *The Great Gatsby* – "It never occurred to me that one man could play with the faith of 50 million people – with the single-mindedness of a burglar blowing a safe" – was beautifully wrought but misdirected. It shouldn't have been written about a gambler. Sport Sullivan, Arnold Rothstein, and their ilk merely walked through a door deliberately left ajar by the lords of baseball.

Here are the few indisputable facts about the Speaker-Cobb-Wood-Leonard affair. Dutch Leonard's allegations were first brought to the attention of Ban Johnson and other AL team executives during the spring of 1926. The former Red Sox–Tigers left-hander felt betrayed by both Cobb and Speaker. During the first few months of his 1925 season with Detroit, Leonard later told Damon Runyon, Cobb had used him so much that Dutch's arm was being wrecked. "When he protested to Cobb, the Tigers manager berated him in the clubhouse in front of the other players, shouting 'Don't you dare turn Bolshevik on me! I'm the boss here!' " Charles Alexander recounted in his Cobb biography.

Cobb had placed Leonard on waivers at the beginning of the 1926 season, despite Dutch's 11–4 mark for the Tigers the year before. The Indians' Speaker then refused to pick Leonard up for a nominal waiver fee, even though Dutch begged his old teammate for a job. Dutch was forced to sign with a Pacific Coast League team for considerably less money.

Leonard had in his possession letters from Joe Wood and Ty Cobb written seven years earlier that appeared to implicate all three men (and Speaker by inference) in some kind of wager that had taken place in the fall of 1919.

That part of the story is not in dispute – but virtually everything else about the controversy is. Leonard's contention was that on the afternoon of September 24, 1919, Tigers Leonard and Cobb and Indians Wood and Speaker all met underneath the stands at Navin Field in Detroit to "talk baseball." As related by Robert Smith, "[Dutch] and Cobb had expressed their strong desire for the Detroit club to finish third, there being no fourth-place money at the time. And a victory over Cleveland – which had already clinched second place [behind the White Sox] – would insure their finishing in the money. Tris Speaker, according to Leonard, then assured Cobb he 'needn't worry about tomorrow's game' because 'you'll win tomorrow.' "

Then, Leonard's story went, since all four players knew how the next day's game would turn out, they figured they should get some action down on it. Cobb dispatched a clubhouse attendant named Fred West to collect the wagers and get the bets placed pronto with a bookie. Leonard originally claimed that he placed a fifteen-hundred-dollar bet, with the other three co-conspirators in for a grand each, although at other times he said that Ty had gone in for two grand. Sure enough, the Tigers won the following day's game, 9–5. Detroit took a commanding lead early in the contest and cruised to victory.

When Leonard's charges became public seven years later, the *New York Times* reviewed coverage of the disputed game and unearthed some interesting observations from reporters there that day: "The sports writers described how the two team edified the crowd by 'good fellowship,' that the only player not offered opportunity to fatten his batting average was Cobb, that Tris Speaker was virtually presented with two triples, while Speaker reciprocated by permitting a triple for Bernie Boland, pitching for Detroit." Indeed, the *Plain Dealer*'s account of the game in question also contained some curious references. "The best thing about this contest was its brevity," the article stated, noting that the contest "did not seem like a real championship game." It took only an hour and six minutes to complete – lightning fast even by the quick standards of the dead-ball era.

A few weeks later in the fall of 1919, Dutch maintained that he'd received letters from first Wood, then Cobb, both lamenting that their arrangement had not yielded the results that they had hoped. Wood's letter, as reprinted in December 1926 by the *New York Times*, said:

> Enclosed please find certified check for sixteen hundred and thirty dollars (1,630.00)

> Dear friend "Dutch":
> The only bet West could get up was $600 against $420 (10 to 7). Cobb did not get up a cent. He told us that and I believed him. Could have put up some at 5 to 2 on Detroit, but did not, as that would make us put up $1000 to win $400.
> We won the $420. I gave West $30, leaving $390, or $130 for each of us. Would not have cashed your check at all, but West thought he could get it up at 10 to 7, and I was going to put it all up at those odds. We could have won $1,750 for the $2,500 if we could have placed it.

If we ever have another chance like this we will know enough to try to get it down early.

Let me hear from you, "Dutch."

Cobb's letter to Leonard pursued a slightly different and oddly plaintive track. Its relevant paragraph is:

> Wood and myself are considerably disappointed in our business proposition, as we had $2,000 to put into it, and the other side quoted $1,400, and when we finally secured that much money, it was about 2 o'clock and they refused to deal with us, as they had men in Chicago to take up the matter with and they had no time, so we completely fell down and of course we felt badly over it. Everything was open to Wood and he can tell you about it when we get together. It was quite a responsibility and I don't care for it again, I can assure you.

It's instructive that both Wood and Cobb felt obliged to cover for Cobb. Wood throws in the gratuitous phrase "and I believed him" referring to Cobb's claim that Ty couldn't get the money down. Ty, meanwhile, makes sure that Leonard knows that Joe was privy to all the machinations between him and West, the go-between to the bookie.

Was part of Dutch's pique that he had been cut out of a little bonanza that Wood, Cobb, and Speaker had enjoyed all those years before? By 1926 Dutch – despite an apparently happy marriage to a one-time vaudeville toe dancer – was behaving erratically, suffering from what today would probably be labeled clinical paranoia. Perhaps he felt like the very friends who turned their backs on him in his hour of need had also denied him a big check seven years earlier – because he wasn't as big a star as they were or in their little clique. Joe Wood speculated years later that Leonard was still steamed at Speaker about a big wager on the 1920 Series that also had gone awry.

The evidence against Cobb, Wood, and Speaker was strong but not necessarily damning. Neither letter specifically mentioned the "fix" of a game. And neither letter referred to Speaker by name. But taken together, they certainly raised a stink. Worst of all, they corroborated at least part of Leonard's story. By 1926 Wood was long retired from professional baseball and had been baseball coach at Yale University for four years. But Speaker and Cobb were living legends, still heavily engaged in the game as player-managers of two high-profile franchises.

Ban Johnson was contacted by Leonard in early spring 1926 but refused to sit down with him. The AL czar first got wind of Leonard's charges that May from several club officials who had seen the letters. Even before he met with Leonard, Johnson rushed off to Cleveland to give Speaker a heads-up. How Spoke may have reacted to Johnson's startling news is not known. Speaker avoided the subject like the plague in the years to come.

Johnson then took a train to Detroit to meet with his loyal lieutenant, Tigers owner Frank Navin. Navin told Johnson that Leonard had already been to see him, threatening to sell the letters to a Detroit newspaper. Leonard had also paid an earlier visit to the Tigers' Harry Heilmann, who'd relayed Dutch's charges to Cobb. Only then did Johnson deign to sit down with Leonard to examine the evidence. In response, Johnson and Navin came up with the classic Gilded Age–and–beyond strategy to combat Leonard: they decided to buy him off. After negotiating with American League counsel Henry Killilea, Leonard agreed to surrender the letters to Johnson for some twenty thousand dollars, which was the amount he claimed the Tigers owed him.

At some point that spring or summer, Johnson hired private investigators to spy on Cobb and Speaker's gambling habits. The private eyes reported that Cobb's gambling was innocuous – it was well known that years earlier Ty had frequented the White House as a poker partner of President Harding's – but that Spoke liked to put action down on practically everything. Tris routinely lost a bundle at the track, they told Johnson. It was not the first time that the American League strongman had sicced gumshoes on Cleveland's star center fielder and player-manager.

By early summer a dozen or more baseball men knew of the charges against Speaker and Cobb, yet the story never broke. Johnson kept mum about Leonard's charges until September 9, when he convened a closed-door meeting of the American League ownership in Chicago. After Johnson briefed them on Leonard's allegations, the owners voted to turn the evidence over to Landis, which Johnson was apparently loath to do. Without a word leaking to the press or public, Johnson quietly met with Speaker and Cobb before the former left for a scheduled hunting trip to Wyoming in mid-October.

We don't know what kind of deliberation may have taken place or whether Johnson put other options on the table. Neither player had hired a lawyer at that point. A not unreasonable conclusion is that John-son reached a quid pro quo with the two legends: resign and immediately retire from the game – and the real reason will be kept under wraps. Johnson later said that his motivation was to spare the players and their families humiliating publicity. The two principals must have agreed to put some daylight between their retirement announcements, probably at Johnson's bidding, in a futile effort to keep the press at bay.

On November 3, 1926, the sporting world awoke to the shocking news that Ty Cobb was retiring – not only as a player but as a manager as well. Things turned ugly in a hurry in the Motor City. In handing Cobb his release, owner Frank Navin cited Cobb's role in the "demoralization" of the Tigers. Cobb quickly retaliated, blaming Navin's meddling for the Tigers' woes. Later, Johnson would tell newsmen that the Tigers dismissed Cobb out of fear that Leonard could sue the club – and win.

There were no public recriminations a few weeks later when the stun-ning news came out of Cleveland. The "venerable Speaker," as he was called in the next day's *Washington Post*, announced that he was leaving the Cleveland Indians to pursue professional opportunities in the truck-ing business. "I considered quitting last year, but the Indians were in sixth place and I didn't want it said that I was leaving a rudderless ship. So I stuck it out another season," Spoke told the wire services.

When asked if he would be joining one of the syndicates seeking to buy the Indians from Mrs. Dunn, Speaker replied, "No. I am taking a vacation from baseball that I suspect will last the remainder of my life."

Spoke retiring as a player wouldn't have been all that surprising – he was, after all, thirty-eight and had lost a step or two in the field, even benching himself for a time the previous season. But quitting as man-ager, too? The skipper who had just guided Cleveland to a remarkable second-place finish a scant three games behind the mighty Yankees? Leaving the club for good? Abandoning his life's passion to go work for a place called the Geometric Stamping Co.? It didn't add up.

The *Plain Dealer*'s editorial the next day spoke for many in trying to make sense of the news:

> Baseball in Cleveland and Tris Speaker have been synonymous for so long that a Speaker-less team will seem contrary to natural law. What Mathew-son was to New York, Cobb was to Detroit, what Johnson was to Washing-ton, Tris Speaker has been to Cleveland. This year, Speaker took a team

that was scheduled by all the wise birds to finish a submerged seventh and led it through a fighting campaign to a final position within two or three hairs' breadth of the championship. This achievement is hailed as a little short of a baseball miracle. We are still a little bewildered, but we feel that no fair objection can be advanced against Speaker's decision. And so, as he goes out, into a new field, we join with all the rest of Cleveland in wishing him good luck, long life, and every happiness.

It wasn't just the *Plain Dealer* that was bewildered. As Harold Seymour put it in *Baseball: The Golden Age*, "All of a sudden, two renowned stars had quit. What lay back of it? Rumors spread, and sportswriters pestered baseball officials for more information." As the holidays rapidly approached, the *New York Times* and other papers were on the verge of breaking the story.

Something closer to the "truth" finally surfaced five days before Christmas. Landis was incensed that Johnson had kept him in the dark much of the year, cutting the commissioner's office out of the decision making. It had taken Johnson weeks to hand over Leonard's evidence after the AL owners' meeting in early September. Fuming, Landis vowed to get to the bottom of the controversy. After sitting down with Cobb and Speaker and their newly retained legal counsel, the commissioner bloodied Johnson's nose by informing the world on December 20 that Speaker and Cobb had been "permitted to resign" in the wake of allegations made by a former teammate that they had cheated on a game in 1919. By going public, Landis broke the gentlemen's agreement that Johnson had reached with Cobb and Speaker, infuriating the AL president.

The story was hyped on front pages across the country. "Baseball Scandal Up Again, with Cobb and Speaker Named," was how the *New York Times* played the story on page one. "Scandal Names Tris and Ty: 'Never Threw a Game,' Says Speaker," was how the *Plain Dealer* headlined it, with four related stories planted on page one. Commissioner Landis released the text of Leonard's letters to the *New York Times*, and in doing so, managed to make statements that were both disingenuous and forthright at the same time – quintessential Landis. In one breath, he informed the press that the reason the truth had been withheld until this point was because "none of the men involved is now associated with baseball" – which was patented nonsense. In the next, he declaimed that "baseball is again on trial, if for no other reason than the peculiar concealment of the Leonard charges" – which happened to be far truer than the *New York Times* could ever imagine.

Baseball was indeed on trial – but Landis and Johnson were doing their damnedest to suppress as much of the truth as they could. The Speaker-Cobb matter was just one of a host of betting affairs that bedeviled the lords of baseball in the mid-1920s – all this several years after the banishment of the Black Sox had supposedly eradicated cheating from the game. One of Landis's first crises after "resolving" the Black Sox scandal was investigating Carl Mays's performance in the 1921 and 1922 World Series. McGraw's Giants scuffed Mays up in both Series. Writer Fred Lieb reported to Landis that he'd heard widespread rumors that Mays was on the take in the '21 Series. Mays's wife, sitting in the box seats, had supposedly flashed a signal to her husband in midgame that the gamblers had given her the cash – and, as if on cue, Mays proceeded to get strafed.

Landis thought enough of the rumors to hire a detective agency to investigate. The private eyes came up empty. Lieb later maintained that Yankee manager Miller Huggins and owner Col. Cap Huston told him that Mays had cheated in both Series.

The charges surrounding Mays were just the beginning of Landis's headaches. Between late 1924 and late 1926, three scandals happened essentially one on top of the other. The first was the comic-tragic chain of events surrounding allegations of a fix in a Giants-Phillies game played in late September 1924. Cozy Dolan, the old Boston National who became McGraw's "Man Friday" as a longtime coach, was accused by the Giants' sophomore center fielder, Jimmy O'Connell, of forcing the youngster to offer a five-hundred-dollar bribe to Phillie shortstop Heinie Sand. The Giants were just two games removed from clinching the pennant over Brooklyn, but certain people wanted to "make the outcome of the pennant race a sure thing," Seymour writes in his account of the affair.

After the Phillies fingered him, O'Connell copped a plea, implicating not only Dolan in the bribery scheme, but second baseman Frankie Frisch, outfielder Ross Youngs, and first baseman George Kelly, three of McGraw's biggest stars. Landis called all four into his office in the first few days of October 1924, beginning with Dolan. Cozy played dumb – a mental condition not totally alien to the baseball lifer. No Mafia button man ever feigned greater ignorance of events. Dolan repeatedly told the commissioner that he couldn't remember what he was doing or what he was thinking or what he may or may not have said to people on that afternoon in question. After gently probing Frisch, Youngs, and Kelly, Landis issued his edict: O'Connell and Dolan would be banished for life, but the three stars were exonerated of all wrongdoing.

The commissioner eventually let it be known to the *Sporting News* that Dolan got such harsh treatment because he had been "evasive" while the three stars had been "straightforward." A couple of months later Landis released a report to "allay the intimations of sportswriters that he was hiding something," in Seymour's words. Landis's report included these sterling examples of the stars' "straightforward" testimony:

> *Youngs*: I have heard talking around and such things mentioning it, but I don't remember who by. You hear fellows talking around that boys that are offering money and something like that. I never heard anything like this, offering money here. This is the first I heard of it.
>
> *Frisch*: On a pennant contender, you always hear a lot of stuff like that, a lot of kidding and some other things. This is all I ever hear.

Why did Landis accept O'Connell's allegations against Dolan and dismiss them against the big boys – particularly given their less-than-reassuring testimony? Certain writers weren't the only people suspecting a whitewash. American League president Johnson, always eager to embarrass McGraw and the senior circuit, demanded a federal probe – a slap in the face that Landis never forgave. Barney Dreyfuss, owner of the Pirates, joined Johnson in demanding that the 1924 World Series be postponed. Dreyfuss pointed out that it defied belief "that two rather obscure members [of the Giants] would go and offer to pay somebody $500 solely of their own money, to have something crooked done that would benefit many other persons besides themselves." The Pittsburgh owner concluded his commentary with a backhanded swipe at McGraw, whom he despised as much as Johnson: "The New York players change, but the manager remains the same."

Landis, chafing that Johnson and Dreyfuss had aired their views in public, refused their request. The World Series between McGraw's Giants and the Washington Senators would go on as scheduled. In the twelfth inning of the seventh and deciding game, a routine grounder hit by the Senators' Earl McNeely struck a pebble and hopped over Giants third baseman Freddie Lindstrom's head, scoring the winning run. Walter Johnson was finally a champion.

The other Johnson, Ban, wasn't through registering his displeasure with Landis and McGraw. The AL president decided that now would be a propitious time to pile on with more damaging information on the Giants' skipper. For several years, Johnson had kept in his hip pocket a sworn statement from Lou Criger, Cy Young's old catcher on the 1903 Boston Pilgrims, claiming that gamblers had approached Criger in a Pittsburgh hotel lobby to persuade him to dump games during the '03 Series against the Pirates. John McGraw and Wilbert Robinson were present when the attempted bribe was offered and made no effort to stop it, Criger's affidavit swore. Criger's impression was that Muggsy and Robbie were in on the scam.

Dreyfuss once again joined Johnson in pressing for a more aggressive investigation of the Criger charge, traveling to Washington to buttonhole Landis at the Series. Again, the commissioner refused Dreyfuss, this time leaving him cooling his heels in a hotel lobby.

The *Sporting News* also clamored for a probe, editorializing, "Who is behind this assault and other assaults on the integrity of the sport? When is the cleaning out, the general cleaning out, going to begin? That's what the fans want to know. Who inspired Dolan?"

Things got even more convoluted after the Series, because it came to light that old Cozy was suing Landis for defamation of character. When Landis learned that McGraw was bankrolling Cozy's "defense," arranging representation by the unctuous William J. Fallon, mouthpiece for gambler Arnold Rothstein and other lowlifes, the commissioner blew his stack. After a couple more weeks of perfunctory fact gathering, Landis retreated to Cuba to do some golfing.

New York district attorney Joab H. Banton decided to join the fracas, promising to prosecute anyone found violating the law. Banton's sleuthing also came up empty. After a few weeks, the DA issued an odd report suggesting that O'Connell "may" have been guilty and that Dolan "brought suspicion onto himself" – two assertions that folks had known all along. Eventually, the hubbub over the affair died, Dolan dropped his lawsuit against Landis, and the commissioner returned from Havana.

The third scandal erupted just as Landis had begun zeroing in on the Speaker-Cobb controversy. And it involved baseball's most disreputable characters: three members of the Black Sox. Swede Risberg, the embittered former White Sox infielder who'd returned to Minnesota to run his family's dairy farm, publicly charged in December 1926 that late in the 1917 regular season, the Detroit Tigers had dumped a slate of games at the bidding of the White Sox. Risberg's allegation was that Detroit's players wanted to make some extra spending cash, so the Bengals tanked against Chicago in several key games down the stretch, enabling the White Sox to hold off the Red Sox. The grateful White Sox, Swede claimed, took up a collection of forty-five dollars per man and paid Detroit's pitchers and starting catcher a bonus for their troubles.

Why had Risberg suddenly come forward after nearly a decade? "They pushed Ty Cobb and Tris Speaker out on a piker bet. I think it's only fair that the 'white lilies' get the same treatment," Risberg told the press. Moreover, his old Black Sox crony (and Speaker foe) Chick Gandil publicly embraced Risberg's claims – and hinted that he could dig up even more sensational dirt.

On New Year's Day, just ten days after Landis had exposed Leonard's allegations against Cobb and Speaker, the commissioner sat down with Risberg in Chicago and questioned him for two hours. Accompanying Risberg to the Chicago meeting was another Black Sox protagonist, George "Buck" Weaver. Long considered the least villainous of the Black Sox, Weaver was desperate to get back into the game and wanted to use this opportunity to show Landis that he was worthy of reinstatement. Buck remained mute during Risberg's meeting with Landis, merely nodding his head from time to time to confirm Swede's recollections. Although he never let on to Risberg or Weaver, Landis was familiar with the substance of Swede's charges. Some four years before, another august member of the Black Sox, outfielder Oscar "Happy" Felsch, had made similar claims about the 1917 season in his lawsuit against club owner Charles Comiskey. Even before Happy's legal action, Landis had discussed the Detroit-Chicago "arrangement" with White Sox catcher Ray Schalk, always considered beyond reproach on matters of gambling. Ban Johnson, of course, knew only too well all the ugly rumors about the 1917 season.

Landis decided to hold public hearings in Chicago on January 5 and

6 to give former members of the Tigers and White Sox a forum to share what they knew. But that provided Tigers owner Frank Navin and White Sox owner Charles Comiskey with nearly a week to concoct a strategy for themselves and their former charges. Yes, the White Sox had indeed given Tigers players some money collected from a pool back then. But it hadn't been a "bribe" to lose to Chicago. It had been a "reward" for Detroit's beating the Red Sox three straight, Frank and Commy divined. Even White Sox second baseman Eddie Collins, formerly believed incorruptible, admitted to having provided some money toward the Tigers' kitty. "It was nothing out of the ordinary to give a player on another team some sort of a gift if he went out of the way to turn in a good performance against one of a team's leading rivals in the [pennant] race," Collins said in a statement that hardly assuaged public suspicions. Collins wasn't alone: in his 1960 autobiography, Ty Cobb mentioned receiving numerous gifts from grateful opponents over the years, including a batch of shirts from the Red Sox.

Barney Dreyfuss, never shy about seizing another chance to stick it to Muggsy, then told the commissioner that during the 1921 season, McGraw's Giants had tried to provide financial incentives to Brooklyn's players to beat Barney's Pirates. McGraw and Brooklyn skipper Wilbert Robinson both hotly denied the charge.

Landis, in the company of a roomful of reporters and the ever-present Will Rogers, listened to the recollections of some forty players on events that occurred nearly a decade before. Risberg smoked cigarette after cigarette as he recounted his story. Gandil backed up most of Risberg's story but was curiously reticent in certain areas. Ty Cobb also testified on the first day, flatly stating that "there never has been a baseball game in my life that I played in, that I knew was fixed," a sweeping declaration that virtually everyone in the crowded room knew was categorically untrue. After Cobb finished he glared at Landis and snarled, "Want to swear me?"

Most of the other "witnesses" stuck to the Navin-Comiskey stratagem and pooh-poohed Swede and Chick's testimony, claiming that the White Sox's pool was just a harmless little "thank you" fund to the Tigers pitchers and catcher Oscar Stanage, no big deal, nothing out of the ordinary. After he finished testifying, former Detroit hurler Bernie Boland gestured toward Risberg and smirked, "You're still a pig!" Moments like that were providing Will Rogers with months' worth of comedic material.

Buck Weaver took the stand late in the evening of day two, having already told the press: "I have been cast out of baseball but I hold no grudge. I only have an ambition to get back into the game. . . . I was innocent in 1919 and I got railroaded on the flimsiest of charges. All I ask is a fair hearing." On the stand, Buck denied having any knowledge of the 1917 scam, explaining that he was out of action that September with a broken finger. Buck also reaffirmed his innocence in the '19 ruse, dramatically asking the commissioner to reinstate him. Landis sat motionless for what seemed like an eternity to the newspapermen in the room, and then said, "Well, drop me a line on that, Buck, and I'll take the matter up at length."

Buck had experienced first-hand the wrath of angry gamblers. In June of that same disputed season of 1917, a thunderstorm struck Fenway Park during the latter innings of a Red Sox–White Sox game, with Boston leading Chicago. When the storm cleared, a group of gamblers who had wagered on the Red Sox vaulted over the railing and fought with Weaver and other Chicago players in a futile effort to stop the game from being resumed. Buck slugged back with such gusto that Boston police arrested him on an assault-and-battery charge that was later dropped.

Ten days after the hearings ended, Landis released his "findings" from the Risberg allegations. The commissioner accepted the notion that the pool was a "gift fund," calling it "reprehensible and censurable" but not criminal. Risberg went back home to Minnesota an even more embittered man, if that were humanly possible. Oddly, Swede's buddy Gandil never did trumpet the charges that supposedly would blow the lid off of baseball. Landis kept Weaver waiting for two full months before writing Buck a letter that broke Weaver's heart all over again. No member of the Black Sox ever gained official reentry to the game. Many of them – Jackson and Weaver included – were reduced to playing in semipro and outlaw leagues, often under assumed names.

After the delightful divertissement with Chick, Buck, and Swede, the commissioner had to refocus energies on his still-incomplete investigation of two of the biggest names in the sport. "Won't these God damn

things that happened before I came into baseball ever stop coming up?"
Landis supposedly barked in frustration that winter.

A month earlier Landis had vowed to dig up the truth when he aired
Leonard's charges against Cobb and Speaker. And who knows? There's
a chance Landis actually meant it at the time. But now Landis turned
skittish – and it's not hard to understand why. Given the circuslike atmosphere of the Risberg hearings, the last thing baseball could afford at
the moment was prolonged public scrutiny of two icons. Uncovering and
punishing "guilt" was no longer Landis's goal. It probably dawned on
the commissioner that exposing more of the game's dirty laundry might
not be in the enlightened self-interest of one Kenesaw Mountain Landis.
The commish had just had his contract extended for another seven-year
term, his salary rising some 30 percent to sixty-five thousand dollars –
handsome pay in the 1920s.

There were three other factors working against a genuine probe of
the Speaker-Cobb mess. First, Dutch Leonard refused to show up at
a hearing to confront his former teammates and alleged co-conspirators
in person. Leonard, with good reason, feared for his life. The patholog-
ical Cobb was eminently capable of harming Dutch. Just after the commissioner heard about the allegations, Landis did go out to California
to meet in private with Dutch. But Leonard, having pocketed twenty
thousand dollars in blood money from Ban Johnson, wouldn't leave his
Fresno farm to make his charges stick.

Second, Cobb and Speaker had wised up and hired themselves capable counsel. The esteemed William H. Boyd, a Cleveland-based attorney recommended by pals in the corporate community, represented
Speaker. Cobb's legal team consisted of the formidable pair of Edward
S. Burke, who had helped Ty and the Tigers out of legal jams in the
past, and James O. Murfin, one of Michigan's most respected litigators
and an adjunct professor at the University of Michigan law school. The
attorneys demanded that Landis rescind the Johnson "order" directing
Cobb and Speaker into retirement.

If Joe Wood's 1963 recollections to Larry Ritter are accurate, the two
icons and their attorneys played hardball with the commissioner. "See,
they got together with an attorney in Detroit, my friend Spoke, and they
got a bunch of stuff together and typewritten and deposited it in a bank

vault in Cleveland, and if they would have chased Cobb and Speaker out of baseball, it would have all come out."

Smoky Joe later regretted having been so candid with Ritter and asked him to destroy the tape and transcript of the interview. Professor Ritter kept Wood's incriminating comments out of *The Glory of Their Times* but never excised the transcript. Along with Ritter's subsequent interview of Wood two years later, the 1963 transcript is on file in the Ritter archives at the University of Notre Dame.

Cobb that winter was also playing political cards, enlisting the help of Georgia's two U.S. senators. By the time the middle of January had rolled around, the two accused superstars had received expressions of support from thousands of fans across the country.

Landis was caught between a rock and a hard place. He knew that if he pressed the charges, Cobb and Speaker may have made good on their threat to tear the game apart. We'll never know exactly what incendiary information was in those files, unless through some miracle the Cobb-Speaker affidavits are still gathering dust in the bowels of a Cleveland bank or law firm.

Finally, and perhaps most importantly, it occurred to the commissioner that he could use the situation to bludgeon Ban Johnson, his archrival. How? By skewering Johnson's original handling of the scandal and blowing apart the clandestine deal that the AL president had reached with the two stars. Any thought that Landis had of going easy on Johnson ended with two events later in January.

On January 17 Johnson angered Landis by holding a press conference in which he blistered the commissioner's decision to go public with Leonard's charges. "The only thing I could see behind [Landis's action] was a desire for personal publicity," Johnson charged. He also confided to newsmen that he loved Cobb and didn't think the Georgian was corrupt. The Peach was "let go," Johnson volunteered, because "he had written a peculiar letter about a betting deal that he couldn't explain and because I felt that he violated a position of trust."

Speaker, on the other hand, was "a different type of fellow," Johnson said. "For want of a better word I'd call Tris 'cute.' He knows why he was forced out. . . . If he wants me to tell him I'll meet him in a court of law and tell the facts under oath." Speaker's habitual gambling – on horses, dogs, cards, anything with action – negated the benefit of the doubt that Cobb enjoyed, at least in Johnson's twisted mind. Spoke wasn't the only member of the Cleveland club with a gambling problem, Johnson implied. As early as 1925 the league had hired "professional men" to trail Speaker and company. Johnson claimed to know all the particulars – who had action on the ponies, who bet on baseball, and what bookies they used. Johnson's barrage against Speaker failed to mention that there was nothing illegal about a ballplayer going to the racetrack. Nor was there a "law" on baseball's books back then that expressly forbade gambling on games.

Johnson concluded his press conference by attacking Landis's handling of the Black Sox affair, claiming that the American League – not the commissioner's office – deserved credit for unearthing the Black Sox scandal and bringing the players to justice. Since the league's handling of the "investigation" had hardly been exemplary and the Black Sox received anything but "justice," it was a preposterous claim.

A week later, Landis got his vengeance. At an emergency closed-door meeting with American League owners on January 24, Landis demanded to know who was leaking information to the press that suggested there was other incriminating evidence about Speaker and Cobb. Stories in various newspapers that week had suggested that the AL owners had, in effect, "blacklisted" the pair. Landis knew going into the meeting that Johnson had planted the stories and wanted to embarrass him in front of his peers. It worked. When Johnson sheepishly conceded that Landis had in his possession all the evidence against Cobb and Speaker, the owners, fed up with Ban's erratic behavior, unanimously imposed a leave of absence. Navin was elected interim league head; not exactly a step up on the ethics ladder, but then, that would have been true of every other owner in the room.

Johnson's hush-hush deal with Speaker and Cobb the previous fall may not have insisted that they "retire" per se, but it clearly proscribed them from playing with another American League club. On January 27 Landis's secretary distributed to newsmen copies of a statement that rescinded Johnson's deal and exonerated the two stars. "These players have not been, nor are they now, found guilty of fixing a ball game. By no decent system of justice could such a finding be made." Landis's words clearly bore the imprint of the two stars' lawyers. Indeed, Cobb's *My Life in Baseball* claims the finding was "dictated" to Landis by Cobb and Speaker's legal team. "I understood and accepted Landis's finding," Fred Lieb wrote years later. "To expel these superstars of baseball on less than conclusive evidence might have given professional baseball a blow from which it could not recover."

"I cannot hold these men guilty if the accuser fails to confront the accused despite all the pressure I have brought upon him," Landis said, referring to Leonard. The statement went on to restore Cobb and Speaker to the active roster of their former teams. Landis's move had been carefully choreographed with all parties, however. That same day, telegrams were sent to Speaker and Cobb from the owners of their former clubs, granting them their unconditional releases and freeing them to sign with other American League clubs. The franchises to which Cobb and Speaker had devoted thirty-three years of their lives, winning a combined four pennants and thirteen batting championships, wanted nothing to do with their tainted player-managers. It probably wasn't a "moral" decision. Navin and Mrs. Dunn no doubt had grown weary of their superstars' egos and big salaries.

Left unwritten and unspoken was Landis's prohibition against Cobb and Speaker ever serving as managers or coaches again. The commissioner was sufficiently concerned about the ethical bearings of the two stars that he didn't want either one of them calling shots in a dugout. In Landis's considered judgment, dugout responsibilities would have made Ty and Tris too tempting a target for gamblers. Landis's ban stuck. Neither man ever managed again. In 1928, when Speaker retired for good, the Pirates quietly queried the commissioner's office about the prospect of bringing Speaker to Pittsburgh as a full-time coach. The Bucs were given an emphatic "no." Other clubs interested in hiring Speaker as manager in the 1930s were given the same brushback. It would be twenty years before the Indians were permitted to bring Speaker back as a part-time spring training coach and advisor. But even then, in the late 1940s and '50s, he never served as a full-time uniformed coach in the dugout.

Landis managed to get one last dig in against Ban Johnson before the Cobb-Speaker affair ended. A day or two after Landis reinstated Tris and Ty, John McGraw of the National League Giants expressed interest in signing Cobb. "Lay off Cobb," Landis told McGraw. Cobb was to stay in the American League, Landis insisted, thus ensuring that Johnson's original decree would be completely overturned.

The Cobb-Speaker debacle did produce one constructive result: Landis insisted that Major League Baseball adopt a rule preventing players from betting of any description on baseball games.

But Landis came out of the affair only slightly less tarnished than Johnson. An essay on Landis's role in the scandal written by dead-ball-era scholar Greg Beston is accurately entitled "Forced to Back Down." When he first got wind of the Leonard charges, Landis tried to reprise his avenging angel role in the Black Sox scandal, attempting to "steal the spotlight" from Johnson, Beston wrote in his 1996 paper. "In the end, though, the judge had no other choice but to back down, thus destroying the myth that the commissioner of baseball had supreme power." Robert Smith wrote that Cobb and Speaker benefited from "Landis's unwillingness to dig much more deeply than a finger's length into any baseball scandal." Historian Glenn Stout recently compared Landis's ambivalence to a seamstress pulling a single thread, then discovering to her horror that she's unraveling the fabric of the whole garment. Landis didn't want to rip up baseball any more than he already had. So he stopped tugging at the Cobb-Speaker thread and stuffed the garment back in the drawer.

In February 1927 Connie Mack ended up signing Cobb for his Athletics at a handsome salary. It was reported to be $40,000 a year, plus a $25,000 bonus for signing and a $10,000 bonus at year's end. Cobb would be a major gate attraction for the A's. Mack had put together the nucleus of a fine young team. He hoped Cobb could show the youngsters how to win.

After dickering with the Yankees' general manager Ed Barrow and the A's new player-coach Eddie Collins, Spoke decided to negotiate in earnest with his old pal Clark Griffith in Washington. His deal didn't quite approach Cobb's. But a thirty-five-thousand-dollar salary, plus gate incentives, helped Spoke get over his humiliation in the Leonard matter.

Barnard and Mrs. Dunn may have grown tired of Speaker. But the fact remains that the Indians backtracked into the second division immediately upon Tris's departure. In the four years before Speaker arrived in 1916, the Indians averaged seventy wins a season for a winning percentage of .457. In the eleven years he played with them, they averaged eighty-two victories a season, winning at a .545 clip. In the four years after he left, they fell to a .480 team, winning just seventy-four games a year. As the Indians' pilot for seven and a half seasons, Speaker compiled a record of 616 wins and 520 losses – a winning percentage of .542.

All these years later, the questions about the Cobb-Speaker-Wood-Leonard ruckus remain vexing. If they were "innocent," why did Speaker and Cobb go along with Johnson's original ultimatum that they quit the game? Why not hire lawyers from the get-go and fight it? Why not at least publicly proclaim their outrage and their determination to clear their good names and not wait for the inevitable revelations to leak out to the press? And why were their actions back in 1919 so brazen? Was cheating so routine back then that ballplayers could collude under the stands, and then exchange nonchalant letters about it without giving it a second thought?

Ultimately, Landis didn't want the real "truth" about the scandal to come out anymore than Johnson did. Instead of mounting a concerted effort to cleanse the game, Landis and Johnson conducted a charade – not just on the incidents described above but on other misdeeds that surfaced in the early to mid-1920s. To the detriment of the game, Johnson and Landis cynically used these "investigations" to settle old scores and try to bully one another. What Speaker, Cobb, Wood, and Leonard did that late September afternoon in 1919 was tawdry. What Landis and Johnson and practically every owner in the game did throughout the early decades of the century was far tawdrier.

With very little thanks to the game's leadership, the role of gambling in baseball began to abate at least somewhat as the 1930s approached. But as the execrable behavior of Pete Rose demonstrates, it's never been completely divorced from the dugout.

As the years wore on, columnists like Henry Edwards, Shirley Povich, and Arthur Daley helped create the image of Landis the Great, the commissioner who ruled with an iron hand – a "diamond autocrat," as Daley labeled him in a 1947 article. All the stories they spread about Landis's "determination to keep baseball free from even the slightest hint of scandal," as Daley put it, may have made for good copy, but they weren't an accurate reflection of Landis's real motivation. Nobody back then wanted to confront the game's seedy realities – not the lords of baseball and certainly not the columnists who covered it. So they all went along with the canard that Kenesaw Mountain Landis had saved baseball from the wretches of gambling.

Ban Johnson's health began to deteriorate soon after the American League owners forced a sabbatical on him in the winter of 1927. He came back briefly to resume the reins of the AL, but died soon thereafter.

On October 10, 1926, just three weeks before Cobb made his startling retirement announcement, baseball experienced a disquieting moment. It was the kind of on-field blunder that caused people from the press box to the cheap seats to scratch their heads. The fact that the sin happened in baseball's cathedral – Yankee Stadium – and was committed by its most revered player – Babe Ruth – makes it all the more irreligious. There were two outs in the bottom of the ninth inning in the seventh and deciding game of the World Series between the St. Louis Cardinals and the New York Yankees. The Cards were protecting a 3–2 lead that had been dramatically preserved two innings earlier when the aging Pete Alexander had come on in relief to strike out Tony Lazzeri with the bases loaded – one of the most poignant moments in the history of the game.

Old Pete wisely wasted a 3-2 pitch to Ruth with the bases empty and two outs in the ninth. With the Bambino on first and cleanup hitter Bob Meusel at the plate, sixty thousand rabid Yankee fans were on their feet, pleading for Meusel to put one in the seats to win or smash one into a gap to send the game into extra innings. Imagine the fans' dismay when Ruth took off for second on an attempted steal and was easily pegged out by Cardinals catcher Bob O'Farrell, ending the game and the Series. The photo of Cardinals second baseman Rogers Hornsby tagging Ruth shows that the Babe never got close to the bag.

Maybe old Jidge's flatulence had finally gotten to his brain. Or maybe he honestly thought he could get a jump on O'Farrell – Ruth had stolen a base on the Cards catcher, many thought foolishly – the day before. Then again it may have been the obverse of "honesty" that was at play. What was an overweight man like Ruth doing taking a risk like that with the Series on the line? If Miller Huggins, the Yankees' manager, had wanted to execute a steal, why not insert a pinch runner? Wouldn't the

Yanks have wanted a faster runner than the Babe on first in that situation?

Ruth had hit four homers previously in the Series – three in one game, a 10–5 Yankees win. If the Babe had been up to hanky-panky, it certainly wasn't in the earlier game. Still, Ruth's base path gaffe caused much head shaking throughout baseball. No doubt innuendo about Ruth's attempted steal reached Landis's and Johnson's ears.

No wonder Landis wanted to dispense with the Leonard controversy. At more or less the same time, he was dealing with accusations against some of the game's most electric personalities: McGraw, Robinson, Cobb, Speaker, Collins, Frisch, Youngs, and Kelly – plus Ruth's troubling play in the Series. On top of all that, the Black Sox had reemerged, smearing the integrity of the game all over again before being smacked down one last time. After Landis thought things through, he couldn't get rid of the Cobb and Speaker matter fast enough.

The truth is that had the Cobb-Speaker-Wood-Leonard story broken when it occurred – in the fall of 1919 – it would have dwarfed what happened in the Series a few days later. The Gray Eagle and the Georgia Peach were much bigger names than Chick and Swede. And because of their perceived roles as pillars of the game, Tris and Ty were bigger names than Shoeless Joe. When the whole ugly mess finally blew over in '27, Damon Runyon sat down with Leonard at Dutch's home in California. "I have had my revenge," Dutch bragged.

Leonard took the twenty-thousand-dollar stash he'd gotten from Johnson and Navin and started a fruit farm and vineyard outside Fresno. Over time he became quite a prosperous gentleman farmer, sending bottles of wine and baskets of dried fruit to his old baseball pals. It's not likely that Wood, Cobb, or Speaker were on Dutch's Christmas list.

One of the most underreported tragedies in baseball history is the sad story of Jimmy O'Connell. Jimmy was a McGraw prodigy – a five-skill star who signed the largest bonus McGraw had ever offered a youngster. The Sacramento kid was on his way to what could have been a brilliant career, hitting .317 in a part-time role in 1924 when Cozy Dolan (and others?) dragooned him into approaching the Phillies' shortstop with a bribe offer. The blackest mark against John McGraw is not that he was a reckless gambler who hung out with hustlers; that was hardly a distinguishing vice in the dead-ball era. It's that Muggsy sat back and let this unsuspecting kid get thrown under a bus while his more established stars – every bit as "guilty" as young Jimmy – slithered away.

Another shady figure that skulked away from reckoning back then was Sport Sullivan, the gentleman crook from Boston. It was Sullivan, at the behest of old crony Hal Chase, who went to the "Big Bankroll," Arnold Rothstein, and formed the cabal that fixed the 1919 Series. Soon after investigators pinpointed him as a target in 1920, the elusive Sullivan disappeared for good. In the last photograph that appeared of Sport in the Boston papers, he had pulled his hat over his eyes – "like a suspect doing a 'perp' walk," Glenn Stout chuckled in a 2004 interview.

No one knows what happened to Sullivan. The Black Sox investigators never questioned him. Maybe Sport knew too much and – à la Jimmy Hoffa – got rubbed out. Rothstein himself was murdered in 1928 by a fellow gambler. Even as the Big Bankroll lay bleeding to death from the gunshot wound, he remained true to the vow of *omertà*; he refused to tell the cops who shot him. In Stout's view, the most plausible rumor about Sullivan is that he slipped away to Mexico, where Sport no doubt figured out how to fix cockfights.

The 1920 World Series brought together one squad that had never appeared in the postseason (Cleveland) with a club with scant World Series experience (Brooklyn). Yet with the press hyping stories that the previous year's Series had been a fraud, both clubhouses joshed about illicit payola. An anecdote recently uncovered by baseball scandal buff Gene Carney, creator of the Web site "Notes from the Shadows of Cooperstown," provides a telling commentary on the players' indifferent mindset during the '20 Series.

In a parody of what supposedly had happened to Joe Jackson the year before, second-string Indians catcher Les Nunamaker woke up one morning during the Series to find that his pillowcase had been stuffed full of cash. Nunamaker didn't know what to make of the situation, so he dutifully turned the money in. The October 12, 1920, *Washington Post* reported that his pillowcase only had sixteen dollars stuffed into it – in Confederate currency, no less! Somebody was having fun at Nunamaker's expense. Player-manager Speaker, Nunamaker's hunting and fishing buddy, may not have snuck the bogus currency into the catcher's hotel room. But surely Spoke was in on it. The Nunamaker episode had all the earmarks of a classic Speaker prank.

So what does it say about baseball back then that many months *before* the 1919 Black Sox went on trial, ballplayers in the succeeding World Series were already spoofing the scandal's seamier moments? It may be difficult to work up sympathy for the Black Sox, but Carney is justified in writing, "The Black Sox paid for the sins of many, not just their own, and they took that infamy with them to their graves."

Kenesaw Mountain Landis was right. Baseball was indeed on trial in the 1920s. Had a real verdict ever been rendered, the game would not have been declared "innocent." Baseball's Moses never did smite the Philistines.

CHAPTER 11

Banished Hero

The nation's capital was giddy at the prospect of the Gray Eagle nesting in center field at National Park. The day after Tris signed with Clark Griffith's club, the *Washington Post* ran an editorial entitled, "Come On, Spoke!"

> Already fandom is talking about a championship and a world's series involving the local team. . . . Tris Speaker has been through an eventful period of his life, and has come out smiling. . . . He has gone through an investigation, however, has been exonerated, and in the eyes of rabid fans, has assumed the position of a near-martyr. It is safe to predict that he will be unusually popular in Washington and that during the coming season the stand will resound frequently with a long-drawn-out and mournful, "Come on, Spoke!"

Johnson and Landis hadn't intended to martyr Speaker – in fact, they had set out to do quite the opposite. But that's not how the episode turned out in the public eye, or at least in the wishful thinking of the *Washington Post*'s editorial staff. The Washington press corps treated his every move that winter and spring with unrelenting enthusiasm. In late February the *Post* reported that Speaker roped calves at a rodeo in Malone, Texas, had been honored by the Dallas Salesmanship Club, and had played in a charity game for an orphans' home.

Spoke told his admirers at the business club: "I am going to give everything I have to help Washington with the pennant, and I hope that this fall all my Texas friends will be able to wire me for world's series tickets." The *Post* noted that "the Texan's jaw clenched a little as he munched the words out. His eyes glistened and his fist tightened. Every word rang as true as steel." One of his luncheon mates asked when he was going to retire. "My dear old mother is 81-years-old, and she recently went all the way to California on a pleasure trip. I ought to be able to play ball until I am 70-years-old." The *Post*'s account saluted the "gray-thatched Texas hero" for withstanding the strain of the scandal "like a true son of the State that produced Davy Crockett, Sam Houston, and other heroes of the Alamo."

With Speaker at the main table was none other than Doak Roberts, the head of the Texas League who first signed Tris to a contract with the Cleburne club twenty-one years before. Doak predicted big things for his former charge in the nation's capital.

Things could not have gotten off to a better start at Griffith Stadium. President Calvin Coolidge came out to throw out the first ball on Opening Day. At the receiving end, of course, was the Nats' prized new acquisition. Tris banged out two hits in his debut as the Senators cruised by the Red Sox, 6–2. It must have given Tris more than a little satisfaction to have beaten Bill Carrigan in Rough's first game back as Boston's skipper – an experience that proved disastrous for the only manager in Red Sox history to have won back-to-back World Series.

Piloting the Nats was their boy-wonder player-manager Bucky Harris. Harris won a world's championship in 1924, then guided the Senators to a second successive pennant the following year. Harris and his boss, Clark Griffith, both hoped that Speaker would fuel the Senators' offense. And for a while, Tris did. But injuries nagged the thirty-nine-year-old all season. He suffered a broken thumb and various leg ailments that kept him out of the lineup. At one point, he was relegated to first base for seventeen games – the only time in Speaker's twenty-two-year career that he played a position other than the outfield.

The Nats had the potential to be a good club. The outfield consisted of Speaker, who hit .327 for the season, Goose Goslin, who hit .334, and Sam Rice, who hit .297. Ossie Bluege at third and Joseph Ignatius Judge, a Washington institution at first, anchored the corners. Harris played second and Bobby "Gunner" Reeves handled short. Pitching depth was the Nats' undoing. Speaker's old pal Walter Johnson was on his last legs, able to appear in only eighteen games that year, winning just five. Hod Lisinbee and Bump Hadley were the Nats' only consistent winners on the mound.

The Senators had a respectable season, finishing sixteen games over .500. But there was no stopping one of the finest teams ever assembled, the indomitable '27 Yankees. The pinstriped juggernaut broke the 1912 Red Sox's record of 105 wins with room to spare, going 110-44 and tearing the Pirates apart in four straight in the Series. There was no need for Babe Ruth to attempt any October base-stealing heroics.

The people of Cleveland did themselves proud when Speaker returned to League Park for the first time in enemy colors on May 14. They presented him with a treasure trove of gifts, including a life-sized color portrait, baskets full of roses, an immense horseshoe wreath of flowers, a fifteen-hundred-dollar chest of silver, and a bejeweled wristwatch. His old friend and ghost writer Henry Edwards noted, "Present after present was given him amid dignified ceremonies, but possibly there was nothing that touched him more than the yells from the grandstand, the pavilion, and the bleachers – 'Hit it against the wall, Spoke! Hit it against the wall!' "

As late as July 25 Spoke was banging plenty of balls off of walls, hitting a sizzling .376 that placed him third in the league. But injuries and exhaustion caused him to drop fifty full points in his batting average. When his club failed to scare the Yankees, Griffith looked at his bottom line and concluded that Spoke wasn't worth the dough. Speaker was earning four or five times the amount of most of his teammates – a disparity not lost on the younger Senators, according to an article written February 8, 1928, by Frank H. Young of the *Post*.

The Speaker deal proved "unpopular" among Washington's players, Young wrote. "This does not mean that the Nats did not like Speaker personally, for he proved himself a fine, likable chap, willing to give his best to the club and to help any of the players, especially the rookies." But the Nats resented Spoke's salary the same way the young Athletics resented Cobb's salary, Young argued.

Stories began surfacing almost right away that suggested Spoke's tenure with the Nats would be brief. On May 18, four days after his emotional return to Cleveland, the Associated Press reported that Speaker was spearheading a syndicate to buy the Indians from Mrs. Dunn. Speaker had allegedly put together a group of Cleveland businessmen, led by a member of the Hanna family, which was offering $580,000 for the franchise. For whatever reason, Mrs. Dunn chose not to entertain the offer from the Speaker-Hanna group.

As the season came to a close there was much speculation that Speaker would take over E. S. Barnard's position as president of the Indians once Barnard was elevated to president of the American League. Speaker must have known in his heart that it was next to impossible for him to become the Indians' president, given Mrs. Dunn's ambivalence toward him and the commissioner's steadfast opposition. Speaker did his best to scotch rumors that he was returning to Cleveland.

Early the following year the Boston Braves were said to have Speaker at the top of their list of managerial candidates. Given Tris's popularity in New England, the Braves' interest made sense. But like every other future story linking Speaker to managerial openings, nothing came of it. McGraw's Giants were said to be interested in acquiring Speaker. But those talks fell through as well.

Next Speaker tarried with Montreal of the International League, which dangled a player-manager job in front of him and hinted at an equity stake in the franchise. But Speaker used Montreal to leverage two offers from big league clubs: the lowly Browns of St. Louis, which needed a gate attraction, and the once and future mighty Mackmen of Philadelphia. Spoke chose to join his hunting companion, rival, and co-conspirator Ty Cobb in Shibe Park. For one brief season, three of baseball's most enduring icons – and oversized egos – would be joined together in the same clubhouse.

"My relations with Connie Mack have always been of the best and it gives me great satisfaction to know I will work under him in 1928," Spoke told reporters upon signing Mack's offer sheet. Mack and Speaker learned their lesson from the year before: Speaker's salary wasn't disclosed. Nevertheless, stories began surfacing even before the A's left for spring training that their younger players resented the big money being paid their geriatric outfielders.

Connie's experiment didn't quite work out. The Peach and the Gray Eagle were hurt much of the season. Cobb only came to the plate 353 times; Speaker had fewer than 200 appearances. Plus Mule Haas, Bing Miller, and Al Simmons proved more than ready to handle the challenges of playing every day. Connie's A's were a mere year away from dominating the league – and the Yankees – for the next three seasons.

Spoke and Mickey Cochrane, the A's all-world catcher, became fast friends and hunting and fishing buddies – a friendship that lasted the rest of their lives. Simmons hit .351 that season with 107 RBIs – amazing productivity in only 464 at bats. Bing Miller hit .329, benefiting enormously, Mack said, from Speaker's coaching on the finer points of outfield play and batting. On May 21, in the first game of a doubleheader sweep against the Nats, Miller and Speaker collided while chasing Gunner Reeves's line drive in left-center. Spoke was knocked unconscious for a few moments, gashed his left leg, and badly bruised his right arm – injuries that hampered him for the rest of the season. Miller also had to come out of the game with a bruised thigh.

Speaker's career should have ended with a bang, but it didn't. The scrappy A's took the Yanks to the wire in '28, winning 98 games to New York's 101. But as John Kieran pointed out in his "Sports of the Times" column on September 30, the Yanks beat the A's in sixteen of their twenty-two head-to-head encounters that year. By late summer Cobb had joined Speaker on the bench, two legends watching youngsters bash a lively ball to places in Shibe Park never dreamed of in the old days. Speaker only got into sixty-four games, batting a paltry .267 – his lowest professional batting average since his half-season in Cleburne twenty-two years before. His finale came on August 30 in the same place where he made his unheralded big league debut two decades earlier: Shibe Park. Mack sent him up to pinch-hit for second-year shortstop Joe Boley. Spoke unceremoniously struck out. It could not have been a happy experience for him to finish his brilliant Major League career sitting on the bench, wearing an unfamiliar uniform in an unfamiliar town.

The early years of Tris Speaker's "retirement" were almost as tumultuous as his last few years in the game. Speaker had a number of offers from businesses in Cleveland eager to have his name and face associated with their company. But the man who had announced two years earlier that he was through with baseball for good wanted to stay in the game – even if it meant going back to the bushes. Plus he may not have been as infatuated with Cleveland as Cleveland was with him. "It isn't that I like the town so much," he once confided. "It's that I know a lot of fine people."

Not surprisingly, he had his heart set on returning to a part of the world he liked a great deal – namely, North Texas. And if he couldn't own or manage a big league club, then he would do the next best thing: get a stake with a club in the high minors. On August 9, 1928, he announced plans to acquire the Dallas franchise in the Texas League. "Baseball is my business. I have made no secret of the fact that I would like to have the Dallas Club at the right price." Initial signals were positive as talks got underway in the fall of 1928. At the last minute, however, the deal fell through. There's no evidence that Landis queered the Dallas deal, but the commissioner almost assuredly vetoed the Pittsburgh Pirates' desire to hire Speaker that fall as a bench coach.

Newark, New Jersey, was far removed from Dallas, but that's where Spoke and Fran ended up. In November 1928 Spoke accepted a two-year offer from Newark Bears owner Paul Block, a newspaper magnate, and club president James Sinnott to become player-manager for their AA franchise. The Associated Press story quoted Sinnott as saying Speaker "expects to put full-time in the outfield," which may have been the ownership's way of hyping ticket sales. Speaker had no intention of playing every day.

In Newark, Spoke replaced his old pal and rival Walter Johnson as pilot. With Bucky Harris stepping down as field manager to take over as Tigers skipper, the Washington Senators' job was given to the greatest star in Nats history. Poor Walter was never temperamentally suited to be the boss in the dugout. Nevertheless, the Big Train took the job and quickly got derailed in the nation's capital – a bumpy ride that was repeated a few years later in the Cleveland dugout as well. It must have pained Speaker to see Johnson get big league managing jobs for which Tris was much better qualified.

The International League back then consisted of such franchises as the Toronto Maple Leafs, the Montreal Royals, the Baltimore Orioles, the Buffalo Bisons, the Reading Keystones, the Rochester Red Wings, and the Jersey City Skeeters. So Tris had some easy train rides and some tough train rides. He was a brilliant contributor as a pinch batter and part-time outfielder. He made his debut for the Bears on May 19, getting a hit in two plate appearances and playing five innings in right. But their 11–3 loss to the Maple Leafs that day was typical of the Bears' performance under Speaker.

If Speaker wanted to use the Newark experience to demonstrate to Landis and others that he deserved the chance to return to the majors as a skipper, it backfired badly. He lasted barely a year in Newark before reaching an accommodation with Block and Sinnott. Block, whose family owned the *Pittsburgh Post-Gazette*, the *Toledo Blade*, and other publications, no doubt was exerting pressure on Speaker to be a gate attraction by playing more. He never got close to chasing the International League pennant. On June 27 the following year, he stepped down as manager.

Speaker in those years clearly hoped Landis would permit him to come back and boss a dugout again. In January 1930 it was reported all over the country that Speaker was in line to become manager of the Brooklyn Dodgers. He was the consensus choice of the two warring factions that ran the Dodgers. Wilbert Robinson had held the dual responsibilities of president and field manager. The compromise between the rival groups in the ownership syndicate was to retain Robbie as president for one more year and to bring in Speaker to run the club on the field. It was a *fait d'accompli*, the *New York Evening World* reported. Except it wasn't. A day or two later, word came out that the deal was off.

A similar dynamic took place ten months later. United Press International reported,

NEW YORK, Oct. 9 (Exclusive)   Out of a past replete with pleasant memory for Boston fans, Tris Speaker, center fielder star of bygone years, is to step into the managerial role with the Boston Red Sox, according to reports circulated in baseball circles here today. . . . Old Spoke, the Texan who failed as a minor league manager with the Newark International League club, is said to have reached an agreement with Bobby Quinn, owner of the Boston club, to become manager of the Sox for the 1931 season.

It was all set, the story said. The official announcement would come as soon as Quinn returned from the American League meetings then going on in Cleveland. Tris would be stepping in for his old teammate Heinie Wagner, who, like Bill Carrigan before him, was unable to turn around the woebegone Sox, who'd finished dead last six years in a row.

Once again, everything was wired for Speaker. And once again, everything got unwired. We'll never know if Landis got ahold of Quinn and nixed the deal, but clearly something happened. Ultimately the Sox job went to the forgettable Shano Collins, who went 73-136, a winning percentage of .349, over the next year and a half. He was replaced by the equally obscure Marty McManus, who took the Sox's winning percentage all the way up to .386 in his year and a half at the helm.

Tris was once again left out in the cold. Maybe then it dawned on him once and for all that he wasn't going to manage again. There was only one other instance over the next decade where Speaker's name was mentioned in connection with a managerial job opening. That was in 1940, when the Cleveland clubhouse mutinied against skipper Oscar Vitt. A couple of stories in the Cleveland papers that fall speculated that Speaker would be among the candidates for the job that eventually went to Roger Peckinpaugh.

Speaker's old pal Harry Hooper pursued a different path after he retired from the game. Like all the other members of the Red Sox glory teams, Hooper grew disgusted with the antics of Joe Lannin and his successor, Harry Frazee. He begged to be traded and was granted his wish in 1921. Charles Comiskey wisely thought that having a person of Harry's bearing might clean up the soiled White Sox clubhouse. Harry stayed five years with Commy, playing his usual brilliant outfield.

In 1930 Harry emulated such teammates as Joe Wood (Yale), Jack Barry (Holy Cross), Stuffy McInnis (Harvard), and his old Northern California pal Harry Wolter (Stanford) by accepting Princeton University's offer to become its baseball coach. When spring drills began in Harry's first year on the job, team members were delighted to discover the Gray Eagle himself helping to conduct practice. Spoke spent several days sharpening the skills of the Princeton players.

Hooper returned to Capitola in 1932 and became actively involved in Franklin D. Roosevelt's presidential campaign, helping to carry the Capitola–Santa Cruz area against incumbent Herbert Hoover. Campaign manager Big Jim Farley, who became FDR's postmaster general, rewarded Harry by making him Capitola's postmaster. Originally Hooper planned to stay in the postmaster position only long enough to get through the worst of the Depression years. But he ended up becoming a fixture in the community and remained in the job until retiring in 1957.

The National Broadcasting Company (NBC) approached Speaker in 1931 about broadcasting baseball games. For parts of the next couple of seasons, Speaker was stationed in Chicago, doing play-by-play from both Wrigley Field (the National League Cubs) and Comiskey Park (the American League White Sox). Sponsor General Electric (GE) would sneak references to Speaker's baseball broadcasts into appliance ads that it ran in the *Chicago Daily Tribune*. In an ad hawking its latest "all steel" icebox (available for ten dollars down and a mere ten dollars a month), GE reminded readers to "Hear Tris Speaker give the play-by-play account of the Cubs and White Sox games. Tune in WLS-ENR at game time each day!" Tris and his Indians pal, Jack Graney, were two of the first ex-ballplayers to become broadcasters. Graney became a beloved radio personality. Tris was, perhaps, something less than beloved behind a microphone, but was nevertheless an important pioneer.

No tape featuring Speaker's call of a game has survived. From the few comments that can be unearthed from columnists who critiqued his performance, it can safely be deduced that not everyone found his scratchy baritone and Texas colloquialisms pleasing. But he did draw plaudits for being able to communicate his knowledge of the game, making him, in effect, one of the first "color analysts." He was considered a good enough commentator to continue calling Cleveland games from time to time over the years. Well into the 1950s, he would stop by radio booths at parks around the country and do an inning or two with his broadcast buddies.

Tris and Fran also went out to Hollywood in 1931. Speaker apparently took a screen test or two, delivering a few perfunctory lines. But after a short time in Tinseltown, Fran and Tris concluded that Hollywood wasn't for them. Nearly two decades later, Speaker, Bob Feller, Lou Boudreau, and other Tribesmen had a cameo appearance in a forgettable matinee feature called *The Kid from Cleveland*.

Having been repeatedly spurned as a manager candidate by the bigs, Spoke once again set his sights on a minor league franchise – this one in a more appealing part of the world. In January 1933 Speaker teamed with E. Lee Keyser, principal owner of the Des Moines franchise in the Western League, and Hollywood comedian Joe E. Brown, to negotiate the purchase of the Kansas City Blues of the American Association. Unlike his effort four years previously to acquire the Dallas club in the

Texas League, this time the talks succeeded. Keyser, Brown, and Spoke took over in time to organize spring training for the 1933 season.

In addition to his responsibilities as field manager, Speaker was also named club secretary, supervising all personnel and contractual issues, including scouting. It proved too much. By the end of May, Spoke decided to give up his job as manager. On May 26 Nick Allen, a former catcher for the Cubs and the Reds, took over as the Blues' manager.

Keyser, Brown, and Spoke no doubt had big plans to create a model minor league franchise, make it click, and attract a lot of people and revenue. But their timing proved disastrous. Just as they took over, the Depression hit with a vengeance. It must have been next to impossible to obtain credit in the first years of operation. With the Dust Bowl further decimating the Midwest, fewer and fewer people could afford the luxury of an afternoon at Muhleback Field. Speaker never volunteered in public how much he lost in the Blues deal. But it couldn't have been pretty. Within a couple of years, he and Keyser sold their interests in the Blues to the Pittsburgh Pirates. Speaker would never again dally in the minors. "Speaker was possessed of a driving mentality," wrote one reporter, "that somehow seemed to bring mediocre players up to his own level. As soon as he quit playing, he lost his inspirational force. He became just another old-timer in the dugout."

By early 1934 Tris had moved semipermanently back to the city where he knew everybody and everybody knew him. Clevelanders were willing to pay him for his troubles – a good thing, because he no doubt needed the dough. He ended up doing what he refused to do five years earlier, profiting off his name and reputation. Spoke signed up as the public face of Peninsular Steel in Cleveland, representing it at local and national functions and playing in a lot of golf tournaments. He joined tony Acacia Country Club, a favorite of steel industry executives. He also played a lot at even tonier Canterbury, site of the 1946 U.S. Open.

Within a few weeks of reestablishing roots in Cleveland, he created Tris Speaker, Inc. The umbrella company's main business was liquor. It allowed him to market his name through a wholesale liquor outfit that came into being soon after Prohibition's repeal. Tris's company acquired office space in the Ninth-Chester Building downtown. It developed a new label: "Gray Eagle Brands." Tris Speaker, Inc., sold Gray Eagle

Brands to restaurants, hotels, and clubs throughout the region. Its logo showed Spoke taking a ferocious cut at the plate. An advertising flier distributed in March 1934 asserted:

> Tris Speaker's remarkable speed and accuracy in fielding, together with other characteristics, and prematurely gray hair made him an outstanding figure in big league ball, and earned him the apt sobriquet of Gray Eagle. Sentiment and appropriateness led Speaker to adopt this name for the particular brands put out under his company's private label. Each product is made to the specifications demanded by Tris Speaker, Inc. Gray Eagle Brands are moderately priced.

The liquor and steel businesses must have treated Speaker better than minor league baseball. He and Fran bought a sizeable home at 17303 Invermere Street in southeastern Cleveland. At the time it was an upscale neighborhood near Shaker Heights. Despite all the bedrooms in the house, they never chose to adopt children. But they appeared to be a devoted uncle and aunt.

Like other cities across the country, Cleveland was desperate in the mid-1930s to exploit interest in boxing. Prizefighting had become a huge business, second only to baseball in terms of fan interest and attendance. But Cleveland's Boxing Commission back then was unable to attract quality fights.

Mayor Harold Burton and members of the Cleveland Boxing Commission approached Speaker in the fall of 1935 to prevail on him to take the job as chairman. On January 9, 1936, it became official. "The new commissioner will have absolute control over boxing and wrestling activities in the city," Mayor Burton declared in making the announcement.

By all accounts, Speaker did a first-rate job putting Cleveland on the boxing map. He was able to work effectively with the other members of the commission, four prominent businessmen and sportsmen. Plus he was able to cash in on his connections across the country. His salary was something on the order of a few thousand dollars per year. But he earned bonuses if the take at the gate were big enough.

By the late '30s and early '40s, Cleveland was attracting more than its share of big-time matches. He stayed as chairman for nearly eight full years. When he finally tendered his resignation, he said it was because his boxing commitments were taking too much time away from Tris

Speaker, Inc., and his work for Peninsular Steel. "His commission has been consistently successful in keeping the sometimes unsavory game 'healthy' in this city," the *Plain Dealer* commented when Speaker resigned.

When a reporter asked Speaker if the controversy surrounding a "much-booed" recent bout triggered his resignation, Speaker laughed and said: "Of course, not. Boos never have bothered me. . . . No, it's just that I can't afford to sacrifice those hours that I take away from business and give to boxing."

In the summer of 1936, Cleveland took enormous pride in native son Jesse Owens's triumphs in the Summer Olympiad in Berlin. The twenty-two-year-old Ohio State University track star, an African American, won four gold medals under the withering glare of Adolf Hitler, giving the lie to Hitler's claims of Aryan supremacy.

On August 25 Governor Martin Davey and Mayor Burton organized a victory parade and rally in Jesse's honor. Tens of thousands of Clevelanders turned out to welcome Jesse home. The Associated Press reported that "In Cleveland's Negro district the welcome reached its noisiest peak. Hundreds of colored boys and girls, dressed in their 'Sunday best,' sat along the curbs. Many rooftops were crowded with enthusiastic greeters. The throng shouted and whistled as those 'who knew him when' sighted the beaming Owens."

Riding in the "gaily decorated" convertible with the mayor and Mr. and Mrs. Jesse Owens was a man who once claimed allegiance to the cause of the Knights of the Ku Klux Klan, Tris Speaker. In the mid-1930s, Speaker's fellow Hubbardite, imperial wizard Hiram Wesley Evans, was still a malevolent force within the national KKK. Like fellow ballplayers Frank Baker, Gabby Street, and Rogers Hornsby, it's unlikely that Speaker was ever more than a "social" member of the Klan, an experience not dissimilar to that of Supreme Court Justice Hugo Black, who belonged to the Klan as a young man and came to profoundly regret it. But even tepid participation in an organization that preached racial genocide was unconscionable.

The man who sixteen years earlier was so pig-headed that he couldn't abide the thought of his friend Ray Chapman memorialized in a Catholic service never commented on the irony of his sharing a dais with a black man. At the rally for Owens, the Olympic gold medalist concluded his remarks by saying, "You say Cleveland is proud of me. I'll turn the tables and say with sincerity that I'm very proud of Cleveland."

Speaker prided himself on his mechanical ability. He could build almost anything on the workbench in his basement on Invermere Street. In early spring 1937 Fran wanted to add a flower box to the second-floor porch off the master bedroom. Tris volunteered to make it himself. On the afternoon of April 11, 1937, Tris put the finishing touches on the flower box, and then called his brother-in-law, Ray Cudahy, to help him install it.

The two men concluded that the most efficient way to get the box up to the second-story porch was for Ray, a six-footer, to stand on his tiptoes and hand it up. Tris went up to the porch and reached down. Here's how the *Plain Dealer* described the harrowing moments that followed:

> The front section of the railing against which Speaker was leaning could not take the strain. Some of the boards were rotten at the base, it was said, and the railing itself was too flimsy to support the former athlete. . . . With a crash the railing broke and Speaker plunged headfirst. Immediately below him was a walk constructed of irregularly shaped pieces of flat slab stone, borders with cobblestones, some smooth, some jagged. As he fell, a distance more than sixteen feet, Speaker glanced off one of Cudahy's shoulders which broke the fall slightly. But it did not prevent him from diving headfirst into the stone walk. He struck one of the jagged border stones with his face when his left arm, broken by the impact, crumpled under him. The blow fractured his skull, and the great ball player should have become unconscious immediately. But he didn't – a fact which [his doctor] thought remarkable.

Horrified, Ray Cudahy hollered for Fran to call an ambulance. Spoke was bleeding profusely. Ray tried to pick him up take him into the house. Spoke told Ray he didn't need help, got up on his own power and sat in a nearby lawn chair. Ray ran into the house and got a blanket to wrap around Tris. "Mrs. Speaker, unstrung by the accident, tearfully awaited the ambulance sent by the Shaker Heights Fire Department," the *Plain Dealer* reported.

Spoke was lucky to be alive. He suffered a fractured skull, a severely lacerated face, and a broken left arm. That evening at Lakeview Hospital, the Indians' longtime physician, Dr. E. B. Castle, described Spoke's condition as critical. Spoke was in intense pain. Dr. Castle and his team had sutured more than a hundred stitches from the base of Spoke's neck to the top of his skull.

Several days passed before Dr. Castle pronounced Speaker out of the woods. Clevelanders shuddered that an awful head injury was going to take Speaker away from them the way one took Ray Chapman away seventeen years earlier.

Three days after the accident, the *New York Times*' John Lardner, one of Ring's four sons, wrote a poignant tribute to Speaker that was published in the *Plain Dealer*.

> It's part of the wonder of baseball that when something happens, good or bad, to a fellow like Speaker . . . the mists disperse from the face of time and the dead past becomes live and green again. . . . I expect that the image of Speaker fielding a ball back in 1916 is clearer and fresher in the mind of the baseball fan than the Hughes-Wilson election in the same year. . . . There never was an outfielder quite like Tristram. He was a natural roamer, as free and easy in the broad spaces of the outfield as a wild horse on a prairie.

The wild horse was stabled in his hospital room for more than a month. Four decades earlier, the metaphorical wild horse had been thrown by a real one, breaking his right arm and collarbone. Now he had been felled by a rickety railing, inflicting similar damage to his head and left side. But he was alive.

Two weeks later, Grantland Rice crafted this touching verse that must have induced a few tears from his "old-time pal."

> Here's to your health, Gray Eagle, in the eyrie you once knew.
> Here's to the grace you brought us – star of a gallant crew.
> Here's to the skill of a master, tops in the big corral.
> Here's to a reigning artist – and here's to an old-time pal.

In early May, Indians' pitching prodigy Bob Feller, all of nineteen years old, paid a visit to Speaker in the hospital. The wire service photo shows Spoke with a huge cast on his left arm. Feller, looking sharp in a window-paned suit and striped shirt that were clearly not purchased in Van Meter, Iowa, is pictured with his arm around Speaker's pillow. A sore arm that spring was preventing Feller from repeating his rookie year heroics.

By early June Speaker was back in the office and attending Indians games. On June 3 the *Plain Dealer* ran a photograph of Speaker serving as "guest broadcaster" on WHK Radio's coverage of the Indians' game that day. Spoke, sporting a fedora, his eyes peeled on the action below, is shown barking into an old upright microphone.

In August 1935 the National and American leagues jointly announced that they were establishing a Hall of Fame to commemorate the one hundredth anniversary of baseball's founding. Baseball had accepted dubious "research" commissioned years earlier by founding father A. G. Spalding that Gettysburg hero Abner Doubleday had "invented" the game in Cooperstown, New York, during the summer of 1839. For baseball's centennial four years hence, the two leagues would create a permanent museum to pay homage to the game's greatest players and contributors. A blue-ribbon advisory group was formed to determine the first slate of inductees.

A year later it was announced that the first five players to be inducted in the new shrine were Ty Cobb, Christy Mathewson, Honus Wagner, Babe Ruth, and Walter Johnson. Among the "pioneer" inductees were John McGraw and Connie Mack, along with Cap Anson, Alexander Cartwright, Ban Johnson, A. G. Spalding, and several others. The old fungo mates from three decades before, Tris Speaker and Cy Young, were somehow left off the initial players' selections, but the oversight was corrected a year later. Spoke received 165 out of a possible 201 votes for admission into the Hall. Four other stars also made the second cut.

On June 12, 1939, the Baseball Museum and Hall of Fame was officially christened before an assemblage of ten thousand people. A grand ceremony featuring a marching band, a red, white, and blue ribbon cutting, and remarks from Commissioner Landis generated front-page news across the country.

The *New York Times*' Arthur Daley took in the festivities and filed this report:

> As the band greeted each man with a fanfare and "Take Me Out to the Ball Game," ten of the eleven living members of the Hall of Fame were introduced to the expectant throng. First came the gaunt 76-year-old figure of

lovable Connie Mack. He was followed by Honus Wagner, Tris Speaker, Larry Lajoie, Cy Young, Walter Johnson, George Sisler, Eddie Collins, Grover Cleveland Alexander, and, with perfect dramatic timing, the one and only Babe Ruth.

Wee Willie Keeler and Christy Mathewson were inducted posthumously. Postmaster General Farley, Harry Hooper's benefactor, "sold" Commissioner Landis the first sheet of the special commemorative stamps that the Roosevelt administration had commissioned for the occasion. One of the highlights of the day for Speaker was introducing Eddie Collins to Honus Wagner; incredibly, the two legends had never met.

Ty Cobb, citing traffic problems, somehow managed to miss the dedication ceremonies, a faux pas not lost on Judge Landis and the organizers of the event. It's entirely possible that the Peach was miffed that the Bambino was getting the spotlight treatment – and not him. Cobb did get there in time to participate in an old-timers' game. A team captained by Eddie Collins lost, 4–2, to a squad captained by Honus Wagner. Before the old-timers took the field, a group of servicemen from Governors Island donned vintage "uniforms" and demonstrated how the game was played back when Doubleday was a lad. It's a shame Abner couldn't have been exhumed for the occasion, because it might have been the first time he'd ever glimpsed the old variation of "rounders," too.

All twenty-five enshrinees had bronze plaques hung in their honor. The initial display included a mid-nineteenth-century ball purportedly dug up on a farm near the Doubleday homestead. The "Doubleday ball" is still a prized possession of the National Baseball Hall of Fame.

Speaker must have taken wry satisfaction that his plaque highlighted a middle initial that, three decades earlier, he had made up out of whole cloth:

TRISTRAM E. SPEAKER
Boston (A) 1909–15
Cleveland (A) 1916–26
Washington (A) 1927
Philadelphia (A) 1928
Greatest centrefielder of his day. Lifetime batting average of .344. Manager in 1920 when Cleveland won its first pennant and World Championship.

In the years to come, Speaker enjoyed going to Cooperstown for induction ceremonies, especially for the enshrinement of such old pals as Sam Crawford and Mickey Cochrane. Unlike other stars, he also could be counted on to participate in charity old-timers' games. In 1944 Speaker was one of the headliners at ceremonies to commemorate the golden anniversary of Connie Mack's career in baseball.

"Softball" was a new phenomenon in the 1930s. It caught on like wild-fire, becoming the favored game of company and community teams. It was even played indoors in some places around the country.

Speaker gambled that he could exploit softball's popularity by establishing an indoor winter circuit – and charging people to come watch it. He called it the National Professional Indoor Baseball League (NPIBL). Spoke approached several former big leaguers, including Bill Wambs-ganss and Gabby Street, persuading them to pilot different franchises – and kick a little start-up money into the kitty. It was officially launched on November 14, 1939, at a well-attended press conference at the Hotel Commodore in New York.

Speaker installed himself as president of the NPIBL, with former Harvard gridiron star Tack Hardwick as vice president. Tris and Tack unveiled an ambitious venture. There were to be eight teams and two divisions in the league. The eastern division consisted of franchises in New York, Brooklyn, Philadelphia, and Boston. Cleveland, Chicago, Cincinnati, and St. Louis formed the western outposts. The New York club was headed by the son of Gen. "Black Jack" Pershing.

The original schedule called for each team to play 102 games – fifty-one at home, fifty-one on the road, with no interleague play until the playoffs began in March. Instead of ninety feet between bases, the distance was sixty feet. And the ball was twelve inches in diameter, somewhat smaller than the softball popular back then. Tryouts would begin immediately, with play scheduled to start in December. The league established headquarters in a midtown Manhattan office building and – a day late and a dollar short – began its marketing campaign.

It was an unmitigated disaster. Speaker and his partners hadn't done their homework on even the most basic issues, such as rental fees and the availability of arenas. All kinds of logistical headaches surfaced immediately. The Chicago franchise of the NIPBL collapsed before it ever played a game.

After a few weeks it became painfully apparent that the American public did not want to pay serious money to watch so-so athletes play softball indoors. On December 22, barely a month after the league was announced with such fanfare, Speaker pulled the plug. "It is hoped that in the future a change in conditions will make it possible to resume," Speaker said in a statement dissolving the league. There was no future; the league fell with a thud.

Tris returned to Cleveland, chastened. He would never again spearhead a big baseball venture. Spoke would stick to pushing liquor, steel, boxing, and his own name in and around Cleveland.

Speaker was nearly fifty-four when the country he had visited in friendship twenty-eight years earlier attacked Pearl Harbor. He was too old to serve in the active military as a pilot or trainer. But he contributed to the war effort in numerous ways. First, he accepted a request to serve as an active member of northeastern Ohio's draft board. Tris become an important advocate for ballplayers enlisting in the service. He also publicly warned men with 2-A or 2-B war-related job deferments that if they quit to play professional ball, they would automatically be promoted to 1-A and drafted into the service. Reprising a role he played in the Great War, Speaker helped sell war bonds by playing in various charity games and hosting different rallies and functions. He also used his capacity as one of the country's leading exponents of prizefighting to bring gratis boxing matches to servicemen all over the world.

Friendship and loyalty cut deep with Tris Speaker. Way back in his first year with the Red Sox, Speaker took a shine to a teenaged boy hawking newspapers on a Boston street corner. The kid, a Jewish immigrant, put his beautiful tenor to good use shilling papers. Spoke was so taken with this Russian émigré who could belt out a Yiddish *nigun*, then, without missing a beat, break into an Irish ballad, that he invited the youngster to entertain the Sox at the Putnam Inn. The kid's act proved so popular that soon he was warbling in the Sox clubhouse at the Huntington Avenue Grounds. Spoke always told the youngster that he found his voice "soothing."

The boy's given name was Max David Weisman. But once the natural southpaw started messing around at the park in pregame warmups, the Sox nicknamed him "Lefty." Lefty's family had immigrated to Boston when their son was barely a year old. Young Weisman left school before his early teens to take the newspaper job. He prided himself, though, on being a "self-educated" man, according to his son Jed, who's now in his early seventies and still living and working in Cleveland. Over time, Lefty became something of a mascot for the Sox. Tris came to view the youngster as almost a surrogate son, says Jed.

When Tris left for Cleveland in 1916, he made a point of telling Weisman, then twenty, that he'd have a job with the Indians if Speaker were ever made manager. Sure enough, Tris made good on his promise. In 1921 the Indians' trainer retired. So Spoke brought his protégé to Cleveland to bandage up his players. The fact that Lefty had no background whatsoever in medicine or hygiene didn't deter Speaker. Lefty took a couple of classes at Cleveland College in health and anatomy. And he learned at the knee of Dr. Edward Castle, the team physician. Over time, Lefty became a respected trainer, making himself so indispensable that he kept the job until the day he died in 1949. Many of his "patients" called him "Doc."

Jed still remembers the thrill of having a baseball immortal come to his and his older brother's bar mitzvahs. The Weisman family still has almost identical photographs of Tris proudly holding up the two bar mitzvah cakes. If the thirty-second-degree Freemason ever expressed any prejudice toward Jews, Jed Weisman never heard it. The Weisman boys always called him "Uncle Tris," even in the Indians' clubhouse where they served as batboys in the late '30s and '40s. Jed remembers Uncle Tris as a gravelly voiced man "with eyes that shined." Tris had a commanding presence about him, what Jed now recognizes as "leadership qualities." Mrs. Speaker, Jed recalls, was a "classy lady," always poised and well coiffed. Fran was quite a beauty in her youth but struggled with her weight in middle age.

Spoke's baritone wasn't in a league with Lefty's tenor, but he loved to sing anyway. Over time, Lefty replaced Ray Chapman in the Jack Graney–Steve O'Neill ensemble. Lefty, who'd been a hustler all his life, shared Spoke's addiction for the ponies. Weisman and Speaker knew every shortcut between Dunn Field and the Thistle Downs thoroughbred track in Cleveland and would often bolt for the track once a ballgame ended. "My mother was fond of saying that we would have been a *lot* wealthier had Dad not had a place in his heart for horses – and wanted to make sure they were well fed," Jed chuckled in a recent interview.

When a sudden heart attack took his friend Lefty away far too soon, Spoke came up from Texas to deliver a eulogy. A half century later, Jed can still summon the image of Speaker choking up. "Goodbye, son," Tris sobbed to the immigrant kid he'd befriended on a street corner forty years before.

It's ironic given his upbringing that another one of Speaker's best pals in life happened to be Jewish. No one in Hubbard knows how Sam Tobolowsky, a nonpracticing Jew, happened to settle in central Texas, but Sam was for many years an important fixture in town. He ran a dry goods store that was a popular gathering spot for farmers and merchants. Sam also served as the chief of the Hubbard Volunteer Fire Department, living in an apartment above the fire station.

Since his mother often had boarders in the house, Speaker liked to bunk with confirmed bachelor Tobolowsky in the firehouse. Over the years, Tris helped Sam raise a lot of money for new fire equipment. Spoke even brought his world champion Indians to town for an exhibition in March 1921 to offset the cost of a new fire engine. Proceeds from that game also went toward fixing up Hubbard's ball yard.

At some point late in his twenties, Speaker purchased a four-hundred-plus-acre ranch just outside town. The silo of his barn was so large it dominated the landscape. He hired old hunting buddy Charlie Vaughn to run the ranch in his absence. It became a standing joke among Cleveland players and sportswriters that Speaker's ranch responsibilities would cause him to show up late for spring training. One year he would tell folks that he couldn't get to camp on time because he was tied up fixing a faulty tractor. The next year it would be because he had to put new seed down.

Tris's brother, Loyd, died in 1921 at age thirty-seven. Jenny, their beloved mother, passed away nine years later at age eighty-three. The woman who had to be talked into letting her son play ball outlived her husband by a third of a century.

Lefty Weisman was just one of many old pals to fete Speaker in March of 1949 on Ralph Edwards's popular radio show, "This is Your Life." Jed Weisman recalls that his dad "surprised" Spoke by singing an Irish ballad offstage – Jed is "90 percent sure" it was "My Wild Irish Rose." Also paying tribute to Tris were Harry Hooper, Bill Wambsganss, and his one-time wunderkind protégé Joe Sewell, by then pushing fifty. Lou Boudreau, still the player-manager of the Indians, offered kind words. Bob Hope and commentator Henry Allen provided comic relief. Sadly, no known tape or transcript has survived. It would be wonderful to know what stories Speaker's pals kidded him about on the air.

Bob Hope's family had moved to Cleveland from Britain while their son was still in short pants. Hope became a lifelong Indians fanatic and, later, part owner of the franchise. The photographs of Hope and Speaker together show the entertainer grinning ear-to-ear, obviously delighted to be pictured with the hero of his teens. Bob and his wife, Dolores, occasionally came to Tucson for spring training games in the '40s and '50s and would socialize with Tris and Fran.

At some point in the early 1940s, Tris shut down Gray Eagle Brands. It's not known whether the enterprise lost its profitability, or Tris sold out to another wholesale liquor distributor, or he just grew tired of the day-to-day strain of running a business. Speaker buff and Cleveland native Fred Schuld, the former head of the Society for American Baseball Research, remembers delivering mail for a vacationing postal carrier in early 1943. One of the pieces of mail that Fred was supposed to deliver was addressed to "Gray Eagle Liquors" on Bolivar Street, near where the Jacobs Field bleachers stand today. Fred, now in his late seventies, distinctly recalls the excitement he felt at the prospect of meeting the great Gray Eagle himself as he delivered the package. Alas, he learned that the business had closed down.

When showman Bill Veeck (as in "wreck," as the popular saying went) acquired the Indians, he generously hired Spoke in January 1947 to serve as a special advisor and "ambassador of good will" for the Indians. As the Associated Press reported, " 'That means [Speaker] will make speeches and explain to the public what we are trying to do,' the publicity-conscious Veeck explained."

Just three weeks later, Veeck announced that Speaker would serve as a part-time coach at the Indians' spring training camp in Tucson. For the first time in two decades, the grounded Gray Eagle would don a Major League uniform in an official capacity. Had Veeck obtained dispensation from the commissioner's office to hire someone previously deemed radioactive? Or in classic showman fashion had Veeck pulled a quickie on Happy Chandler? The owner may have executed a slick bait-and-switch on Chandler; positioning Spoke's hiring as strictly a public relations move, then quickly flipping him over to coach, which is what Veeck had planned all along. Regardless of how it evolved, Veeck announced that Speaker would be working with the Indians' outfielders in camp. Rookie Dale Mitchell would be Spoke's special project. "If anyone can make a great outfielder out of Mitchell, Speaker is the guy," Veeck said.

Speaker was indeed the guy to teach the nuances of outfield play to young Indian outfielders. But Dale Mitchell wasn't destined to become Speaker's star pupil. Maybe Veeck knew that all along, too. Lawrence Eugene Doby, late of Camden, South Carolina, became Tris Speaker's great latter-day protégé. Doby, a veteran of both the navy in World War II and of the Negro Leagues, was the first African American ballplayer in the American League. Doby made his debut for the Indians on July 5, 1947, just eleven weeks after Jackie Robinson had broken the color barrier with the Brooklyn Dodgers.

The eventual Hall of Famer was a terrific athlete but not a natural outfielder. Doby had played mainly second base in the Negro Leagues and the minors. Over the next few springs, Speaker conducted a tutorial in outfield play for Doby, spending endless hours under the hot Tucson sun teaching young Larry how to position himself and read different defensive situations.

In June of 1949 Speaker talked to Shirley Povich of the *Washington Post* about his star pupil. "I've never seen a young ballplayer with such a high potential," Spoke raved. "I get a personal pleasure out of working with a kid who can do so many things so well."

A *Sport Magazine* photo from 1952 shows Speaker conducting a hitting clinic in Tucson, encircled by such Indians stars as Doby, Luke Easter, Ray Boone, and slugger Al Rosen. It's one of those posed photographs where the participants look a little *too* attentive and enthusiastic. Larry Doby is shown with his hands perched on his knees, literally leaning on every word being spoken by a man who once professed membership in the Ku Klux Klan. Doby proved to be a brilliant student. He acquitted himself with great dignity in a career that lasted a dozen more years. Larry was inducted into the Hall of Fame forty years after his mentor passed away.

Speaker stayed with the Indians in a part-time capacity throughout most of the next decade, even after Veeck sold his controlling interest in the club. Señor Al Lopez once said that the aging Speaker could "still spot a batter's weakness quicker than most of us." General manager Frank Lane and others in the Indians organization always appreciated Spoke's willingness to work with their most promising young players in Daytona Beach, or represent the club in the community, or serve as a sounding board on personnel issues. Spoke's second tenure with the Tribe happened to coincide with the second golden era of Indians' baseball. Then again, maybe it wasn't a coincidence. Maybe the old duffer's Tucson tutorials paid huge dividends. The year after Speaker was hired as spring training coach, the Indians beat the Boston Braves in the World Series – the same way the Tribe had won the Series the year after Tris was hired as field manager in 1919. Speaker had a direct hand in the only two world championships ever won by the Cleveland Indians.

In 1951 Speaker received a telegram notifying him that he was the first inductee into the brand-new Texas Sports Hall of Fame. A dinner was held to honor the Texas hall's first group of inductees. Speaker was seated with golfer Ben Hogan, who along with Rogers Hornsby, Doak Walker, and others, was among the later honorees. The following year, Spoke joined Cy Young and Napoleon Lajoie in being elected the first members of the Cleveland Indians Hall of Fame.

Illness and accidents continued to dog Tris Speaker. In 1942, five years after he barely survived his terrifying spill, he contracted pneumonia and returned to the hospital under the care of Dr. Castle. It was touch-and-go for a few days, but the fifty-four-year-old Speaker pulled through. After returning home, he allowed himself to be photographed sitting outside in a lawn chair, smiling as one of his beagles gamboled on the lawn.

Spoke drove a car the way he rode a horse: hard. On February 8, 1952, it nearly cost him his life. Speaker narrowly avoided injury while driving solo from Ohio to Texas. Outside Clarksville, Tennessee, Spoke was passing a truck on a two-lane highway when the truck abruptly turned left, colliding into the right side of Speaker's car and sending it careening off the road. The passenger side of Speaker's car was heavily damaged, according to the Tennessee highway patrol report. The Associated Press account of the accident quoted Spoke as saying, "I'm thankful Mrs. Speaker wasn't riding with me."

In July 1954, in the midst of another great Indians drive toward the pennant, sixty-six-year-old Spoke suffered a serious heart attack at home. As had happened seventeen years before, he was rushed to Lakeview Hospital. The coronary laid him up for months and forced him to give up golf, pretty much for good. Spoke's physicians gave him special medication that he was supposed to have with him at all times, lest he have another episode.

At the 1946 U.S. Open at Canterbury Country Club, Spoke served as a celebrity host. The June 13 *New York Times* pictured Spoke showing his golf grip to "Jug" McSpaden and Vic Ghezzi. It's one of the few pictures extant that shows Spoke – the player whom Pirates owner Barney Dreyfuss wouldn't sign forty years earlier because of his cigarette habit – actually smoking a cigarette. Spoke's fellow Texan Ben Hogan, with whom he shared so many personality traits – good, bad, and, like smoking, indifferent – three-putted the seventy-second hole and missed a playoff with Ghezzi, Byron Nelson, and eventual winner Lloyd Mangrum by one stroke.

Spoke always had a soft spot in his heart for kids – especially needy or disabled youngsters. Over the years, he played in scores of exhibition and old-timers' games to raise money for orphanages and children's charities. As the years went by, the Golden Outfield of Spoke, Cat, and Duffy would reunite to raise money for worthy causes. It started in September 1930 when Duffy and Spoke put aside their personal differences and joined with Hoop to raise money for Children's Hospital of Boston and a needy ballplayers' fund. In July 1938 the beneficiary was the hospital fund of the Veterans of Foreign Wars. In September 1947 it was the Babe Ruth Foundation Fund.

Tris was also an integral part of the organization that gave rise to the National Easter Seals Society. Together with founder Edgar F. Allen and members of the Cleveland Rotary Club, Speaker played a lead role in the Society for Crippled Children, becoming a first vice president in 1942. Over the years, he and Fran stayed active in the philanthropy, helping to establish a special summer camp for disabled kids called Camp Cheerful. Tris visited the camp nearly every summer, donating thousands of dollars and raising tens of thousands of dollars more.

In 1953 President Eisenhower hosted a luncheon to honor America's forty greatest living athletes. When Tris Speaker emerged from the White House, reporters asked him how things had gone with the president. "Well," said the man who had drawn applause from chief executives as varied as Taft, Wilson, and Coolidge, "I called him Mr. President, and he called me Tris."

CHAPTER 12

Twilight

We tell ourselves that he had success far beyond the measure allotted to most men, and good friends and the happiness that comes to those who spend their lives doing what they most want to do. But still the sadness remains that the Gray Eagle flies no more. — Gordon Cobbledick

Some twenty-two months before Tris Speaker died, he was one-third of the answer to a question posed to contestant Charles Van Doren on the television quiz show "Twenty-One." Mixed in with brain teasers on Spanish geography, classic French architecture, and earth science that evening was this stumper: "Name the three players in the history of baseball who amassed more than 3,500 hits in their major league careers."

The Columbia University doctoral candidate in English literature had been defending champion on "Twenty-One" for ten consecutive programs. In those couple of months, Van Doren had become a national heartthrob. A handsome bachelor and the son and nephew of noted writers, Van Doren had already won more than $100,000 – serious money in the winter of 1956–57 – on what had become television's first "reality show" sensation.

As the show's producers had coached him, Van Doren paused dramatically before correctly answering: "Ty Cobb, Cap Anson, and Tris Speaker." The studio audience clapped on cue, amazed that an Ivy Leaguer would have such a grasp of baseball minutia. Had the audience known the truth – that Van Doren was given the answers ahead of time, that in fact "Twenty-One" and other quiz shows of the 1950s were big fat frauds – perhaps it would have applauded less enthusiastically. Once again, a trusted American institution had toyed with "the faith of 50 million people."

In the half century that's passed since "Twenty-One" went off the air, thousands of men have played big league baseball. But only three have joined Speaker, Cobb, and Anson in the 3,500-hit club: Pete Rose, Henry Aaron, and Stan Musial. There's no more exclusive fraternity in sports.

It's fascinating that Musial also scaled the rare plateau of 3,500 hits, because Bob Ryan of the *Boston Globe* believes that Speaker and Musial are the two immortals whose achievements have somehow been ignored in the pastime's history. Speaker was eclipsed in the public's mind first by Ty Cobb, then by Joe DiMaggio, Ryan pointed out in a recent interview. "Stan the Man" was overshadowed by the volcanic Ted Williams and undercut by his own self-effacing personality.

On September 30, 1954, during warmups before the second game of the Indians-Giants World Series, wire service photographers made a special request. They arranged for the Giants' precocious center fielder, who had made a sensational catch the previous day, to be pictured with a retired center fielder whose legend revolved around sensational catches.

Tris Speaker, just three months after suffering a heart attack, showed up for the photo opportunity nattily turned out in a polka-dotted bow tie and checkered blazer. Willie Mays was wearing his home Giants uniform and a self-conscious smile. The photographers had the Gray Eagle "demonstrate" his batting technique, fingering a bat handle with his left-handed grip.

Arthur Daley, the eminent columnist of the *New York Times*, witnessed the exchange between Mays and Speaker. " 'Cup your hand as if you're giving Willie advice,' shouted a lens snapper," Daley wrote the next day. " 'No, siree,' laughed Tris. 'I can't give this boy any advice. He knows all the answers already.' Willie shuffled his feet in embarrassment."

Such influential commentators as Daley, Shirley Povich of the *Washington Post*, Joe Williams of the *New York World-Telegram*, Gordon Cobbledick of the *Cleveland Plain Dealer*, and syndicated columnist and broadcast personality Bob Consodine remained unabashed Speaker fans long after the Gray Eagle had turned completely gray. Scores of times through the decades they would extol Speaker's unmatched defensive genius. Whenever a member of the New York press corps would attempt to elevate DiMaggio over Speaker in the pantheon of great center fielders, Povich would burn up his typewriter keys. No one could cover ground like Spoke, Shirley wrote a dozen times over the years. Not

Cobb. Not Milan. Not DiMaggio. Not Piersall. Not Mantle. Only Mays was in Speaker's class as a fly hawk, in Shirley's oft-written opinion.

In his *SuperStars of Baseball*, the *St. Louis Post-Dispatch*'s Bob Broeg wrote, "[Speaker] had considerable career advantages over the great DiMaggio if you'll accept what Branch Rickey would call 'quantitative quality.' " Tris played nine more seasons than Joe, scored 491 more runs, compiled 1,301 more hits, laced 404 more doubles, pounded 93 more triples, and pilfered 403 more bases. It's difficult to compare the dead-ball era, of course, with the one in which DiMaggio played. Joe had 361 career homers to Tris's 115. It's also difficult to deny the implications of certain numbers, especially these: DiMaggio had only two seasons with more than twenty assists, with a high of twenty-two; Speaker four times had *thirty* or more assists. In 1923, well into the lively ball era, Speaker assisted on twenty-six put-outs – at the age of thirty-five, no less. Speaker was credited with more than three times the number of assists DiMaggio collected in his career.

"Joe DiMaggio? An authentic great," wrote the acerbic Joe Williams in 1951. "But you and Toots Shor can have him. Make mine Speaker."

Speaker, clearly jealous of the adoring press that DiMaggio was getting in the late 1930s, belittled him with the comment that there were fifteen better outfielders in baseball than Joe – a remark he quickly came to regret. At first he denied saying it, even though Bob Consodine had him on tape, and a half dozen or more correspondents, plus Horace Stoneham, president of the Giants, eavesdropped on the interview. Then Spoke wrote an angry letter to the *Sporting News*, expressing outrage that they had published his criticism of Joltin' Joe. Eventually, the tempest died down, but not before Speaker was lampooned in a cartoon that accompanied a Jimmy Powers column in the *New York Daily News*.

Many of the columnists' reminisces of Speaker came during the '40s and '50s when he would visit spring training camps in his capacity with the Indians. There was something about Speaker's presence in the warmth of the bleachers that would cause sportswriters to begin waxing nostalgic. "One of this reporter's vivid boyhood memories is the indelible picture of Tris Speaker catching a fly ball," Daley wrote in 1952. "There never was a more graceful outfielder. The Gray Eagle, playing inordinately shallow, would flit back and in a swooping motion of his arms gather in a fly ball, waist high and off to the side, with exquisite grace."

Daley's tribute came after watching Spoke's "disconcerting" performance in an old-timers' game. "A simple fly ball floated out to Speaker the incomparable. He looked like Babe Herman blinded by the sun. He ran uncertainly in circles, falling all over his feet. The Speaker of old actually could have caught it in his back pocket. The old Speaker didn't catch it at all. The ball struck him on the glove fortunately and bounced foolishly away. Time marches on!"

Of the thousands of players who have galloped through center field over the past century, only two have made the "Graces look like jades," to invoke Grantland Rice. And they were pictured together that autumn afternoon in 1954 at the Polo Grounds.

Time, thank heavens, has indeed marched on. Darker-skinned men are no longer "boys" in the popular vernacular. Ed Walton, now in his early seventies and retired in Bridgeport, Connecticut, served the Boston Red Sox in many capacities: as historian, scribe, and scout. But perhaps his most enduring contribution to the franchise is that he brought the aging Joe Wood back into the Red Sox family. It was Walton who interceded with the club and arranged for Smoky Joe to be invited to various Fenway gatherings. Ed's proudest moment came when he introduced Smoky Joe to Rocket Roger Clemens, one fireballer to another.

The Fenway clubhouse through which Walton wheeled Wood was a much different place than the one Smoky Joe inhabited in the second decade of the century. Wood, Speaker, and the other old "Masons" could barely abide people whose Christianity was not all that different from their own. It would have been unthinkable for them, or for the "K.C.s," for that matter, to tolerate the varying ethnicity of the modern Major League clubhouse.

Despite his son Bob's persistent efforts, Joe Wood has never been inducted into the Hall of Fame. In the late 1960s writer Eugene Murdock interviewed Smoky Joe. When Murdock asked him about the 1919 controversy with Dutch Leonard, Wood motioned to Murdock to turn off the tape recorder. According to Scott Longert, sports archivist at the Western Reserve Historical Association, Joe then lamented that he'd never get into the Hall of Fame because he was tainted by the Leonard debacle.

Humorist Ogden Nash once compiled an alphabet-driven "Line-up for Yesterday" of great ballplayers, hinging his verse on the first letter of their last names. " 'S' is for Speaker," Nash mused:

Swift centerfield tender
When the ball saw him coming,
It yelled, "I surrender!"

Tris Speaker died exactly the way he should have: doing something he loved in Texas's great outdoors. Spoke and his pal Charlie Vaughn headed forty miles east on the morning of December 8, 1958, to fish Lake Whitney in western Hill County. The Army Corps of Engineers had created the lake seven years earlier to control flooding on the Brazos and Nolan rivers. Spoke didn't pack the heart medication that had been prescribed since his heart attack four and a half years earlier. His doctors had redoubled their warnings to him earlier that year when he spent a few days in the hospital with chest pains. A carefree day casting for bass, catfish, and crappie didn't seem to be the kind of activity that would trigger a coronary.

After they'd finished fishing for the afternoon, Charlie, Tris, and a couple of other pals were maneuvering the boat onto its trailer hitch. The exertion of getting the boat out of the water, then backing the car into position in those days before power steering, proved too much for Tris's heart. He keeled over and was carried into the backseat of the car by Charlie and the others. One of them took another car and raced to the nearest telephone. A physician from Hill County named H. P. Sammons was summoned. The wire service accounts the next day said that Dr. Sammons arrived "within minutes" but a more realistic timetable given travel distance would be thirty to forty-five minutes, perhaps longer.

There was nothing that Sammons could do. "Tris opened his eyes and whispered, 'My name is Tris Speaker.' Then he died. I have an idea he knew what was taking place," Dr. Sammons said to the press later that day.

Fran, who rarely accompanied her husband on his trips to Texas to go hunting and fishing, happened to be in Hubbard and got the news from a devastated Charlie. She was inconsolable.

The funeral took place in Hubbard three days later. The Reverend William Fleener, the rector of Hubbard's Episcopal Church, presided.

His eulogy noted the biblical invocation of a lifespan of "threescore and ten" – which was Spoke's precise age at death. Before the official service began, two Catholic priests comforted a weeping Fran at the bier. The Wolfe Funeral Chapel seated only two hundred, so hundreds of mourners stood outside. Near the casket was placed a faded photograph of Spoke's first professional team, the 1906 Cleburne Railroaders of the North Texas League.

The encomiums and flowers came flooding in. The American League, the National League, Commissioner Ford Frick, the Hall of Fame, the Red Sox, the Yankees, the Baseball Writers Association of America, and Cleveland's Society for Crippled Children all sent wreaths. Commissioner Frick and former American League president Will Harridge led baseball's official delegation to the funeral. "There's not much you can say at a time like this. It's a shame we're losing so many of the old stars. These are the players who have meant so much to the game," said Frick. The Indians sent a large contingent to Hubbard, including club vice president George Medinger, road secretary Spud Goldstein, and former Tribesman Dale Mitchell. Fellow Texan Rogers Hornsby told the Associated Press, "You just can't say anything too nice about Tris."

Frank Lane, the Indians' general manager who was instrumental in keeping the aging Spoke involved with the club, volunteered, "You don't replace Tris Speaker. He was a Cleveland institution. We're really going to miss him."

The Cleveland press gave their institution the send-off he deserved, with huge front-page coverage and numerous stories inside. The *Plain Dealer* highlighted Tris's role as first vice president of the Society for Crippled Children, mentioning that he helped start the society's Camp Cheerful and frequently visited, spending hours with the kids. Said William B. Townsend, the society's director: "Speaker's death is a great loss to our society and the national organization in which he was an advisory member. Tris had a tremendous interest in our children."

Joe Sewell, the Alabama prodigy who helped Spoke secure the pennant in 1920, told the *Plain Dealer* that Speaker was "one of the greatest managers I ever played for and one of the finest persons I ever came in contact with in baseball. He was like a second father to me."

"Thousands of fans remembered Speaker grazing in center field," the *Plain Dealer* noted on its front page in a passage clearly shaped by Cobbledick. "The term is used advisedly. The great fielder would bend over, pluck a few blades of grass, and chew them industriously. . . . He seemed to know at the exact moment the ball struck the bat precisely where the ball was going. And if it was going out into his territory, he tore out like a frightened antelope – and he always got there. He made tough catches look easy."

Napoleon Lajoie, whom Speaker had replaced in the hearts of Cleveland fans, offered, "He was one of the greatest fellows I have ever known, both as a baseball player and as a gentleman. . . . He will always be remembered as one of the game's greats." Former Tribe pitcher George Uhle said, "He was the best – the greatest I ever saw in center."

The *Plain Dealer* tribute also made note of the 1919 feud between Spoke and former teammate Chick Gandil. Spoke and Chick went toe-to-toe at least twice and possibly three times that season. The contretemps started in late May at Comiskey, then were renewed a few weeks later at Dunn Field. In their first dustup, both dugouts emptied and formed a circle around the combatants. " 'Why don't you stop the fight?' one of the White Sox asked of [umpire] Tommy Connolly. 'Who is getting the best of it?' asked Connolly, whose view of the battle was hidden by a cordon of players. 'Speaker has Gandil down.' 'Well,' said Tommy, 'let them go for another minute. Gandil has it coming to him,' " remembered the *Plain Dealer*. But Gandil, who'd boxed professionally in Mexico under an assumed name, still wanted a piece of Speaker, so they took it under the stands in Cleveland after a later game. Tris licked him all over again. Henry Edwards compared the Speaker-Gandil melee to the Jess Willard–Jack Dempsey fight that had taken place in Toledo that same summer of '19.

That fall, Speaker and Henry Edwards were eating breakfast together in a Cincinnati hotel on the morning of the first game of the 1919 World Series. Gandil and a White Sox teammate happened to be a few tables away.

"I am one of those who believe in not harboring a grudge," Speaker told Edwards. "I don't want to see Gandil not giving his best because of that fight I had with him. I am going over to shake hands with him and wish him and the White Sox luck." And he did, Edwards recalled.

In a beautiful column wrought from the heart, Gordon Cobbledick paid homage to his departed friend a few days after Spoke's death. Cobbledick set his piece in the press box at Fenway Park during a Tribe-Bosox game played a few years earlier. A skeptical young reporter within Cobbledick's earshot was quizzing Speaker about Tris's fielding prowess. Just as the other reporter was beginning his interrogation, Jimmy Piersall of the Sox made a nice running catch in center field. " 'So, sassed the reporter, 'you're going to tell me you could have made that catch, you playing that shallow center I've heard so much about?' Tris mulled the question over briefly, his eyes twinkling. 'No I couldn't,' he admitted. Then he added with a grin, 'Not at my age.' " Cobbledick continued:

> As someone who is old enough to have seen much of Tris Speaker at the peak of his glorious career, I can attest that the only catches he didn't make were the ones that couldn't be made. There may never be another like him. But it won't be for his superb professional gifts that he will be missed. It will be because he was a good and kindly and understanding man, and because he was a warm and friendly man.

Often, Cobbledick remembered, Tris would sit near him in the press box, "observing shrewdly and commenting wisely on the action as it unfolded on the field." In the 1930s and 1940s when he had no official capacity with the club, he and Fran would come to the games "simply because he, and she, loved the game that had brought them together and that had been such a big part of their lives."

In the *Cleveland News*, columnist Hal Lebovitz recalled how complimentary Speaker always was of the contemporary player. When asked the inevitable question comparing modern players to those from the old days, "He would reply, with his gravelly voice, 'I think the boys today might be a little better.' " Concluded Lebovitz: "He never played the big man."

Bill Wambsganns, who played with and for Spoke for a decade with the Tribe, paid him the ultimate ballplayer's tribute: "I can't conceive of anyone more forceful as a player or manager. He was a fighter. . . . All of us loved the guy."

Another outfielder who was beloved by teammates and "never played the big man," was Spoke's old outfield mate Harry Hooper. It took one of the great right fielders in baseball history three and a half decades to be inducted into the Hall of Fame. But thanks in no small measure to some resourceful advocacy from his son John, the veterans committee finally voted Harry into Cooperstown in 1971. Larry Gardner was among those who made the pilgrimage to Cooperstown to congratulate Harry. Seated next to Harry that afternoon in the group shot was Blossom Seely's onetime beau and vaudeville partner, Rube Marquard, still looking dapper in his eighties. If Rube scalped his tickets to that year's induction ceremony, he got away with it.

Harry passed away at age eighty-seven while being operated on for an aneurysm. As he was being wheeled into surgery, he squeezed John's hand and said, "Don't worry, son. I've had a good life."

The final Golden Outfielder, Duffy Lewis, served for many years as the traveling secretary of the Boston Braves, eventually retiring to a small village in New Hampshire. He and Spoke supposedly buried the hatchet as they chatted at various old-timers' games. Duffy's death in 1979 attracted virtually no attention. Not unlike Louis Sockalexis a half century before, Duffy was buried in an unmarked grave until local Sox fans raised the money for an appropriate headstone.

Two years before he died, Tris Speaker sat down with Bob Rule, a columnist with the *Houston Press*, at a spring training game in Tucson.

He had a lot of thrills, Speaker allowed, but the "greatest thrill of all" was that moment in 1920 when the Indians clinched the World Series against Brooklyn at home on Dunn Field. "Fans poured onto the field and started after me, Charlie Jamieson cut across the infield and started after me, too. He would have jumped all over me. But I held onto that ball and headed for the box seats where mother was sitting right back of the third base with the club president. I took the ball and gave it to her, then gave her a great big kiss and stayed there and hugged her for about five minutes."

Rule noted that "when the fans witnessed this show of affection for his mother, they roared an ovation the great Speaker has never forgotten. 'It was something to remember,' Speaker said, looking away from you just for an instant. It was a blustery day, and that moisture in his eyes could have been caused by the wind." The crowd gathered behind the Indians' dugout cheered Jenny for a good ten minutes after Speaker hustled off to join his mates in the clubhouse. "Mother often told me it was the greatest thrill of her life, too," Speaker told Rule.

Rule also coaxed Speaker that afternoon into naming his all-time team. It was impossible to pinpoint just one pitcher, Speaker said. So he tabbed three: Walter Johnson, Christy Mathewson, and Lefty Grove, whom Spoke saw go 24-8 with an ERA of 2.58 the one year they played together. Picking one catcher was also too tough, so Tris offered two: Bill Dickey and Mickey Cochrane. Speaker chose George Sisler over Lou Gehrig at first. Honus Wagner, of course, was his pick at short. "At second base I've always debated between Eddie Collins and Nap Lajoie but I've always sort of leaned to Collins because of his speed. For third base, I've always had a lot of respect for Jimmy Collins of the old Boston club and Larry Gardner of the 1920 Cleveland team." It's instructive that Spoke didn't reference Gardner's glory days with the Red Sox but chose to remember him as a Tribesman.

In the outfield, Speaker named Cobb, Ruth, and Shoeless Joe Jackson. "His outfield, of course," Rule concluded, "is lacking of the very greatest of them all – Speaker."

Rule even got Spoke to address a delicate subject: Shoeless Joe's alleged involvement in the 1919 Black Sox scandal. "Well, it isn't an easy thing to decide on. I don't think Joe knew he was doing anything wrong but at the same time you can see how baseball had to bar him for life because he apparently did take the money. It was just unfortunate that he was influenced by others. Joe, of course, was very easily led."

" '[Jackson's situation] was right pitiful,' Speaker said in his kindly manner. 'I've heard it said that the only thing that bothered Jackson was the fact that the money was delivered to him in a dirty envelope and put under his pillow,' " Rule quotes Speaker as saying.

Jackson may well have been "right pitiful" and "easily led," but Speaker's account of the Black Sox scandal perpetuates two of its biggest myths: that the money was somehow spirited to Jackson and that he was essentially an unwitting accomplice. Neither is true – and Speaker, who studied Jackson's suspicious play during the '19 series, almost certainly knew that. If Rule asked Speaker about the Dutch Leonard controversy or anything else about baseball's days as a gambling emporium, he kept it out of his column. Reporters knew that Speaker would clam up if queried about the painful events of 1926–27.

Few of Tris Speaker's Texas baseball haunts are around anymore. The Hubbard ball yard he helped fix up in 1921 was torn down a few years back. For years, all the teams in the area, including Hubbard High, used the field. Now the property is a water treatment facility. To this day, Hubbard's Little League is still named after Tris, who supported it generously in the latter years of his life.

Waco's North Texas League field where Speaker irked his manager by showing up late for his professional debut – the old park at East Webster and Eighth in the south end of town – is now a body shop on one side and an AT&T storage facility on the other. *Se Habla Espanol* is painted by hand on the outside wall of the repair shop.

John McGraw's stomping ground in Marlin – a hallowed mecca in the dead-ball era – has sadly fallen into disrepair. Ball games haven't been played there in years. The backstop and metal bleachers are completely shriveled and rusted out, although a ramshackle fence still encircles the field. Huge weeds now grow where Buck Herzog and Art Fletcher and Fred Merkle and "Laughing Larry" Doyle once fielded grounders. On that field, having been released by the Red Sox at a tender age, Spoke begged the Giants' skipper for a chance to compete for a job. McGraw turned him down flat, which must have made for a long ride home to Hubbard, whether by car, train, or horse. Five and a half years later, the pride of Hubbard returned in triumph to that same diamond, not only as an established star touring the country with baseball's elite, but as a hunter who had just bagged a bunch of duck and quail and was eager to share it with his buddies. The railroad tracks that linked the field to Marlin's famous bathhouses have been ripped up, too. Today, the area around Marlin's old park is dominated by a Texas youth correctional facility with rugged barbed wire fences.

A few years ago, Marlin's Main Street Project commissioned a local artist to capture the town's colorful history on two outdoor murals. One mural is devoted to the legacy of Marlin's miraculous mineral waters. The town billed itself back then as the "South's Greatest Health Resort"; its motto was "Where Life Giving Waters Flow." The other depicts three ballplayers with "Giants" across their chests walking through a field of bluebonnets. A pair of bonneted ladies are flirting with the players, waving hankies and triggering smiles from the fellows in uniform. If local folklore is to be believed, much more than hankies got waved at the players. Marlin back then was home to a raucous red-light district conveniently situated near the train station. "New York Giants – 1913" is inscribed on one of the ballplayer's bats – a clear reference to that long-ago afternoon when the population of Falls County must have tripled with all the folks who crashed the field to see Commy and Muggsy's touring all-stars.

Cleburne, the North Texas League town for which Speaker played in the summer of '06, has done a nice job preserving its old ball yard. The field has always been part of City Park, the village green in the center of town. Today a well-manicured diamond with a first-class backstop shares the park with tennis and basketball courts. The day after Speaker's death in December 1958, the Cleburne City Council voted to name the field in Spoke's honor – a resolution that generated press coverage across the country, including the *New York Times*. Cleburne posted a sign near the backstop to remind folks that a Texas immortal had gotten his start in professional ball right there. At some point in the 1970s, the sign fell apart; it's never been replaced.

On March 7, 1973, fifteen years after Speaker's death, a tornado came ripping through Hubbard's downtown just after dawn. Seven people were killed before the funnel cloud dissipated. Among the two hundred homes and businesses damaged or destroyed was the Speaker homestead at Third and Bois d'Arc. The twister obliterated the offices of the *Hubbard City News*, the weekly newspaper that has served the community for more than a century. Also decimated was the First State Bank, a magnificent Beaux-Arts edifice with a pleasing cupola that graced Magnolia Avenue for many decades. Locals recall with a wry smile that the only thing left standing inside the stately old bank was its vault. Many of the leveled buildings were never rebuilt. To this day, Hubbard's downtown has a pockmarked feel.

For years, the wooden signs greeting motorists as they enter the city limits on Routes 31 and 171 have featured a colored carving of Speaker swinging a bat, along with a notation that says, "Home of Tris Speaker, Hall of Famer." In 1966, near Sam Tobolowsky's volunteer fire department, the state historical committee erected a plaque. It reads:

Twilight

TRIS SPEAKER
1888–1958
A legend in his own time, Tris Speaker was born, educated, and buried here. Known as the Grey Eagle he was the first Texan named to the National Baseball Hall of Fame, first man elevated to the Texas Sports Hall of Fame. Was on Boston's 1912 and 1915 World Series winning teams. Managed Cleveland Indians in their first pennant win, 1920. At 18 began professional play at $50 a month. Became a smart, able businessman. Never wasted big money of playing career. Always "came home" to Hubbard. Here he was lifetime member of volunteer fire department.

The "Tris Speaker–Hubbard Sports Hall of Fame" honors the man who always came home. It occupies one room in the beautifully restored Old Hubbard High School, which dates back to 1906 – two years after Speaker graduated. One of the incandescent stars of our national pastime shares crowded space with mementos from Hubbard High's sports teams. Encased in one display next to Spoke's is a collection of Hubbard High cheerleading outfits as they've evolved through the years, along with a set of aging pompoms.

Generously donated by the ballplayer's niece, Miss Tris Speaker Scott, the Speaker display includes the life-sized color portrait the Indians gave him when he returned to Cleveland in 1927 after leaving the team under a cloud a few months before. It captures Speaker in action in center field, eyes intently locked onto a fly ball, mouth slightly agape, legs beginning to churn, hands ready to pounce – the pose Tris struck some eight thousand times in his career. The glove on his right hand looks almost comically tiny.

Speaker's display also highlights other artifacts from his years in Cleveland, a scrapbook that includes the Cobbledick and Lebovitz tributes to Speaker, a photograph from the late 1940s of Tris and Fran with Bob and Dolores Hope that – judging from the goofy grins all around – must have been snapped well into the cocktail hour, and a replica of Tris's plaque at the Ted Williams Hitters Hall of Fame in Florida. Other pictures show the old rodeo wannabe happily astride various horses, sometimes in full cowboy attire, sometimes not. There's also a rare photograph of Speaker posing in a convertible (the famed Chalmers "30," perhaps?) that must have been taken right after the Red Sox's Series triumph in 1912. We'll never know how much Speaker got paid to drape a banner across the roadster that read, "Boston to Texas: Velie Motor Cars and Hartford Tires," but hopefully it offset the cost of gas for the cross-country trip. Miss Scott and other members of the Hubbard Garden Club volunteer their time in managing the Hubbard exhibit, along with restaurateur Billy Mack Waller.

Jon McConal, a columnist for the *Fort Worth Star-Telegram*, came down to Hubbard in April 2000 to cover the opening of the hall of fame. He interviewed Miss Scott, then in her late seventies, about her recollections of Uncle Tris. "He would come to my classroom and talk to students," Miss Scott told McConal. "He would bring a baseball game ticket. 'See this ticket? Anybody who has one of these can get into the game. But they start misbehaving and they can get thrown out. Life is the same way.' "

Spoke had misbehaved in baseball – but his misdeeds paled in comparison to those of many owners and players of his generation. Still, given the harsh punishment that Commissioner Landis meted out to the Black Sox, Spoke knew that he was fortunate not to have been banished from the game he loved. Unlike Buck Weaver and Chick Gandil and all the rest, he was able to make a livelihood in the game – not as a Major League manager as he would have preferred, but as an executive in the minor leagues and later as a broadcaster and part-time coach. By the time he was visiting Miss Scott's classrooms on his way to Tucson in the '40s and '50s, gambling's role in baseball – we can only hope – was less pernicious.

At the Texas Sports Hall of Fame down the road in Waco, the Speaker exhibit is surprisingly small, given that he was its first inductee in 1951. The baseball display is dwarfed by the space given those other red-blooded Texas institutions: football and golf. Spoke's pinstriped jersey from the 1916 Indians hangs near Rogers Hornsby's complete Cardinals uniform, including some very scratchy-looking woolen socks. A plaque next to Speaker's jersey informs visitors of his remarkable offensive season in 1916, the year he finally overtook Cobb in the batting race.

Also encased is a portrait shot that depicts an impish Speaker wearing a Boston jersey with a large collar, tie string, and no buttons – a style that went out of vogue soon thereafter. There's just the faintest trace of a smile on Speaker's twenty-year-old countenance. Early in life virtually every photograph taken of Speaker showed him tight-lipped. Later in life, almost every picture showed him grinning ear-to-ear, eyes twinkling.

Punch in "Tris Speaker" on the museum's computer and up pops a video reel of Spoke swinging a bat in the mid-1950s, clearly shot during spring training in Tucson. Since it's in slow motion the viewer can appreciate Speaker's inside-out swing. Even in his sixties, Spoke's Ichiroian follow-through shoots the head of the bat toward left field, making it easy to imagine a double laced hard down the third base line – something that Spoke did four or five hundred times.

Had he been more forthcoming with the press early in his career, or if he had played in New York or been permitted to manage after 1926, Speaker would have left a deeper legacy. Had Speaker and Joe Wood not met with Ty Cobb and Dutch Leonard under the stands at Navin Field that fateful afternoon, it could have been Tris Speaker piloting the Yankee machine of the '30s and '40s, not Joe McCarthy. Or even better: it could have been Tris Speaker managing the club that *broke up* the Yankee dynasty of the '30s and '40s – maybe even into the '50s, too.

The Red Sox's current ownership team can't turn back the clock and eliminate the boorishness and greed of long-ago owners Joseph Lannin and Harry Frazee. But they can pay homage to the franchise's greatest team ever by commemorating the Golden Outfield with a placard in right field next to the numbers of Ted Williams, Bobby Doerr, Carl Yastrzemski, and the other Sox immortals. And in Spoke's hometown museum, the player Grantland Rice called "perfection on the field" certainly merits space all to himself, away from the pompoms.

"You can write Speaker down as one of the two models of ball playing grace," Rice wrote a decade after Spoke's retirement. "The other was Napoleon Lajoie. Neither ever wasted a motion or gave you any sign of extra effort. They made hard plays look easy."

In his *Historical Baseball Abstract*, Bill James tried to put Speaker's supernatural skills into perspective by asking readers to imagine a ball-player who hit like George Brett and fielded like Cesar Geronimo.

Folks in Hubbard take great pride in their native son, although only a few know much about him. At the Wade Funeral Home across the street from where Speaker grew up, a picture of the ballplayer hangs in a hallway, along with a summary of career highlights. Don Sims, who doubles as a volunteer sportswriter for the *Hubbard City News* (his goal is to get the name of every youngster on Hubbard High's teams into his articles because "that's important for our kids"), helps to run the funeral home. He proudly takes the photograph off the wall, then somewhat sheepishly admits that he doesn't know much about Speaker beyond the teams for whom he played. When told that Connie Mack and Babe Ruth both thought he was the best outfielder they'd ever seen, Don grins and says in a soft drawl, "Well, how 'bout that?"

Justice of the Peace Gene Fulton, a student of Hill County history, has a similar reaction when told of the high esteem in which contemporaries held Speaker. On the wall behind Gene's desk hangs a lithograph of the bathhouse from Hubbard's salad days as a resort in the 1910s and 1920s – back when boarders could stay at "Mrs. Speaker's" for five dollars a week.

Billy Mack Waller, the Speaker buff who runs the Country Kitchen restaurant, remembers the aging Speaker's deep voice and the kindly way he greeted youngsters when he came to visit Hubbard in the 1950s. "Tris was a good guy – not a rebel like Ty Cobb," Billy volunteers. A dozen or more articles about Speaker hang in Billy's restaurant, along with some yellowed photographs and Tris's old fishing rod, courtesy of Charlie Vaughn. When a visitor explains to Billy his intention to write a book about Speaker, Billy shakes his hand and says, "I've been waiting forty years for somebody to do that."

Octogenarian Bill Jarvis remembers that Speaker was friendly and approachable but "had a touch of reservation" about him. Bill and his brother-in-law, Lowell Wilkes, clearly recall how honored the town's leadership was when Speaker came home to celebrate the twenty-fifth anniversary of Hubbard's Lion Club in 1954. Tris loved to go dove hunting with his great pals Vaughn and Tobolowsky, Jarvis says. Whenever he was home, Speaker enjoyed pulling up a stool at Sam's dry goods store, or "Daddy Sam" Ryan's grain store, or Dill Onstott's grain store, or Waller's service station, sit a spell, and swap stories.

In 1954 Speaker arranged for a party of Hubbard pals to go the Giants-Indians World Series. Sam Tobolowsky led a group that included nine-year-old Sonny Murphy, an avid baseball fan who went on to become

Bill Jarvis's son-in-law. Sonny was killed in a tragic accident while still in his thirties. Seeing the World Series in the company of Hubbard's living legend was the thrill of Sonny's life, he always told his father-in-law.

Fairview Cemetery is a half mile or so southeast of town. It's set back off of Route 31 – the highway to Waco – in a grove of live oak, cedar, cypress, and crepe myrtle trees. Hubbard's cemetery is as green and pastoral as central Texas ever gets.

A pole with a huge American flag dominates the middle of the graveyard. The people of Hubbard erected it in 1997 to commemorate the "U.S. and Confederate veterans buried within these sacred grounds."

The simple gravestone of Tristram and Mary Frances Cuddihy Speaker lies at the base of the flagpole. Their epitaph reads:

Tris Speaker	Mary Frances Cuddihy Speaker
Baseball Hall of Fame	Married 1925
April 4, 1888	December 9, 1889
December 8, 1958	November 1, 1960

Just beyond a copse of cypress trees is the family plot. One side of the tombstone is inscribed "Poer"; on the other, "Speaker." Archery Oscar and Jenny, Tris's father and mother, are buried there, as is brother Loyd, the young man who never quite found himself. Nearby are Tris's paternal grandparents, Henry and Eliza, the brave pioneers who uprooted themselves from Maryland to Ohio to Illinois to Texas, only to watch their two oldest boys ride off to wage war against the Union.

A few years ago the town placed a metallic gray eagle on top of the flagpole to pay homage to "the Gray Eagle" buried below. Speaker's gravestone faces east and the eagle's eyes peer north – the points on a compass that a fatherless young Texas boy somehow found the courage to conquer.

"I feel better in the outfield, in center field, with room to swing my elbows," Speaker once said. "I think maybe the feeling was born in me down in Texas. I got used to the idea of space all around me. I was raised to it."

Bill Moyers's conviction is correct: Speaker was, indeed, the consummate Texan, blusterous and big-hearted, narrow-minded and ingenious, all at the same time. Sir Tristram's flaws were many – but they never trumped his virtues. For a half century, the Gray Eagle's epic journey traced the arc of our national pastime, in all of its splendor and seediness.

In September 1920 Speaker's admirers among Cleveland's business and sporting elite presented him with a spectacular white horse to celebrate the city's first-ever American League pennant. A couple of days after his Indians clinched the flag, player-manager Speaker donned the full cowboy regalia – a Stetson, chaps, spurs, six-shooters, a lariat, the whole shootin' match – and rode his new steed around Dunn Field at a ceremony to honor the fans. Barely a month had passed since the horror of Ray Chapman's death; the gathering must have been a catharsis for everyone. Cleveland's newspapers reported that thousands of fans rose as one to roar their approval as Speaker spurred the horse around the park. Hubbard City's cowboy acknowledged the cheers by doing a little trick riding, eliciting louder and louder applause. Finally, Tris climbed out of the saddle, waved his Stetson to the crowd, and disappeared. He had to get his team ready for the World Series.

"Far off I hear the rolling, roaring cheers," Grantland Rice once penned.

> They come to me from many yesterdays,
> From record deeds that cross the fading years,
> And light the landscape with their brilliant plays,
> Great stars that knew their days in fame's bright sun,
> I hear tramping to oblivion.

Notes

INTRODUCTION

The Grantland Rice verse, "When Speaker Swings Out for a Fly," came from the files of Cleveland baseball history buff Fred Schuld.

Willie Mays's quote about the joys of playing center field was taken from the Academy of Achievement Web site devoted to Mays (www.achievement.org), which also features video of Willie's interview.

Speaker is generally credited with four unassisted double plays in his career. But research done in the 1980s by historian and statistician Marty Appel indicates that he made two other unassisted double plays; hence the total of six. Appel's documentation is on file at the National Baseball Hall of Fame.

Several versions of the Gomez-DiMaggio story have appeared in print over the years and are referenced in different books and Web sites. Baseball buff Lynwood Wells of Martinsville, Virginia, inspired the use of the story.

CHAPTER 1. OCTOBER 1912

There are many accounts of the 1912 World Series, from Durso's *Baseball and the American Dream* to Golenbock's *Fenway: An Unexpurgated History of the Boston Red Sox*. Contemporary newspaper accounts and Stout and Johnson's *Red Sox Century*, however, were my main sources. The William Howard Taft–Newport story comes from Durso's chapter on Honey Fitz. The 1903 Series references come from Stout and Johnson and from Ryan's *When Boston Won the World Series*.

The "Carrigan, Carrigan" verse comes from Durso. The Royal Rooters–mounted police episode has been widely chronicled; Golenbock has a particularly good description of it. The Wood brothers' fisticuffs with the hapless Buck O'Brien was first reported by Fred Lieb, Hugh Fullerton, and others, then recounted by Stout and Johnson.

Information on the 1912 Giants comes from a number of sources, principally Alexander's *John McGraw* and Ritter's *The Glory of Their Times*. The Spink quote likening Speaker's voice to a mastiff's came from *The Ultimate Baseball Book*. The description of Speaker's batting style comes from several magazine pieces, notably Meany's article in *Baseball Digest*.

The Snodgrass-Hooper story comes from Ritter; the Gardner-Berry story and the anecdote about Larry's Vermont home now being a beauty parlor comes from Vermonter Tom Simon, former chairman of the Dead-ball Era Committee of the Society for American Baseball Research (SABR) and author of *Green Mountain Boys of Summer*.

I also relied heavily on the *New York Times* and *Boston Globe*'s account of game seven—and the *Boston Post*'s account of game eight, since it dispelled certain myths about what happened in the fateful tenth inning. The *Times* and the *Globe* also had great descriptions of the raucous rally the day after the Series ended at Faneuil Hall. The statement about Joe Wood's hand turning numb was taken from his son Bob's 2002 interview with me.

Speaker's criticism of DiMaggio was referenced in Richard Ben Cramer's *Joe DiMaggio: The Hero's Life*; at the time it happened in 1939, it was widely covered by the likes of Bob Consodine, Joe Williams, Jimmy Powers, and other columnists. Spoke's niece, Miss Tris Speaker Scott, recounted in an April 2000 Jon McConal column in the *Fort Worth Star-Telegram* the story about Spoke having fun with his faux middle initial.

Ban Johnson's hiring of private detectives to tail Cobb and Speaker has been described in a number of books and essays, including Alexander's piece in the Ohio Historical Society's *Timeline*. Information on Speaker's mid-to-late-life activities comes from numerous sources, principally wire service and Cleveland newspaper accounts. Speaker was such a hero in Cleveland that his every move was carefully chronicled.

Stout's quotes about Speaker's bulldog persona came from a 2003 interview. Ryan's quote on the dead-ball era's system of justice comes from his '03 Series book.

CHAPTER 2. TEXAS FRONTIER CHILD

The genealogical information on the Speaker family comes from both the in-house National Archives Census databases and Cleo Davis's dogged research. The Speaker brothers' Civil War experiences are recounted in records maintained at the National Archives. There's also a good Internet service called the Civil War Soldiers and Sailors System (www.itd.nps.gov/cwss), as well as various Web sites on Texas cavalry units. Information on Camp Douglas came from www.illinoiscivilwar.org.

Information on Hill County's past came from a combination of Mrs. Davis's research, *The Handbook of Texas Online* (www.tsha.utexas.edu/handbook), and various interviews conducted in Hubbard and Hillsboro from 2002 through 2004. The Speaker family's real estate purchases in Hubbard were documented by Mrs. Davis's research of municipal records. The flier listing Mrs. Speaker's room for rent for five dollars a week is on display at Nancy York

Ryan's charming antique shop in Hubbard. Nancy is the daughter of another Hubbard baseball great, Texas League legend Tony York.

The profiles of Speaker by Cobbledick and Greene provided much of the information on his childhood, as did a 1912 *Sporting Life* piece that was republished in 1920 in the *Cleveland Plain Dealer*. Bylined autobiographical articles that Spoke "authored" in 1911 in the *Boston Post* and five years later in the *Cleveland Press* also provided background and quotes.

CHAPTER 3. TEXAS LEAGUER

The Cobbledick and Greene profiles again provided much of the background for Speaker's minor league career. Spoke's 1911 and 1916 autobiographical newspaper articles also provided a number of direct quotes. The *Waco Times-Herald* account of his professional debut appears in the archives of the Hall of Fame, as does Speaker's claim that the Cleburne club won the North Texas League pennant in 1906. Background on Cleburne comes from the *Handbook of Texas Online*.

Spoke's Major League debut was also chronicled in the files of the Hall of Fame, as was Grantland Rice's account of his first glimpse of Speaker in a Little Rock uniform.

The Cy Young information comes from a variety of sources, including Stout and Johnson, Alexander's Ohio Historical Society piece, *Baseball Digest* articles by Tom Meany and Morton Roth, and Golenbock's book.

CHAPTER 4. BOSTON, 1908

Goodwin's *The Fitzgeralds and the Kennedys* provided much of the background on the Boston of 1908. Professional baseball's birth in Boston has been described in many publications, most notably Stout and Johnson's and Sullivan's.

In addition to the Goodwin book, much of the information on Honey Fitz came from Martin Nolan's article that helped commemorate the *Globe's* 125th anniversary. It appears on the *Globe* Web site (www.boston.com/globe/search).

The '03 "Tessie" stories appear in the books by Ryan and Golenbock, as well as in numerous anthologies. The Hal Chase–Highlander stories came from Nemec's *Great Baseball Feats, Facts, and Firsts*. Background on the Taylor family came from Goodwin, Stout and Johnson, Durso, Golenbock, Sullivan, and Walton.

Ritter's book provided much of the background on Joe Wood, as well as a Wood Web site (www.thediamondangle.com) that quotes his son, Bob. The K.C.-Mason dynamic in the Sox clubhouse has been addressed in numerous books and anthologies, including Ed Walton's history of the Sox. Walter Johnson's quote about Joe Wood has also been widely recounted. The Charley Hall quote about Wood's natural athletic abilities comes from the Wood Web site.

Mike Sowell's *The Pitch That Killed* and Stout and Johnson provided much of the background on Rough Carrigan. A 2004 interview with Glenn Stout produced the description of Sport Sullivan and Boston's gambling scene in the early 1900s.

CHAPTER 5. EARLY YEARS IN BOSTON

Paul Zingg's biography of Harry Hooper provided much of the information on the old Huntington Avenue Grounds, as well as the glory days of spring training in Hot Springs, which Zingg magnificently researched. The Young-Taylor story comes from Stout and Johnson.

Information on Harry Hooper's childhood and early days in professional ball comes from Zingg and Ritter. Descriptions of the 1909 Sox roster and exhibition tour came from Stout and Johnson, as well as Zingg. The background on Ty Cobb comes from Ritter, Alexander's biography, and Fred Lieb's *Baseball As I Have Known It*. The "mollycoddle" quote comes from various Web site biographies of Cobb and was also highlighted in Ken Burns's PBS documentary, "Baseball."

The perspectives on the Golden Outfield come from such columnists as Arthur Daley in a 1951 column and Grantland Rice in a 1937 column, as well as from various anthologies. The Doc Powers fundraising exhibition anecdote comes from Zingg's book.

Boston's 1911 spring training in California was recounted by Zingg and various articles in the *Los Angeles Times*. The wire services then picked up the story as the Sox traveled up the coast for exhibition games in the Bay Area.

The story about the Rough-Spoke brawl was printed in Stout and Johnson. The anecdote about the slightly less dead dead ball came from Nemec's book.

CHAPTER 6. CHAMPIONSHIP SEASON

Zingg, Golenbock, and Stout and Johnson were the primary sources behind the early Fenway folkore, as were the Carrigan diaries at the Sports Museum of New England. Ritter's book and Thomas's book on his grandfather, Walter Johnson, were the principal sources behind the Big Train–Smoky Joe face-off. The anecdote about "dead bodies being strewn all over Idaho" came from *The Ultimate Baseball Book*.

Dan Holmes at the Hall of Fame provided background information on Speaker's hitting heroics in the 1912 season. Nemec, Alexander, and Lieb described the circumstances surrounding the Cobb Hilltop Park incident.

Ryan, Stout and Johnson, various online baseball biographies, and Murnane's own writing provided the background on T. H. Murnane. The George M. Cohan gambling anecdote came from Stout and Johnson. Durso's book also provided an excellent perspective on the 1912 Series, as did Zingg's.

Carrigan's diaries at the Sports Museum of New England provided several newspaper accounts of the '12 Series, not just Murnane's. The O'Laughlin "infallible" story has been printed in several anthologies.

Lieb and Stout and Johnson were the principal sources behind the Sox's disaffection with McAleer's decision to start Buck O'Brien in game six of the Series.

CHAPTER 7. LAST YEARS IN BOSTON

The Buck O'Brien quartet story comes from Stout and Johnson. The *Cleveland Leader* poem on Cobb, Jackson, and Speaker came from the files of Fred Schuld.

Wilfrid Sheed's marvelous essay on Mack in *The Ultimate Baseball Book* provided much of the background for the section on Connie.

The primary source for the recounting of the world tour comes, of course, from Jim Elfers's wonderful book. An old Franklin Lewis column in Fred Schuld's files also helped, as did Stout and Johnson's description of Speaker's contract negotiations with the new Federal League. The background information on Jim Thorpe came from various on-line biographies. The Shore-Ruth-Mays background comes from a variety of sources, including Smith's *Baseball in the Afternoon*, Sullivan's history of the Red Sox, and Sowell's *The Pitch That Killed*.

The 1915 season sources include Zingg, Stout and Johnson, Dan Holmes at the Hall of Fame, the *Globe*'s T. H. Murnane, and the excitable N. J. Flatley at the old *Boston American*. On-line bios and Lieb provided much of the information on Old Pete Alexander. Sullivan included the quotes from Cobb and Ruth's joint interview reminiscing about the defensive brilliance of the '15 club.

CHAPTER 8. EARLY YEARS IN CLEVELAND

Smith, Sullivan, Walton, the Greene profile, Stout and Johnson, and various newspaper accounts are the sources behind Spoke's banishment from the Sox in early 1916. Speaker got a royal reception when he arrived in Cleveland; he dominated front pages for days, with photos, lithographs, and cartoons, only a small fraction of which I referenced.

The historical perspective on Cleveland came from an on-line biography of Mayor Tom Johnson (www.hb.edu/school/primary/resources) and facts cited in Sowell's book, as well as from *Baseball in Cleveland* and *League Park*, publications of the SABR.

The origin of the nickname "Indians" comes from the *Plain Dealer*.

The archival library at the Massachusetts Institute of Technology and its "Technology's War Record" provided the background on Speaker's service in the naval aviation unit stationed in Cambridge.

CHAPTER 9. WORLD CHAMPION MANAGER

Eugene Murdock's *Baseball Players and Their Times*, coupled with old Henry Edwards and Ed Bang columns, provided the background for Spoke's early years in Cleveland and ascension to the manager's position.

Sowell, of course, is the primary source behind the Chapman-Mays story, coupled with an old Joe Williams column and testimonials from Ed Bang in the *News*. Chappie's death and funeral generated, not surprisingly, a huge amount of coverage in the Cleveland papers.

The Speaker platoon system has been examined by everyone from columnist H. G. Salsinger in Detroit to Bill James in the *Historical Baseball Abstract*. Slim Caldwell's unusual alcohol cessation treatment was described by Sowell and commented upon in several Cobbledick columns written years after the fact.

Most accounts of Speaker's spectacular catch against Joe Jackson claim that it happened in the thick of the 1920 pennant race. It didn't: it happened in May of that year, as Sowell correctly points out.

With Edwards doing his ghostwriting, Spoke served as a columnist at the 1919 World Series. His observations about the White Sox's suspicious play were published years later by Edwards, then reprinted in 1948 by the *Plain Dealer* in its nostalgia column. Spoke's comments about the Black Sox make for fascinating reading and call into question Spoke's professed ignorance of the scandal during the waning days of the 1920 regular season.

Joe Wood's long-dormant 1963 interview with Larry Ritter contained Smoky Joe's quotes about the White Sox and Tigers' suspiciously mediocre play late in the 1920 campaign.

The wonderful anecdote about Uncle Wilbert Robinson and the publicity stunt is described in www.baseball-fever.com/archive.

Sportswriters Henry Edwards and Damon Runyon provided most of the background for the '20 Series.

President Wilson's congratulatory telegram was reported by the wire services, which also described Cleveland's victory celebration run amok.

Wire service accounts provided the information on Spoke's Canadian hunting cabin. The *Los Angeles Times* printed the Port Bay hunting club column from outdoor columnist Tom Marshall. Wire service accounts reported on Spoke's near world-record calf roping time at the Hillsboro rodeo.

CHAPTER 10. SCANDAL

Seymour's *Baseball: The Golden Age*, Smith's *Baseball in the Afternoon*, Lieb's *Baseball As I Have Known It*, the writings of scandal buff Gene Carney ("Notes from the Shadows of Cooperstown," www.baseball1.com/Carney), Alexander's *Ty Cobb*, and the essay "Forced to Back Down" by SABR member Greg Beston are the primary sources on the various scandals that wracked baseball in the 1910s and 1920s.

Once Landis "went public" with the charges against Cobb and Speaker, it became front-page news, followed quickly by Risberg's sensational charges. Scandal buff Carney unearthed the wonderful gag that the Indians pulled with Confederate currency, which was reported in the *Washington Post* in the middle of the '20 Series.

Wood's 1963 interview with Ritter, obtained from the University of Notre Dame archives, included the remarkable revelation about how Cobb, Speaker, and their lawyers compiled damaging information about corruption that they threatened to take public if Landis didn't reinstate them.

CHAPTER 11. BANISHED HERO

Contemporary accounts in the *Washington Post* and *New York Times* provided much of the background for the 1927 and 1928 seasons. The *Post* covered Spoke's arrival in the nation's capital with breathless enthusiasm. The *Plain Dealer* did a superb job covering Spoke's initial return to Cleveland in May 1927. Wire service accounts covered the various job offers that came Spoke's way during this period, as well as rumors about Major League managing positions. The Hall of Fame's files included a description of Speaker's last performance in a Major League uniform. He struck out at Philadelphia's Shibe Park, the very park where in the fall of '07 he made his Major League debut.

The *New York Times* covered Speaker's stint with the Newark Bears. His ill-fated involvement with the Kansas City Blues was covered by the wire services. Spoke's broadcasting days were covered by the *Chicago Daily Tribune* and the Cleveland papers—although not with the kind of intensity that a biographer would have liked. Fred Schuld's methodical research provided the background information on Gray Eagle Brands and Spoke's leadership of the Cleveland boxing commission. The Cleveland papers and Jed Weisman provided background on his work for the steel industry. Spoke's dalliance with indoor softball was widely covered by the wire services and the Cleveland papers.

Speaker's near-fatal fall in 1937 was front-page news in the Cleveland papers for days. Arthur Daley's account in the *New York Times* was the primary source behind the description of the Hall of Fame induction ceremonies. Speaker's draft-board statements were covered by the wire services.

Two interviews with Lefty Weisman's son Jed were the primary sources behind the Spoke-Lefty friendship. Wire service accounts provided information on Spoke's car accident and health issues in the 1950s. The Cleveland papers covered Spoke's involvement with the Society for Crippled Children. Alexander's Ohio Historical Society piece is the source of the Ike-Spoke story.

CHAPTER 12. TWILIGHT

The *New York Times* covered the Van Doren TV episode. A 2004 interview with Bob Ryan produced the analogy between Speaker and Stan Musial.

Arthur Daley's October 1, 1954, column in the *New York Times* provided the background on the Mays-Speaker photo opportunity at the Polo Grounds. The Ogden Nash poem also came from the files of the ever-vigilant Fred Schuld.

Spoke's death and funeral received front-page treatment in the Cleveland papers and were widely covered by the wire services. As part of their tribute to Spoke, the *Plain Dealer* reprinted some classic Henry Edwards columns and recounted its past editorials about Spoke. The Baseball Hall of Fame archives included several detailed articles about Spoke's funeral arrangements.

The Bob Rule column in the *Houston Press* is on display at the Speaker museum in Hubbard, as are various articles from the Cleveland papers related to his death and funeral, including a reminiscence about the horse that was presented to Spoke as a gift in 1920 and the reception Spoke and his horse were given by Cleveland fans.

The interviews with various folks in the Hubbard community were conducted in March 2004. The visit to the Speaker museum in Hubbard and to the Texas Sports Hall of Fame also took place in March 2004, as did visits to the old ball fields in Cleburne and Marlin.

The Grantland Rice verse at the end comes from Seymour's *Golden Age*.

Bibliography

Note: For specific Web sites used as sources, please refer to the Notes.

UNPUBLISHED SOURCES

Cleo Davis, Hill County genealogist and historian. Interviewed numerous times by author, 2002–2004, Hillsboro TX.

James Elfers, author and historian. Interviews by author, February–April 2004, Newark DE.

Dan Holmes, historian. Interview by author, April 2004, National Baseball Hall of Fame, Cooperstown NY.

Richard Jarvis, retired businessman. Interview by author, March 2004, Hubbard TX.

Richard Johnson, curator, Sports Museum of New England. Interviewed numerous times by author, 2002–2005, Cambridge MA.

David Kelly, historian and archivist, Library of Congress. Interviews by author, November 2001 and June 2004, Washington DC.

Scott Longert, sports archivist, Western Reserve Historical Association. Interview by author, April 2005, Cleveland OH.

Massachusetts Institute of Technology, Archival Library, Cambridge MA. Technology's War Record.

National Archives, Washington DC. Consolidated Civil War Service Record. Census databases.

Bob Ryan, columnist, *Boston Globe*. Interview by author, May 2004, Boston MA.

Fred Schuld. Interviewed by author numerous times, 2004–2005, Cleveland OH.

———. Personal collection. Cleveland OH.

Miss Tris Speaker Scott, retired teacher. Interview by author, January 2002, Hubbard TX.

Don Sims, funeral home executive and sportswriter. Interview by author, March 2004, Hubbard TX.

Mike Sowell, author and historian. Interview by author, November 2003, Stillwater OK.

Sports Museum of New England, Cambridge MA. Rough Carrigan diaries.

Glenn Stout, author and historian. Interview by author, October 2003, Alburg VT.

Billy Mack Waller, restaurant owner. Interview by author, March 2004, Hubbard TX.

Jed Weisman. Interviews by author, July and August 2004, Cleveland OH.

Craig T. Wolff, author and baseball writer. Interview by author, January 2004, New York NY.

Bob Wood. Interview by author, February 2002, Keene NH.

Joe Wood. Transcript of interview by Lawrence Ritter, 1963. Lawrence Ritter Collection, Hesburgh Library, University of Notre Dame, South Bend IN.

———. Transcript of interview by Lawrence Ritter, 1965. National Baseball Hall of Fame and Museum, Cooperstown NY.

PUBLISHED SOURCES

Alexander, Charles C. *John McGraw*. Lincoln: University of Nebraska Press, 1987.

———. "Triple Play: Cleveland's Hall of Fame Triumverate." *Timeline* (Ohio Historical Society), April–May 1992, 2–17.

———. *Ty Cobb*. New York: Oxford University Press, 1984.

Astor, Gerald. *The Baseball Hall of Fame Fiftieth Anniversary Book*. New York: Prentice Hall, 1989.

Broeg, Bob. *SuperStars of Baseball*. South Bend IN: Diamond, 1994.

Chadwick, Bruce, and David Spindel. *Memories and Memorabilia of New England's Team*. New York: Abbeveill, 1992.

Cobbledick, Gordon. "Tris Speaker . . . The Grey Eagle." *Sport Magazine*, July 1952, 34–37, 68–73.

Cramer, Richard Ben. *Joe DiMaggio: The Hero's Life*. New York: Simon and Schuster, 2001.

Durso, Joseph. *Baseball and the American Dream. The Sporting News* compendium. New York: Sporting News, 1986.

Elfers, James E. *The Tour to End All Tours*. Lincoln: University of Nebraska Press, 2002.

Golenbock, Peter. *Fenway: An Unexpurgated History of the Boston Red Sox*. New York: Putnam, 1992.

Goodwin, Doris Kearns. *The Fitzgeralds and the Kennedys*. New York: St. Martin's, 1987.

Greene, Lee. "The Grey Eagle," *Sport Magazine*, June 1960, 35–36, 75–80.

Honig, Donald. *In the Dugout: Fifteen Big League Managers Speak Their Minds*. Chicago: Follet, 1977.

Keane, Kerry, Raymond Sinibaldi, and David Hickey. *The Babe in Red Stockings*. Champaign IL: Sagamore, 1992.

Bibliography

Lieb, Fred. *Baseball As I Have Known It*. New York: Coward, McCann and Geoghegan, 1977.

Mathewson, Christy. *Pitching in a Pitch*. New York: Stein and Day, 1977.

Meany, Tom. "The Grey Eagle Was a Lion at Bat." *Baseball Digest*, February 1959, 56–61.

Murdock, Eugene. *Baseball Players and Their Times*. Westport CT: Mecklen, 1991.

Nemec, David, ed. *Great Baseball Feats, Facts, and Firsts*. New York: Signet, 1987.

Okrent, Daniel, and Harris Lewine, eds. *The Ultimate Baseball Book*. Boston: Houghton Mifflin, 1979.

Reichler, Joseph L., ed. *The Baseball Encyclopedia*. New York: Macmillan, 1969.

Ritter, Lawrence S. *The Glory of Their Times*. New York: Morrow, 1966.

Roth, Morton. "Best Center Fielder of All Time: How About Speaker?" *Baseball Digest*, July 1987, 65–69.

Ryan, Bob. *When Boston Won the World Series*. Philadelphia: Running Press, 2002.

Seymour, Harold. *Baseball: The Golden Age*. New York: Oxford University Press, 1971.

Simon, Tom, ed. *Green Mountain Boys of Summer: Vermonters in the Major Leagues, 1882–1993*. Shelburne VT: New England Press, 2000.

Smith, Robert. *Baseball in the Afternoon: Tales from a Bygone Era*. New York: Simon and Shuster, 1993.

Society for American Baseball Research. Various essays and papers written by SABR members, including "Forced to Back Down" by Greg Beston, 1996, South Weymouth MA, www.sabr.org.

Sowell, Mike. *The Pitch That Killed*. New York: Collier, 1989.

Stout, Glenn, and Richard Johnson. *Red Sox Century*. Boston: Houghton Mifflin, 2000.

Sullivan, George. *The Picture History of the Boston Red Sox*. Boston: Bobbs-Merrill, 1979.

Thomas, Henry W. *Walter Johnson: Baseball's Big Train*. Lincoln: University of Nebraska Press, 1995.

Walton, Ed. *Red Sox Triumphs and Tragedies*. New York: Stein and Day, 1980.

Zingg, Paul. *Harry Hooper: An American Baseball Life*. Chicago: University of Illinois Press, 1993.

Bibliography

Magazines
   Baseball Digest
   Baseball Magazine
   Literary Digest
   Sport Magazine
   Sporting News

Newspapers
   Boston American (and *Record-American*)
   Boston Globe
   Boston Herald
   Boston Post
   Chicago Daily Tribune
   Cleveland Plain Dealer
   Cleveland Press
   Fort Worth Star-Telegram
   Los Angeles Times
   New York Times
   New York World-Telegram
   Waco Times-Herald
   Washington Post

Index